ENGLISH & COMMUNICATION *for* COLLEGES

2nd Edition

Carol Henson, Ed. D.
Clayton State College
Morrow, Georgia

Thomas L. Means, Ed. D.
Louisiana Tech University
Ruston, Louisiana

SOUTH-WESTERN EDUCATIONAL PUBLISHING

International Thomson Publishing

South-Western Educational Publishing is a division of International Thomson
Publishing Inc. The ITP trademark is used under license.

Library of Congress Cataloging-in-Publication Data

Henson, Carol.
    English and communication for colleges / Carol Henson, Thomas
Means. -- 2nd ed.
      p.   cm.
    Rev. ed. of: Fundamentals of business communication. c1990.
    Includes bibliographical references and index.
    ISBN 0-538-71138-8 (alk. paper)
    1. English language--Business English.   2. English language-
-Grammar.   3. Business communication.   4. Business writing.
I. Means, Thomas L.   II. Henson, Carol. Fundamentals of business
communication.   III. Title.
PE1479.B87H457   1995
808´.06665--dc20   95-44121
                                                        CIP

Editor in Chief: *Peter McBride*
Project Manager: *Penny Shank*
Production Coordinator: *Tricia Boies*
Editor: *Alan Biondi*
Internal Design: *Pronk & Associates*
Photo Editors: *Fred Middendorf and Devore Nixon*
Marketing Manager: *Carolyn Love*

1 2 3 4 5 6 7 8 9 VH 03 02 01 00 99 98 97 96 95

Printed in the United States of America

Employers of postsecondary graduates tell us that communication is one of the most important skills they look for in job applicants. Unfortunately, many students lack the communication skills that will make them competitive in the job market. The goal of English and Communication for Colleges, *second edition, is to help students in postsecondary programs improve their skills so that they can communicate effectively in the workplace.*

This new edition of *English and Communication for Colleges* supplements the traditional teaching of grammar and writing with new and innovative approaches. Chapters are shorter in the second edition to provide concentrated instruction on key topics. The text provides thorough coverage of grammar, punctuation, and style and introduces the types of communications generated in the workplace. It presents the mechanics of writing, describes issues of format and style, and reviews the seven *C*s of writing—courteous, considerate, concise, clear, concrete, correct, and complete. Students learn to plan, organize, edit, and proofread messages.

This edition thoroughly covers basics of workplace communication—letters, memos, e-mail, and reports. Memos receive particular attention because of their extensive use in the workplace. The text also introduces contemporary issues such as multiculturalism, ethics, critical thinking, and collaborative writing.

Organization

English and Communication for Colleges, second edition, is an extremely versatile textbook. It can be used as a text for the following:

- two semester courses—a one-semester business English course and a one-semester business communication course

Preface

- two quarter courses—a one-quarter business English course and a one-quarter business communication course
- a one-semester business English course
- a one-semester business communication course
- a one-semester business communication course with a grammar review
- a one-semester business communication course with a job interview or an oral presentation
- a program of 8, 10, or 12 weeks concentrating on business communication
- a program of 8, 10, or 12 weeks concentrating on business English

The textbook contains 46 chapters organized into 9 parts. Part 1 introduces the importance and purposes of business communication and the role electronic communication plays in today's offices.

Parts 2 and 3 provide an intensive review of the rules governing grammar, punctuation, abbreviation, capitalization, and number expression for written business communications. Part 2 also provides a two-chapter grammar review that focuses on common grammatical errors. This review is included to meet the needs of schools that do not offer a separate grammar course.

Part 4 introduces students to the basics of effective business writing. Students learn how to plan and organize messages. Then they systematically learn to construct messages—from word selection, to sentence construction, to paragraph building. Following message construction, students review techniques for effective editing and proofreading.

Part 5 of the textbook is new. In this new edition, the entire part focuses on memo writing, including correct formatting of memos, uses and abuses of memos, and guidelines for writing effective memos.

Part 6 presents formats and specific methods for developing effective routine, good-news, bad-news, and persuasive letters. Students apply the concepts of direct and indirect structure to plan, organize, and compose documents.

Part 7 discusses the report writing process. In this edition, report writing has been expanded to three chapters, enabling a more detailed coverage of this topic. A fourth chapter was added to cover methods for writing specialized workplace documents such as news releases, proposals, agendas, and minutes.

Part 8 covers nonverbal communication, listening, and oral communication. This section has been expanded to help students enhance their oral communication skills in one-to-one conversations, group settings, and meetings. Students can apply these oral communication concepts in their workplaces or as they plan, organize, and deliver oral presentations.

Part 9 completes the text by providing comprehensive, up-to-date instructions on career communications, including resumes, letters of application, application forms, job interviews, and follow-up letters.

Key Features

English and Communication for Colleges, second edition, includes these important features:

- **Chapter Objectives.** Each chapter begins with a list of learning objectives.
- **Marginal Notations.** New in the second edition, marginal notations provide students with additional information to reinforce and support the text. Each notation is identified as one of four categories:

  —*Across Cultures*—Notations that introduce international and cultural differences in communication.

  —*Extra! Extra!*—Notations that build on concepts presented in the textbook.

  —*Legal/Ethical*—Notations that introduce legal or ethical communication issues.

  —*On the Job*—Notations that contain workplace information and tips.
- **Full-Color Visual Aids.** A variety of full-color photographs, illustrations, and full-length documents are used to assist learning. Numerous full-page illustrations show students how to format letters, memos, and reports correctly.
- **Bold Terms.** Key terms are highlighted in each chapter and included in the glossary in Appendix E.
- **Icons.** Critical thinking and collaborative writing exercises are identified with attractive graphical icons.
- **Checkpoints.** Checkpoints are provided in each chapter to provide continuous reinforcement as students study the text. Answers to the checkpoints are in Appendix F.
- **Common Grammar Error Review.** Chapters 13 and 14 contain a detailed review of the most common grammar trouble spots. This review may be used in combination with or separate from the thorough grammar coverage in Parts 2 and 3.
- **Chapter Summary.** The main points are summarized at the end of each chapter to reinforce the material presented.
- **Communication Activities.** The following end-of-chapter communication activities may be used in class or assigned as homework:

  —*Discussion Questions* that check students' comprehension of main points emphasized in each major section and their achievement of learning objectives for each chapter.

  —*Practical Applications* that reinforce the content and instruction presented in each chapter.

—*Editing and Proofreading Applications* that apply the grammar and English mechanics presented in Parts 2 and 3. Commonly misspelled and misused words are included in the business documents that students edit, proofread, and revise.

—*Spelling and Word Usage Applications* in Parts 2 and 3 that provide opportunities for students to determine correct spelling and usage of commonly misspelled and misused terms.

- **Appendixes.** The text contains seven appendixes.

—*Appendix A* reviews the commonly misspelled and misused words applied in Parts 2 and 3.

—*Appendix B* contains a list of standard and two-letter postal abbreviations.

—*Appendix C* provides formatted models of business documents.

—*Appendix D* provides the commonly used proofreader's marks and shows examples of how to use them in the editing and proofreading exercises.

—*Appendix E* is a glossary of all terms highlighted in the text.

—*Appendix F* contains solutions to the checkpoints.

—*Appendix G* provides a brief overview of the Internet and gives e-mail addresses for the authors.

Instructional Tools

Instructional supplements include an instructor's annotated edition of the textbook, an instructor's edition of the enrichment activities, a printed and computerized test bank, and transparency masters.

Instructor's Annotated Edition of Textbook

The comprehensive instructor's edition contains a complete instructor's manual and template solutions. To assist the instructor, the manual provides class schedules for quarter and semester plans.

Each chapter in the instructor's edition contains numerous annotations to assist instructors during class discussions. Annotated text includes the following:

- Checkpoint answers shown on text pages
- Marginal teaching notes and suggestions
- Transparency master icons indicating when to use each transparency
- Short answer keys shown on text pages

Additionally, each chapter contains a chapter overview, teaching suggestions, and long solutions to the communication activities at the end of each textbook chapter.

Instructor's Edition of *Enrichment Activities*

The instructor's edition provides solutions to all *Enrichment Activities*—study guide questions, exercises, and case studies in a convenient format. Solutions are overprinted on the student exercises.

Evaluation and Testing Materials

This new edition provides numerous opportunities to evaluate student learning. Printed and microcomputer versions of all tests are included.

- **Chapter Tests.** Each chapter has a Quick Quiz.
- **Part Tests.** A test may be administered after completing each of the nine parts in the text.
- **Pretests.** Two pretests that may be used to determine student understanding of grammar and punctuation principles at the beginning of the course are available for Parts 2 and 3 (Chapters 3–21).
- **Business English Exam.** A test covering Parts 1–3 (Chapters 1–21) may be administered to evaluate student abilities on the business English part of the text.
- **Business Communication Exam.** A test covering Part 1 (Chapters 1–2) and Parts 4–9 (Chapters 22–46) may be administered to evaluate student progress on the business communication part of the text.
- **MicroSWAT III.** All tests are available on *MicroSWAT III* software. These computerized versions are available for IBM®[1] compatible and Macintosh®[2] computers. Instructors may generate tests from the computerized test bank by selecting specific questions, adding their own questions, or allowing the computer to select questions randomly.

Transparency Masters

Forty-six transparency masters are available to assist with the discussion of the chapters. Formatted letters and memorandums, checklists, and summaries of key points support and supplement the chapter material.

Student Learning Tools

The student supplemental learning package provided with the second edition of *English and Communication for Colleges* includes enrichment activities and a template.

---

[1]IBM is a registered trademark of the IBM Corporation.
[2]Macintosh is a registered trademark of Apple Computer, Inc.

- *Enrichment Activities.* This component provides study guide objective questions, exercises, and case studies. One exercise in each *Enrichment Activities* chapter, identified by a template icon, may be completed by using material that is in Revision and Composition Applications Template Diskette.
- **Revision and Composition Applications Template Diskette.** Two computer exercises are provided for each chapter. One of the template exercises also is in the workbook. The template disk may be used with IBM compatible and Macintosh computers and Windows®[3] software. Keys to these exercises are provided in the up-front pages of the instructor's edition of the textbook.

Acknowledgments

We wish to extend our appreciation to all those who helped us create this book. For their expertise and significant contributions, we are deeply grateful to the following individuals:

Lois Bachman
Mary Lea Ginn
Susan Merrill
Marion Burk Wood

Also, we appreciate the valuable assistance of the following reviewers who provided many helpful suggestions for the second edition:

Vanessa Arnold, The University of Mississippi, University, Mississippi
Paige P. Baker, Trinity Valley Community College, Athens, Texas
Janice Brown, Athens Area Vocational-Technical College, Athens, Georgia
Billie Miller Cooper, Consumnes River College, Sacramento, California
Ann Cunningham, Branell Institute, Chattanooga, Tennessee
Virginia Dochety, Sawyer College at Pomona, Pomona, California
Andrew Halford, Paducah Community College, Paducah, Kentucky
Mary K. McClanahan, Loveland, Colorado
Donna Madsen, Kirkwood Community College, Cedar Rapids, Iowa
Arenda Maxwell, American Institute of Business, Des Moines, Iowa
Dale A. Neeck, Blackhawk Technical College, Janesville, Wisconsin
Jill Nesheim, Aaker's Business College, Grand Forks, North Dakota
Douglas Okey, Spoon River College, Canton, Illinois
Betsy Ray, Indiana Business College, Indianapolis, Indiana

---

[3]Windows is a trademark of Microsoft Corporation.

Penny Sherrill, Wright Business School, Oklahoma City, Oklahoma
Tony Sweet, National Education Center, Louisville, Kentucky
Colleen Vawdrey, Utah Valley State College, Orem, Utah
Richard R. Williams, Grayson County College, Denison, Texas
Dr. Andrea Wise, Georgia College, Milledgeville, Georgia
Nancy J. Zitsch, Computer Learning Network, Altoona, Pennsylvania

Carol W. Henson
Thomas L. Means

Contents

Part 3 MECHANICS OF WRITING   187

Part 4 BASICS OF EFFECTIVE WRITING   277

Part 5 WRITING MEMOS   339

Concepts in Communication

Communication is an essential element of your personal and professional life. Communication skills enable you to convey thoughts and ideas and have them understood by receivers. Without the ability to communicate, the contributions a person can make are extremely limited.

Chapter 1 examines the nature of communication, the process used to communicate and some of its barriers, the types of communication, and the media used to communicate. Because people spend so much time communicating, making wise choices when trying to communicate is critical to your success.

Chapter 2 introduces selected electronic technologies used to communicate. These technologies enable senders to create, edit, send, and store communications quickly and efficiently. Electronic technologies discussed include computers, e-mail, facsimile, and optical disk storage.

Chapter 1 The Communication Process
Chapter 2 Electronic Communication

The Communication Process

OBJECTIVES

After studying this chapter and completing the chapter activities, you will be able to do the following:

1. List the purposes of communication.
2. Describe the communication process.
3. Discuss barriers to communication.
4. List the forms of communication within organizations.

WHAT IS COMMUNICATION?

The process you use to send and interpret messages so that they are understood is called **communication.** When communicating, you go through the process so quickly and naturally that you don't realize a process is being used. In the business environment, this process is called **business communication.** *Being an effective communicator is critical to your personal and professional lives.*

Accurate communication does not occur unless the receiver attaches the same meaning to the message as the sender intended. The basic responsibility of accurate communication lies with the sender.

Effective communication requires that (1) the receiver interpret the message as the sender intended and that (2) the communication achieve its purpose.

★ The effective communicator is the one who gets things done.

The Importance of Communication

Research indicates that adults spend about two-thirds of each day communicating. Responding to friends, maintaining relationships with co-workers and supervisors, interpreting messages, and persuading customers are all ways people interact. Studies also indicate that managers spend more than 50 percent of their time attending meetings, making telephone calls, writing, and listening.

Communication skills include the ability to use language accurately—use grammar properly, choose words precisely, and spell correctly. They also include the ability to speak, teach, counsel, debate, and listen. Your success within any organization will depend on your ability to use these communication skills.

The Purposes of Communication

Communication is used to fulfill five basic purposes:

1. *To establish and build goodwill.* Your ability to establish and build relationships with co-workers, clients, and customers has a major effect on your professional development and advancement. Good relationships result in **goodwill**—the favorable reputation that an individual or a business has with its customers. Any communication that helps to develop a better relationship between you and the receiver builds goodwill.
2. *To persuade.* Motivating or persuading others to act in a certain way depends on your ability to convince them that they will benefit from such an action.

Build goodwill among your co-workers by turning them into friends.

3. *To obtain or share information.* Information is one of the most valuable resources of an organization. You must communicate to obtain the information you need and to share information you have.

4. *To establish personal effectiveness.* When you receive a message that is accurate, easy to understand, and error free, you form a positive image of the sender. However, if a message is full of errors, you evaluate the sender as careless or thoughtless—a person with whom you do not want to do business. Because you are constantly being evaluated by your ability to communicate, you must do it well.

5. *To build self-esteem.* Positive comments or reactions from other people increase your self-esteem. Such positive reinforcement causes you to feel good about yourself and your chances for success. If your supervisor complimented you on a report you wrote, you would feel good about yourself. Communication is a major building block of self-esteem.

THE COMMUNICATION PROCESS

Before the communication process begins, you create or develop an idea. To communicate the idea, you will use the communication process. The communication process, shown in Figure 1–1, consists of five components: (1) the sender, (2) the message, (3) the receiver, (4) the feedback, and (5) the channel.

Usually, the communication process is interpersonal (between persons). However, it may occur between a person and a machine, such as a computer, or it

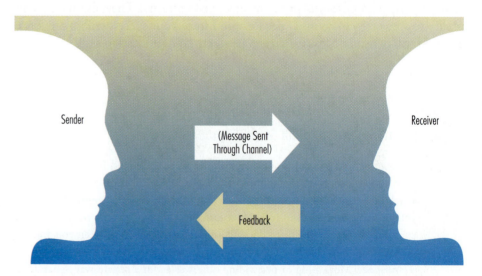

Sender

(Message Sent Through Channel)

Receiver

Feedback

Figure 1–1 The main components of communication are sender, message, receiver, feedback, and channel.

may occur between two machines. Computers, printers, or facsimile devices can exchange information.

The Sender

The **sender** is a person or thing that originates a message and initiates the communication process. When you are the sender, you have the primary responsibility for accurately conveying the complete message in a manner that can be easily understood. If you fulfill this responsibility, the receiver is likely to interpret the message as intended. By applying what you know about the receiver, you can anticipate the receiver's response and adjust the message as necessary.

The Message

A **message** is a set of symbols that represent meaning. It can be composed of either verbal or nonverbal symbols or both. **Verbal symbols** are words used when speaking or writing. Letters, memorandums, reports, brochures, catalogs, manuals, and annual reports are composed of verbal symbols. These symbols are also used when speaking face-to-face or on the telephone, participating in a conference or a meeting, or delivering a speech.

Nonverbal symbols, such as gestures, posture, facial expressions, appearance, time, tone of voice, eye contact, and space usually accompany verbal symbols. Nonverbal symbols help to convey attitudes.

Nonverbal symbols also help the receiver interpret verbal symbols. If verbal and nonverbal symbols conflict, receivers generally attach more importance to the nonverbal symbols than to the verbal symbols. For example, if a salesperson says a customer's account is important but keeps the customer waiting, the customer may conclude that his or her account is not very important. The salesperson's nonverbal communication may cause the customer to take his or her business elsewhere.

The Receiver

A person or machine to whom a message is sent is the **receiver.** When you are the receiver, your responsibility is to give meaning to the verbal and nonverbal symbols used by the sender. The meaning receivers give to messages depends on their respective educational backgrounds, experiences, interests, opinions, and emotional states. *Miscommunication* results if the receiver gives the message a different meaning than the sender intended.

The Feedback

Feedback is the response of a receiver to a message. Feedback may be nonverbal—a smile, a frown, a pause, or a blank stare. Feedback may be verbal—a telephone call or a letter. Any response—even no response—is feedback.

Feedback is a critical component of the communication process because it helps the sender determine whether the receiver has understood the message. Feedback tells you when to clarify a message, provide additional information, or modify the message. To be meaningful, feedback must accurately reflect the receiver's reaction to the message.

The Channel

The mode a sender selects to send a message is the **channel.** Letters, memorandums, and reports are the most common channels for written messages. One-to-one conversations, telephone conversations, and meetings are common channels of oral messages.

Selecting the appropriate channel becomes more significant as the importance or sensitivity of the message increases. When trying to resolve a sensitive issue with a customer, for example, you must carefully weigh the merits of communicating by telephone or by letter. Using the telephone indicates a sense of urgency and allows immediate feedback. On the other hand, a letter enables the sender to explain a position and provides a record of the message. Often, using both channels is appropriate—you might discuss the situation over the telephone and then follow up with a letter.

CHECKPOINT 1

The Purposes and Process of Communication

Answer the following questions:

1. When communicating, what is the main purpose of the sender?
2. When communicating, what is the main purpose of the receiver?
3. What is the purpose of each of the following communications?
   a. You give your supervisor your sales figures for last month.
   b. Your supervisor tells you that your report was well done.
   c. A woman's clothier advertises in a local newspaper.

Check your answers in Appendix F.

COMMUNICATION BARRIERS

Although the primary goal of communication is for the receiver to interpret the message as the sender intended, frequently this goal is not achieved. *Communication barriers* can interrupt the communication process (see Figure 1–2). Learning to recognize external and internal communication barriers will help you plan your messages and become a more effective communicator.

External Barriers

Conditions outside the receiver and the sender that detract from the communication process are called **external barriers.** Examples include environmental factors, such as lighting, heat, humidity, comfort, and noise.

The appearance of a written document also may be an external barrier to communication. A document can create an external barrier if it is smudged; contains errors in content, spelling, or grammar; or is presented in an inappropriate

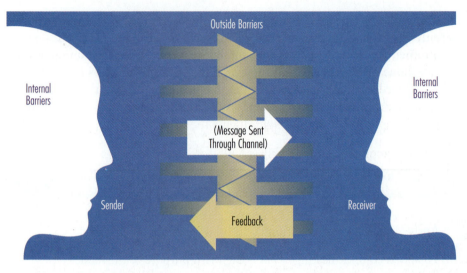

Figure 1–2 Barriers can interfere with effective communication.

format. You could become so distracted with the appearance of the document that you fail to comprehend its content.

Another external barrier to communication within an organization is an "authoritarian climate." In such an environment, decisions and policies often are made and implemented by command. Consequently, workers may stop offering suggestions because they may feel that making suggestions is useless.

Conversely, in an open climate in which ideas and information are welcomed, communication flows easily. Workers feel that supervisors and managers are receptive to their ideas, which facilitates communication. Most managers in progressive organizations realize the importance of maintaining open communication. They know that being sensitive to employees' attitudes and ideas encourages creativity and growth.

Internal Barriers

People have different personalities, educational backgrounds, experiences, cultures, statuses, and biases. These **internal barriers** affect a sender's willingness and ability to express messages and a receiver's ability to interpret them.

In meetings, extroverts (outward, outspoken, and outgoing individuals) are apt to express ideas and appear to be very knowledgeable. Introverts (inward, quiet,

An "authoritarian climate" typically hampers communication. Sometimes, however, it is effective. For example, research indicates that in the military, authoritarian is the most effective type of leadership.

and shy individuals) may not express their opinions until someone asks for them. One-to-one conversation is easier for extroverts than introverts. To avoid a communication barrier, extroverts need to make sure they think before they speak. For introverts to avoid the barrier, they need to make sure they speak.

FORMS OF COMMUNICATION IN ORGANIZATIONS

Employees communicate externally or internally and formally and informally. These messages may be written, oral, or electronic.

External and Internal Communication

External communication originates within a company and is sent to receivers outside the company. Communication with clients, customers, sales representatives, governmental agencies, advertising agencies, and transportation agencies is external.

Internal communication originates and is sent to receivers within a company. For example, a memorandum from a supervisor to an employee is an internal communication.

Formal and Informal Communication

Formal communication occurs through established lines of authority. As Figure 1–3 illustrates, communication may travel down, across, or up lines of authority.

Communication that travels down the hierarchy from a superior (supervisor, manager, or executive) to subordinates is *downward communication.* Instructions from a project manager to project team members travel downward. Policies established by the board of directors and company officers are relayed downward to department managers and then to other employees.

Communication among peer—persons of the same status—is *lateral (or horizontal) communication.* A memorandum from one department head to another is an example of lateral communication. Lateral communication encourages cooperation between departments and divisions of an organization.

Upward communication refers to communication from subordinates to superiors. When employees convey to their supervisors their suggestions for improving production, their attitudes and feelings about their jobs, or their perception of the

For written business messages, the memo is the most commonly used format.

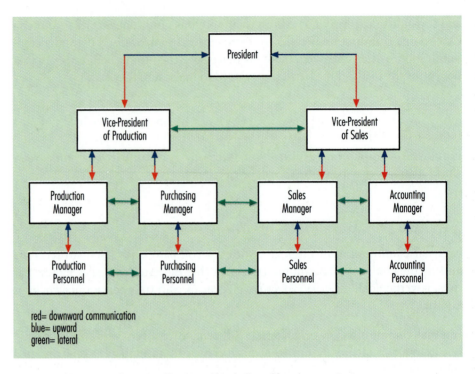

Figure 1–3 Messages travel in various directions within the lines of formal communication.

organization, they are communicating upward. Likewise, managers' recommendations to company officers are upward communication.

Informal communication is unrelated to established lines of authority. It may be written or oral. Sharing interests over lunch or during breaks and socializing after work are examples of informal communication. Often referred to as the *grapevine,* informal communication is usually a rapid communication channel, although not always an accurate one.

Written, Oral, and Electronic Communication

Letters, memorandums, and reports are common forms of written business communication. **Letters** are external documents that may be addressed to business associates, customers, and clients.

Memorandums, often called *memos,* are internal documents used to communicate with one or more co-workers. Because co-workers are the receivers, memos are usually less formal than letters.

Letters can be formal or informal—the degree of formality depends on the sender's relationship with the receiver.

Reports are designed to provide meaningful information to a group of people. They may be formal documents, such as research studies or proposals to top management, or informal documents, such as memo reports.

Agendas, minutes of meetings, speeches, brochures, business directories, legal documents, office manuals, and announcements are other forms of written communication used in business. Written communication is used in the workplace for three reasons:

1. It provides a record of information exchanged. For example, a price quoted in a written bid cannot be disputed.
2. It can be revised until the final message is logical and clear. This factor is especially important when complex information must be explained.
3. It enables the receiver to analyze a message and refer to it as many times as necessary.

Generally, **oral communication** can be sent quickly and provides immediate feedback to the sender. You may use oral communication (one-to-one conversations and telephone conversations) when seeking opinions, explaining procedures, providing counseling, or building relationships.

Written messages may be composed, edited, and transmitted on a computer. An exact copy of a message may be transmitted by a facsimile receiver. These written electronic messages are forms of **electronic mail** or *e-mail.* Oral messages may be sent over the telephone and stored electronically in a computer for playback later on a **voice mail** system. E-mail and voice mail are discussed in greater detail in Chapter 2.

CHECKPOINT 2

Forms of Communication

Refer to Figure 1–3 to identify each message according to the following categories:

Downward, upward, or lateral

Internal or external

Oral or written

1. A lunchtime conversation between administrative assistants.
2. A memo from the vice president of sales to supervisors in the sales department.

(Continued on next page)

Forms of Communication Continued

3. A presentation to the president by the vice president of production.
4. A letter containing a proposal from the vice president of sales of Company A to the vice president of sales of Company B.
5. A memo from employee to supervisor informing the supervisor that the employee will be on jury duty next Thursday.

Check your answers in Appendix F.

Summary

Communication is the process used to exchange ideas. Components of the process include the sender, the message, the receiver, the feedback, and the channel. Barriers to effective communication often complicate the process. Obstacles that originate outside the sender or the receiver are external barriers; those that originate within the sender or the receiver are internal barriers.

The purposes of communication are (1) to establish and build goodwill, (2) to persuade, (3) to obtain or share information, (4) to establish personal effectiveness, and (5) to build self-esteem.

Communication within an organization takes various forms: external and internal; formal and informal; and written, oral, and electronic.

Discussion Questions

1. What are the purposes of communication?
2. Refer to Figure 1–1 and explain how the communication process works. Refer to Figure 1–2 and discuss barriers to communication.
3. List forms of communication within an organization.

Practical Application

Indicate whether each of the following symbols is verbal, nonverbal, or both.

1. A handshake
2. A memo
3. A picture on your desk
4. A letter from a client
5. A conversation with your supervisor

Editing and Proofreading Application

Proofread the following message. Prepare a revised and corrected message on separate paper.

Recently, production of your assembly line has been falling. The number of items your produce ever day is falling and the number of faulty items is increased. I cannot stand why you are unable to improve I need your help in deciding what to do next.

Chapter 2

Electronic Communication

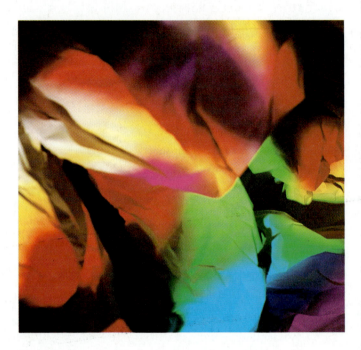

OBJECTIVES

After studying this chapter and completing the chapter activities, you will be able to do the following:

1. Identify equipment and software used to create and edit documents.
2. Identify technologies used to send documents electronically.
3. Define types of media used for storing documents.

CREATING A DOCUMENT

Technology has had a tremendous impact on the way messages are sent and received. Word processors, microcomputers, facsimile machines, teleconferencing facilities, and electronic mail systems are just some of the technologies used in today's electronic office.

Word/information processing is the broad term used to describe the movement of information from origination to storage. *Origination* (creation) is the first stage in the life cycle of a document. *Storage* is the last stage in the life cycle of a document. Documents can be stored in computers, on disks, or in file cabinets. Keyboards, dictating machines, scanners, and voice recognition equipment provide efficient means for creating documents.

Keyboard

A **keyboard** has alphabetic, numeric, and function keys that are used to create, format, edit, and revise documents. A **mouse** is a hand-held device that enables the user to move quickly and efficiently on a computer screen. Other effective devices for moving around on a computer screen are a trackball roller, a touch-screen, and a light pen.

Dictating Machine

With **machine dictation**, the originator speaks into a microphone or a telephone, and the message is recorded onto a magnetic medium. Only the originator's time is required to create a document. The originator also can dictate at a convenient time and place. A transcriber later listens to the recording and keys the message to produce a final copy. Desktop, portable, and centralized dictation systems are available.

Scanner

A **scanner** converts printed text into a digital form that can be read by a computer or a word processor. As text is scanned, it appears on the screen in the correct format. Updating a printed manual is relatively easy using a scanner. The scanner reads the printed pages and records them in digital form on a disk. The keyboarder calls the manual to the screen and keys only the revisions.

An **image scanner** can read graphs, charts, or photographs. Once scanned, these images can be integrated into text documents. Hand-held and desktop scanners are available.

The technology you now use on the job will change dramatically in the future.

A serious drawback to dictating into a machine is the lack of feedback. Feedback tells the sender that the receiver understands the instructions as well as the message.

Many companies use scanners to determine inventories.

Voice Recognition Equipment

Voice recognition technology allows spoken words to be reproduced in printed form on a computer screen. As you speak into a microphone or a headset, the voice sounds are converted into digital impulses that are then compared with sound patterns recorded in the computer's memory. If the two match, the spoken words will be displayed on a computer screen.

EDITING A DOCUMENT

Editing includes keying, proofreading, printing, and revising a draft document to achieve a final form. Electronic workstations, word processors, computers, and application software simplify the editing process.

Electronic Workstations

An **electronic workstation** consists of a keyboard, a monitor or display screen, a printer, a central processing unit, and a storage device. The **screen,** also called a monitor, displays the document as it is keyed, and the **printer** produces the hard copy.

A **central processing unit** (CPU) contains computer chips that control the operating functions of a workstation. These microprocessors work with the software (programmed instructions) to process text, perform mathematical calculations, sort information, and so forth. As information is keyed, it is recorded on a storage device. The storage device may be internal (hard disk) or external (floppy disk).

Word Processors

Word processors are similar to personal computers in that some word processors make calculations through the use of software. A word processor that performs only word-processing functions is called a *dedicated word processor*. Although dedicated word processors are still being used, the trend is toward using workstations that can handle more than word processing.

Computers

Computers range in size and power from large supercomputers to small notebook computers that can fit in a briefcase. The most common workstation is the

personal computer (PC), also called a **microcomputer.** The personal computer has made office technology less expensive and more accessible to workers at all levels. A personal computer is preferred over a word processor because it can handle different applications with a change in software.

Application Software Packages

Application software provides instructions to a computer on how to perform particular functions. Software interacts with the logic of the computer to perform the desired operations. Word-processing software is the most popular application software. Spreadsheet programs, database management software, graphics programs, and desktop publishing software are examples of other widely used application software programs.

Word Processing

Word-processing software enables the user to enter, format, revise, and print text efficiently. Text can be added, deleted, moved, revised, italicizied, converted to bold, put in a contrasting type face, and much more. WordPerfect[1] and Microsoft Word[2] are word-processing software programs.

---

[1]WordPerfect is a registered trademark of WordPerfect Corporation.
[2]Microsoft Word is a registered trademark of Microsoft Corporation.

Document Analysis

Document analysis software, sometimes called a *style checker,* detects possible errors in grammar, punctuation, spelling, capitalization, abbreviation, and number display. It can detect possible violations of the principles of effective writing, such as the use of passive voice or weak words. The reading level of the document and other statistics are presented at the end of the analysis.

Spreadsheet

Spreadsheet software is an electronic worksheet consisting of rows and columns. Rows are read across a spreadsheet and columns are read down. The point at which a row and column intersect is called a *cell.* Formulas are entered within cells to add, subtract, multiply, or divide the various columns and rows. By using formulas, you can change one figure in a spreadsheet and all related figures will be updated automatically. Spreadsheet programs include Lotus 1-2-3[3], Excel[4], and Quattro Pro[5].

Database Management

Database management software provides a way to store and retrieve information on a computer. Client or customer information often is stored in a database. Specific information needed, such as the date of the last order or payment record, can be retrieved quickly by searching the database. Among the database software programs available are dBASE[6] and Paradox[7].

Graphics

Graphics software is used primarily for two purposes: (1) to analyze data and (2) to create visual aids to support presentations. **Analytical graphics software** converts numbers, which may originate from a spreadsheet or a database, into meaningful charts and graphs, such as line charts, bar charts, and pie charts. Such visuals enable managers and other professionals to analyze data easily. **Presentation graphics software** is used for creating visual aids, such as transparencies and slides. Graphics software packages include Harvard Graphics[8] and Corel Draw[9]. See Chapter 36 for a discussion of the creation and use of visual aids.

★ The city taxation department in your hometown probably has developed or soon will develop a database that contains property records for all residents.

---

[3]Lotus 1-2-3 is a registered trademark of Lotus Development Corporation.
[4]Excel is a registered trademark of Microsoft Corporation.
[5]Quattro Pro is a registered trademark of Borland International, Inc.
[6]dBASE is a registered trademark of Borland International, Inc.
[7]Paradox is a registered trademark of Ansa Software, a Borland company.
[8]Harvard Graphics is a registered trademark of Software Publishing Corporation.
[9]Corel Draw is a trademark of Corel Systems, Inc.

Desktop Publishing

With **desktop publishing software,** a personal computer and a high-quality printer can produce documents of typeset quality. Businesses use desktop publishing software to produce newsletters, brochures, advertisements, reports, and other publications that previously were prepared by commercial printers. Text can be formatted in different type sizes and styles. Spacing between lines, called *leading,* can be adjusted to add more or less white space to give the desired effect. Copy can be formatted in newspaper columns, and graphics and scanned images can be combined with text. PageMaker®[10], Ventura Publisher®[11], and First Publisher®[12] are examples of desktop publishing software.

Windows

Windows®[13] software makes a computer and software easier to use—*user friendly.* Several software programs can run at the same time on the same computer. Using a mouse or another device, a computer user can move easily among programs. For example, a user can use word-processing and spreadsheet programs at the same time. Then the work done by the two programs can be combined to produce one document.

Communication Software

Communication software enables a microcomputer with a **modem** (a device that converts computer signals to telephone signals) to send and receive messages over telephone lines. Users can read electronic bulletin boards and access databases containing research data, travel options, stock market prices, and more. Communication software programs include Crosstalk®[14], ProComm®[15], and Smartcom®[16].

Group Decision Support Systems

Group decision support systems software employs effective group characteristics and the computer's calculating capacity to improve member performance within a group. Individual group members prepare various sections of a report that can be integrated into a complete final report.

---

[10]PageMaker is a registered trademark of Aldus Corporation.
[11]Ventura Publisher is a registered trademark of Ventura Software, Inc.
[12]First Publisher is a registered trademark of Software Publishing Corporation.
[13]Microsoft Windows is a registered trademark of Microsoft Corporation.
[14]Crosstalk is a registered trademark of DCA/Crosstalk Communications, Inc.
[15]ProComm is a registered trademark of Datastorm Technologies, Inc.
[16]Smartcom is a registered trademark of Hayes Microcomputer Products, Inc..

Integrated Software

An **integrated software** package contains word-processing, speadsheet, database, graphics, and communication programs. These programs can run simultaneously, and documents in one program can be integrated (merged) into another program. Integrated software packages include Microsoft Works®[17] and Symphony®[18].

CHECKPOINT 1

Origination and Production of Documents

Match the equipment and software on the left with the correct function or definition on the right.

1. Graphics

2. Desktop publishing

3. Personal computer

4. Word processing

5. Scanner

6. Dictation equipment

7. Spreadsheet

a. Software that enables text to be keyed, stored, and revised easily.

b. A device that reads and converts paper documents into a form that can be read by a computer.

c. A device used for recording documents to be keyed.

d. A CPU that uses word processing and other software applications software.

e. Software that can produce documents of typeset quality.

f. Software that provides an electronic worksheet.

g. Software that designs illustrations or charts.

Check your answers in Appendix F.

SENDING A DOCUMENT

Traditional means of sending documents, such as hand delivery, interoffice mail, the U.S. Postal Service, and private carriers like Federal Express, are still widely used. Distribution by electronic methods, however, provides faster and more efficient delivery.

---

[17]Microsoft Works is a registered trademark of Microsoft Corporation.
[18]Symphony is a registered trademark of Lotus Development Corporation.

Communication sent electronically travels over a local or wide area network. A **local area network** (LAN) connects various workstations within a building or nearby buildings. A **wide area network** connects a nationwide or worldwide network. These networks use telephone lines, microwaves, and satellites.

Electronic Mail

Electronic mail (e-mail) is a system by which written messages are sent and stored by means of a computer. An e-mail message is keyed and edited at a workstation and then transmitted to one or more receiving workstations. The receiver views the message on a monitor and may save, delete, print, or respond to the message. E-mail allows the sender to transmit messages almost instantaneously and avoids the problem of "telephone tag" (repeatedly calling and missing the receiver).

An electronic mail system may be an internal system that runs on a LAN, or it may be a public system. For a subscription fee e-mail services such as MCI Mail®[19], CompuServe®[20], and US Sprint's Telenet®[21] enable users to send, receive, and store messages in these services' mailboxes.

Electronic mail messages can also be transmitted through the use of the Internet, which is connected to thousands of computers around the world. Users can access card catalogs from many libraries and transcripts of U.S. Supreme Court opinions, as well as send e-mail messages to fellow students and instructors on college campuses. An Internet connection and the Internet address of other users allow you to collaborate with students in your class or other universities. The vast amount of information available through the Internet attracts new users regularly. For more on the Internet, see Appendix G.

★ Because of networking, many personal computer users have access to large databases and large, powerful computers.

★ Campus e-mail systems facilitate communication among students, faculty, and administration.

Facsimile

Exact copies of documents can be sent electronically using a **facsimile** (fax) device. A facsimile device scans an image and converts it to digital form. The digitized image travels over telephone lines and is converted back to its original form on the receiving end. Fascimiles can be sent using a fascimile machine or a computer modem. Although a facsimile device can transmit any form of printed

---

[19]MCI Mail is a registered trademark of Dow Jones & Company, Inc.
[20]CompuServe is a registered trademark of CompuServe, Inc., and H&R Block, Inc.
[21]Telenet is a registered trademark of US Sprint.

information, it is particularly useful for sending graphics or images, such as blueprints, engineering drawings, and photographs.

Teleconferencing and Videoconferencing

A **teleconference** uses the telephone to link two or more persons in two or more locations. The simplest form of teleconference is an **audioconference,** which is a long-distance telephone conference call. If more than two persons are involved, speakerphones may be used.

A **videoconference** is a more sophisticated form of a teleconference. Video conferencing allows members to see as well as hear each other. Voices, images, and data are transmitted over telephone lines. Video conferences may be full-motion video or freeze-frame video. Full-motion video is the most sophisticated form of videoconference because every continuous movement is broadcast. With freeze-frame video, images change every few seconds.

Voice Mail

Voice mail is a valuable solution to the problem of telephone tag among busy people. Messages are dictated into a voice mail system using a push-button telephone. The verbal message is stored in a "voice mailbox" for retrieval by the receiver.

STORING A DOCUMENT

Messages usually must be saved so they can be retrieved later for reference or distribution to others. The most common storage method is to file printed documents in file cabinets, on shelves, or in trays or boxes. However, because of the high cost of storing paper, other means of storage and retrieval, such as magnetic disks, microforms, and optical disks, often are used.

Magnetic Disks

Information keyed on a computer usually is saved to a flexible or hard magnetic disk for later reading or printing. A **flexible diskette** (floppy disk) is a removable storage medium that can store at least 260 pages. A **hard disk** provides storage for thousands of pages. A hard disk is usually built into a computer and cannot be removed.

Microforms

Documents that must be stored for extended periods of time often are microfilmed. Reduced images of paper documents are stored on microfilm, which may be formatted into **microforms,** such as roll film, microfiche, or jackets. Checks and accounting records often are microfilmed and stored for specific periods of time.

Optical Disks

Optical disk technology combines a scanner with a computer workstation. A document is scanned into a computer, viewed on a screen, indexed for accurate retrieval, and stored on a disk. To store a document, a laser beam burns the images into a disk. Capacity of an optical disk depends on the disk size—5.25, 8, 12, or 16 inches. Optical disks can store all forms of information—text, data, and images.

EXTRA, EXTRA!

★ The 3.5-inch disk is the most popular size flexible disk and is a common storage medium.

Sending and Storing Documents

Match the equipment and technologies on the left with the correct function or definition on the right.

1. Electronic mail
2. Facsimile
3. Flexible diskette
4. Teleconferencing
5. Hard disk
6. Voice mail

a. A device that transmits an exact copy of text or graphics electronically.

b. A storage medium that is built into a computer and is usually not removable.

c. A method of using the telephone or another media to link two or more persons.

d. A system that stores text messages in a voice mailbox.

e. A system by which messages can be sent using a LAN and stored electronically.

f. A removable storage medium.

Check your answers in Appendix F.

★ Because electronic communication technology is progressing so rapidly, you must read continually to stay up to date. *Computer World, Business Week,* and *The Wall Street Journal* are good sources of information about technology

Summary

Automation has improved the speed and efficiency of sending messages. New equipment, software, and technologies have had a tremendous impact on communication and document production.

Equipment, technology, and methods used to create a document include keyboards, dictation machines, scanners, and voice recognition equipment. Documents may be created and edited on dedicated word processors and computers with applications software, such as word-processing, document analysis, spreadsheet, database management, graphics, desktop publishing, Windows, communication, group decision support systems, and integrated software.

Documents may be sent by electronic mail or facsimile and may be stored on flexible diskettes, hard disks, microforms, or optical disks. Teleconferencing, videoconferencing, and voice mail are commonly used forms of electronic communication.

Discussion Questions

1. What types of equipment and software may be used to create and edit documents? Describe the uses of each type of software.
2. Identify technologies used to send documents electronically.
3. List and describe three types of storage media.

Practical Applications

1. Describe a system you might use to store and retrieve documents in an automated office.
2. How would an electronic workstation for a company in Japan differ from one in the United States?

Editing and Proofreading Application

Use a word processor or a computer and a word-processing software program to revise the following message. Correct any spelling, punctuation, or grammar errors using a spell-checking program and a document analysis program if available.

Thank your for you're recent request for more informmation about hour new exorcise program. A brochure detailing the steps in the program the benefits and the cost is inclosed.

Meany participants have made treemendus progress in acheiving there personal goals. To arrange a time to see our facilities and talk to a councilor, call 555-3100.

Grammar Review

As communication skills become increasingly important to employers, the need to understand grammar basics also grows in prominence. Of course it should, because grammar is the framework of language—and language, in turn, is the vehicle you use to communicate.

Part 2 presents grammar from an interesting perspective. First, it tackles grammar on a need-to-know basis; that is, it emphasizes the principles you are most likely to confuse or misuse. Second, it presents a two-chapter review of 18 of the most common errors avoided by good communicators. Technical terms are relatively few and used only when they are needed to simplify discussion and when they cannot be avoided without causing confusion.

Part 2 presents a strong foundation for understanding the language and avoiding its most common abuses and misuses. As you proceed through Chapters 3 through 14, you will want to remind yourself of the importance of grammar to successful communication—and the importance of successful communication to business success.

Part 2

Chapter 3

A Language Foundation

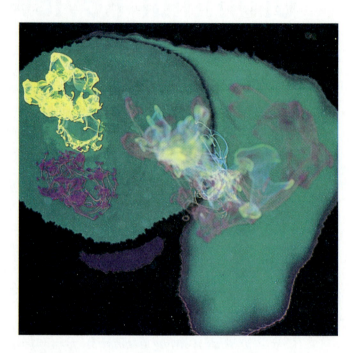

OBJECTIVES

After studying this chapter and completing the chapter activities, you will be able to do the following:

1. Name the eight parts of speech and explain their routine functions.
2. Identify the parts of speech in sentences.
3. Describe subjects and predicates and explain how they function in sentences.
4. Describe clauses and phrases and distinguish between the two.

PARTS OF SPEECH

A dancer destined to stardom had no formal dance training; he knew virtually none of the technical terms for dance moves and steps. At an audition, he was unable to perform basic moves only because he did not understand the dance terms and directions. Fortunately, the choreographer was patient enough to explain the moves. Then, armed with explanations, the young dancer gave an outstanding performance! He became one of the legends of popular dance.

As you read the following brief introduction to grammar terms, you may come across words that are unfamiliar to you. These terms will be easy for you to understand once their definitions and usage are explained. So, let's begin!

Eight basic terms, called the *parts of speech,* describe all the words in the English language. These terms are

nouns	pronouns	verbs	adjectives
adverbs	prepositions	conjunctions	interjections

We will begin our discussion with *nouns.*

★ Armed with basic grammar terms, you will be able to understand the following chapters more easily.

Nouns

Nouns are words that name *people, places,* or *things.* Written with lowercase letters, **common nouns** identify people, places, or things *in general.* Written with capital letters, **proper nouns** identify *specific* people, places, or things. Note the distinction between lowercase and capitalized words in these examples:

★ Our language contains countless numbers of nouns. You can probably list hundreds with little effort.

PEOPLE		PLACES		THINGS	
friend	Jack	city	New York	computer	IBM
sister	Mae	park	Central Park	car	Ford

The list above includes a few *compound nouns* written as two separate words. Compound nouns also can be written as one word, or they can be hyphenated:

ONE WORD	TWO OR MORE WORDS	HYPHENATED WORDS
textbook	editor in chief	sister-in-law
storyboard	bulletin board	runners-up

Your full name is a proper compound noun. So are all other full names, including company and organization names, such as *Temple University* and

★ Always be sure to capitalize proper names.

International Business Machines Corporation. For a complete discussion of nouns, see Chapter 4.

Pronouns

Pronouns serve as short, convenient replacements or substitutes for nouns. **Personal pronouns,** which refer to people, places, and things, are very familiar. Here is a list of singular and plural personal pronouns:

SINGULAR PRONOUNS	PLURAL PRONOUNS
I, you, he, she, it	we, you, they
me, you, him, her, it	us, you, them
my, your, his, her, its	our, your, their
mine, yours, his, hers, its	ours, yours, theirs

The nouns to which the personal pronouns refer in a sentence are their **antecedents.** For example:

> John said *his* manager wants *him* to work with Roberta on *her* committee. (The pronoun *his* serves as a substitute for John's; *him,* for John; *her,* for Roberta's.)

> Betty and Marcia said that *they* would help Carl because *he* has so much to do. (The pronoun *they* refers to Betty and Marcia; *he* refers to Carl.)

Nouns and pronouns work hand in hand, as their similar names hint. Remember that *pro* means "for"; therefore, think of *pro + noun* as a "substitute *for a noun.*" Refer to Chapters 5 and 6 for a detailed discussion of pronouns and pronoun-noun agreement.

★ Create your own examples using the pronouns *I, you, he,* and so forth. Can you identify the noun for which the pronoun is a substitute in each example?

Verbs

A **verb** is a word that indicates action or a condition or a state of being. When a verb indicates action, it describes what a noun or pronoun is doing, or what is being done to a noun or pronoun. For example:

> Bob is keying his proposal. (The verb *is keying* shows the action that the noun *Bob* is performing.)

> The proposal is being keyed. (The verb *is being keyed* shows what is being done to the noun *proposal.*)

★ Two or more words can form one verb just as two or more words can form one noun.

Instead of action, some verbs show a condition or a state of being. For example:

> Ms. Tyler *is* the chief financial officer. (The verb *is* shows no action; it indicates Ms. Tyler's state of being.)

> She *was* formerly the treasurer. (The verb *was* shows no action; it indicates the state of being for the pronoun *she*.)

In the previous examples, consider the words *is* and *was* as equal signs: Ms. Tyler = chief financial officer; She = treasurer.

Verbs tell time; they indicate *when* the action occurred, when the action will occur, or if the action is occurring right now. **Verb tense** is a verb form that indicates time (present, past, future, and so forth). For example:

> She *is* chief financial officer. (The **present tense** verb *is* describes a current state.)

> She *was* treasurer. (The **past tense** verb *was* describes a former state.)

> She *will be* president. (The **future tense** verb *will be* describes a state that has not yet taken place.)

Two, three, or four words often are combined to form one verb phrase. In the following sentences, the words in italics are verb phrases:

> She *has managed* many ad campaigns. Both managers *have been evaluating* the latest offer. This proposal *must have been developed* by the Planning Committee.

See page 38 in this chapter for a brief discussion and examples of verb phrases. See Chapter 7 for an in-depth discussion of verbs.

See page 38 in this chapter for a brief discussion and examples of verb phrases. See Chapter 7 for an in-depth discussion of verbs.

ACROSS CULTURES

- When you hear new citizens speaking English, be patient and understanding. Verb tenses often pose a serious problem for them. Learning English as a second language is a long-term project.

CHECKPOINT 1

Nouns, Pronouns, and Verbs

Identify the underscored words as nouns (N), pronouns (P), or verbs (V).

Theresa Amato[1], the manager of our Data Processing Department, <u>has submitted</u>[2] her revised expense budget to the Finance Committee. When <u>she</u>[3] receives official approval, she <u>will process</u>[4] our orders for new equipment. Everyone in the <u>Data Processing Department</u>[5] hopes that the budget <u>will be approved</u>[6] quickly so that we can have <u>our</u>[7] new <u>computers</u>[8] in operation by next month.

Check your answers in Appendix F.

Adjectives

An **adjective** is a word that describes a noun (person, place, or thing).

an *intelligent* child	an *efficient* engineer
a *meticulous* worker	a *friendly* agent
a *residential* area	an *uninhabited* island
a *mountainous* terrain	a *clean* city
an *expensive* car	a *cherrywood* desk
a *color* printer	her *new* furniture

In the previous examples, the adjectives precede the nouns they describe. Another common pattern places nouns before adjectives by using forms of the verb *to be* (am, is, are) to connect the adjectives to the nouns. In the following examples, note how the forms of the verb *to be* joins adjectives to nouns:

That car is *expensive*. (The adjective *expensive* describes the noun *car*.)

Maria and Paul were *helpful*. (The adjective *helpful* describes Maria and Paul.)

As you can see, the verbs *is* and *were* permit adjectives to describe nouns in these examples. Using the same pattern, adjectives can describe pronouns:

It is *expensive*. (The adjective *expensive* describes the pronoun *it*.)

They were *helpful*. (The adjective *helpful* describes the pronoun *they*.)

For more information on adjectives, see Chapter 9.

Adverbs

An **adverb** can describe a verb, an adjective, or another adverb, as described below.

Adverbs can describe verbs. For example, in the sentence "Antonio is keying his proposal," the verb is *is keying*. Let's add adverbs that describe this verb:

Antonio is keying his proposal *carefully*. (How is Antonio keying? Carefully.)

Antonio is keying his proposal *quickly*. (How is Antonio keying? Quickly.)

Continue with *cautiously, slowly,* and *meticulously,* and then add adverb examples of your own. In each case, an adverb will answer questions such as "How" or

★ *Carefully* and *quickly* describe the action of "keying." Adverbs can describe verbs.

"When" or "Where" about the verb.

> Place all the boxes *here*. (Where?)

> She ordered the merchandise *yesterday*. (When?)

Adverbs can describe adjectives. For example:

> He bought a *very* expensive car. (The adverb *very* describes the adjective *expensive*.)

> He bought an *incredibly* expensive car. (*Incredibly*, an adverb, describes the adjective *expensive*.)

Adverbs can describe other adverbs. For example:

> Yu-lan processed the forms *very quickly*. (*Very*, an adverb, describes *quickly*, another adverb, to intensify its meaning.)

> Yu-lan processed the forms *rather quickly*. (*Rather*, an adverb, describes *quickly*, another adverb, to intensify its meaning.)

Using the same base sentence, insert the adverbs *extremely* and *somewhat* to describe *quickly*. For additional information on adverbs, see Chapter 10.

★ Q: How quickly? A: *Very* quickly. Q: How quickly? A: *Rather* quickly. Adverbs can modify other adverbs.

Adjectives and Adverbs

Identify all adjectives in the following sentences. (Hint: Be sure to determine what each adjective describes.)

1. An expert investment analyst, Sandra Goode, recommended buying stock in Allied Industries.
2. Ms. Goode considers Allied Industries a solid stock with excellent potential.
3. She gave us an informative prospectus on Allied.
4. We enjoyed reading about its progressive management style.

Identify all adverbs in the following sentences. (Hint: Be sure to determine what each adverb describes.)

5. Ms. Goode quickly provided us with the prospectus.
6. She patiently explained why she approved of Allied's stock.
7. We eagerly listened to Ms. Goode's rationale, and we are seriously thinking of buying stock.
8. Because we are very aware of the risks involved, we will buy only a few shares.

Check your answers in Appendix F.

Prepositions

A **preposition** is a word that is linked to a noun or pronoun to form a phrase. Some examples of prepositions are

in	on	before	to	with	for
by	about	above	between	from	off

A preposition begins a **prepositional phrase,** which is a group of words that begins with a preposition and ends with a noun or noun substitute. Here are examples:

in the afternoon	*before* noon	*on* the bus
for Eve and him	*between* you and me	*from* Joanne

Every preposition has an **object,** which is the noun or noun substitute that ends a prepositional phrase. In the previous examples, the objects are *afternoon, noon, bus,* and so forth. Now, notice how prepositional phrases are used in sentences:

The Budget Committee will meet *in the afternoon.*

This morning I met Marty *on the bus.*

For more information on prepositions, see Chapter 11; for additional information on prepositional phrases, see page 39 in this chapter.

Conjunctions

The words *and, but, or,* and *nor* serve to join; these connecting words are called **conjunctions.** What do they join? They join words, phrases, or clauses—two or more of anything. For example:

Three nouns—Maria, Cheryl, *and* Rachel

Two prepositional phrases: She will assign the project to Maria and Cheryl *or* to Charles and Sean.

Two pronouns: She *and* I will complete the project.

Two adverbs: It runs smoothly *and* quietly.

Two independent clauses: Beatriz is in charge of the project, *but* Tony will finish it for her.

★ These are called *coordinate conjunctions;* later, you will be introduced to *subordinate* and *correlative* conjunctions, as well.

Interjections

Interjections, which are short exclamations, are fairly common in everyday speech but are rarely used in business writing. Note these examples:

Wow! What an unbelievable sale!

Great! I appreciate your rushing these samples to me.

For additional information on conjunctions and interjections, see Chapter 12.

Prepositions, Conjuctions, and Interjections

Identify the italicized words as prepositional phrases (PP), conjunctions (C), or interjections (I).

Congratulations![1] I am very pleased to hear *about your promotion,*[2] *and*[3] I wish you success *in your new position.*[4] *On Thursday or Friday,*[5] after we meet *for our annual budget review,*[6] I plan to take a few minutes to discuss your new job *and*[7] the challenges ahead.

Check your answers in Appendix F.

SENTENCES

A **sentence** is a group of words that contains a subject and a predicate and expresses a complete thought. The sentence is the core of all communication. When forming sentences, the parts of speech are arranged into subjects and predicates.

The Subject

The **subject** of a sentence is either the person who is speaking, the person who is spoken to, or the person or thing spoken about, as described below.

The person who is speaking (or writing), always identified by *I* or *we*. For example:

"I already wrote to IBC International; we must estimate these costs conservatively."

The person who is spoken to, always identified by *you* (either singular or plural). For example:

"You did an excellent job, Catherine; you will be pleased to hear that the raises have been approved." "Sign the voucher and attach it to your order." (*You* is the understood subject of *sign* and *attach*.)

The person(s) or thing(s) spoken about. For example:

"Angela is going to accept the transfer to Toronto." (subject: Angela) "Your car is still in excellent shape." (simple subject: car; complete subject: your car) "All government agencies will be affected by the recent changes." (simple subject: agencies; complete subject: all government agencies)

The Predicate

The second part of a sentence, called the *predicate*, is simply the rest of the sentence. The **predicate** is everything in the sentence said by, to, or about the subject:

> Norma <u>is the chief candidate for executive director.</u> (The predicate is everything that follows the complete subject, *Norma*.)

> The union members <u>are losing thousands of dollars each week that they are on strike.</u> (The predicate is everything that follows the complete subject, *The union members*.)

You can try a simple visual technique that will help you both to understand and to reinforce the partnership between subjects and predicates. Use a single underscore to identify the subject of a sentence; use a double underscore to identify the predicate. For example:

> <u>Norma</u> <u>is the chief candidate for executive director.</u>

> <u>The union members</u> <u>are losing thousands of dollars each week they are on strike.</u>

See Chapter 8 for an in-depth discussion of subject-verb agreement.

★ To be sure that you have identified the predicate accurately, locate the verb. The verb is the most important part of the complete predicate.

Subjects and Predicates

CHECKPOINT 4

Identify the complete subject in each sentence.

1. The Budget Committee will meet in the afternoon.
2. I met Julian on the bus this morning.
3. The panel will be named during the summer.
4. I doubt that the proposal will be approved.

Identify the complete predicate in each sentence. (Hint: First find the complete subject. The complete predicate is simply the rest of the sentence.)

5. You will receive a copy of the signed contract.
6. Andres and Akira are considering transfers to our new office.
7. McFarland Industries, Inc., has been our supplier for years.
8. That company used to audit our books.

Check your answers in Appendix F.

CLAUSES AND PHRASES

Two additional terms will complete your brief look at the basics of the English language. These terms are *clauses* and *phrases*. A **clause** is a group of words with a subject and a predicate; a **phrase** is a group of words with no subject or predicate. For a more detailed explanation, let's begin with *clauses*.

Clauses

A clause is labeled **independent** if it can stand alone as a complete sentence. Note these examples:

> Dr. DeMarco is scheduled to speak on Thursday morning. (This is an independent clause with a complete subject (Dr. DeMarco) and a predicate: (the rest of the sentence).)

> One of our sales managers has developed an excellent training manual. (This is an independent clause with a complete subject (One of our sales managers) and a predicate (the rest of the sentence).)

A clause is labeled **dependent** if it cannot stand alone as a complete sentence. Dependent clauses do not convey complete messages by themselves. For example:

> unless she is delayed in London

> which we plan to use in all future training sessions

The following dependent clauses (in italics) must be attached to independent clauses to make any sense:

> Dr. DeMarco is scheduled to speak on Thursday morning *unless she is delayed in London.*

> One of our sales managers has developed an excellent training manual, *which we plan to use in all future training sessions.*

Phrases

A **phrase** is a group of words that does not contain a subject and a predicate. The three kinds of phrases you will use most often are verb phrases, prepositional phrases, and infinitive phrases.

A **verb phrase** is a group of words that functions as one verb. For example:

> Frank *was eating* when we called him. (The verb phrase is *was eating*.)

The IBC Corporation *has been supplying* us with these products. (The verb phrase is *has been supplying*.)

A **prepositional phrase** is a group of words that begins with a preposition and ends with a noun or noun substitute. For example:

Place both cartons *on the desk*. (The prepositional phrase is *on the desk*.)

The boxes *in the office* belong *to him*. (The prepositional phrases are *in the office* and *to him*.)

An **infinitive** is a verb form that consists of a present tense verb preceded by the word *to* (*to run, to eat, to schedule*). An **infinitive phrase** is a group of words that is formed with an infinitive and any modifiers the infinitive may have. For example:

She wants *to schedule conference dates*. (The infinitive phrase is *to schedule conference dates*.)

To run five miles a day is my goal. (The infinitive phrase is *To run five miles a day*.)

★ You can convert any present tense verb into the infinitive form by preceding it with the word *to*. If you change this sentence to "To *walk* five miles a day . . ." you would still be using an infinitive phrase as the subject of the sentence.

CHECKPOINT 5

Clauses and Phrases

Identify the underscored word groups as dependent clauses (DC), independent clauses (IC), infinitive phrases (IP), prepositional phrases (PP), or verb phrases (VP).

At Monday's status meeting,[1] our vice-president said that expenses must be lowered.[2] She is concerned about high costs.[3] She intends to review all budgets carefully[4] and to slash unnecessary expenses.[5] All department managers will be invited[6] to a budget meeting on Tuesday; if you cannot attend,[7] please call Jennifer Logan.[8]

Check your answers in Appendix F.

Words can be classified as eight parts of speech according to their function: nouns, pronouns, verbs, adjectives, adverbs, prepositions, conjunctions, and interjections. When creating sentences, arrange the parts of speech to form subjects and predicates. In addition, clauses, groups of words with a subject and a predicate, and phrases, groups of words with no subject or predicate, have distinct roles in forming effective sentences.

Summary

Discussion Questions

1. Name the eight parts of speech and explain how each part functions in the English language.
2. What is the relationship between nouns and personal pronouns? Use examples to illustrate the relationship.

Spelling and Word Usage Application

Spelling counts! Note the correct spelling of the following words:

accommodate	approximately	education	personnel
sincerely	recommendations	convenience	statement

Rewrite the following sentences, correcting all misspelled words:

1. For our personel banquet, we need to accomodate 150 people.
2. Please read the written statment, fill in the enclosed form, and return both of them to us at your conveneince.
3. The committee received excellent reccommendations for them.
4. We sincerly hope that your project is successful.
5. You should complete your high school educaton.
6. Aproximately 11 percent have returned their papers.

If necessary, refer to Appendix A for the correct usage of these words:

accept/except   principal/principle

Practical Applications

Part A. Provide a word that corresponds to the part of speech indicated for each blank in the following paragraph.

Please be sure to give (noun)[1] a copy (preposition)[2] the expense summary that you and (pronoun)[3] compiled. Then, when you and I (verb)[4] next week, we can look for ways to cut (adjective)[5] expenses. Only by (adverb)[6] reviewing all expenses can we be sure to cut costs (conjunction)[7] increase profits.

Part B. Identify the complete subject in each sentence.

1. Corinne Bates and Ryan Poole are candidates for the job.
2. I will attend the meeting if it begins no earlier than 2 p.m.

3. For the most part, the witnesses have been very cooperative.
4. The company's auditor has been here all week.

Part C. Identify the complete predicate in each sentence.

1. The chief executive officer presided over the meeting.
2. Roger and Anne signed the letters and stuffed the envelopes.
3. Braddock Inn is the site for the reunion.
4. Do you want to join us at the seminar?

Part D. Identify the independent (I) and dependent (D) clauses in each sentence.

1. Can you meet us in the lobby before noon?
2. The professor assigned Chapters 1–3 in the textbook.
3. Because he has the qualifications, Bernardo was selected to chair the committee.
4. Please call us when you have the opportunity.

Part E. Identify verb phrases (VP), prepositional phrases (PP), and infinitive phrases (IP) in each sentence.

1. Ames and Sons has been manufacturing the product for many years.
2. To walk once around the track is difficult for my father.
3. I will be able to participate in the program on Saturday.
4. The researcher plans to study the data carefully.

Editing and Proofreading Application

Identify errors in parts of speech and make a corrected copy of the following message.

> The text book that my sister-in-law Edna given me have been especially helpful. Her choice is not a surprise because Edna is well educate and careful selects appropriate books to help hers relatives. Last year, she supply me with software that helped me develop speedy and accurate data-entry skills in our new computer. Edna are kind to the entire family; we are fortunate that she married mine brother.

Nouns

OBJECTIVES

After studying this chapter and completing the chapter activities, you will be able to do the following:

1. Identify nouns in sentences, and categorize them as either proper nouns or common nouns.
2. Identify the four noun forms.
3. Distinguish between the need for a singular noun and the need for a plural noun in a sentence.
4. Apply rules to form the plurals of most English nouns.
5. Determine when a possessive noun form is required, and form the possessive correctly for both singular and plural nouns.

INTRODUCTION TO NOUNS

Nouns—proper, common, and compound—are discussed in Chapter 3; review pages 29–30 before proceeding with Chapter 4.

A **noun** is a word used to *name* people, places, or things. Think of some words you use to identify *people:*

attorney, attorneys	neighbor, neighbors
editor in chief,	editors in chief

Some routine words you use to identify *places:*

town, towns	state, states
suburb, suburbs	desert, deserts

Some everyday words you use to name *things:*

printer, printers	cable, cables
airplane, airplanes	workshop, workshops

Consider this sentence: "Only one *architect* in this *city* designs *bridges.*" To talk about this person [architect], this place [city], and this project [bridges], you must name them. Pause for a moment to think of other nouns. How does each noun name a person, place, or a thing?

★ When someone is *nominated,* he or she has been *named. Nominate* and *noun* are both derived from the same Latin root, *nomen,* which means *name.*

PROPER NOUNS AND COMMON NOUNS

People, places, and things—these three classifications help you to *identify* nouns, but these groupings do little to help you *use* noun forms correctly. It is more helpful to sort all nouns into one of two very broad categories: *proper* and *common.*

Proper Nouns

A **proper noun** is distinctive because it names a specific person, place, or thing. Proper nouns are always distinguished by capital letters:

Specific people:	Mary Ann	Mr. Yukimura	Ms. Mendelson
Specific places:	Seattle	Orange County	United States
Specific things:	Bic pens	Canon copiers	Ford Escort

As you see, sometimes you need two or more words to identify *one* person, place, or thing—that is, *one* proper noun. One noun, proper or common, that requires two or more words is called a **compound noun.**

Common Nouns

A **common noun** is a word that identifies a person, place, or thing in a general way. Here are examples of common nouns that refer to people:

By gender: man, woman, boy, girl

By age: infant, baby, child, youth, teenager, retiree

By occupation: teacher, doctor, mechanic, newspaper reporter

By interests: baseball fan, skier, reader, movie-goer

This list classifies only *people.* You also can list many classifications for places and for things. Common nouns can be *compound* (*editor in chief, vice-president, son-in-law, attorney general*).

Proper and Common Nouns

A. On a sheet of paper, label three columns **People, Places, Things.** In each column, list three proper nouns and three common nouns.

B. List the nouns in each of the following sentences. Then identify each noun as a proper noun (PN) or a common noun (CN).

1. The two clerks are working in the Silverman Building.
2. Every terminal is connected by cable to our main computer.
3. The photographer, Amy Cordova, submitted all the proofs to the department.
4. Star Industries distributes products for several different companies in Tennessee.
5. Fred Ausiello approved all the layouts, but the president of the company has not seen them yet.
6. One judge has announced her retirement early next September.

Check your answers in Appendix F.

★ Nouns as well as verbs and adjectives change forms: verbs, to show tense (as in *print, prints, printed, printing*); adjectives, for comparisons (as in *clear, clearer, clearest*).

NOUN FORMS

An English noun has only four forms. The base form is the **singular form,** which signals one person, place, or thing. From this base form, three other noun forms can be developed: the plural form, the singular possessive form, and the plural possessive form.

The **plural form** indicates two or more persons, places, or things. This form usually uses an *s* to signal "more than one." The **singular possessive form** indicates ownership by one person, place, or thing. This form usually uses an *'s* to signal ownership. The **plural possessive form** indicates ownership by two or more persons, places, or things. This form usually uses an apostrophe to signal ownership.

In the following examples, note that the signal is always added to the base form (the singular form):

				SIGNAL
Singular:	auditor	president	clerk	—
Plural:	auditors	presidents	clerks	s
Singular Possessive:	auditor's	president's	clerk's	's
Plural Possessive:	auditors'	presidents'	clerks'	s'

Read the preceding examples aloud. Notice that you pronounced *auditors, auditor's,* and *auditors'* the same. In speaking, you do not distinguish among these three forms; you leave that chore to the listeners. But not so in writing. The writer must use signals to tell the readers which words are plural and which words are singular or plural possessive. The signal for plurals is the *s* ending on almost all nouns. The signal for possessives is the *apostrophe.*

2 · CHECKPOINT · *Noun Forms*

Complete the following sentences.

1. A noun has_____forms.
2. The base form for every noun is its _____form.
3. From the base form, the other noun forms that can be created are the_____.
4. In English, the signal for plurals is _____.
5. In English, the signal for possessives is _____.

Check your answers in Appendix F.

NOUN PLURALS

Most noun plurals may be formed by using one of three rules. These rules for forming plurals are easy to learn and apply.

Rule 1—For Most Nouns

Add *s* to the end of most nouns to form the plural. This rule applies to most nouns in our language. Note how the rule applies to the various applications below:

★ The first rule applies to most nouns! Consider it THE rule for forming plurals.

	SINGULAR	PLURAL	SINGULAR	PLURAL
Common Nouns	pamphlet	pamphlets	frame	frames
	employee	employees	department	departments
Proper Nouns	Smith	the Smiths	Denton	the Dentons
	Corvette	Corvettes	Neanderthal	Neanderthals
Abbreviations	CPA	CPAs	R.N.	R.N.s
Numbers	10	10s	1990	1990s

Note how plural nouns (in italics) are used in these sentences:

> In the *1980s*, we granted 23 new *franchises;* in the *1990s*, we plan to grant 75 more.

> Our target market is *supervisors* and *managers* in their *30s*.

> We polled 75 *CPAs* in two *regions* to obtain their *responses*.

> Our *agents* in both *districts* asked that we schedule our *meetings* during the summer *months*.

The next two rules cover a limited number of nouns. Because the application of each of these rules results in plurals that end in *s*, you should continue to consider *s* as the signal for plural nouns.

Rule 2—For Singular Nouns That End in *s, x, z, sh,* and *ch*

Add *es* to any singular noun that ends in *s, x, z, sh,* or *ch*. Say the following singular-plural pairs aloud:

SINGULAR	PLURAL	SINGULAR	PLURAL
lens	lenses	tax	taxes
Lopez	the Lopezes	bush	bushes
Lynch	the Lynches	wrench	wrenches

In each case, you probably noticed that you added one syllable whenever you said the plural form aloud. The *es* ending on these plurals represents that extra syllable, that added "iz" sound that you hear in "lens.*iz*," "tax.*iz*," and so forth.

Rule 3—For Nouns That End in y

Nouns that end in *y* form their plurals in one of two distinct ways. The first will sound familiar: add an *s* to form the plural of any noun ending in *y* when the *y* follows a vowel (*a, e, i, o,* or *u*). Here are examples of plurals that follow this rule:

delay, delays   tray, trays
key, keys   relay, relays

With the exception of proper nouns, nouns that have a **consonant** (all letters except vowels) before the final *y*, change the final *y* to *i* and then add *es*.

SINGULAR	>	>	>	>	>	PLURAL
city		citi		citi + es		cities
territory		territori		territori + es		territories

EXTRA, EXTRA!

★ If you are unsure about the plural of a noun that ends in *y*, you may want to consult a dictionary.

---

3   *Noun Plurals*

CHECKPOINT

Complete the following sentences.

1. The most common rule for forming plurals is to_____.
2. Form the plural of nouns that end in *s, x, z, sh,* or *ch* by _____.
3. Form the plural of a noun ending in *y* when the *y* follows a vowel (for example, *delay*) by_____.
4. Form the plural of a noun ending in *y* when the *y* follows a consonant (for example, *company*) by_____.

Form the plural of each singular noun.

5. bank_____   7. inventory_____
6. lunch_____   8. boy _____

Check your answers in Appendix F.

SPECIAL PLURAL FORMS

On a daily basis, you use three pairs of nouns that are irregular because they follow none of the previously mentioned rules: *man-men*, *woman-women*, and *child-children*. Because they are so familiar, these plurals are easily recognizable.

Irregular nouns are nouns that do not form their plurals by adding an *s* or *es*. They may change their vowels (*tooth*, *teeth* or *foot*, *feet*), or they may change their consonants (*life*, *lives* or *shelf*, *shelves*).

Foreign Words

Because the *s* ending is standard for English plurals, plurals that do not end in *s* may sound odd. English claims a considerable number of such words, mostly borrowed from Latin and Greek. By becoming familiar with the words in the following list, effective communicators can use them with ease. Notice that alternative forms have two plurals from which to choose; effective writers use either of the alternatives:

ACCEPTABLE

CHANGE	SINGULAR	PLURAL
1. -um to -a	curriculum	curricula or curriculums
	datum	data
	medium	media or mediums
2. -us to -i	alumnus	alumni
	stimulus	stimuli
3. -a to -ae	alumna	alumnae
	formula	formulae or formulas
4. -is to -es	crisis	crises
	analysis	analyses
5. -ion to -ia	criterion	criteria or criterions
-ix to -ices	matrix	matrices
-ex to -ices	index	indices or indexes

★ Although the plurals *crises and analyses* end in *s*, they are formed in an unusual way.

Nouns Ending in o

Nouns that end in *o* form their plurals in one of two ways. Many simply add *s* to form their plurals:

SINGULAR	ADD s	SINGULAR	ADD s	SINGULAR	ADD s
ratio	ratios	radio	radios	piano	pianos

★ All musical terms ending in *o* form their plurals by adding only *s*, for example, *soprano-sopranos* and *contralto-contraltos*.

Others add *es* to form their plurals:

SINGULAR	ADD es	SINGULAR	ADD es	SINGULAR	ADD es
tomato	tomatoes	potato	potatoes	veto	vetoes

Clearly, you must use a dictionary whenever you are in doubt.

Compound Nouns

Compound nouns, you will remember, are formed from two or more words. In each case, note how the compounds are spelled.

Rule 1—Compound Nouns—Spelled as Separate Words

Compound nouns may be spelled as separate words; in this case, the most important word is made plural:

SINGULAR	PLURAL
editor in chief	editors in chief
vice president	vice presidents

Rule 2—Compound Nouns—Joined by Hyphens

Compound nouns may be joined by hyphens; in this case, the base form is made plural:

SINGULAR	PLURAL
brother-in-law	brothers-in-law
daughter-in-law	daughters-in-law

Some modern hyphenated compounds form their plurals on the last element of the compound:

hand-me-down   hand-me-downs   tie-in   tie-ins

Rule 3—Compound Nouns—Spelled as One Word

Compound nouns may be spelled as one solid word; the plural is formed by adding *s,* adding *es,* or changing the *y* to *i* and then adding *es* (depending on the word ending). Treat these words as one word, not as the combination of two words

letterhead   letterheads   textbook   textbooks

Proper Names

When forming plurals, treat a proper name like any other noun with this exception: Add only *s* to all proper nouns that end in *y;* ignore the "change *y* to *i* . . ." rule with proper names.

In the following examples of proper-noun plurals, the word *the* is inserted before the plurals to simulate real-life use:

John Haggerty   the Haggertys   Rosemary Portera   the Porteras

★ This exception preserves the base spelling of a person's name. The spelling *Haggertys* is obviously closer to the base than *Haggerties*!

★ Dictionaries provide invaluable usage guides; for example, for *data,* the entry reads "noun plural but singular or plural in usage." Learn to rely on a dictionary for such help.

One-Form Nouns

Some nouns have only one form. Depending on the noun, that one form may be always plural or always be singular:

> Always plural: thanks, scissors, belongings

> Always singular: news, mathematics, headquarters

Titles

Occasionally you may need to form the plural of a name with a courtesy title such as the singular *Mr. Smith.* In such cases, make either the title or the name plural, not both:

Miss Smith	Misses Smith	the Miss Smiths
Mr. Smith	Messrs. Smith	the Mr. Smiths

ACROSS **CULTURES**

• The plural of *Mister* is the French word *Messieurs,* the abbreviation of which is *Messrs.*

CHECKPOINT 4 — Special Plural Noun Forms

Form the plural of each singular noun. Use a dictionary if necessary.

1. bulletin board
2. woman
3. vice-president
4. Miss DeGroat
5. Williamson (last name)
6. floppy disk
7. Mr. Ramirez
8. motto

Check your answers in Appendix F.

POSSESSIVE NOUNS

Possessive nouns have two signals: the apostrophe (') and the apostrophe plus *s* ('s). Because these are the *only* signals, they are your *only* choices when forming possessive nouns.

Forming Possessive Nouns: Two Basic Rules

Add an apostrophe plus *s* ('s) to all singular nouns, both common and proper:

SINGULAR NOUN + 's	=	SINGULAR POSSESSIVE
man	+ 's	=	one *man's* opinion
executive	+ 's	=	an *executive's* word
Mr. Ross	+ 's	=	Mr. *Ross's* district
district attorney	+ 's	=	the *district attorney's* actions

Add only an apostrophe (') to any plural if it ends in *s:*

PLURAL NOUN + '	=	PLURAL POSSESSIVE
executives	+ '	=	three *executives'* goals
district attorneys	+ '	=	the *district attorneys'* ideas

The important words in this last rule are "if it ends in *s.*" Which plurals do not end in *s*? Irregular plural nouns (such as *men, women, children,* and *alumni*) and some compound nouns are examples of plural forms that do not end in *s.* For these exceptions, add an *'s* to form their possessives; in other words, apply the rule for singular nouns:

PLURAL NOUN + 's	=	PLURAL POSSESSIVE
women	+ 's	=	both *women's* investments
children	+ 's	=	good *children's* books
brothers-in-law	+ 's	=	my two *brothers-in-law's* cars

Forming Possesive Nouns

5 **CHECKPOINT**

Form the possessive of each of the following nouns.

1. factory
2. Cathy Ruiz
3. children
4. committees

5. sales representatives
6. nurses
7. committee
8. Personnel Department

Check your answers in Appendix F.

Using Possessive Nouns Correctly

If you remember that possessive nouns describe or modify other nouns (just like adjectives), you will use these nouns correctly.

SINGULAR POSSESSIVE NOUN

Alan's file	*client's* home	*manager's* seminar

PLURAL POSSESSIVE NOUN

lawyers' files	*clients'* homes	*managers'* seminars

In speaking and writing, people sometimes take shortcuts by omitting "understood" words. In the following sentences, note how the missing understood words (in parentheses) can disguise the need for the possessive:

"Jean's office is much larger than Yuan's (office)."

"Jon's computer is newer than Mae's (computer)."

CHECKPOINT

6 Identifying Correct Noun Forms

Select the correct word and identify its form: plural (P), singular possessive (SP), or plural possessive (PP).

1. Angelo informed all the (managers, manager's, managers').
2. The only estimate that was accepted was my (supervisors, supervisor's, supervisors').
3. All (divisions, division's, divisions') forecasts must be submitted promptly.
4. This (memos, memo's, memos') conclusions have little validity.
5. None of these (memos, memo's, memos') offer valid conclusions.
6. As soon as we have the (presidents, president's, presidents') approval, we will send you our purchase order.
7. The (Kleins, Klein's, Kleins') real estate holdings were purchased by Satterlee Enterprises.

Check your answers in Appendix F.

Nouns are the words used to name people, places, and things. Proper nouns are distinctive and are capitalized, such as *International Cargo, Inc.* Common nouns are general words and are written in lowercase letters, such as *company*.

The primary rule for forming noun plurals (add *s* to the singular form) applies to most nouns. Three lesser rules cover virtually all other nouns. To form noun possessives, add *'s* to singulars and plurals that do not end in *s* and add an apostrophe to all plural forms that do end in *s*.

Summary

Discussion Questions

1. Describe the system for signaling readers that a noun is plural. Explain why this system offers listeners less help than it offers readers.
2. When is a possessive form of a noun required? How does a possessive noun function as an adjective?

Spelling and Word Usage Application

Note the correct spelling of the following words:

referred	specifications	permanent	annuity
mortgage	immediate	assistant	foreign

Rewrite the following sentences, correcting all misspelled words.

1. The payment on Harry's anuity will be nearly $1,500.
2. The following foriegn countries are cooperating on the project: Italy, Australia, and New Zealand.
3. The spesifications revealed that the morgage will be fully paid in the year 2015.
4. Sara suggested that we hire a permenent asistant for the job instead of a temporary one.
5. This is the contract to which Ms. D'Antonio refered.
6. Paul told the reporters that we need an imediate answer.

If necessary, refer to Appendix A for the correct usage of these words:

forth/ fourth   addition/ edition

Practical Applications

Part A. Select the correct word in each of the following sentences.

1. Only three of the (prototypes, prototype's) are available.
2. The (HMOs, HMO's) policies are explained in this brochure.
3. We plan to review all these (expenses, expenses').
4. We will replace all our (computers, computer's) next year.
5. This (disk's, disks') storage capacity is inadequate.

Part B. Write ten sentences using each of the following possessive noun forms.

1. employees'
2. employee's
3. Smiths's
4. memo's
5. municipality's
6. woman's
7. women's
8. food's
9. telephones'
10. editors in chief's

Part C. Write ten sentences using each of the following proper and common nouns.

1. bank
2. Bank
3. college
4. College
5. store
6. Store
7. magazine
8. Magazine
9. anthology
10. Anthology

Editing and Proofreading Application

Identify all errors in noun usage, word usage, and spelling in this excerpt from a performance appraisal; write a corrected copy.

This evaluations of Angelica Ford, one of the perminent full-time administrative assistants' in the Finance Department, cover her first six month's of employment, a periods from January 20 through July 20, 199-. Angelica quickly mastered the basics' of her job, in which she assist three mortgage banker's. She processes paperwork imediately. She handles complicated financial specifications' flawlessly. Her communication skill's is good, and she handles foriegn clients in a professional manners. As a result, in the past six months all client's comments have been exceptionally positive.

On the basis of this positive evaluations, we are proceeding with a six-month raise request for Angelica, and we will schedule future evaluation's of Angelica on an annul basis.

Chapter 5

Pronouns

OBJECTIVES

After studying this chapter and completing the chapter activities, you will be able to do the following:

1. Identify personal, intensive, reflexive, and interrogative pronouns.
2. Use nominative, objective, and possessive case personal pronouns correctly.
3. Use *who*, *whom*, *whoever*, and *whomever* correctly in your writing.
4. Identify the correct pronouns in pronoun phrases, after the word *than*, and in appositives.
5. Use intensive, reflexive, and interrogative pronouns to improve your sentences.

CLASSIFICATION OF PRONOUNS

Pronouns are ideal substitutes for *nouns,* and they help to communicate the *nominative, objective,* and *possessive* forms to listeners and readers. They play a major role in speaking and writing. In addition, they help writers avoid repetition and immaturity in their sentences. Note this example:

> John and Bea recently earned degrees in accounting; John and Bea aspire to be CPAs. Too, John and Bea are looking forward to starting an accounting practice. John and Bea have confidence in John's and Bea's future success.

You can see that the use of pronouns would have greatly improved the paragraph above.

Unlike nouns, pronouns do not have a base form. As a result, the nominative, objective, and possessive case *personal pronouns* vary according to their use in a sentence. In addition to personal pronouns, communicators also can use *intensive, reflexive,* and *interrogative pronouns* to enhance their writing significantly.

A careful look at the various types of pronouns and their functions will be helpful. Let's begin with *personal pronouns.*

★ Remember that the base form of a noun is the *singular form.*

COMMONLY USED PRONOUNS

To best exemplify the changing "faces" of personal pronouns, note these pronouns that refer to the writer(s) or speaker(s): *I, me, my, mine, we, us, our,* and *ours.* How can you determine which pronoun to use in a given sentence? The relationship of the pronoun to other words in the sentence will influence your selection. Because *nominative case pronouns* play a very important role in our communications, let's examine them first.

Nominative Case

A **nominative case pronoun,** sometimes referred to as a *subjective case pronoun,* may be used as a subject or a *predicate nominative.* A **predicate nominative** is a noun or pronoun that refers to the subject and follows a form of the verb *to be* (*am, is, are*). Note these nominative case pronouns:

★ *Who* and *whoever* are also nominative forms. For example: "*Who* is she?" "*Whoever* is here will have to wait."

PERSON	SINGULAR	PLURAL
First (person(s) speaking)	I	we
Second (person(s) spoken to)	you	you
Third (person(s) spoken about)	he, she, it	they

The following two rules indicate when nominative case pronouns are used.

Rule 1: Use a nominative case pronoun when it is the subject of a sentence. For example:

Carla and *I* voted for him.

They completed the project on time.

Rule 2: Use a nominative case pronoun after a form of the verb *to be* (am, is, was) or a verb phrase ending in *been* or *be.* In these situations, the pronoun serves as a *predicate nominative.* Note these examples:

It is *she* who received all the attention.

It must have been *he* who sent the fax.

If I were *they,* I would handle this differently.

Objective Case

★ Notice that the form for the second person (the person spoken to) is the same for nominative and objective, singular and plural—*you.*

★ *Whom* and *whomever* are also objective forms. For example: "To *whom* is she leaving her money?" "They will employ *whomever* they interview the second time."

An **objective case pronoun** may be used as a direct or indirect object of a **transitive verb,** which is a verb that denotes action and takes objects. A **direct object** is a noun or pronoun directly affected by the action of the verb. (They chose *me.*) An **indirect object** is a noun or pronoun that receives the verb's action. (They gave *me* a gift.) An objective case pronoun may also be used as an object of a preposition. Note these objective case pronouns:

PERSON	SINGULAR	PLURAL
First (person(s) speaking)	me	us
Second (person(s) spoken to)	you	you
Third (person(s) spoken about)	him, her, it	them

The general rule for the use of objective case pronouns has the following three parts:

Rule 1: Use an objective case pronoun when it is the *direct object* of a transitive verb, a verb that denotes action. In this situation, a pronoun answers the question "what" about the verb:

Please send *them* by express mail. (Send what? Send *them.*)

Buy *it* at the pharmacy. (Buy what? Buy *it.*)

Rule 2: Use an objective case pronoun when it is the *indirect object* of a transitive verb. In these sentences, a pronoun receives the verb's action:

He bought *her* a bracelet. (Bought whom? Bought *her.*)

The manager gave *us* the tickets. (Gave whom? Gave *us.*)

Rule 3: Use an objective case pronoun as the *object of a preposition;* here, a pronoun answers the question "whom" about the preposition:

Give the memo to *me.* (To whom? To *me.*)

I made it available for *her.* (For whom? For *her.*)

CHECKPOINT 1

Personal Pronouns

Select the correct word in the following sentences.

1. Bob and (I/me) plan to attend the budget meeting.
2. Mario gave the computer printout to (I/me).
3. You can see (he/him) tomorrow at the meeting.
4. (Them/They) discovered the mistake in time.
5. It was not (I/me) who called this morning.
6. (He/Him) originated the idea to renovate the building.
7. I made it available for (they/them) to analyze today.

Check your answers in Appendix F.

Possessive Case

A pronoun that indicates ownership or possession is a **possessive case pronoun.** Unlike nouns, pronouns do not need an apostrophe to signal possession; instead, the following possessive case pronouns do the job:

PERSON	SINGULAR	PLURAL
First	my, mine	our, ours
Second	your, yours	your, yours
Third	his, her, hers, its	their, theirs

★ *Whose* is also a possessive form. For example: "*Whose* are these?" "*Whose* books are on the table?"

Follow the three rules below in pronoun selection:

Rule 1: To indicate ownership, use *my, your, his, her, its, their,* or *our* when the pronoun immediately precedes the noun it modifies:

These are *our* folders.

Your speech was very inspiring.

Rule 2: To indicate ownership, use *mine, yours, his, hers, ours,* and *theirs* when the pronoun is separated from the noun it modifies or when the noun is omitted:

The clothes are *hers.*

Those are *theirs.*

Rule 3: Precede a **gerund** (a verb form that ends in *-ing* and serves as a *noun*) with a possessive case pronoun:

My going to the party surprised her.

The firm was aided by *your* witnessing the accident.

The words *its* and *it's; their, there,* and *they're;* and *your* and *you're* frequently are interchanged incorrectly by writers. Study them carefully to avoid misusing them.

Its or It's

The possessive case pronoun *its* is a self-contained word showing ownership. An apostrophe is not necessary. For example:

Its color is very bright; *its* design is eye-catching.

On the other hand, the contraction *it's* is a shortened version of *it is* or *it has.* An apostrophe is inserted in place of the missing letters. For example:

It's raining; *it's* rained every day this week.

Their or There or They're

The possessive case pronoun *their*, like other pronouns, does not need an apostrophe to indicate ownership. For example:

Their call came this morning; *their* news is exciting.

The second spelling, *there*, is a *demonstrative pronoun.* A **demonstrative pronoun** is a pronoun that answers the question "where" in a sentence:

Put the newspapers *there*. The computer is in *there*.

There is also frequently used as an *expletive.* An **expletive** is used to invert a sentence (the verb precedes the subject). In the following sentences, *there* is used as an expletive:

There are pens on the desk. *There* is paper in the drawer.

The third spelling, *they're*, is a contraction of *they are.* For example:

They're here already; that is unusual because *they're* usually late.

Your or You're

The possessive case pronoun *your* is used to indicate both singular and plural ownership. For example:

Is *your* suit new? Ladies, *your* suggestions are helpful.

On the other hand, the contraction *you're* is a shortened version of *you are.* Note this example:

You're welcome! We hope *you're* able to visit again.

★ Be certain that you understand the differences between the possessive forms *their, its,* and *your* and the contractions *they're, it's,* and *you're.*

Possesive Case

Select the correct form in the following sentences.

1. Sachi said that (you/your) singing was very professional.
2. (Its/It's) (their/they're) choice to make.
3. (His/He) working overtime helped to complete (our/ours) work.
4. (Their/There) suggestions are both intelligent and logical.
5. The notes are (he's/his), but the ideas are (hers/her's).
6. (You're/Your) correct about all aspects of the job.
7. The new computer on the mahogany desk is (our's/ours).

Check your answers in Appendix F.

Who and Whom

The application of *who* and *whom* puzzles many writers who otherwise have little difficulty in selecting correct nominative and objective pronoun forms that refer to people. The following guidelines can help to eliminate any question that you may have about the use of *who* or *whom* in your writing and speaking:

Rule 1: Use the nominative form *who* when the subject of a verb is needed. If you can substitute other nominative case pronouns such as *he*, *she*, *we*, or *they*, then *who* is the correct choice. For example:

Who should attend? (*He/She* should attend.)

Who are here? (*They* are here.)

Rule 2: Use the nominative form *who* as a *predicate nominative*:

She is *who*? (She is my cousin.)

The leaders are *who*? (The leaders are *they*.)

Rule 3: Use the objective form *whom* as the direct object of a transitive verb. If you can substitute other objective case pronouns such as *him*, *her*, *them*, or *me*, then *whom* is the correct choice:

Tom selected *whom*? (Tom selected *him/her*.)

Whom did they call this morning? (They did call *them* this morning.)

★ *Who* and *whom* can be used as either singular or plural forms.

Rule 4: Use the objective form *whom* as the object of a preposition:

To *whom* should I give the box? (I should give the box to *him*.)

The receipt is for *whom*? (The receipt is for *them*.)

Whoever and Whomever

Whoever is the nominative form and follows the same guidelines as *who* and other nominative case pronouns. *Whoever* is used as the subject of a verb and as a predicate nominative.

Whoever is chosen I will support. (*She/He* is chosen.)

Whoever will help us will be thanked. (*He/She* will help us.)

Whomever is the objective form and follows the same guidelines as *whom* and other objective case pronouns. *Whomever* serves as the direct object of a verb and the object of a preposition.

Thomas will award *whomever* he wants. (He wants *them*.)

Give the dictionary to *whomever* she suggests. (She suggests *him/her*.)

★ Remember, if *he* would be correct, then use *who*; if *him* would be correct, then use *whom*.

★ A helpful reminder is that hi**m**, the**m**, who**m**, and who**m**ever are all objective case pronouns. They all also have a common bond—the letter "**m**."

---

3 CHECKPOINT

Who and Whom

Select the correct pronoun in each of the following sentences.

1. The woman (who/whom) we worked for is now working at the Acme.
2. (Whoever/Whomever) answers the telephone will win the prize.
3. To (who/whom) should I deliver the package?
4. Where is the man (who/whom) we saw last night?
5. (Who/Whom) caused the accident?
6. We will answer to (whoever/whomever) the committee chooses.
7. The accountant you recently hired is (who/whom)?

Check your answers in Appendix F.

Pronoun Phrases

If phrases such as *we bankers* and *us bankers* appear in sentences, selecting the correct pronouns is relatively easy. Just follow this guideline: Temporarily omit the noun *bankers* and say the sentence aloud to determine which pronoun fits. For example:

> (*We/Us*) bankers are meeting today. (Which is correct? *We* are meeting? *Us* are meeting? *We* is correct.)

> Direct the speech on interest rates to (*we/us*) bankers. (Which is correct? Direct the speech to *we*? Direct the speech to *us*? *Us* is correct.)

Personal Pronouns Following Than

When the word *than* is used to indicate comparison, select an objective case pronoun after *than* in a complete thought. The statement "I watched her rather than *him*" means that *I watched her instead of watching him.* Select a nominative case pronoun after *than* when it introduces an incomplete thought. For example:

> I key documents faster than (*he/him*). (keys documents)

He is the correct pronoun form. How can you be sure? Say aloud "than he what?" The answer to the question is "than he keys documents." Therefore, *he* is the correct pronoun. For example:

> She has more vacation days than (*I/me*). (This sentence is stating that she has more vacation days than *I have.*)

> Len gave more to charity than (*they/them*). (This sentence is stating that Len gave more to charity than *they gave.*)

★ "I key documents faster than he" is a complete sentence but an incomplete thought. Say the sentence aloud and complete the thought: "I key documents faster than *he* keys documents."

Pronouns in Appositives

An **appositive** is a noun or pronoun that renames another noun or pronoun that immediately precedes it. Pronouns that rename nouns that precede them should agree in case form. In the following sentence, *Tom, Jay,* and *she* is an *appositive.* The nominative pronoun *she* must agree with the subject *graduates:*

> The new graduates, Tom, Jay, and *she*, are interviewing for management-trainee positions.

The appositive renames the subject of the sentence (graduates) and therefore must be in the nominative case.

> As soon as you arrive, give the documents to *us*, Sam and *me*.

Sam and *me* is an appositive that renames *us*, the object of the preposition *to*. Because *us* is an objective case pronoun, *me*, also an objective case pronoun, is correct.

INTENSIVE PRONOUNS

An **intensive pronoun** is a compound pronoun form created by joining a pronoun with *self* or *selves*, such as *myself* and *yourselves*. Use intensive pronouns to provide emphasis in a sentence. For example:

> I *myself* completed the project in two days.

> You *yourselves* are responsible for this budget.

Use the singular forms of intensive pronouns as follows:

TO EMPHASIZE	FOLLOW IT WITH
I or me	myself
you	yourself
she or her	herself
he or him	himself
it	itself

Use the plural forms of intensive pronouns as follows:

TO EMPHASIZE	FOLLOW IT WITH
we or us	ourselves
you	yourselves
they or them	themselves

★ *Hisself, theirself,* and *theirselves* are incorrect forms; do not use them. They are *always* wrong.

Selecting Pronouns

Select the correct pronoun in each of the following sentences.

1. All of you (yourself/yourselves) deserve the credit.
2. You (yourself/yourselves) are an inspirational speaker.
3. The attorneys, Gladys and (he/him), represent the Thompsons.
4. We are celebrating for the assistants, Lou and (she/her).
5. No one deserves more credit than (he/him).
6. The salespersons at Allied sold more cars than (they/them).
7. (We/Us) students look forward to the end of the term.

Check your answers in Appendix F.

REFLEXIVE PRONOUNS

A **reflexive pronoun** is also a compound pronoun form that ends in *self* or *selves*. However, a reflexive pronoun refers to a noun or pronoun that appears earlier in a sentence. For example:

> We found *ourselves* reminiscing at the reunion. (The reflexive pronoun *ourselves* refers to *we.*)

> The accountant gave *himself* an overdue raise. (The reflexive pronoun *himself* refers to *accountant.*)

A pronoun that ends in *self* or *selves* should only be used to emphasize or to refer to an earlier noun or pronoun. Reflexive pronouns should not be used instead of other personal pronouns, such as *I* or *me.*

★ Avoid the wrong uses of pronouns ending in *self* or *selves*: "Kim and *myself* (should be *I*) are bank tellers. Bring the safe deposit box forms to me and *herself* (should be *her*)."

INTERROGATIVE PRONOUNS

An **interrogative pronoun** begins a question that leads to a noun response. Interrogative pronouns are *who, whose, whom, which,* and *what*; notice that they all begin with the letter *w.* Here are questions beginning with interrogative pronouns:

> *Who* is in your office?
>
> *Whose* are these?
>
> *What* are your plans?

> *Whom* do you want to call you?
>
> *Which* of those are important?

Identifying Correct Pronouns

Identify the correct pronoun in each of the following sentences.

1. Judy gave the graphs to Robert and (me/myself).
2. Tom wrote (hisself/himself) a reminder and left it on his desk.
3. Rae and (myself/I) will document the information.
4. Terri did the work (hersself/herself).
5. The systems analysts directed the work (theirselves/themselves).
6. We three, Victor, Jane and (I/myself), approve of your suggestion.
7. We (ourself/ourselves) are responsible for this error.

Check your answers in Appendix F.

Summary

Pronouns, which serve as noun substitutes, take different forms depending upon their relationship to other words in a sentence.

Some of the most frequently used pronouns are personal nominative case pronouns (I, you, he, she), personal objective case pronouns (me, us, them), and personal possessive case pronouns (its, their, your, his, hers). Effective communicators follow the guidelines for other nominative and objective personal pronouns to avoid incorrect usage of the pronouns *who, whom, whoever,* and *whomever,* as well as the pronouns that follow the word *than.* Compound pronouns ending in *self* and *selves* (myself, yourself, ourselves) have two special roles. They are used to provide emphasis (intensive pronouns) and to refer to a noun or pronoun that appears earlier in a sentence (reflexive pronouns). In addition, pronoun phrases and pronouns in appositives, if used correctly, enhance written communication.

Because pronouns have a vital role in effective communication, writers and speakers must become proficient in their use.

Discussion Questions

1. Mention two rules that indicate when nominative case pronouns are used, and give examples to illustrate nominative case pronoun usage in sentences.
2. When does a compound pronoun form that ends in *self* or *selves* serve as a reflexive pronoun in a sentence? Serve as an intensive pronoun in a sentence?

Spelling and Word Usage Application

Note the correct spelling of the following words:

nineteen	its	secretary	possession	software
pronunciation	presence	occurred	pastime	listening

Rewrite the following sentences, correcting all misspelled words.

1. It's purpose is to train a secretery to use computer softwear.
2. What is the correct pronounciation of the caller's name?
3. The speaker's presents at the school was very inspirational.
4. My favorite pasttime is lisening to classical music.
5. What occured at the conference that is of interest to us?
6. They are in possesion of ninteen certificates of deposit.

If necessary, refer to Appendix A for the correct usage of the following words:

hear/ here   stationary/ stationery

Practical Applications

Part A. Select the correct answer from the choices in parentheses.

1. Tyrone (hisself/himself) put the stock in the storeroom.
2. The trainer will work with (whoever/whomever) has completed the first module.
3. John and Betty (theirselves/themselves) decorated both trees.
4. If I were (he/him), I would not attend tonight's meeting.
5. The toddler (itself/herself) put the puzzle together.
6. She gave Rodolfo and (he/him) the copy of the printout.
7. We (ourself/ourselves) prepared the itinerary.
8. Did Li-ming see Peter and (he/him) at the morning session?

9. The two unabridged dictionaries (themself/themselves) made the carton too heavy.
10. The supervisor approved of (he/his) relocating to the other plant.

Part B. Correct any errors in nominative, objective, and possessive case personal pronouns.

1. Gloria's outdated typewriter was her to keep.
2. Did May ask for the operator whom assisted her?
3. We voted for they for treasurer and parliamentarian.
4. It's Appendix A is incomplete.
5. Him working on the budget keeps him busy.
6. Give the election ballots to we recorders.
7. Leah and her asked the guard to let them in.
8. Their's new statistics textbooks have arrived.
9. Me and she are pleased with the accounting results.
10. Mine watch appears to be slow; we will be late for the meeting.

Editing and Proofreading Application

Edit the following paragraph, and correct all errors in noun usage, pronoun usage, and spelling. Rewrite the paragraph correctly.

Thank your for you're inquiry about the position off marketing representive for our company. We need three new representative's ourself and also know of two additional openings with are sister company. We are enclosing a job description and the salary range for peoples holding this type of job. Follow these procedures to submit you application: (1) attach a cover letter printed on high-quality stationary, (2) attach your up to date resume, and (3) attach a completed employment aplication form. Please send these items to I or the sales manager at your convenence.

Chapter 6

Pronoun-Noun Agreement

OBJECTIVES

After studying this chapter and completing the chapter activities, you will be able to do the following:

1. Identify the antecedents of pronouns.
2. Use personal and relative pronouns that agree with their single or compound antecedents in person, number, and gender.
3. Select correct indefinite and demonstrative pronouns.
4. Avoid unclear pronoun-antecedent relationships in your writing.

AGREEMENT OF PERSONAL PRONOUNS WITH ANTECEDENTS

In Chapter 5, a pronoun was defined as a part of speech that substitutes for a noun. Sometimes a pronoun refers to a noun that precedes it in a sentence, so that the noun itself does not need to be repeated. The noun is called the *antecedent* of the pronoun, and the pronoun must agree with its antecedent in person, number, and gender.

Person: Use a first-person pronoun to represent the person(s) speaking (I, we). Use a second-person pronoun to represent the person(s) spoken to (you). Use a third-person pronoun to represent the person(s) spoken about (he, she, it, they).

Number: Use a singular pronoun (he, she) to refer to an antecedent that is a singular noun. Use a plural pronoun (they) to refer to an antecedent that is a plural noun.

Gender: Use a masculine pronoun (his) to refer to an antecedent that is a masculine noun. Use a feminine pronoun (her) to refer to an antecedent that is a feminine noun. Use a gender-neutral pronoun (such as *it*) to refer to an antecedent that is a gender-neutral noun (such as *table*).

In the examples below, the antecedents are italics and the pronouns are in bold:

John encouraged **his** staff.

Anyone can state **his** or **her** opinion on the matter.

When *David and I* drafted the proposal, **we** sent it to Ms. Jones.

The British *man* **who** completed the two projects received a promotion.

In the previous sentences, each pronoun agrees in every respect with its antecedent.

★ Although the antecedent of a pronoun is usually a noun, it can also be a pronoun as in the sentence about *David and I.*

Third-Person Pronoun Agreement

Writers do not have many problems matching first- and second-person pronouns with their antecedents. On occasion, however, communicators find that third-person pronouns present problems in gender and number.

The gender of the antecedent in a sentence is not always obvious. For example, nouns such as *manager, nurse, astronaut, president, systems analyst,* or *worker* could apply to either gender. The practice of using *he* (or *him* or *his*) when gender is unknown is no longer acceptable because it can offend many people. Two alternatives will help alleviate this problem:

Rule 1: Use both masculine and feminine pronouns to agree with an antecedent if its gender is unknown:

A good *manager* consults with **his** or **her** staff.

A *doctor* tends to **his** or **her** patients without favoritism.

Rule 2: Change the antecedent to a plural form and use the gender-neutral plural pronoun *their*:

The *students* completed **their** work on time.

The *astronauts* cooperate 100 percent with **their** peers at NASA.

As mentioned before, third-person pronouns also must agree with their antecedents in number. Here are examples:

Maria keyed **her** decision on **her** computer.

The *students* keyed **their** decisions on **their** computers.

A problem may arise when applying the number-agreement principle to a collec-

★ Many communicators find sentences overly wordy, such as: "The assistant listens to **his** or **her** supervisor's voice mail messages and then gives them to **him** or **her**." Communicators prefer the second alternative (see No. 2 on this page).

tive noun (jury, panel, committee). You must first determine whether the group is acting as a unit or individually. Note these examples:

Singular: "The *committee* submitted **its** report."
"The *jury* reached **its** decision."

In the previous sentences, the collective nouns (committee, jury) act as single units that give one committee report and reach one jury decision. Therefore, the singular pronoun **its** is correct. Note the following examples:

Plural: "The *police* were given **their** assignments."
"The *members* of the Board of Directors volunteered **their** opinions."

In the previous sentences, the nouns (police, members) performed as individuals with individual assignments and individual opinions. In these situations, the plural pronoun **their** is correct.

Nouns such as *school*, *company*, or *corporation* are always singular even though they employ many people.

Compound Antecedents

A **compound antecedent** is an antecedent that consists of two or more elements. "Agreement in number" may present a problem if an antecedent is compound. To eliminate errors when this occurs, follow these three principles:

Rule 1: When two or more elements are connected by *and*, use a plural pronoun to refer to the antecedent:

After *David and I* drafted the proposal, **we** sent it to Ms. Jones.

The *manager and the administrative assistant* planned **their** itinerary.

Rule 2: If two or more elements of a compound antecedent are joined by *or/nor*, *either/or*, and *neither/nor*, (a) use a *singular* pronoun if all elements are singular and (b) use a plural pronoun if all elements are plural. Note these examples:

Singular: *Faye or Tom* can work on **her** or **his** papers now.
Neither Lars nor Hal has completed **his** book report.

Plural: The *trainees or their supervisors* will finish **their** statistical computations.
Neither the *men nor the women* plan to share **their** profits on the sale.

★ Compound antecedents can be tricky. Practice composing sentences using both you and one of your friends as subjects. For example: "After *Jim and I* leave work on Fridays, **we** go to a club to dance."

Rule 3: If the elements are connected by *or/nor*, *either/or*, or *neither/nor* and one part of the antecedent is singular and the other part is plural, the pronoun must agree in number with the part that is closest to the *verb*:

Singular: *Neither the boxers nor the manager* expressed **his** (or **her**) opinion.
Either the engineers or the architect will give **her** (or **him**) suggestions for renovation.

If applicable, place the plural item last and use a plural verb and pronoun:

Plural: *Neither the manager nor the boxers* expressed **their** opinions.
Either the architect or the engineers will give **their** suggestions for renovation.

CHECKPOINT 1

Agreement of Pronouns with Antecedents

Select the correct pronouns.

1. Neither the Board of Directors nor Robert Chang presented (their/his) case clearly.
2. Neither Robert Chang nor the employees presented (their/his) cases clearly.
3. Sally and Julio are pleased to donate (their/his and her) combined winnings to the charity.
4. The workers were satisfied with (their/his and her) raises.
5. The guideline provided the union members with the fact (they/he or she) needed.
6. The new electrical engineer will receive (their/his or her) first project.
7. Either Richard or Tara has to share (their/his or her) computer.

Check your answers in Appendix F.

Indefinite Pronoun Agreement

An **indefinite pronoun** refers in *general* terms to people, places, and things. Some pronouns in this category are always *singular*, such as: *one, each, every, anybody,* and *anything.*

Every auditor had an opportunity to ask **his** or **her** questions.

Each of the data operators is concerned about **his** or **her** job.

One of the students left **his** or **her** notebook in the room.

Other indefinite pronouns are always *plural,* such as *many, few, both,* and *several:*

> *Many* will hand in **their** questionnaires.

> *Few* accountants receive **their** CPAs.

> *Several* share **their** expertise on college transfer.

Some indefinite pronouns, such as *all, any, some, more,* and *most,* can be either singular or plural depending on the noun or object of the preposition that follows them:

> **Singular:** *Most of the report* had **its** spelling checked.
> *Some of the merchandise* has arrived, and **it** will be tagged today.

> **Plural:** *Most of the reports* have **their** spelling checked.
> *Some of the suits* have arrived, and **they** will be tagged today.

Indefinite Pronoun Agreement

CHECKPOINT 2

Select the correct pronouns.

1. Some of the team members were pleased with (their/his or her) new uniforms.
2. One has already returned (their/his or her) library books.
3. Each has had (their/his or her) turn.
4. Every data operator appreciates (their/his or her) vacation.
5. Each of the auditors received (their/his or her) bonus.
6. All the rock salt has been received, and (they/it) will be inventoried.

Check your answers in Appendix F.

PRONOUNS WITH SPECIAL USES

Two categories of pronouns that are quite important in effective writing are *relative pronouns* and *demonstrative pronouns.* Each category has its own special function for communicators. First, let's take a careful look at the role of *relative pronouns.*

Relative Pronouns

A **relative pronoun,** such as *who, whom, whose, which,* and *that,* begins a dependent clause that relates to a person, place, or thing that appears earlier in the sentence. *Who, whom,* and *whose* are used to relate to people; *which* is used to relate to *things;* and *that* may be used to relate to either *people* or *things.* For example:

My brother *Raymond*, **who moved to California**, will be visiting in June.

The *man* **whom we hired** is a finance expert. (*whom* is the object of the verb *hired*)

The *credit manager*, **whose accomplishments are many**, is receiving a promotion.

My *Mustang*, **which is three years old**, looks brand new.

The neighbor **that called** wanted to borrow my ladder.

Review the usage of *who* and *whom* in Chapter 5 if necessary.

EXTRA, EXTRA!

★ Pet owners who consider their pets to be an important part of the family do not refer to that pet as "it." Instead, the owners probably refer to the pet as "him" or "her," such as "He is a wonderful dog."

3 CHECKPOINT

Relative Pronoun

Select the correct relative pronouns.

1. Dr. Gardinia, (which/whom/who) I have just met, is a dentist.
2. The soldier (which/whom/who) left early is my first cousin.
3. The catcher (who's/whose) play won the game was hurt.
4. The clothes (who/that) were old were donated to charity.
5. Both Mario and Pam, (which/who) work for Jack and James, started to drive ice cream trucks in April.
6. The radio station (that/who) plays classical music has many loyal listeners.
7. The man (which/whom/who) stood next to the subway entrance witnessed the accident.

Check your answers in Appendix F.

Demonstrative Pronouns

A **demonstrative pronoun** points to a *specific* person, place, or thing. The four *demonstrative pronouns,* all beginning with the letters "*th,*" are *this, these, that,* and *those.*

This, which is singular, points to a person or thing *near* the speaker; *these,* which is plural, points to people or things *near* the speaker. For example:

This is the insurance policy that I recommended.

These are the professionals you are to counsel.

That, which is singular, points to a person or thing that is *not near* the speaker; *those*, which is plural, points to people or things that are *not near* the speaker. For example:

That counselor has been available since last summer.

Those programs are better than the original software.

★ Substituting "them" for "those" is grammatically incorrect and should be avoided. Don't say "Please hand me *them* papers." Instead, say "Please hand me *those* papers."

Demonstrative Pronoun

Select the correct demonstrative pronouns.

1. (This/These) are the graphs on the desk.
2. (Those/These) were the accountants' offices that we passed.
3. (This/That) had helped us many years ago.
4. (This/Those) is very helpful in every respect.
5. (That/Those) are the negotiating team's suggestions.
6. Where are (that/those) lists you mentioned?
7. (Those/This) is not the insurance policy they selected.

Check your answers in Appendix F.

CLEAR PRONOUN REFERENCES

One way to ensure clarity in your writing is to be certain that a pronoun-antecedent relationship is clear and unambiguous. Note these examples:

Incorrect: The supervisor told the employee that **she** made a mistake. (Who made the mistake? The supervisor? The employee?)

Correct: The supervisor admitted her own mistake to the employee.

Incorrect: The directors shared the information with the actors that they deserved to win the awards. (Who deserved the awards? The directors? The actors?)

Correct: The directors said to the actors, "You deserved to win the awards."

To check the clarity of pronoun-antecedent relationships in your sentences, you should remember that a pronoun functions as a substitute for a *noun* or other

★ Pronoun-antecedent relationships must be *obvious* to your readers and listeners if you want your meaning to be crystal clear.

noun substitute. Remembering a pronoun's purpose will eliminate errors such as these:

> **Incorrect:** The president *mailed a letter* of explanation; **this** satisfied everyone. (The word *this* cannot substitute for "mailed a letter.")

> **Correct:** The president mailed a letter of explanation; **his mailing** satisfied everyone.

One last recommendation for pronoun use pertains to consistency in selecting either first- or second- or third-person pronouns in any one sentence. For example:

> **Incorrect:** Before keying **your** proposal, **one** should check **his** or **her** statistics.

In the previous sentence, the shift from second person (your) to third person (one/his or her) creates an awkward and ineffective sentence. Note this correction:

> **Correct:** Before keying **your** proposal, **you** should check **your** statistics.

★ Another choice is, "Before keying *one's* proposal, *one* should check *his* or *her* statistics."

---

5 | **CHECKPOINT**

Clear Pronoun Preference

Select the correct answer.

1. They listen to experts on the subject; (expert advice/it) causes people to think.
2. Shoshana told Ms. Johnson that (she is/Ms. Johnson is) obligated to attend the meeting.
3. The statement is to be issued tomorrow; (the statement's issuance/this) is what we want.
4. The coaches communicated to the team members that (they/the coaches) were not doing their very best.
5. She studied hard for her Economics 101 test; (this/studying) improved her grade.
6. The attorneys told their clients that (the clients/they) will incur additional expenses on the case.
7. Select correct pronouns in every case; (it/accurate pronoun selection) will improve your writing.

Check your answers in Appendix F.

Pronouns frequently refer to nouns and noun substitutes called *antecedents,* which precede pronouns in sentences. Clear and obvious pronoun-antecedent relationships lead to effective writing that does not have more than one meaning.

Careful use of relative pronouns will improve writing skills. Communicators use *who, whom,* and *whose* to refer to people; *which* to refer to things; and *that* to refer to either people or things. In addition, the correct application of demonstrative pronouns, such as *this, these, that,* and *those,* will eliminate vague references in sentence writing.

Similarly, *pronoun-compound antecedent* relationships often cause problems and deserve close attention. The antecedent element next to the verb indicates whether a singular or a plural pronoun is needed for "agreement in number."

Writers who follow basic grammar rules such as pronoun-antecedent agreement will communicate in a manner that their receivers understand more easily.

Discussion Questions

1. How do you identify the antecedents of pronouns in sentences?
2. List the relative pronouns and comment on the specific function of each in a sentence.

Spelling and Word Usage Application

Note the correct spelling of the following words:

discrepancy	receipt	negotiable	illustrate
lieutenant	schedule	necessity	exceed
vehicle	precisely	instructor	

Rewrite the following sentences, correcting all misspelled words.

1. Their appears to be a discrepency in the reciept.
2. According to our scheduel, one U.S. Army corporal and one lieutenent will address the students in tomorrows assembly.
3. The salary offer for this job opening is negoitiable if anyone asks.
4. A private vehical is a neccessity for people who do not have access to public transportation.
5. Can you ilustrate and explain presisely what you mean?
6. Your parent's and your driver education instructer will give you ample reasons why you should not excede the speed limit.

If necessary, refer to Appendix A for the correct usage of the following words:

advise/ advice   it's/ its

Practical Applications

Part A Identify the antecedent of the italicized pronouns.

1. Gus keyed the first two pages of *his* proposal.
2. The chairperson stated, "I believe everyone will be able to complete *his* or *her* work on schedule."
3. After Sid cleaned the display case, *he* arranged the ceramics on the shelves.
4. Ling Mai and Chou Xiang have renewed *their* visas.
5. The woman *who* volunteered the information will testify.

Part B Correct the errors in pronoun-antecedent agreement. Write your answers on a sheet of paper.

1. Every student took their seat in the auditorium.
2. After one works so diligently to finish the project on time, we expect it to be accepted by the administration.
3. Each of the retailers changed their mind about the display.
4. Either Ms. Morganti or Mr. Gold is going to state their side of the story.
5. The leaders of the federation offered its opinions on the matter.
6. Tonick Bros., Inc., submitted their bid for repaving the road.
7. Maya and I, which suggested the renovation, have been assigned to draw up the plans.

Part C Select the correct pronoun.

1. Anyone at all can volunteer (their/his or her) answer.
2. Each young girl and all the men received (its/their) parts for the play.
3. Ann, (who/whom) just graduated, is studying for the CPA test.
4. Either he or she will present (their/his or her) views.
5. In this company, a vice-president does (their/his or her) best to follow the wishes of the president.
6. The coach gave the members of the baseball team (its/their) individual assignments.
7. My dishwasher, (who/which) is about to be replaced, has started to leak.

Editing and Proofreading Applications

Correct all errors in pronoun agreement, word usage, and spelling in the following excerpt of a report. Write a corrected copy.

In order to collect data and the opinions of the township residents, a house-to-house survey was completed the weeks of July 10 and July 17. Here are some of the findings: (1) most household have two or more dependants which are still in school; (2) some of the residence either disapproved off or were not willing to give his or her opinions about the township recretional areas; (3) a few people surveyed had all ready recieved questions such as this in the mail and had all ready returned the three-page questionairre to the township building; (4) most township familys whom have lived here 15 or more year's support the ideas of the township directors; (5) all those surveyed congratulated themselves for putting up with the recent construcsion in there neighborhood; and (6) adherence to the scooper-dooper policy, who had been put in force in March, is not a problem for him or her.

Overall, those people in this township are extremely cooperative and indicate that they will continue they're support of are leaders.

Verbs

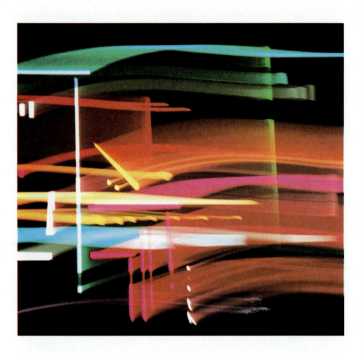

OBJECTIVES

After studying this chapter and completing the chapter activities, you will be able to do the following:

1. Define and describe types of verbs.
2. Use verb phrases correctly in your writing.
3. Identify the principal parts and tenses of verbs.
4. Use the past, past participle, and present participle forms of regular and irregular verbs correctly.
5. Identify transitive and intransitive verbs in your sentences.
6. Use active and passive voice correctly.
7. Determine the correct choice among pairs of troublesome verbs.

TYPES OF VERBS

Every sentence must have a verb in order to be complete. A careful look at the types of verbs, their principal parts and tenses, and their special characteristics will help you continue to improve your communication skills.

Verbs are either *action* or *linking* verbs. Linking verbs include *state-of-being* verbs and *condition* verbs. An explanation and examples of action and linking verbs follow.

★ Verbs express what the subject of the sentence is doing or what is being done to the subject.

Action Verbs

Action verbs help to create strong, effective sentences. Action verbs can take objects and indirect objects. Here are examples with the verbs in **bold**:

> Mr. Gomez **teaches** me Finance 102.

> Juniata **purchased** a stock certificate.

An *action verb* can also be used without an object or indirect object:

> Tony **ran** fast.

> Gabrielle **wrote** legibly.

★ The indirect object is the receiver of the action. In the statement, "Mr. Gomez teaches me Finance 102," *me* is the indirect object.

State-of-Being Linking Verbs

State-of-being linking verbs, sometimes called *to be* verbs, do not have objects or indirect objects; instead, these verbs have *predicate nominatives* and *predicate adjectives*. The verb *to be* has many different forms to denote the present, past, or future state of being. Here are some examples:

> The new president **is** Mr. Jongg. (The predicate nominative, *Mr. Jongg*, is linked to the subject by the verb *is*.)

> The old software programs **were** expensive. (The predicate adjective is *expensive*.)

> Gloria **will be** happy with the renovations. (The predicate adjective is *happy*.)

Condition Verbs

A **condition linking verb** does not have an object or an indirect object; instead, it connects an adjective to the subject. Condition linking verbs either refer to a

condition or appeal to the senses. Examples are *taste, smell, seem, appear,* and *become.* Note these sentences:

> The assistant **appears** cooperative.

> The health food **tastes** delicious.

A verb that appeals to the senses and is not used as a linking verb can have an object. For example:

> They **hear** music.

> The child **tastes** the cookie.

VERB PHRASES

Frequently, sentences have a main verb and helping verbs. The combination of a main verb, either action or linking, preceded by a helping verb or verbs forms a verb phrase. The most common helping verbs are forms of the verb *to be* and forms of the verb *to have.* Examples are *is, are, was, were, has, have,* and *had.* For example:

> Sally **spoke** to her peers. (The verb is *spoke.*)

> Sally **has spoken** to her peers. (The main verb is *spoken;* the helping verb is *has;* thus the verb phrase is *has spoken.*)

Additional helping verbs include *can, could, may, might, must, ought, should, will,* and *would.* For example:

> Sally **could have spoken** to her peers. (The main verb is *spoken;* the helping verbs are *could have;* the verb phrase is *could have spoken.*)

In order for a verb to be classified as a helping verb, it must have a main verb to help. Compare these sentences:

> Jim **has assisted** Ms. Quinn. (The helping verb *has* precedes the main verb *assisted.*)

> Jim **has** a new computer. (The verb is *has.*)

> Jane **will be looking** for it. (The helping verb *will be* precedes the main verb *looking.*)

> Jane **will be** here. (The linking verb is *will be.*)

Verb Phrases

Identify the verb phrase in each of the following sentences.

1. He has spent his money on new office equipment.
2. Ms. Yokohama was elected president for the second time.
3. The bank teller was taking a lunch break.
4. We might have been driving all night.
5. They had left early the night before.
6. The plaintiff should have thought of that earlier.
7. We have had a constructive meeting with the builders.

Check your answers in Appendix F.

PRINCIPAL PARTS OF VERBS

All verb forms are derived from four basic **principal parts**: The *present, past, present participle,* and *past participle.* Here are sentences illustrating the verb *call* in its principal parts:

I **call** her every day. (*present* form)

I **called** her yesterday. (*past* form)

I **am calling** her today. (*present participle* form)

I **have called** her many times. (*past participle* form)

Do not use a helping verb with the *past form*, but always use a helping verb with present participles and past participles. For example:

Timothy and Julia **spoke** yesterday. (*past* form)

Timothy and Julia **are speaking** now. (*present participle* form)

Timothy and Julia **have spoken** daily. (*past participle* form)

VERB TENSES

Two groups of **verb tenses** discussed in this section, *simple tenses* and *perfect tenses,* enable verbs to express time. Selecting the correct tense is important if a listener or reader is to know when an action takes place. A helping verb is used

★ Do not substitute past participle forms for past tense forms. Do not write, "He done the project" when you mean "He did the project." Don't say "He seen the film" when you mean "He saw the film."

with a main verb to indicate several, but not all, of the verb tenses. Let's begin with the *simple tenses* (*present*, *past*, and *future*).

Simple Tenses

A **present tense verb** expresses present occurrences (what is happening now). For example:

> Computer services **sell** information.

> Georgia **teaches** a course in merchandising.

Add an *s* to the present tense of a regular verb when it is used with a third-person singular pronoun (*he, she, it*) or a singular noun. For example:

Compare:
he walk**s**	she walk**s**	it run**s**	telephone ring**s**

with:
I walk	you walk	they run	telephones ring

A **past tense verb** expresses action recently completed. Add *ed* to the present tense of a regular verb to form the past tense. The spelling of some irregular verbs changes to form the past tense, such as *see* and *saw*. For example:

Past Tense of Regular Verbs
he walk**ed**	she talk**ed**	it sputter**ed**

Past Tense of Irregular Verbs
I did	you bought	they came

A **future tense verb** expresses an action or condition yet to come. The future tense is formed by placing the helping verb *will* before the main verb:

> I **will vote** on election day.

> The accountants **will consult** with their clients.

When using the first person (I, we) in *formal* circumstances, place *shall* instead of *will* before the main verb.

> We *shall* attend the benefit in his honor.

Perfect Tenses

A **perfect tense verb** describes the action of the main verb in relation to a specific time period that is in the past, from the past to the present, or in the future. The

★ The present tense form of a verb does not end in *s* when used with first-, second-, or third- person plural.

three perfect tenses are *present perfect*, *past perfect*, and *future perfect*. Form the perfect tense by preceding the past participle form of the main verb with either *have*, *has*, or *had*.

A **present perfect tense verb** indicates continuous action from the past to the present. *Has* or *have* precedes the past participle form of the main verb:

George **has voted** in every election since 1986.

They **have jogged** every day since the beginning of the month.

The technician **has checked** all the charts since she was hired.

A **past perfect tense verb** indicates action that began in the past and continued to the more recent past when it was completed. *Had* precedes the past participle form of the main verb:

George **had voted** in every election until last week.

They **had jogged** every day until this past Monday.

The technician **had checked** all the charts by last Friday.

A **future perfect tense verb** indicates action that will be completed at a specific point in the future. *Will have* precedes the past participle form of the main verb:

Including next year, George **will have voted** in every election since 1986.

By May 31, they **will have jogged** every day since the beginning of the month.

By next Tuesday, the technician **will have checked** all the charts.

2 Verb Tenses

CHECKPOINT

Correct any verb tense errors in the following sentences.

1. Including next week, Phyllis visited her parents five weeks in a row.
2. They take inventory monthly or had someone do it for them.
3. By this coming Friday, Courtney has completed the work.
4. The tellers eat lunch in the cafeteria and have followed this practice every day since the first of the year.
5. You will enjoy the company picnic that takes place Saturday.
6. The students study daily and did all their homework.

(Continued on next page)

Verb Tenses, Continued

7. He has keyed the data into the computer and will have completed the report on time.

Check your answers in Appendix F.

★ If the present form of a verb ends in *e* (wri*te*/dri*ve*), form the present participle by dropping the *e* before adding the *-ing* (wri*ting*/dri*ving*).

REGULAR AND IRREGULAR VERBS

A **regular verb** is a verb that expresses its past and past participle forms by adding *ed* to the present form. Present participle forms of regular verbs are constructed by adding *ing* to the present form. For example:

PRESENT	PAST	PRESENT PARTICIPLE	PAST PARTICIPLE
compute	computed	computing	computed

An **irregular verb** is a verb for which the past and past participle forms are constructed irregularly. Here are some examples:

PRESENT	PAST	PRESENT PARTICIPLE	PAST PARTICIPLE
know	knew	knowing	known
lend	lent	lending	lent
do	did	doing	done
bring	brought	bringing	brought
choose	chose	choosing	chosen

The English language contains many irregular verbs. Consult a dictionary if you are not sure of a correct verb form.

Regular and Irregular Verbs

3 CHECKPOINT

Select the correct verb in each of the following sentences.

1. Last year we (hold/held) the charity auction the first Sunday in March.
(Continued on next page)

TRANSITIVE AND INTRANSITIVE VERBS

A **transitive verb** is a verb that must have an object to complete the meaning of a sentence. For example:

Tara *did*. (*Did* what? Not complete)

Tara *did the assignment*. (Complete)

Clark *suggested*. (*Suggested* what? Not complete)

Clark *suggested a profitable method*. (Complete)

An **intransitive verb** is a verb that does not need an object to complete the meaning of a sentence. For example:

The recruits *laughed*.

The merchandise *is* here.

Intransitive verbs may need predicate nominatives or predicate adjectives or adverbs but never objects. Here are additional examples:

He *will be* treasurer. (*Treasurer* is a predicate nominative.)

The merchandise *is* out-of-date. (*Out-of-date* is a predicate adjective.)

The recruits *laughed* loudly. (*Loudly* is an adverb.)

ACTIVE AND PASSIVE VOICE

Voice indicates whether the subject is doing the action or receiving the action of a verb. **Active voice** means that the subject of a sentence is doing the action. Here are examples:

John **completed** his report using his computer.

The young sprinter **won** the race.

My supervisor **caught** the Beijing flu.

For the most part, use the active voice in business writing; the active voice creates a clear, sharp picture in the listener's or reader's mind.

Passive voice means that the subject of a sentence is receiving the action. The passive voice is formed with the past participle and a form of the *verb to be*. Here are some examples:

The report **was completed** by John.

The race **was won** by the young sprinter.

The Beijing flu **was caught** by my supervisor.

Passive voice is preferred in the following situations.

Rule 1. Use passive voice when the subject cannot be identified or identifying the subject is not beneficial. For example:

Property taxes **will be increased** beginning January 1.

Rule 2. Use passive voice to emphasize the receiver of the action rather than the performer of the action. For example:

Our ex-lawyer **was disbarred** recently.

Rule 3. Use passive voice to reduce the impact of a negative situation. For example:

The summary **was not received** on time.

4 CHECKPOINT   *Active and Passive Voice*

Change the passive voice to the active voice in the following sentences.

1. The garage was painted by Julie.
2. Cable costs will be increased by the company owners in May.
3. The tests were taken by the students.
4. The overdue check was not received by the creditor.
5. Ten pages were printed by the copy center.
6. The speech was given by Mai.
7. The race was run by many French citizens.

Check your answers in Appendix F.

TROUBLESOME VERBS

Some verb pairs pose problems for writers. The pairs include *set/sit, lay/lie, raise/rise,* and *may/can.* To select the correct verb of any of these pairs in a given situation, first decide if you need a transitive verb (one that takes an object) or an intransitive verb (one that does not take an object). Let's start with *set/sit.*

Set or Sit

Set, which means to place an object somewhere, is a transitive verb and takes an object:

> I **set** the dining room table for dinner. (*Set* what? Set the table.)

Sit, which means to be seated, is an intransitive verb and does not take an object:

> I **sit** at the table every day.

Lay or Lie

Lay, which means to put down, is a transitive verb and takes an object:

> I **lay** the perishables down carefully. (*Perishables* is the object of *lay.*)

Lie, which means to rest in a horizontal position, is an intransitive verb and does not take an object:

> I **lie** on the couch daily.

EXTRA, EXTRA!

★ The *i* in *sit, lie,* and *rise* will help you remember that they are *i*ntransitive verbs and do not take objects.

Raise or Rise

Raise, which means to lift, is a transitive verb and takes an object:

> I **raise** the flag in the schoolyard every weekday. (*Flag* is the object of *raise.*)

Rise, which means to get up, is an intransitive verb and does not take an object:

> The sun **rises** earlier here.

★ If it is not a clear-cut situation where you are requesting permission and if you are not certain of the receiver's ability, then you will probably want to select **can** instead of **may**.

May or Can

May is used to express permission:

> **May** I participate in the picnic races?

Can is used to express the ability or power to do something:

> **Can** you do 40 pushups daily?

When you are seeking permission, do not substitute *can* for *may*.

Troublesome Verbs

Select the correct verb in each pair of troublesome verbs.

1. (Sit/Set) the report at the back of my desk.
2. When you arrive in the lobby, (sit/set) until I arrive.
3. She will (lie/lay) on the chaise for an hour or two.
4. Did he (lie/lay) the clothes on the bed as I requested?
5. (Can/May) I leave the office before four today?
6. The rainfall causes the water to (raise/rise) over the bank.
7. (Can/May) she type 70 words per minute on the computer?

Check your answers in Appendix F.

Summary

Verbs are important in effective writing because they give sentences meaning and direction. Learning to distinguish between action and linking verbs, simple and perfect tenses, transitive and intransitive verbs, and active and passive voice can be helpful in verb selection. Study the characteristics of both regular and irregular verbs to familiarize yourself with the many options available as you continue to improve your communication skills.

Remember to keep a dictionary close to your writing desk or table; refer to it whenever you have a question about verb form.

Discussion Questions

1. What are the differences between the past tense verb form and the past perfect verb form of regular verbs? Discuss their construction and function.
2. Define a *transitive verb* and illustrate its use in a sentence. Also, define an *intransitive verb* and illustrate its use in a sentence.

Spelling and Word Usage Application

Note the correct spelling of the following words:

seize	impatient	absence	importance
noticeable	courtesy	criticism	occasion
opportunity	commission	beginning	special

Rewrite the following sentences, correcting all misspelled words.

1. Students should sieze the oportunity to show cortesy and respect to their elders.
2. Jordan's continued absense on the job became very noticable to his peers and his supervisor.
3. Are you pateintly or impateintly waiting for your commision check?
4. Constructive critisism is very helpful for begining golfers.
5. What is the spesial occassion for which you are dressed in a suit and tie?
6. The importanse of our meeting today depends on it's final outcome.

If necessary, refer to Appendix A for the correct usage of the following words:

your/ you're   affect/ effect

Practical Applications

Part A
Identify all main verbs (MV) and helping verbs (HV).

1. Since joining the firm, Lucian has worked in the mailroom.
2. The local high school may clinch the title.
3. The article stated that they might win the award.
4. The hospital has had more than six heart transplants performed there.
5. We will start the training program on July 1.

Part B
Correct any errors in verb form.

1. The nurse gone out of his way to care for the child.
2. Lie your report on my desk next to the other ones.
3. Some residents of the town has traced their ancestry.
4. Faye learned the business and begins looking for customers.
5. The officers am budgeting an extra $5,000 for tax payments next year.

Part C
Select the correct verb.

1. I (choose/chose) the materials last week.
2. The delegates should (raise/rise) from their seats when the president arrives.
3. Harold (will be/will have been) elected next week.
4. Gladstone Bros. (has complained/have complained) about the competition's prices.
5. By the end of the summer, I (painted/had painted) all the rooms in the apartment.

Part D
Designate whether the main•verb in each sentence is transitive (T) or intransitive (I).

1. Sitting on that hard chair is uncomfortable.
2. The stockbrokers were very successful.
3. Can I have permission to use the car?
4. Kay has had mumps and chicken pox in her lifetime.
5. With the computer installation next year, the employees will have the opportunity to maintain their own files.

Editing and Proofreading Application
Correct all errors in verb form and spelling in the following message.

Speaking with you this passed Wenesday and meeting some of the administrators I have heard so much about was a pleasure. Ed, as you requested, the following day I survey the market to comparison shop laser printers for home use. The dot matrix and ink-jet printers owns by many of are employees are becomed either out dated or insufficient for the work that they do at home.

My complete report are attached by me; the report include the discounted prices, features, apearance, power, memory, ease of use, size, and overall eficiency of five diffrent laser printers. Also include is my recomendation for purchase and a convenient financial arrangment for our employees. If requested, we will lent them the money for the printer of there choice, and a pay roll deduction for the cost plus 5 percent interest will be spreaded over 12 months.

After you has had an opportunity to readed the report in full, let's met in the conference room at you're convenence to make final arrangements and notifys interested employees. We have had so many inquirys about laser printers that I known an opportunity to purchase printers will improve the moral of our staff.

Subject-Verb Agreement

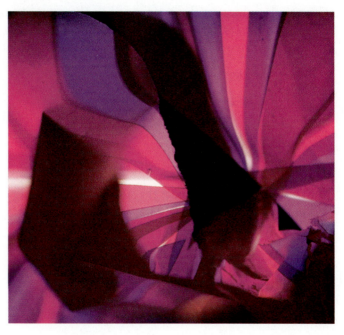

OBJECTIVES

After studying this chapter and completing the chapter activities, you will be able to do the following:

1. Identify the simple, complete, and compound subjects in sentences.
2. Select the simple, complete, and compound predicates in sentences.
3. Use verbs that agree with their subjects in all situations.

Chapter 8

★ The subject may be a noun or a personal pronoun, such as *I, you, he, she, it, we,* and *they*, which substitutes for a noun.

THE SUBJECT IN A SENTENCE

A **subject** is either the person who is speaking, the person who is spoken to, or the person, place, or thing spoken about.

The Simple Subject

The **simple subject** is the main word in the *complete subject* that specifically names what the sentence is about. The simple subject of a sentence is never in a prepositional phrase. Here are examples with the simple subject in **bold**:

> **John**, the young journalist, writes articles.

> The **chair** behind the girl is vacant.

The Complete Subject

The **complete subject** includes the simple subject plus all the sentence that is not part of the *complete predicate* (discussed on next page). The complete subjects are in **bold** in these sentences:

> **John** writes articles.

> **John, the young journalist**, has written articles.

> **Sally, whose office is near mine**, is very capable.

A Compound Subject

A **compound subject** is two or more simple subjects joined by conjunctions such as *and, or, nor, not only/but also* and *both/and*. Note these compound subjects in **bold**:

> **John** and **Sally** work for our company.

> His **brother** or my **sister** will accompany us.

When two nouns in a subject refer to one person, the article *the* (or *a*) is omitted before the second noun:

> The **teacher** and **counselor** *is* my friend.

When two nouns in a subject refer to two people, the article *the* (or *a*) is placed before both nouns:

The **teacher** and the **counselor** *are* my friends.

THE PREDICATE IN A SENTENCE

The discussion of a predicate is divided into three brief sections: the simple predicate, the complete predicate, and a compound predicate.

The Simple Predicate

The **simple predicate** is the verb in the *complete predicate*. Here are examples with the simple predicate in **bold**:

John **writes** articles.

John, the young journalist, **has written** articles.

Sally, whose office is near mine, **is** very capable.

★ The verb *is* is a form of the verb *to be*. Such verbs can cause problems in agreement because their forms are irregular.

The Complete Predicate

The **complete predicate** is everything in the sentence said by, to, or about the subject; it always includes the main verb of the sentence. Whatever is not included in the *complete subject* of a sentence belongs in the *complete predicate*. Here are examples with the complete predicate in **bold**:

John **writes articles**.

John, the young journalist, **has written articles**.

Sally, whose office is near mine, **is very capable**.

A Compound Predicate

A **compound predicate** consists of two or more verbs with the same subject; the verbs are connected by conjunctions such as *and, or, nor, not only/but also,* and *both/and.* Note these sentences:

John and Sally **discussed** the matter and **concluded** that we are handling this situation incorrectly.

The engineer not only **complained** but also **refused** to finish the project.

★ The compound verbs that appear in bold in these sentences are regular verbs in the past tense. Notice that they all have *ed* endings.

CHECKPOINT 1

Subjects and Predicates

Identify the simple or compound subjects.

1. My mother-in-law and father-in-law moved to California.
2. Behind the sofa is the suitcase to be carried to the camp.
3. The executive travels extensively on her job.
4. Lloyd and Betty are sophomores at the state college.

Identify the simple or compound predicates.

5. The tenor and soprano have sung together before.
6. The den, including its wallpaper and window treatment, has been redecorated completely
7. They shopped, cooked, and set the table to prepare for the party.

Check your answers in Appendix F.

★ Some communicators who make sure that their written sentences have subject-verb agreement may not be as careful in their oral communications. The agreement guidelines should be applied to both speaking and writing.

SUBJECT-VERB AGREEMENT

Good communicators make sure that their subjects and verbs always agree (he walks, they walk). Grammatical errors in subject-verb agreement offend the receiver and label the person who erred as a careless writer or speaker. Follow these guidelines to avoid errors.

Agreement in Number

Remember that third-person singular pronouns and singular nouns require a singular verb that ends in *s* when the present tense is used. For example:

> Joy **telephones** her parents daily.

> Ari **drives** to his client's warehouse every Monday.

Third-person plural pronouns and plural nouns require a plural verb that does not end in *s* when the present tense is used. For example:

> Joy's parents **telephone** her daily.

> The musicians **record** their music when they have a chance.

Agreement in an Inverted Sentence

If a sentence is inverted (predicate precedes subject), putting the sentence in normal order will help you check subject-verb agreement:

Inverted order

Among the recruit's many strengths *is* her *ambition*.

Normal order

Her *ambition is* among the recruit's many strengths.

Inverted order

In the box *are* two *bags* of apples.

Normal order

Two *bags* of apples *are* in the box.

Intervening Phrases

Do not be confused by words or groups of words that intervene between the subject and the verb. The intervening words do not affect subject-verb agreement and should be ignored. Note these examples with the intervening words in bold and the subjects and verbs in italics:

The *manager* **of the sports teams** *is traveling* to New Orleans.

The *members* **of the audience** *have* different reactions.

In the first example, the singular subject *manager* requires the singular verb *is traveling*. In the second example, the plural subject *members* requires the plural verb *have*. In both cases, the intervening phrases are ignored. Here are two additional examples:

A *professor*, **rather than the college administrators**, *represents* the institution at the convention. (professor *represents*)

My *assistants*, **along with the company comptroller**, *work* overtime on this project. (assistants *work*)

★ Some inverted sentences may have compound subjects following the verb. If this is the case, the verb must be plural. An example is "In the vase **are** a *rose* and a *gardenia*."

★ Temporarily cross out or cover any prepositional phrases (*see* Chapter 11) in your sentences. The remaining words will highlight your subject and verb and help you achieve subject-verb agreement.

Subject-Verb Agreement

Select the correct verb in each sentence.

1. The class (is having/are having) mid-term examinations.
2. The electrician and the plumber (is scheduled/are scheduled) to begin work this afternoon.
3. In what conference room (is/are) the five applicants for this job?
4. Here, among your files, (is/are) the report.
5. The representative of the committee (is/are) to attend the next meeting.
6. The employees who relocated (is/are) happier.
7. There in the room, with all her clothes, (is/are) her photograph albums and tapes.

Check your answers in Appendix F.

★ The verb *come* is a present tense plural form; it agrees with *a number*.

A Number, The Number

When used as a subject, the expression **a number** is considered to be plural and needs a plural verb. Here are examples:

> *A number* of inquiries **come** to our office each day.

> There **are** *a number* of tourists at our concert.

When used as a subject, the expression **the number** is considered to be singular and needs a singular verb. Note these sentences:

> *The number* of inquiries **has decreased** since last month.

> *The number* of attorneys in Philadelphia **is** on the rise.

Names of Companies

Names of companies are usually considered singular. Although a firm's name may end in *s* or include more than one individual's name, it is still one business; therefore, it is treated as a singular noun. The sentences on the next page include company names and exemplify subject-verb agreement.

Gordon, Rodriguez, and Ramirez **is representing** the plaintiff.

Komuro Bros. **manufactures** women's clothing.

Richards and Green **is** a bank holding company in the Northeast.

Amounts

An amount that is plural in form takes a singular verb if the amount is considered to be one item. For example:

One hundred dollars **is** *a* generous wedding gift.

Two dollars **is** given to the six-year-old child for every baby tooth that falls out.

An amount that is plural in form takes a plural verb if the amount is considered to be more than one item:

Fifty one-dollar bills **are** in my wallet.

A Number, The Number, Companies, Amounts

Select the correct verbs.

1. A significant number of recommendations (was/were) made.
2. A.C. Smoltz Bros. (print/prints) business cards and stationery.
3. Fifty cents (is/are) ample allowance for a five-year-old.
4. The number of interested travelers (increases/increase) with discounted prices.
5. Essex, Ltd. (are/is) distributing English bone china.
6. Twenty-five dollars (are/is) my annual gift to the university.
7. McGill Bros. (are/is) well known for quick service.

Check your answers in Appendix F.

Compound Subjects Joined by And

Because errors in subject-verb agreement commonly occur with compound subjects, take a careful look at some special guidelines.

1. Usually a compound subject joined by *and* is plural and requires a plural verb. For example:

   Mei-ling and Yuan **are visiting** their parents in Wuxi.

2. However, sometimes compound subjects are treated as one item and require a singular verb. For example:

   Peanut butter and jelly **is** popular in the grammar school.

   In this case, the singular verb *is* is used. Other examples of compound subjects treated as one item are bacon and eggs, corn beef and cabbage, and peaches and cream.

3. If *each, every, many a,* or *many an* precedes a compound noun, always use a singular verb. For example:

   Many an *investor and homeowner* **has supported** this tax increase.

CHECKPOINT 4

Subject-Verb Agreement With And

Select the correct verbs.

1. Every man, woman, and child (are enjoying/is enjoying) Super Sunday activities.
2. Each staff person and each manager (is covered/are covered) by health insurance.
3. The executive and his assistant (is/are) aware of the study.
4. Each sales representative and each store manager (hope/hopes) to receive a bonus at the end of the year.
5. Every paper carrier and magazine deliverer (have been sent/has been sent) Season's Greetings cards.
6. My mentor, Jose Medina, and my teacher, Faye Long, (is/are) responsible for my advancement.
7. Ham and eggs (is/are) no longer considered to be a healthy breakfast dish.

Check your answers in Appendix F.

Compound Subjects Joined by Or/Nor

When a compound subject is joined by *or, nor, either/or,* or *neither/nor,* the verb agrees with the subject that is closest to the verb. Here are some sentences illustrating this guideline:

> *Tracey* or *Hal* **seems** to be well qualified for the position.
>
> Either *George* or his *sisters* **are** catering the buffet.
>
> Neither the *supervisors* nor the *security guard* **has seen** the criminal.

★ The conjunction *nor* is usually combined with *neither* or appears after some other negative, such as *not, no,* or *never.*

5 | *Subject-Verb Agreement With* Or/Nor

CHECKPOINT

Select the correct verbs.

1. Every executive or assistant (is/are) to attend the conference.
2. Neither Greg nor his cousins (is/are) interested in the suggestion.
3. Either Mr. Velez or his employee (is/are) responsible for the error.
4. The assistants or their supervisor (is/are) permitted to sign for them.
5. Neither the astronauts nor the design engineer (was/were) in attendance.
6. Either Toni or Kelly (draw/draws) well enough to finish Bob's sketch.
7. Each word or paragraph (has been/have been) spell-checked on the computer.

Check your answers in Appendix F.

Summary

A clear knowledge of nouns, pronouns, and verbs and a conviction that subjects and verbs must agree in every respect will help you become an efficient communicator. Guidelines, such as those presented in this chapter, provide a basis for referral when you are unsure of the principles covering agreement in number. Other rules are helpful as well, particularly those that pertain to inverted sentences, intervening phrases, a number, the number, names of companies, an amount, and compound subjects. By following the recommendations in this chapter, you will develop the skill and confidence needed to create effective business communications.

Discussion Questions

1. Prepositional phrases present a problem for communicators who want to achieve subject-verb agreement. What suggestions do you have to help communicators select the appropriate verb? Explain and give two examples.
2. Define the terms *simple subject*, *complete subject*, and *compound subject*, and illustrate their uses in sentences.

Spelling and Word Usage Application

Note the correct spelling of the following words:

rhythm	grammar	all right	indispensable
necessary	calendar	development	permissible
mathematics	international	tutor	

Rewrite the following sentences, correcting all misspelled words:

1. Sachi's tudor told her that writing in her grammer book was alright.
2. Changing the meeting time on you're calender is not neccessary.
3. A sense of rhythem is indispensible for aspiring musicians.
4. Early developement is affected with out love and attention.
5. Smoking is permissable on most intranational flights.
6. Mathmatics students where told that they were not required to take the final exam.

If necessary, refer to Appendix A for the correct usage of the following words:

all ready/ already   allot/ a lot

Practical Applications

Part A

Identify the simple or compound subject in each sentence.

1. The two actors with several years of training are more professional.
2. Neither the tellers nor the loan officers understand the directive.
3. Every one of the secretaries worked overtime on Monday.
4. Both of the team members that were benched were also fined.
5. Stan and Chloe's sister won a merit scholarship.

Part B
Identify the simple or compound predicate in each sentence.

1. Each of us has her suit pressed and ready to wear.
2. The employees have listened carefully and have heeded our advice.
3. Some of the report is intelligible and appropriate.
4. The residents will scrape the walls and woodwork before painting them.
5. Careful reading, enjoying both the plot and its development, enhances the reader's enjoyment.
6. He should have played in the opening football game.
7. The teenagers fussed and fumed over the tedious homework assignment.

Part C
Correct any errors in verb form.

1. All executives has been offered early retirement incentives.
2. Where is the speaker and the introducer sitting on the stage?
3. The committee were unified in the decision.
4. Neither of her remarks were meaningful.
5. While keying in the data, Hal and Julia was distracted by the noise.
6. The seashore house, together with the furnishings, are a very tempting purchase.
7. Priscilla, while looking for the missing proposals, have found the documents prepared by Tilden.
8. Neither Ms. Huang nor her former students plans to attend the reunion.

Part D
On a separate sheet of paper, write two inverted sentences, two sentences with compound subjects, and two sentences with compound predicates. Identify the simple subject (SS), complete subject (CS), simple predicate (SP), and complete predicate (CP) in each sentence.

Part E
On a separate sheet of paper, write a sentence that begins with *everyone* or *somebody*, a second sentence that begins with *a number*, and a third sentence that has a singular compound subject joined by *neither/nor*.

Editing and Proofreading Application

Correct all errors in subject-verb agreement and spelling in the contents of the following message.

To provide you with an additional opportunity to enhance you're financial security and over come any retirement fund deficeincy, the Board of Directors have unanimously voted to institute a new stock purchase plan effective Febuary 1. This plan are voluntary and provide you with a chance to acquire company stock. Heres important information about the offer:

1. You can elects to make contributions through payroll deduction's.

2. The dollar amount you contributes are applied toward the purchase price of the stock. You will receives a 5 percent discount on the market price; the company pay all brokerage fees.

3. As soon as you receives a stock certificate, you begin to earn dividend's and may vote as a stockholder.

All staff members, including recent hires, is eligable. If you is interested in this investment opportunity, just fill in the attached questionnairre and return it to Room 264 within 20 days. If their is any questions you want answered, call me at Ext. 1234.

Chapter 9

Adjectives

OBJECTIVES

After studying this chapter and completing the chapter activities, you will be able to do the following:

1. Define *adjective* and tell what questions adjectives answer about nouns.
2. Identify the correct use of articles, nouns, and pronouns used as adjectives, proper adjectives, and compound adjectives.
3. Use the positive, comparative, and superlative forms of regular and irregular adjectives easily and accurately.
4. Apply helpful guidelines for using adjectives.
5. Avoid pitfalls in adjective selection.

THE ROLE OF THE ADJECTIVE

An **adjective** is a word that describes or limits nouns or noun substitutes. Adjectives are referred to as **modifiers**. *Modify* means to limit, describe, or define. Here are examples of adjectives at work:

> She is reading a book.
>
> She is reading a **well-written, interesting** book. (The adjectives *well-written* and *interesting* describe *book*.)
>
> He wants a job.
>
> He wants a **new, exciting**, and **challenging** job. (The adjectives *new*, *exciting*, and *challenging* describe *job*.)
>
> **Casey's stylish** suit was perfect for **Dot's** wedding. (The adjectives *Casey's stylish* describes *suit*; *Dot's* modifies *wedding*.)

Adjectives answer the following questions about nouns:

1. Which one? *this* proposal, *those* appointments
2. How many? *six* calls, *few* tourists
3. What kind? *ambitious* student, *creative* teacher

Adjectives add specificity, meaning, and life to communication. Their use in business communication, however, is somewhat limited because they are not very concrete.

★ Notice that the second sentence that describes the book is much livelier than the first sentence that has just one adjective—the word *a*.

SOME SPECIAL ADJECTIVES

The commonly used words *the*, *a*, and *an*, as well as other adjectives that sometimes function as nouns and pronouns, need to be studied to ensure their correct use. Let's look at the **articles** first; the words *the*, *a*, and *an* are articles.

Articles

Rule 1. Place the article *the* before a noun to designate that the noun is specific, not general. For example:

> **The** man (a specific man)
>
> **The** toy (a specific toy)

★ Remember that the word *a* converts to *an* before a word that begins with the *sound* of a vowel, not necessarily an *actual* vowel (a, e, i, o, u).

Rule 2. Place the article *a* before a noun that begins with a consonant sound to designate that the noun is general, not specific:

A man (a nonspecific man)

A toy (a nonspecific toy)

Rule 3. Place the article *an* before a noun that begins with the sound of a vowel:

an honorable leader (The consonant *h* in the word *honorable* is silent; the word begins with the sound of *o*.)

an attractive child

an idea that will work

CHECKPOINT 1

Articles and Other Adjectives

Identify the adjectives in each of the following sentences:

1. The tall Christmas tree is decorated with Gayle's colorful glass ornaments.
2. Once a motivated student learns how to study, he or she will gain self-esteem.
3. Please complete these three homework assignments by Thursday.
4. Good managers seek good ideas from administrative assistants.
5. The new automobile features tinted glass windows and a manual high-powered transmission.
6. The results of Ms. Ortiz's consumer survey was mailed to four local distributors.
7. This Northern Italian restaurant is patronized by college-age students and workers of all ages.

Check your answers in Appendix F.

Nouns and Pronouns Used as Adjectives

Nouns or pronouns that precede and modify other nouns and answer questions such as *which one* or *what kind* are used as adjectives. Note these examples:

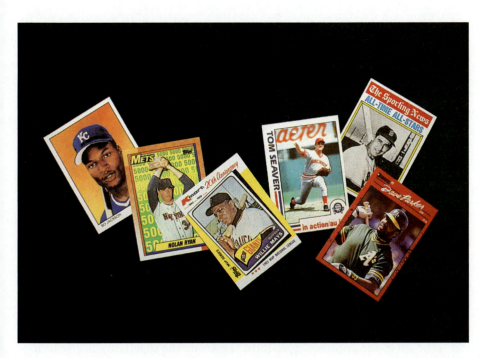

Many youngsters collect **baseball** cards. (Usually a noun, *baseball* serves as an adjective describing the "kind" of cards.)

Is **her** project completed? (The pronoun *her* serves as an adjective describing "which" project.)

Did you see **my mathematics** assignment? (The pronoun *my* and the noun *mathematics* are used as adjectives to identify which assignment.)

Proper Adjectives

Proper nouns that precede and modify other nouns serve as **proper adjectives**. Begin proper adjectives with capitals in written communication. These sentences illustrate the use of proper adjectives:

Burton is proud of his **New York** accent.

Our family thoroughly enjoys **Thanksgiving** dinner.

Chinese food in China is different from **Chinese** food in America.

★ If a noun is being modified (*bicycle* tires, *designer* clothes), classify the modifier as an adjective.

Compound Adjectives

A **compound adjective** is two or more hyphenated words that precede and modify nouns. Some examples are *well-known, long-term,* and *high-level.* Note their use in these sentences:

> The **well-known** mystery writer is signing copies of his book.
>
> Vivian is selling **long-term** health care insurance policies.
>
> Leonard tries to avoid **high-level** administrative meetings.

COMPARISON OF REGULAR ADJECTIVES

A change in the form of adjectives is called **comparison**. Adjectives have the three *degrees* for comparison: the *positive* degree, the *comparative* degree, and the *superlative* degree.

To create the comparative degree of regular adjectives, either add *-er* or *more* or add *-er* or *less* to the positive degree form. To create the superlative degree of regular adjectives, either add *-est* or *most* or add *-est* or *least* to the positive degree form. The rules below illustrate the use of each degree.

Rule 1. Use the positive degree to describe one item:

> The box is a **big** carton.
>
> She is a **beautiful** baby.
>
> Ryan is an **efficient** worker.

Also use the positive degree to express equality:

> He is as **big** as you.
>
> They are as **quick** as the game-show contestants.
>
> She is as **efficient** as the former assistant.

Rule 2. Use the comparative degree to describe two items:

> The box is a **bigger** carton than the first one.
>
> She is a **more beautiful** baby than Calley's daughter.
>
> Ryan is **less efficient** than Charles.

★ Memorize the spelling and pronunciation of the three degrees of adjective comparison. The same degrees apply to adverbs, which we will discuss in Chapter 10.

★ Two items are being compared in each of these sentences; that is why the comparative degree is used.

Rule 3. Use the superlative degree to describe three or more items:

The box is the **biggest** carton of the three.

She is the **most beautiful** baby of them all.

Ryan is the **least efficient** of the new employees.

Comparison of Regular Adjectives

Identify all adjectives in the following sentences. Write (C) after all comparative degree adjectives and (S) after all superlative degree adjectives.

1. Their house is clearly the largest and most beautiful on the block.
2. Jeremy, the kinder of your two uncles, is invited to join us on our sailboat.
3. The antique dealer, the most knowledgeable of the three, appraised the clock at $6,000.
4. Liberty Place is the taller of the two new modern buildings downtown.
5. A quick-witted applicant is needed for this job.
6. That actress has a better British accent for the part than the other person who tried out for the role.
7. Is the latest budget you are following the most effective one of all?

Check your answers in Appendix F.

HELPFUL GUIDELINES FOR USING ADJECTIVES

To know whether to use *-er* or *more* or *less* for the comparative form or to use *-est* or *most* or *least* for the superlative form, follow the rules below.

Rule 1. If an adjective has one syllable, add *-er* or *est* to the positive form for the comparative and superlative degrees:

POSITIVE DEGREE	COMPARATIVE DEGREE	SUPERLATIVE DEGREE
loud noise	louder noise	loudest noise
soft cloth	softer cloth	softest cloth
brief report	briefer report	briefest report

Rule 2. If an adjective has two syllables, add *-er* or *more* or *less* for the comparative degree and add *-est* or *most* or *least* for the superlative degree. Use the adjective form that sounds the least awkward.

POSITIVE DEGREE	COMPARATIVE DEGREE	SUPERLATIVE DEGREE
pleasant friend	more pleasant friend	most pleasant friend
forthright mayor	less forthright mayor	least forthright mayor
greedy person	greedier person	greediest person

Rule 3. If an adjective has three or more syllables, add *more* or *less* for the comparative degree and add *most* or *least* for the superlative degree:

POSITIVE DEGREE	COMPARATIVE DEGREE	SUPERLATIVE DEGREE
innocent child	more innocent child	most innocent child
intelligent idea	less intelligent idea	least intelligent idea
effective plan	more effective plan	most effective plan

COMPARISON OF IRREGULAR ADJECTIVES

A few frequently used adjectives do not form their comparisons in the usual manner (adding *-er* or *more*, *-est* or *most*). These are called **irregular adjectives**. Examples are *good, bad, little, many,* and *much*. Note this breakdown:

POSITIVE DEGREE	COMPARATIVE DEGREE	SUPERLATIVE DEGREE
good book	better book	best book
bad result	worse result	worst result
little amount	less amount	least amount
many reports	more reports	most reports
much laughter	more laughter	most laughter

3 CHECKPOINT

Helpful Guidelines and Irregular Adjectives

Select the correct adjective(s) in each sentence.

1. Of all the union leaders, they are the (most efficient/ efficientest) of them all.

(Continued on next page)

2. They were (most nervous/more nervous) speaking individually than they were participating in a panel.
3. His new idea is (worst/worse) than the first one.
4. That is the (reasonabler/more reasonable) price of the two.
5. Her homemade fudge is the (most sweet/sweetest) I have ever tasted.
6. Of the two colors, the (better/best) choice is navy blue.
7. Did you notice that Kay's room is (cleaner/more clean) than Yale's?

Check your answers in Appendix F.

PITFALLS

To avoid misusing adjectives, look closely at the use of double comparisons and absolute adjectives, incorrect placement of adjectives, and common errors made with a few specific adjectives. Let's begin with the double comparison.

Double Comparison

Double comparison is the use of two forms of comparative degree adjectives (or superlative degree adjectives) to describe a noun. To avoid double comparison, do not combine *-er* and *more* and *less* in the comparative degree and do not combine *-est* and *most* and *least* in the superlative degree. Select either an ending or an insertion of a word, but do not combine the two. For example:

WRONG	CORRECT
more better	better
most loudest	loudest
least proudest	least proud

Absolute Adjectives

Some adjectives cannot be compared because they do not have degrees; they are already at the maximum level of their potential. These adjectives are referred to as **absolute adjectives**. Some examples are *perfect, square, round, complete, excellent,* and *unique.* When you use these words in your sentences, use them alone or precede them with the terms "more nearly" or "most nearly." For example:

Her suggestion is the **most nearly perfect** of all of them.

★ If you have always referred to items as "rounder (or squarer) than another item," remembering to place "more nearly" before *round* or *square* will require practice.

Your yard is **more nearly square** than your neighbor's.

My science project is **more nearly complete** than my history project.

The food at Tim's restaurant is **excellent**.

CHECKPOINT 4

Double Comparisons and Absolute Adjectives

Select the correct adjective in the following sentences.

1. Their dorm room is (more immaculate/more nearly immaculate) than their friends' room.
2. That situation is the (most nearly unique/most unique) case I have ever heard.
3. Norm ran the (quickest/most quickest) race of all.
4. My beliefs are (more intense/most intense) than my sister's.
5. The comedian's jokes were (less funnier/less funny) this time than last time.
6. Participating in the event was the (most hard/hardest) thing I have ever done.
7. This diamond is (rounder/more nearly round) than the other one.

Check your answers with Appendix F.

★ If *else* were omitted in the second sentence, the result would be, "He produces more transcripts than anyone in the pool." This implies that he is not a member of the pool but is instead an outsider, which is not what the writer means.

Using More Than Any Other; More Than Anyone Else

When comparing one member of a group with another member of the same group, use *any other* or *anyone else*. Here are examples:

He produces more transcripts than **any other** transcriber.

He produces more transcripts than **anyone else** in the pool.

Repeating Modifiers in a Compound Subject

To indicate that two people in a compound subject are two different people, insert the articles *the*, *a*, or *an* or insert possessive pronouns before each element of the compound subject. Note these:

My teacher and **my mentor** are meeting with me.

The local politician and **the attorney** are running for office.

If the compound subject refers to only one person, omit the modifier before the second element.

My teacher and mentor is meeting with me.

The local politician and attorney is running for office.

Less *versus* Fewer

Less refers to amount and is used with *singular* nouns. For example, "Gladys makes **less** money than she did previously." *Fewer* refers to number and is used with *plural* nouns. For example, "They published **fewer** copies of his new book."

This *versus* That; These *versus* Those

Demonstrative pronouns, such as *this, these, that,* and *those,* frequently function as adjectives. Examples are:

This report is excellent, but **these** reports are incomplete.

That suggestion will help, but **those** other suggestions are useless.

Incorrect Placement of Adjectives

In order to do their job, adjectives should be placed near the nouns they modify. In most cases, adjectives are effective if they immediately precede the nouns. For example:

A new chicken barbecue *restaurant* is opening on York Road.

Four incorrect *messages* taken by the new employee incurred the supervisor's wrath.

If you choose to place adjectives after nouns, be sure that they serve the specific purpose you intended. Here are two examples:

The night—**cold** and **damp**—chilled the campers.

The night is **cold** and **damp**, chilling the campers.

More Adjective Pitfalls

Identify all adjectives in the following sentences.

1. That tool is the handier of the two.
2. This maintenance contract expires in July.
3. The manufacturing company produced fewer machines and made less money in 1994.
4. My cousin and best friend is accompanying me on my vacation to the Southwest.
5. Julia has presented more seminars than any other member of ABC.
6. That surprise gift we selected for him is a certificate for a hot-air balloon ride.
7. This recipe has less salt than the original one.

Check your answers with Appendix F.

Summary

By correctly interspersing adjectives in your communications, you will enliven your writing and give it meaning and specificity. The accurate use of positive, comparative, and superlative forms of regular and irregular adjectives enhances your writing. Helpful, too, is knowing how to use articles, absolute adjectives, and proper adjectives in your communications. In addition, avoiding double comparison and other pitfalls of adjective use can provide clarity to your sentences. Last and most importantly, following the guidelines for comparison of adjectives will help you develop skill in their use.

Discussion Questions

1. Many writers contend that adjectives do more than modify nouns; they actually make writing "come alive." Do you agree or disagree? Comment on the role and importance of adjectives in your writing.
2. The articles *the*, *a*, and *an* are among the most commonly used words in the English language. What purpose do the articles serve, and what are the guidelines for their use?

Spelling and Word Usage Application

Note the correct spelling of the following words:

congratulate	mediocre	acknowledge	liable
government	prejudice	disappear	professor
graduate	unattended	achieved	discrimination

Rewrite the following sentences, correcting all misspelled words.

1. Let me congradulate you on your new job in local goverment.
2. Predjudice and descrimination have no place in education.
3. The proffessor was unhappy with the mediocer grades acheived by the students.
4. The dollar's couldn't just dissappear from my wallet.
5. Young children are liabel to cross the street unatended.
6. Did the gradate acknowlege the role of the teacher?

If necessary, refer to Appendix A for the correct usage of the following words:

lay/ lie   assure/ ensure/ insure

Practical Applications

Part A

Identify the adjectives in these sentences.

1. That shoe felt good on my foot; I usually cannot wear that kind.
2. They will broadcast the debate on credit card interest rates in an hour.
3. I received fewer holiday cards this year than last year.
4. The elder statesman spoke well and presented an excellent appearance.
5. An insurance agent was called in to offer an expert opinion on the merits of the policy.

Part B
Select the correct words within the parentheses.

1. Sachi's plan is the (most perfect/most nearly perfect) of the ones submitted.
2. The campers are (more hungry/more hungrier) than they were yesterday.
3. My sister and (my assistant/assistant) are joining me.
4. Everyone wants a (self confident/self-confident) person as an advisor.
5. Be sure to complete (an/a) unit each day.
6. The young boxer is the (tallest/taller) of the two.
7. Of what relative are you the (proudest/most proudest)?

Part C
Select an adjective from the list for each blank. Use each adjective only once.

better	best	a	an	These	Those
well-known	well known	bigger	more		

1. I am glad that you are _____ than you were yesterday.
2. _____ books on this desk belong to the library.
3. I cannot wait more than _____ hour for you.
4. Is that _____ question that I hear?
5. Joshua, who knows many professional athletes, does not know any _____ soccer players.
6. This carton is _____ than the one at the store.
7. He read _____ books than his brother.
8. _____ coupons that you want are at June's house.

Editing and Proofreading Application

Correct all errors in the use of adjectives and in spelling in the following message.

Thank you for your well-wrote letter of application for the position of communication specialist. My supervizor and administrator are looking for the most perfect candidate of all to fill the opening; you may very well be those person.

Your qualifications indicate that you are the most capablest communication specialist to answer our helpwanted advertisement. We hope that you can find time in your busier schedule to visit us during the next too week's for a interview. Are company will be pleased to pay you're expenses.

Mr. Chan, please call us collect at the telephone number that appears on our letterhead so that we can make promppt arrangements to meet with you. We are more interested in filling this opening as soon as possable.

Adverbs

OBJECTIVES

After studying this chapter and completing the chapter activities, you will be able to do the following:

1. Use adverbs correctly to modify action verbs, adjectives, verb phrases, and other adverbs and to add variety to your communications.
2. Choose the proper adverb degree in each situation, selecting positive, comparative, or superlative form.
3. Avoid common pitfalls in adverb use, use nouns as adverbs in special situations, and use conjunctive adverbs to connect independent clauses.

Chapter 10

THE ROLE OF THE ADVERB

An **adverb** is a word that modifies an action verb, an adjective, or another adverb. Most adverbs end in *ly*. Notice the adverbs and adjectives in the following examples:

ADJECTIVES	ADVERBS
fashionable dress	She dressed *fashionably*.
quick response	He responds *quickly*.
intelligent answer	They answer *intelligently*.

An adverb answers the questions *how, when, where, how often,* or *to what extent* about an action verb, adjective, or other adverb. Here are examples with the adverbs in **bold**:

How? He wrote the paper **correctly**.

When? He wrote the report **yesterday**.

Where? He wrote the report **here**.

How often? He wrote the report **twice**.

To what extent? He wrote the report very **speedily**.

Now, let's look more closely at the role of the adverb as it modifies action verbs, adjectives, and other adverbs. Nouns often are used as adverbs, as you will see.

Modifying Action Verbs

Adverbs modify action verbs but not linking verbs. Linking verbs are modified by adjectives, as in "She *appears* **happy**." or "George *is* **intelligent**." Action verbs require adverbs. Here are some additional examples:

How? She *gave* it to me **gladly**.

When? He *will mail* it **tomorrow**.

Where? They *are skating* **here**.

How often? The dog *sat* up and *begged* **just once**.

Adverbs that answer the question *to what extent* usually modify adjectives and other adverbs, not action verbs.

★ Because a few adjectives end in *ly*, such as *brotherly, costly,* and *timely,* you cannot always distinguish adverbs from adjectives by the *ly* ending.

★ The way a word is used in a sentence determines its part of speech.

Nouns Used as Adverbs

You may have noticed in the preceding examples that words such as *yesterday* and *tomorrow* functioned as adverbs. These words answered the question *when* about the verbs. Remember that *yesterday*, *tomorrow*, and other nouns are sometimes used as adverbs in sentences; in these situations, they are considered to be adverbs. Here are some examples:

The school children went **home**. (Usually a noun, *home*, serves as an adverb answering the question *where*.)

We met **yesterday** to discuss our meeting **tomorrow**. (Both *yesterday* and *tomorrow* answer the question *when*.)

Let's shop **Saturday**. (*Saturday* answers the question *when*.)

---

1 CHECKPOINT

Action Verbs and Nouns Used as Adverbs

Identify the adverb(s) in each sentence and tell what question is answered about the action verb.

1. The modern living room is decorated beautifully.
2. The chief financial officer should arrive Tuesday.
3. The shaggy-haired puppy is asleep there.
4. Ms. Galveston, the accountant, calculated this yesterday.
5. The sophomore student called his mentor twice.
6. The Italian tenor sang very forcefully.
7. Hal plans to attend the data processing meeting soon.

Check your answers in Appendix F.

Modifying Adjectives

An adverb usually answers the question *to what extent* about an adjective that it modifies. Here are examples:

The cookies Granny bakes are **very** good. (The adverb *very* describes the adjective *good*.)

That new project is **tremendously** complex. (The adverb *tremendously* describes the adjective *complex*.)

Modifying Other Adverbs

An adverb also can answer the question *to what extent* about another adverb in a sentence. For example:

> The grammar school pupil did her work **too quickly**. (The adverb *too* modifies the adverb *quickly*.)

> We purchased the new printer **very recently**. (The adverb *very* modifies the adverb *recently*.)

Accompanying Verb Phrases

Because adverbs modify action verbs and verb phrases that include action verbs, adverbs such as *never* or *always* frequently appear in the middle of verb phrases. Look at these examples:

> I have **never** tasted shellfish. (The adverb *never* modifies the verb phrase *have tasted*.)

> That has **already** been ordered. (The adverb *already* modifies the verb phrase *has been ordered*.)

> She has **rarely** suggested a solution. (The adverb *rarely* modifies the verb phrase *has suggested*.)

EXTRA, EXTRA!

★ Adverbs such as *never, always, hardly,* and *already,* which may be included in a verb phrase, modify verbs but are not part of the verbs themselves.

Conjunctive Adverbs

A special group of adverbs called *conjunctive adverbs* includes words such as *therefore, moreover, however, nevertheless,* and *furthermore.* A **conjunctive adverb** is a transitional word that joins two independent but related sentences. Here are examples:

> They remained at work late; **therefore**, they were able to complete the project.

> The student works after school as a messenger; **moreover**, she waits on tables in the evening.

> Jorge wants to study medicine; **however**, his parents need his assistance in the family's store.

★ Notice that the conjunctive adverbs *therefore, moreover,* and *however* introduce the second independent clause in each sentence.

2 CHECKPOINT — Adverbs as Modifiers

Identify the adverb(s) in each sentence and tell what word(s) it modifies.

1. John Clarke, the consultant, will leave very soon.
2. They are exceptionally concerned about the problem.
3. She is not too happy with her final grades.
4. The counselor's advice is not quite right.
5. You have to think extremely quickly on game shows.
6. The instructors are to meet here tomorrow.
7. I had always visited her.

Check your answers in Appendix F.

COMPARISON OF ADVERBS

Like adjectives, adverbs have three degrees of comparison: *positive, comparative,* and *superlative.* Adverbs usually show their comparative form by adding *-er* or *more* or *less* to the simple form (positive degree). Adverbs show their superlative form by adding *-est* or *most* or *least* to the simple form. Here are examples:

★ Like adjectives, adverbs cannot show their comparative form using a combination of *-er* and *more*; either one can be used, but both cannot be used together.

POSITIVE DEGREE	COMPARATIVE DEGREE	SUPERLATIVE DEGREE
arrived *late*	arrived *later* than she	arrived *latest* of all
clearly written	*more clearly* written	*most clearly* written
acted *greedily*	acted *less greedily*	acted *least greedily*
keyed *fast*	keyed *faster* than he	keyed *fastest* of all

Adverbs and Comparisons

Select the adverb that belongs in each sentence.

1. The exercise enthusiast decided to run (fast/fastly).
2. Don't wait for me; I will eat (lately/later).
3. On his birthday, Jay acted (more friendly/most friendly) than he did at our previous meeting.
4. The CPA audited the books (very carefully/very careful).
5. Of them all, this one works (more efficiently/most efficiently).
6. Among Sue, Lynn, and Steve, he arrived (earlier/earliest).
7. She works (quickly/most quickly) trying to impress Arnold, her supervisor.

Check your answers in Appendix F.

PITFALLS

A few troublesome adverbs can cause problems for communicators. These adverbs are *where, badly, never, not, really, surely,* and *well.* They are discussed in this section to help you use them correctly.

Where *or* That

The conjunctive adverb *where,* which refers to "at or in a place," should not substitute for *that* in these sentences: "I notice in your memo **that** the meeting is canceled" and "I saw in the magazine **that** he is considering running for office." *Where* is used correctly in "I never go **where** I am not wanted."

Bad *or* Badly

The adjective *bad* follows the linking verbs *feel* or *look,* as in "Don't *feel* **bad** about your absence" and "He *looks* **bad**." The adverb *badly* describes how something is done, as in "Candy *hurt* her hand **badly**" and "Allen *wrecked* his truck **badly**."

Never *or* Not

Although *never* and *not* both denote a negative situation, they should not be used interchangeably. Use *never* when you mean *not ever,* as in "I have **never**

★ The only time you should use *badly* after the verb *feel* is when your fingers are not working properly and your sense of touch is clumsy. Then the word *badly* describes your inadequate sense of touch.

smoked." and "They have **never** been late for a cast rehearsal." Use *not* in short-term negative situations, as in "I have **not** smoked since Monday" and "They have **not** been late recently."

Real *or* Really

Real, an adjective, means *genuine*, as in "This is a **real** diamond." and "He testified that this is a **real** antique." *Really*, an adverb, means *actually*, as in "Did you **really** see him?" and "He **really** enjoys giving to charity."

★ In expressions such as "I *really* like him," *really* means *truly* or *genuinely*. "I like him very much" is another way to express the same sentiment.

CHECKPOINT 4
Adverb Pitfalls

Select the correct word in each sentence.

1. He receives (really/real) joy listening to Christmas carols.
2. I feel (badly/bad) about their moving on Wednesday.
3. I spied in the help-wanted ads (that/where) your company is looking for a word-processing operator.
4. You won't believe it; he has (not/never) arrived.
5. Delia is (real/really) an expert in tournament bridge.
6. Saburo is the first to admit that he plays first base (badly/bad).
7. The college (that/where) you went to school is expanding.

Check your answers in Appendix F.

Sure *or* Surely

Sure, an adjective, means *certain* or *positive*, as in "The small computer businesses are **sure** to be on their mailing list" and "Are you **sure** the residents will buy this product?" *Surely*, an adverb, means *certainly*, as in "We were **surely** sorry to lose him to our competitors" and "**Surely**, you can understand our logic."

Good *or* Well

Good, always used as an adjective, means *suitable* or *praiseworthy*, as in "We received a **good** response from our questionnaire" and "She told the group the **good** news." *Well*, usually used as an adverb, modifies an action verb and answers the question *how*, as in "He communicates **well** with others" and "The fashion models carry themselves **well**." Remember, however, that *well* is used as an adjective when referring to *health*. "Carly feels **well** today."

More Adverb Pitfalls

Select the correct word in each sentence.

1. Bernadette remarked, "He has a (really good/real good) collection of miniature cars."
2. Scott felt (well/good) about his participation.
3. (Sure/Surely), you can't mean that!
4. We are pleased that you are feeling so (well/good) after your surgery.
5. The reconstructed equipment seems to be working (real good/ really well).
6. They will (surely/sure) finish the assignment on time.
7. Gail and Bud feel (badly/bad) about your predicament.

Check your answers in Appendix F.

★ To *feel well* means "to be in good health"; to *feel good* means "to be in a good mood" or "to be contented or satisfied." For example: "That music makes me feel **good**."

Summary

Adverbs, which modify action verbs, adjectives, and other adverbs, add variety to communication. Nouns sometimes function as adverbs. Adverbs are written in three degrees for comparison—positive, comparative, and superlative. The guidelines for selecting the correct adverb form in a given situation are the same guidelines that apply to adjectives, which were discussed in Chapter 9. Knowing and applying these guidelines will make adverb selection easy for you.

Adverbs should be placed near the words that they modify in order to avoid confusion. Some adverbs such as *where, badly, never, really, surely*, and *well* persist in presenting problems for communicators. In addition, adverbs that modify verb phrases and conjunctive adverbs that join independent clauses deserve special attention.

A close look at adverbs, with their special role and characteristics, should serve you well as you continue to strive for better communication skills.

Discussion Questions

1. Compare the role and characteristics of adverbs with the role and characteristics of adjectives.
2. Define the adjectives *sure* and *good* and the adverbs *surely* and *well.* Use each of these words in a sentence. When is the word *well* used as an adjective?

Spelling and Word Usage Application

Note the correct spelling of the following words:

changeable	loose	advertisement	library
forty	preferred	restaurant	receive
participating	envelope		

Rewrite the following sentences, correcting all misspelled words:

1. We will be taking a group of fourty kindergarten children to the storytelling session at the main liberry.
2. There restrictions appear to be changable depending on the circumstances.
3. José will recieve a copy of the latest advertisment by five o'clock today.
4. The restaruant serves lose sugar instead of sugar packets to it's patrons.
5. The teenagers prefered participateing in sports to watching them on television.
6. If you want my opinion, send me a sample of your new stationary and be sure to include an enveloppe.

If necessary, refer to Appendix A for the correct usage of the following words:

quite/ quiet/ quit   choose/ chose

Practical Applications

Part A

Select the correct word in each sentence.

1. Our meeting at the restaurant was (pure/purely) coincidental.
2. Files can be accessed (fastest/faster) by using the newer of the two systems.
3. The featured alto sang (very beautifully/very beautiful) at the service.
4. Request travel information to the world's (more/most) enticing vacation spots.
5. Jayne's neighbors feel (bad/badly) about her misfortune.

Part B
Identify and correct errors in the use of adverbs and adjectives in each sentence.

1. Alicia has never met the comptroller yet.
2. This fabric feels incredible smooth when you touch it.
3. The company is real pleased with the employee's progress.
4. The principal spoke good at the ceremony.
5. The stockbroker felt badly about the decline in the stock market.
6. Mr. Shinoda could not understand why Joe reads slow.
7. Arrange your itinerary early so that you will have a real successful business trip.

Part C
Select the correct word for each sentence.

1. Don't talk (most quickly/quickly) when you give instructions.
2. The campers are (really/realy) eager to go fly-fishing.
3. We see a need for a retreat (occasionally/occasional).
4. Please do your homework (silently/most silently).
5. The girls loved their (kindly/kind) aunt (deep/deeply).
6. Of all the vacationers, she dressed the (most stylishly/more stylishly).
7. Of the two contestants, Sherrie answered (most intelligently/ more intelligently).
8. I read in your letter (that/where) the company is decreasing health-care benefits.

Editing and Proofreading Application

Correct all errors in adverbs, adjectives, and spelling in the contents of this memo sent to all sales agents.

In the last few months' we have been great effected by the suddenly decline of the stock and bond markets. Our sales adgents are complaining most bitterly then ever about they're decreasing commission's. We want you to know that we full understand your discontent and your surprise about the unexpectedly downturn in the economy.

Be assure that we are watching the situation careful and will due everything we can to see that your income is not affected to severe in the coming months.

Mean while, encourage you're clients to sell their holdings cautious and assure them that you will monitor their accounts dayly and keep them apprised frequent. We all look foreword to a rapidly recovery in the markets and in the economy.

Chapter 11

Prepositions

OBJECTIVES

After studying this chapter and completing the chapter activities, you will be able to do the following:

1. Identify prepositions and prepositional phrases in your communications.
2. Use prepositional phrases as adjectives or adverbs in your writing.
3. Avoid the incorrect use of troublesome prepositions and prepositions that require special consideration.
4. Select the correct prepositions in combination with other words.

INTRODUCTION TO PREPOSITIONS

A **preposition** is a word that usually indicates direction, position, or time. A preposition is linked to a noun or noun substitute to form a phrase. Here are examples with the prepositions in **bold**:

Direction: She walked **into** the classroom.

Position: She stood **behind** the open gate.

Time: She left work **before** lunch.

Most prepositions are short words that appear to be unimportant. On the contrary, however, they are very important because they create major differences in meaning when used correctly. Note these examples:

Ian arrived **at** the designated time.

Ian arrived **before** the designated time.

Ian arrived **after** the designated time.

The following list contains some of the most commonly used prepositions:

about	behind	for	through
above	below	from	to
across	beneath	in	toward
after	beside	into	under
against	between	like	until
along	beyond	of	up
among	by	off	upon
around	concerning	on	with
at	during	out	within
before	except	over	without

★ This list is a mere sampling of commonly used prepositions.

THE ROLE OF A PREPOSITION

Prepositions introduce phrases called *prepositional phrases*. A **prepositional phrase** begins with a preposition and ends with a noun or noun substitute that functions as the *object* of the preposition. In addition, one or more adjectives that modify the object may appear in a prepositional phrase. Here are examples:

Place the carton **behind** the tall cabinet. (The preposition is *behind;* the object is the noun *cabinet; the tall* are modifiers; the prepositional phrase is *behind the tall cabinet.*)

Gary believes that the ability to cross-country ski is **beyond** him. (The preposition is *beyond;* the object is the noun substitute [pronoun] *him;* the prepositional phrase is *beyond him.*)

Prepositional Phrases Used as Adjectives

Prepositional phrases may be used to modify nouns and noun substitutes in sentences. Prepositional phrases can have the same function as adjectives and answer questions such as *what kind* or *which one* about the words they modify. Here are examples:

> Robert is **among** those here. (The prepositional phrase *among those* modifies the noun *Robert*.)

> They, **without** a doubt, are the most considerate people I have ever met. (The prepositional phrase *without a doubt* modifies the noun substitute [pronoun] *they*.)

Prepositional Phrases Used as Adverbs

Prepositional phrases may be used to modify action verbs, adjectives, or adverbs. Prepositional phrases can have the same function as adverbs and answer questions such as *when, where, why, how,* or *to what extent* about the words they modify. For example:

> **After** lunch, Marla filed the papers. (The prepositional phrase *after lunch* answers the question *when* about the verb *filed*.)

> The vase belongs **on** the shelf. (The prepositional phrase *on the shelf* answers the question *where* about the verb *belongs*.)

> Ms. Torres is very knowledgeable **about** the subject. (The prepositional phrase *about the subject* modifies the adjective *knowledgeable*.)

> He walked quickly **without** her. (The prepositional phrase *without her* modifies the adverb *quickly*.)

EXTRA, EXTRA!

★ In this sentence, *without her* not only modifies the adverb *quickly* but also answers the question *how* about the verb *walked*.

Prepositional Phrases

Identify each prepositional phrase, tell which word it modifies, and tell if it is used as an adjective (ADJ) or an adverb (ADV).

1. The executives acted without empathy.
2. Your donation to your favorite charity is greatly appreciated.
3. Please do not call Mr. Tanaka until tomorrow.
4. You had just gone on break when the comptroller called.
5. Place the table between the two new computers.
6. They plan to open a new store around the corner.
7. The filing cabinet you are looking for is behind my desk.

Check your answers in Appendix F.

TROUBLESOME PREPOSITIONS

Several prepositions pose problems for communicators. If you follow the guidelines below, you will avoid errors in your writing.

Between *or* Among

The preposition *between* is used to connect two nouns or noun substitutes to the rest of a sentence. The preposition *among* is used to connect three or more nouns or noun substitutes to the rest of a sentence. Here are examples using these two prepositions in sentences:

> **Between** Nan and Paul, who is the better tennis player?

> Choose **between** the red or blue scarf.

> **Among** Mark, Nan, and Paul, who is the best tennis player?

> Choose one **among** the three scarves to complement your suit.

In *or* Into

The preposition *in* refers to *position*. The preposition *into* refers to *motion* or *movement.* Here are examples that clearly show the difference:

> After the statistician walked **into** the office, she looked for the data **in** the cabinet.

> While Ray was working **in** the laboratory, he was called **into** the conference room to be questioned.

★ In this sentence, Ray is *positioned in* the laboratory but was asked to *move into* the conference room.

Beside *or* Besides

The preposition *beside* means "next to" or "by the side of." It is not interchangeable with the preposition *besides*, which means "in addition to." Here are the two words used in sentences:

> Set the package **beside** the one on the couch.

> The dog sits **beside** his owner on the patio each morning.

> **Besides** the recent innovation, the company is known for its past successes.

> **Besides** that, what else is new?

Troublesome Prepositions

Identify and correct any errors in the use of prepositions.

1. She placed the paperweight besides the electric pencil sharpener on the desk.
2. The fruit was divided between the four boy scouts.
3. Beside pasta, we are having a salad and homemade apple pie.
4. Don't worry! I will look into the safe deposit box for the bond.
5. The contest among the two finalists ended in a tie.
6. Beside that, I am not available; I have to accompany my mother to her car.
7. Between the three vacation choices, I prefer cruising to Alaska.

Check your answers with Appendix F.

With Regard To, In Regard To, *or* As Regards

The prepositions *with regard to*, *in regard to*, and *as regards* can be used interchangeably, but only in the exact form in which they appear. The words *with* or *in* precede the word *regard;* the word *as* precedes the word *regards*. Note these examples:

With regard to your suggestion, we think it might work.

In regard to the position, we know that Alva will be filling it.

As regards our championship team, we expect to win again. (The preposition *as regards* is correct; but if it sounds awkward, substitute *with regard to* or *in regard to*.)

Like *or* As

The preposition *like* requires an object. The conjunction *as*, which is used to introduce a clause, does not require an object. *Like* and *as* may not be used interchangeably. Note these examples:

The firm plans to buy a printer just **like** its other one.

We hope to hire another employee **like** Lisa.

★ In the combination *as regards*, both elements end in *s*. In *with regard to* and *in regard to*, none of the elements ends in *s*.

★ The word *as* can also be used as an adverb to modify an adjective, as in "I am just *as* contented to stay at home."

Recite the poem **as** it appears in your book.

As your instructor suggested, check each step after completing it.

SPECIAL CONSIDERATIONS WHEN USING PREPOSITIONS

This section discusses guidelines that pertain to the use of *over* and *opposite* and the omission of *of* after *off*, *at* or *to* after *where*, *for* after *like*, and prepositions at the end of sentences. Communicators who follow these guidelines will use prepositions wisely.

Use of Over

Writers have a tendency to insert the word *with* after the word *over*. Omit *with* after *over!* Note these examples:

INCORRECT	CORRECT
We want this project *over with*.	We want this project **over**.
When the winter is *over with*, you can make plans.	When the winter is **over**, you can make plans.

CHECKPOINT 3

Additional Troublesome Prepositions

Identify the correct word in each sentence.

1. (As regard/As regards) your second question, I am not in a position to answer it.
2. (As/Like) a flame in the night, Stephanie brightened the room as she approached.
3. I will be happy when this semester is (over with/over).
4. (With regard/With regard to) the agenda, let's include the report.
5. (Like/As) I told you before, I must work overtime this Friday evening.
6. Is your recuperation period (over/over with)?
7. The new scout tried to behave (like/as) the other scouts in his troop.

Check your answers with Appendix F.

Omitting Of *after* Off

Eliminate the word *of* after the word *off* in sentences. For example:

INCORRECT	CORRECT
Flo took the book **off of** the shelf.	Flo took the book **off** the shelf.
The ball rolled **off of** the roof.	The ball rolled **off** the roof.

Omitting At *or* To *After* Where

Some people incorrectly ask "Where are you going to?" or "Where is the book at?" Eliminate the words *at* and *to* after the word *where*. For example:

INCORRECT	CORRECT
Where should I deliver the bag **at**?	Where should I deliver the bag?
Where did the children go **to**?	Where did the children go?

Use of Opposite

Many communicators unnecessarily add the word *to* after the preposition *opposite*. Note this example:

INCORRECT	CORRECT
The school is opposite **to** the township building.	The school is opposite the township building.

When used as a noun, the word *opposite* should be followed by the word *of*, as in "Her lifestyle is the **opposite of** mine" and "The president's viewpoint is the **opposite of** Congress's." If the word *opposite* is preceded by the word *the* in a sentence, *opposite* is used as a noun.

★ In this sentence, the word *to* after *opposite* serves no logical purpose; it doesn't help to clarify the meaning of the sentence. Therefore, *to* should be omitted.

Omitting For *After* Like

In informal communications, some people tend to insert the word *for* after the word *like*. This practice is incorrect and should always be avoided. For example:

INCORRECT	CORRECT
They would **like for** you to provide the data now.	They would **like** you to provide the data now.

★ Inserting the word *for* after *like* is a bad habit that should be broken as quickly as possible.

Prepositions at the End of Sentences

Try to avoid ending a sentence with a preposition. For example:

> **Wrong:** "Whom did you donate the money **to**?" "I need a book to write my notes **in**."

> **Right:** "**To** whom did you donate the money?" "I need a book **in** which to write my notes."

Do not reorganize a sentence to avoid ending the sentence with a preposition if an awkward construction results, such as "**For** what are you looking?" A sentence appropriately ends with a preposition only if moving the preposition results in an awkward construction.

4 CHECKPOINT

Selecting Prepositions

Identify the correct word in each sentence.

1. Where did you say you were (studying/studying at)?
2. My parents' opinions are the (opposite/opposite of) hers.
3. He would (like/like for) the waiters to be at work by noon.
4. Did the book fall (off of/off) this shelf?
5. Where in New York is your supervisor (going to/going)?
6. The post office is (opposite/opposite to) the supermarket.
7. They would (like for/like) you to sing at their wedding.

Check your answers with Appendix F.

PREPOSITIONS WITH OTHER WORDS

Sometimes other words, most often verbs, are followed by specific prepositions. Here are some examples:

1. Agree *to* rules and procedures; agree *upon* or *on* a plan; agree *with* a person.
2. Angry *at* a situation; angry *with* a person.
3. Different *from* not different *than.*
4. Discrepancy *in* (when the object is singular); discrepancy *between* (when the object is plural).
5. Identical *with* not identical *to.*

6. Part *with* something; part *from* a person.
7. Plan *to* not plan *on*.
8. Retroactive *to* not retroactive *from*.
9. Speak *with* (when two or more people converse); speak *to* (when one person does all the talking).

★ A sentence exemplifying the use of *retroactive to* is "We expect a 3 percent pay raise **retroactive to** the first of the year."

5 Prepositions with Other Words

Identify the correct word choice in each sentence.

1. Jan's thoughts are (identical to/identical with) mine on the topic.
2. The teachers (agreed upon/agreed with) the union's proposal.
3. The child cannot (part from/part with) her blanket for more than ten minutes.
4. The new stationery you are using is (different from/different than) your old letterhead.
5. Let's plan (on touring/to tour) the facility while we are in Cincinnati.
6. We hope you are not (angry at/angry with) us for suggesting that.
7. They detected a (discrepancy in/discrepancy between) this year's and last year's numbers.

Check your answers with Appendix F.

Prepositions, frequently very short in length, play an important part in communications. They introduce prepositional phrases that function as adjectives, modifying nouns and noun substitutes. They also introduce phrases that function as adverbs, modifying action verbs, adjectives, and adverbs. The prepositions themselves usually denote direction, position, or time.

Learning to avoid the incorrect use of troublesome prepositions considerably improves communications. In addition, memorizing the correct prepositions to be used with other words helps communicators to master basic English.

Discussion Questions

1. When students are asked to select the most important parts of speech in the English language, they usually chose nouns and verbs, not prepositions. Defend the importance of prepositions by discussing their role and special characteristics.
2. Discuss reasons for and reasons against ending a sentence with a preposition.

Spelling and Word Usage Application

Note the correct spelling of the following words:

aggressive	freight	liability	parallel
clientele	turnpike	intercede	relevant
representatives	criticism		

Rewrite the following sentences, correcting all misspelled words:

1. We prefer forceful and tactful sales represetives to aggresive ones.
2. This seminar topic is not relevent to our clientell.
3. Our company has not incurred any libility from the accident involving the frieght trains.
4. We will not intersede in that matter.
5. Did you know that the turn pike runs paralell to Route 80?
6. Josefina was put on probation because she was not able to take suggestion's and critisism.

If necessary, refer to Appendix A for the correct usage of the following words:

cite/sight/site   than/then

Practical Applications

Part A

Select the correct word in each sentence.

1. The land was divided (among/between) Jeb and Brett.
2. Let's go (into/in) the garage to find the radial tires.
3. Who is attending the meeting (beside/besides) you?
4. (With regard to/With regards to) your cousin, when will he arrive?
5. The team manager (agreed upon/agreed with) the owner of the club.

Part B

Find and correct errors in the use of prepositions.

1. The accountant refused to hire an assistant as the one sent by the temporary agency.
2. As soon as this assignment is over with, I am taking a well-deserved break.
3. Where did you say the house is at?
4. The administration building is opposite to the old mansion on the corner.
5. The professor would like for us to research the topic this weekend.
6. She is no different than any other professional employee.
7. Be aware of a discrepancy in Tom's and Unis's reports.

Part C

Identify the prepositional phrase(s) in each sentence.

1. Their health-care benefit program is identical with ours.
2. Parting from her long-term companions is difficult for her.
3. Between you and me, this film should win an Oscar.
4. None of my relatives are coming except her.
5. What is Kim doing to help besides driving to the restaurant?
6. Below the kitchen sink, you will find the cleaning fluid.
7. The manager left the information-processing meeting before lunch.
8. To find the gas station, drive around the corner and down the street.

Editing and Proofreading Application

Correct all errors in preposition usage, spelling, and word usage in the following message.

As you know, our company will be relocating on the very near future. We has sold the building, the buisiness, and the inventory as of March 1. All employees will start this week to prepare for our move to Lafayette Creek, which is between 15 miles from here, opposite to the Methodist church. The store to the new location is newest and more modern then this one, and you will enjoy the cleaner and best surroundings. We plan to occupy the new premises during June 1.

Because the new store is only 15 miles a way, commuting should continue to be easy for everyone. You will also be happy to hear that starting June 1, the day of the grand openning, all employees will receive a 1 percent pay raise.

You will be sent additional details in regards to the move within the next two weeks. Our relocation should be benificial for everyone, and we are certain that all employees will be very pleased when the move is over with.

Conjunctions and Interjections

OBJECTIVES

After studying this chapter and completing the chapter activities, you will be able to do the following:

1. Use coordinate, correlative, and subordinate conjunctions correctly.
2. List pitfalls pertaining to conjunction use and avoid those pitfalls.
3. Create sentences that use parallel construction.
4. Recognize interjections and use them in appropriate situations.

INTRODUCTION TO CONJUNCTIONS

A **conjunction** is a word that joins two or more words, phrases, or clauses. Note the conjunctions that appear in **bold** in the following sentences:

> Clara **and** José worked overtime.

> **Not only** Clara **but also** José worked overtime.

> **When** Clara worked overtime, José joined her.

Each of the previous sentences illustrates a different kind of conjunction. The first sentence uses a coordinate conjunction; the second sentence, a correlative conjunction; the third sentence, a subordinate conjunction. Let's take a closer look at each category, beginning with coordinate conjunctions.

COORDINATE CONJUNCTIONS

A **coordinate conjunction** joins words, phrases, and clauses of equal grammatical rank. *Equal grammatical rank* means that the connected elements are the same part of speech. For example, the connected elements may be nouns, verbs, prepositional phrases, or independent clauses. The coordinate conjunctions are *for, and, nor, but, or,* and *yet.* The list below shows guidelines for using coordinate conjunctions and includes examples of their use.

- **For.** Use *for* primarily as a preposition and also as a coordinate conjunction. Use *for* as a coordinate conjunction when the second independent clause explains the first independent clause in a compound sentence. For example:

  Leo is studying computer science, **for** he plans to be a systems analyst. (The conjunction *for* joins two independent clauses.)

- **And.** Use *and* to mean "in addition to." For example:

  The teacher **and** the principal spoke outside the room. (The conjunction *and* joins two nouns.)

- **Nor.** Use *nor* with a negative word such as *neither* or *not.* For example:

  Max did not agree with Craig, **nor** did he agree to take part in the arrangements. (The conjunction *nor* joins two clauses.)

- **But.** Use *but* in an opposing situation. For example:

  Tien wanted to attend the workshop, **but** she couldn't spare the time. (The conjunction *but* joins two clauses.)

★ Can you think of a sentence that uses *nor* with *not?*

- **Or.** Use *or* to present a choice. For example:

  They plan to swim **or** to hike this weekend. (The conjunction *or* joins two verbs.)

- **Yet.** Use *yet* in an opposing situation to mean *but nevertheless*. For example:

  Management says it wants to avoid a strike, **yet** it hasn't made an acceptable offer. (The conjunction *yet* joins two clauses.)

★ In the sentence "Ms. Long manages ably *and* efficiently," *and* joins two adverbs—elements of equal grammatical rank.

Coordinate Conjunctions

Select the correct words within the parentheses.

1. The assistant keeps the records methodically (and/but) neatly.
2. Try to hire Bella, (yet/for) she is well qualified for the job.
3. Leon is a recent graduate (and/or) a good worker.
4. Ms. Rubin does not agree with your remark (nor/or) does she agree with your philosophy.
5. Danielle behaves well, (but/and) Sean behaves better.

(Continued on next page)

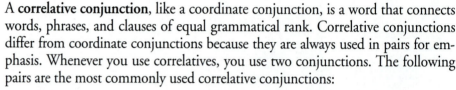

Coordinate Conjunctions, Continued

6. Plan to go with us (yet/or) go with them on Tuesday.
7. We hoped to join you, (and/yet) we didn't plan for it early enough.

Check your answers in Appendix F.

★ Use *neither . . . nor* when expressing a negative situation; use *either . . . or* when expressing a positive situation.

CORRELATIVE CONJUNCTIONS

A **correlative conjunction**, like a coordinate conjunction, is a word that connects words, phrases, and clauses of equal grammatical rank. Correlative conjunctions differ from coordinate conjunctions because they are always used in pairs for emphasis. Whenever you use correlatives, you use two conjunctions. The following pairs are the most commonly used correlative conjunctions:

both . . . and	neither . . . nor
either . . . or	not only . . . but also

These sentences illustrate the use of correlative conjunctions:

Both Greg **and** Barbara applied for the teaching position.

Either Greg **or** Barbara applied for the teaching position.

Neither Greg **nor** Barbara applied for the teaching position.

Not only Greg **but also** Barbara applied for the teaching position.

2 CHECKPOINT

Correlative Conjunctions

Select the correct words within the parentheses.

1. Neither he (or/nor) she is helping us on this project.
2. Not only Hal (but also/but) June is qualified.
3. Either one (or/nor) the other is satisfactory in this situation.
4. Both Alberto (and also/and) Gloria are related to my parents.
5. Either she is ready for this (or/nor) she isn't.
6. Neither of them are here (nor/or) did they call.
7. Not only Lance (but/but also) Rosalind arrived.

Check your answers in Appendix F.

SUBORDINATE CONJUNCTIONS

A **subordinate conjunction** joins elements of unequal grammatical rank. It is used primarily to connect dependent clauses with independent clauses. Here are sentences illustrating the use of *after*, a subordinate conjunction:

> **After** the semester ended, the junior class traveled to Europe.
>
> The junior class traveled to Europe **after** the semester ended.

In the previous sentences, the subordinate conjunction *after* introduces a dependent clause. The list below shows other common subordinate conjunctions:

after	as though	provided	though	whenever
although	because	since	unless	where
as	before	so that	until	while
as if	if	that	when	

Here are some additional sentences that use subordinate conjunctions:

> **Although** we couldn't attend, we sent a donation.
>
> They saw her **as** they were leaving the factory.
>
> **As if** we could solve the problems, the men asked us for help.
>
> Mr. Tompkins searched for the parts **while** he was shopping.
>
> **When** we can, we donate used clothes to the thrift shop.
>
> Jules and Beth will visit **provided** they are allowed.

EXTRA, EXTRA!

★ Both of these sentences are complex sentences; each has one dependent clause and one independent clause.

EXTRA, EXTRA!

★ When you check your answers in Appendix F, you will see that more than one conjunction is acceptable for some of these sentences.

CHECKPOINT 3

Selecting Conjunctions

Supply an appropriate conjunction for each sentence.

1. The pilot started the left engine _____ the co-pilot checked the passenger list.
2. You purchased a fax machine _____ you purchased a copier for your home office.
3. As _____ we could do anything about it, they came to us for money.
4. We will plant the flowers _____ the warmer weather arrives.

(Continued on next page)

Selecting Conjunctions, Continued

5. _____ you wish to succeed, you must be diligent.
6. The sales manager was depressed _____ sales had decreased.
7. I will not be able to work overtime _____ I have a doctor's appointment.

Check your answers in Appendix F.

PITFALLS

Generally, communicators have success selecting correct conjunctions; however, a few trouble spots are worth mentioning. These trouble spots include the incorrect use of *being that* and *the reason is because*. These pitfalls also include the incorrect use of some conjunctions, which leads to ungrammatical sentences. Let's take a look at some of the trouble spots.

★ Never substitute the expression *being that* for *because.*

Being That *or* Because

Being and *that* can be used together in a sentence such as "Are you being that way on purpose?" As you can see, *being that* is not a subordinate conjunction and should not be used as one. For example:

Incorrect

Being that she has arrived, we can get ready to go.

Correct

Because she has arrived, we can get ready to go. (The conjunction *because* indicates that a reason will follow.)

The Reason Is Because *or* The Reason Is That

Although both *because* and *that* are used as subordinate conjunctions, *because* should not be used after *the reason is*. The expression *the reason is that* is grammatically correct because *that* introduces a noun clause that is not a subordinate clause. For example:

Incorrect

The reason is because they don't have sufficient credit.

Correct

The reason is that they don't have sufficient credit. (The conjunction *that* introduces the noun clause *they don't have sufficient credit*, which functions as a predicate nominative and renames the subject *reason*.)

Using Parallel Construction

Remember that two kinds of conjunctions—coordinate and correlative—join words, phrases, and clauses of equal grammatical rank. Subordinate conjunctions join words, phrases, and clauses of unequal grammatical rank. If conjunctions are used incorrectly, unparallel constructions will result.

A construction that is not parallel will have a conjunction that joins unmatched elements. An adverb may be joined to a prepositional phrase or a verb phrase may be joined to a noun. Constructions that are not parallel are ungrammatical. Note these examples:

Incorrect

Customers want *not only* good service *but also* to be treated with courtesy. (A correlative conjunction joins a noun with an infinitive verb phrase, which is an unparallel construction.)

Correct

Customers want *not only* good service *but also* courtesy. (A conjunction joins two nouns, which is a parallel construction.)

Customers want *not only* to receive good service *but also* to be treated with courtesy. (A conjunction joins two verb phrases, which is a parallel construction.)

Incorrect

The expert works cleverly *and* with speed. (A coordinate conjunction joins an adverb with a prepositional phrase, which is not a parallel construction.)

Correct

The expert works cleverly *and* speedily. (A conjunction joins two adverbs, which is a parallel construction.)

The expert works speedily when a deadline is approaching. (A subordinate conjunction *when* joins an independent clause and a dependent clause, which is a parallel construction.)

★ Remember that an infinitive phrase must begin with the word *to*.

★ Parallel construction is smooth and does not sound awkward. Parallel construction helps to improve clarity in writing.

Pitfalls

Supply the correct word(s) for each sentence.

1. (Being that/Because) the weather was cloudy, the photographs of the beach scene were just fair.
2. The word processor keys accurately and (with speed/speedily).
3. The reason is (that/because) she is not fluent in French.
4. Sketching and (to paint/painting) are among his many talents.
5. (Because/Being that) the auditors are here, the conference room is occupied.
6. The supervisor wants either James (and/or) me to lead the project.
7. You are expected to finish on time and (with accuracy/ accurately).

Check your answers in Appendix F.

Before you move on to the next section, you may want to review the discussion of conjunctive adverbs in Chapter 10. Conjunctive adverbs serve as conjunctions in sentences.

INTERJECTIONS

An **interjection** is a word or expression that has no grammatical relationship with other words in a sentence. An interjection is used primarily to express strong emotion; therefore, it is usually followed by an exclamation point. Some examples are:

Great!   **Oh!**   **Help!**   **Ouch!**   **No!**   **Super!**

Here are sentences that use interjections:

Great! I'm glad you are joining our team.

Oh! That is something to think about.

Help! Do you hear that daily from your customers?

Ouch! That really hurts.

Don't pass this by. **No!** It is too good an opportunity.

Your idea is sure to work. **Super!**

★ Business communicators use interjections sparingly unless they frequently write sales communications and advertisements.

In specific situations such as sales promotions, interjections add color and vitality. However, interjections should not be used routinely in business writing.

Conjunctions are words that connect two or more elements to create smoothly written and coherent sentences. Coordinate conjunctions and correlative conjunctions join words, phrases, or clauses of equal grammatical rank. Subordinate conjunctions, which usually join dependent clauses to independent clauses, connect elements of unequal grammatical rank. Avoiding trouble spots, such as the use of conjunctions and constructions that are not parallel, helps to create effective communications.

Interjections are words and expressions that convey emotion and that are not grammatically connected to other words in a sentence. Interjections are used sparingly in business communications.

The discussion of coordinate, correlative, and subordinate conjunctions and of interjections completes the coverage of all parts of speech in the English language. Chapters 3-12 are designed to prepare you for the remaining chapters in this textbook. These chapters provide a valuable review and a solid base for creating effective letters, memos, and reports.

Summary

Discussion Questions

1. When using coordinate and correlative conjunctions in your writing, how can you be sure that your constructions are parallel? What disadvantages result from constructions that are not parallel?

2. Define the word *interjection*. Give several examples of interjections and discuss their role in business writing.

Spelling and Word Usage Application

Note the correct spelling of the following words:

confident	gratitude	miscellaneous	privilege
advertising	criticize	graduation	precede

Rewrite the following sentences, correcting all misspelled words.

1. I am confidant that the miscelaneous items in the child's gift box will please her.
2. The companies advertiseing budget for this year far exceeds that of last year.
3. Its important that you express you're graditude for the assistance you have received.
4. Why criticise him? It wont do any good.
5. He has the priviledge of addressing your class at your gradation ceremony.
6. Preceed your writting with at least three months' research.

If necessary, refer to Appendix A for the correct usage of the following words:

allude/ elude   council/ counsel/ consul

Practical Applications

Part A

Identify all conjunctions.

1. Merry and Bob worked hard, but Faye didn't.
2. Either Carl or Mae knew when the late shipment arrived.
3. Since the new journalists arrived, the planning and scheduling meetings have ended early.
4. He desires not only wealth but also peace and quiet.
5. Unless all of us agree, we and they will not profit nor succeed in our business.

Part B
Correct any errors in conjunction use.

1. Dr. Garth plans to attend the conference, unless Dr. Bodinsky will not be able to attend.
2. Whether the filing systems vary from branch to branch, the banker cannot make a general statement about them.
3. Janet needed six fillings for she rarely brushed her teeth.
4. I would prefer to work in either accounting and real estate.
5. I wanted to help the supervisor, and the summer positions were all filled.
6. Not only Ann but Betty graduated in the top ten of the class.
7. The reason is because we are short of money.

Part C
Select the correct word(s) in parentheses.

1. (Super!/Super,) We have a winner.
2. (Because/Being that) you are qualified, we are considering you for the position.
3. He exclaimed, "(Wow!/Wow,) That new software saves us several hours each week."
4. The house painter works slowly and (sloppily/sloppy).
5. (Help!/No!) There has been an accident.
6. Either you (nor/or) your assistant is responsible for this statement.
7. Please call me (whenever/as if) it is convenient for you.
8. (That/While) we are at the meeting, we will mention the telephone call.

Editing and Proofreading Application

Correct all errors in conjunctions, interjections, and spelling in the following message.

Until my family has enjoyed your dellicious canned soups for a number of year's, I purchase four or five cans each time that I go to the supermarket. My sons recent expereince with your old-fashioned vegetable soup, however, is a great disappointment.

Not only did he find a bone in the soup, but he found some meat. In order that my son is a vegetarian, this displeased him grately. At first, we decided to overlook the incident; yet our friends and family, who also use your products, advised me to write to you. Being that we are such good customers, I decided to follow their advise.

I am enclosing a copy of my son's dentist bill for the problem caused by the bone; please reemburse me as soon as possible. In edition, we expect something for the displeasure he felt before he found the meat in his "meatless" vegetable soup. Why am I asking for some satisfaction? The reason is because your advertisments declare that you are the consumer's friend.

I expect to here from you speedily and with understanding. This may restore my faith in you or you products.

A Grammar Review: Ten Common Errors

Chapter 13

OBJECTIVES

After studying this chapter and completing the chapter activities, you will be able to do the following:

1. Apply the guidelines for forming and using noun plurals and possessives.
2. Use past participle and past tense verb forms accurately.
3. Apply the agreement rules for contractions, subjects-verbs, and nouns-pronouns in your communications.
4. Identify pronouns to be used as subjects and objects.

ELIMINATING TEN GRAMMATICAL ERRORS

In business writing and speaking and in job interviews, every grammatical error can cause miscommunication, as well as cause your readers and listeners to distrust your message. What can you do to eliminate communication errors? For now, you can focus on ten common errors that pertain to noun plurals and possessives, past participle and past tense verb forms, various forms of agreement, and pronouns used as subjects or objects. Your awareness of these errors will help you avoid them and help you develop error-free messages.

ERRORS IN NOUN PLURALS AND POSSESSIVES

This section presents two common errors that pertain to the formation of singular possessive, plural possessive, and simple plural nouns.

Error Number 1. Incorrect Use of Plural Nouns and Possessives

Words such as *manager's*, *managers'*, and *managers* are pronounced alike but are not spelled the same. In the first word the apostrophe precedes the *s*, in the second word the apostrophe follows the *s*, and in the third word the apostrophe is omitted altogether. The apostrophe identifies the singular possessive noun *manager's* and the plural possessive noun *managers'*. These two forms often are confused with the simple plural form *managers*, which has no apostrophe.

Find the Errors

1. Several manager's have requested data.
2. Several executive's representatives are present today.
3. Hilda owes about two thousand dollars on her taxs.
4. The Kennedies live next door. (Name is Kennedy)
5. Mens' clothes are sold in this store.

Corrections

1. Several **managers** have requested data. (Simple plural, not possessive)
2. Several **executives'** representatives are present today. (Plural possessive noun)
3. Hilda owes about two thousand dollars on her **taxes**. (To form the plural, add *es* to nouns that end in *x*.)
4. The **Kennedys** live next door. (To form the plural, do not change *y* to *i* in proper names.)
5. **Men's** clothes are sold in this store. (An irregular plural noun, *men* forms its plural possessive like a *singular* possessive ['s].)

Error Number 2. Singular Possessive Nouns

For most nouns, the singular possessive form (such as *manager's*) is pronounced the same as its plural form (*managers*) and plural possessive form (*managers'*). To determine if a singular possessive form is needed, create an "of phrase" (*budget of the manager*); if the phrase makes sense, the possessive case is needed. To form the singular possessive, add *'s* regardless of whether or not the noun ends in *s*.

Find the Errors

1. One managers budget has been reviewed.
2. One supervisors' budget was turned in late.
3. An attorneys brief has been filed.
4. The young actresses role as an executive pleased her.
5. The young actors' role in the play is very short.

Corrections

1. One **manager's** budget has been reviewed. (singular possessive ['s])
2. One **supervisor's** budget was turned in late. (singular possessive ['s])
3. An **attorney's** brief has been filed. (singular possessive ['s])
4. The young **actress's** role as an executive pleased her. (singular possessive ['s])
5. The young **actor's** role in the play is very short. (singular possessive ['s])

ACROSS CULTURES

- If you are learning English as your second language, beware of these common errors caused by plural and possessive nouns.

CHECKPOINT 1

Noun Plurals and Possessives

Select the correct answer in each sentence.

1. Several (employees/employee's) are displeased with the offer.
2. One (operators/operator's) job is being eliminated.
3. The (accountant's/accountants) are arriving July 6.
4. Two (womens'/women's) boutiques are on Main Street.
5. Do you know any (actuaries/actuary's)?
6. How many (executives'/executives) have desks on this floor?
7. The two (managers'/manager's) stores will open today.

Check your answers in Appendix F.

ERRORS IN PAST PARTICIPLE AND PAST TENSE VERB FORMS

This section presents two common errors that pertain to the incorrect use of past participles and past tense verb forms.

Error Number 3. Incorrect Use of Past Participles

Past participle verb forms include *seen, been, gone, spoken, known, written, taken,* and *grown.* Past participle forms must be preceded by helping verbs such as *has, have,* or *had.*

Find the Errors

1. I been to several concerts lately.
2. Luis already seen the movie you recommended.
3. They gone to the restaurant to reserve our table.
4. Toshi spoken to us about the problem.
5. If I known about it, I wouldn't have called her.

Corrections

1. I **have been** to several concerts lately. (Past participle *been* needs helping verb *have.*)
2. Luis already **had seen** the movie you recommended. (Past participle *seen* needs helping verb *had.*)
3. They **have gone** to the restaurant to reserve our table. (Past participle *gone* needs helping verb *have.*)
4. Toshi **has spoken** to us about the problem. (Past participle *spoken* needs helping verb *has.*)
5. If I **had known** about it, I wouldn't have called her. (Past participle *known* needs helping verb *had.*)

★ Practice eliminating helping verbs with past tense verb forms and adding helping verbs to past participle verb forms to improve your skills.

Error Number 4. Incorrect Use of Past Tense Verbs

Past tense verb forms do not have helpers. Some examples of past tense forms are *saw, was, went, spoke, knew, wrote, took,* and *grew.* Placing *had, has,* or *have* before past tense forms is incorrect. For a thorough review of verbs, refer to Chapter 7.

Find the Errors

1. The managers already have went to the meeting.
2. Hannah has wrote to the airlines about the delay.
3. Roy and she have took advantage of the discount.
4. My supervisor had saw how hard I worked on the report.
5. The tree has grew three inches since we last spoke.

Corrections

1. The managers **already went** to the meeting. (Past tense verb *went* does not need helping verb *have.*)

2. Hannah **wrote** to the airlines about the delay. (Past tense verb *wrote* does not need helping verb *has*.)

3. Roy and she **took** advantage of the discount. (Past tense verb does not need helping verb *have*.)

4. My supervisor **saw** how hard I worked on the report. (Past tense verb *saw* does not need helping verb *had*.)

5. The tree **grew** three inches since we last spoke. (Past tense verb *grew* does not need helping verb *has*.)

ERRORS IN VARIOUS FORMS OF AGREEMENT

This section presents four common errors that involve subject-verb agreement, noun-pronoun agreement, and agreement using correlative conjunctions.

Error Number 5. Misunderstanding of Agreement Rules

Grammar has several agreement rules. One agreement rule states that two singular subjects joined by *either . . . or* or *or* create a singular construction and require a singular verb. The same rule applies to *neither . . . nor*. A second agreement rule

★ Remember that a dish such as pie and ice cream is considered to be one dessert and requires a singular verb, as in "Pie and ice cream *is* my favorite dessert."

indicates that two singular subjects joined by *and* usually create a plural construction and require a plural verb.

Find the Errors

1. Either Virginia or Victor are handling that project.
2. Gloria and Hector has recommended the new site.
3. Suzanne or Derek have the report you need.
4. Neither Mr. Syms nor Ms. Long know about the mailings.
5. Janine or Lance were assigned to this department.

Corrections

1. Either Virginia or Victor **is handling** that project. (Two singular subjects joined by *either . . . or* require a singular verb [is].)
2. Gloria and Hector **have recommended** the new site. (Two singular subjects joined by *and* require a plural verb [have].)
3. Suzanne or Derek **has** the report you need. (Two singular subjects joined by *or* require a singular verb [has].)
4. Neither Mr. Syms nor Ms. Long **knows** about the mailings. (Two singular subjects joined by *neither . . . nor* require a singular verb [knows].)
5. Janine or Lance **was assigned** to this department. (Two singular subjects joined by *or* require a singular verb [was].)

★ Note—if the noun closer to the verb is plural instead of singular, a plural verb is required, as in "Either the girl or the boys are in charge."

CHECKPOINT 2

Verb Form and Agreement

Correct any verb form or agreement errors in the following sentences.

1. Amy had wrote to the gas company about her bill.
2. A long time was took by the auditors to check the books.
3. The child grown very quickly in the last year.
4. They seen their teacher at the park.
5. The violinist or the pianist are providing the music.
6. Neither Bart nor Tara are joining us at the meeting.
7. Chicken salad and egg salad is two of my favorite foods.

Check your answers in Appendix F.

★ By covering the interrupters with your hand, you can disregard them easily when checking subject-verb agreement.

Error Number 6. Misunderstanding of Subject-Verb Agreement

Intervening phrases or other interrupters between the subject and the main verb often confuse communicators. Knowing when a singular or a plural verb is required takes skill and practice. Remember to ignore interrupters when determining subject-verb agreement.

Find the Errors

1. The members of the association in that district has called today.
2. Anne Williams, who is one of the competitor's directors, are visiting in May.
3. All tellers and the vice president of the bank is to attend the training.
4. The book, which helps those who want to become practical nurses, are selling for $15 this week.
5. Marla and Perry, who belong to the team, is being considered for the Olympics.

Corrections

1. The members of the association in that district **have** called today. (Plural verb *have* agrees with plural subject *members.*)
2. Anne Williams, who is one of the competitor's directors, **is** visiting in May. (Singular verb *is* agrees with singular subject *Anne Williams.*)
3. All tellers and the vice president of the bank **are** to attend the training. (Plural verb *are* agrees with plural subject *tellers* and *vice president.*)
   Or: The vice president and all tellers of the bank **are** to attend the training. (Notice how reconstructing the sentence can help readability.)
4. The book, which aids those who want to become practical nurses, **is** selling for $15 this week. (Singular verb *is* agrees with singular subject *book.*)
5. Marla and Perry, who belong to the team, **are** being considered for the Olympics. (Plural verb *are* agrees with plural subject *Marla* and *Perry.*)

Error Number 7. Incorrect Use of Contractions

In the contractions *here's*, *where's*, and *who's*, the *'s* substitutes for *is*, a singular verb. Sentences that start with contractions such as these are inverted sentences, which means the subject follows the verb. First, find the subject. If the subject is singular, then *'s* is correct. If the subject is plural, drop the *'s* and change the construction to *Here are*, *Where are*, or *Who are*, whichever is appropriate.

★ People tend to talk first and think later. Thus, people often say *Here's* and *Where's* without considering whether a singular or a plural subject follows.

Find the Errors

1. Where's the copies of the report?
2. Who's the sales representatives in Chicago and Tampa?
3. Here's the keys to the office and the desk.
4. Where are the new application form?
5. Here are the latest copy of the product price list.

Corrections

1. **Where are** the copies of the report? (Plural verb *are* agrees with plural subject *copies*.)
2. **Who are** the sales representatives in Chicago and Tampa? (Plural verb *are* agrees with plural subject *representatives*.)
3. **Here are** the keys to the office and the desk. (Plural verb *are* agrees with plural subject *keys*.)
4. **Where's** the new application form? (Singular verb *is* agrees with singular subject *form*.)
5. **Here's** the latest copy of the product price list. (Singular verb *is* agrees with singular subject *copy*.)

3 *Agreement*

CHECKPOINT

Correct errors in the following sentences.

1. The fans in the audience is impatiently awaiting the star.
2. Annette and Lloyd, who recently met, has started to date.
3. The items, in the desk in the office, was discarded yesterday.
4. My sister who lives in Maine has wrote to me once a week.
5. Where's your textbook and notebook on economic geography?
6. Here's the information and the papers you requested.
7. Who's the people that are coming to the party?

Check your answers in Appendix F.

★ Use the *gender-neutral* pronoun *it* if neither *masculine* nor *feminine* gender applies.

Error Number 8. Misunderstanding of Personal Pronoun Agreement

Make each personal pronoun, such as *they*, *it*, or *she*, agree with the specific person, place, or thing to which it refers (its antecedent). The pronoun must agree in number (singular or plural) and gender (masculine, feminine, or gender-neutral).

Find the Errors

1. Each of the women presented their forecast.
2. Both executives stated that he or she would cooperate.
3. Every employee has the right to see their personnel file.
4. UCLA wants their staff to adopt these new procedures.
5. The man offered their assistance to the senior citizen.

Corrections

1. Each of the women presented **her** forecast. (Singular feminine pronoun *her* agrees with *each* in number and *women* in gender).
2. Both executives stated that **they** would cooperate. (Plural pronoun *they* agrees with plural antecedent *executives.*)
3. Every employee has the right to see **his or her** personnel file. (Singular pronoun *his or her* agrees with *every employee.*)
4. UCLA wants **its** staff to adopt these new procedures. (Singular pronoun *its* agrees with singular antecedent *UCLA.*)
5. The man offered **his** assistance to the senior citizen. (Singular masculine pronoun *his* agrees with singular masculine antecedent *man.*)

ERRORS IN PRONOUN SELECTION

This section presents errors that pertain to incorrect pronoun selection when pronouns are used as subjects or objects.

Error Number 9. Misunderstanding of Nominative Pronouns

In communications, you must select either the nominative or objective form of a pronoun, depending on which is needed for noun-pronoun agreement. How do you know which form is correct? Error number 9 implies that objective pronouns are frequently but incorrectly used as subjects. Remember to use only nominative pronouns (*I, you, he, she, it, we, they, who,* and *whoever*) as subjects.

Find the Errors

1. My supervisor and me went to the airport early.
2. Ms. Hamilton said that Mark, Lana, and him should discuss these problems.
3. When Art and her drove to the train, they were delayed.
4. Jack and them will complete all the work on time.
5. The athletes and whomever else are there will see that the door is locked.

Corrections

1. My supervisor and **I** went to the airport early. (Use nominative pronoun *I* as a subject.)
2. . . . Mark, Lana, and **he** should discuss these problems. (Use nominative pronoun *he* as a subject of *should discuss.*)
3. When Art and **she** drove to the train, they were delayed. (Use nominative pronoun *she* as a subject of the verb *drove.*)

★ To determine which pronoun or pronouns to use in a compound subject, split the subject into parts. For example, in the sentence "Jack and I went to the store," split the subject into two pieces: *Jack* went and *I* went. This practice highlights the need for the nominative pronoun *I* instead of the objective pronoun *me.*

4. Jack and **they** will complete all the work on time. (Use nominative pronoun *they* as a subject of the verb *will complete*.)
5. The athletes and **whoever** else are there will see that the door is locked. (Use the nominative pronoun *whoever* as a subject of the verb *are*.)

Error Number 10. Misunderstanding of Objective Pronouns

Use an objective pronoun form (*me, you, him, her, it, them, us, whom,* and *whomever*) as the object of a preposition in a prepositional phrase.

Find the Errors

1. The project will be challenging for you and I.
2. They will celebrate with Claire and he.
3. Without Adam and she the team has no chance to win.
4. The materials were written by Rachel and they.
5. You can use the conference room after Lance and we.

Corrections

1. The project will be challenging for you and **me**. (Use objective pronoun *me* as the object of preposition *for*.)
2. They will celebrate with Claire and **him**. (Use objective pronoun *him* as the object of preposition *with*.)
3. Without Adam and **her** the team has no chance to win. (Use objective pronoun *her* as the object of preposition *without*.)
4. The materials were written by Rachel and **them**. (Use objective pronoun *them* as the object of preposition *by*.)
5. You can use the conference room after Lance and **us**. (Use objective pronoun *us* as the object of preposition *after*.)

Pronoun Selection and Agreement

Select the correct pronoun in each sentence.

1. Each of the agents asked if (they/he or she) could join us.
2. Both tenants mentioned that (they/he or she) will move.
3. Every student has the opportunity to meet with (their/his or her) teacher on conference night.
4. The college gives financial aid to Roy and (them/they).
5. Your hospitality toward Bruce and (I/me) is appreciated.
6. The tax preparer said that you and (she/her) should bring your records up to date.
7. (Him/He) and they have been friends since childhood.

Check your answers in Appendix F.

This chapter covers ten common grammar errors that communicators should avoid. First, remember that most noun plurals are formed by adding *s* or *es*, singular possessives are formed by adding *'s*, and most plural possessives are formed by adding an apostrophe. For most nouns, these three forms are pronounced the same.

Past participle verb forms must be accompanied by helping verbs, but past tense verb forms do not need helping verbs. Remember that nominative pronouns are used as subjects and objective pronouns are used as objects of prepositions in prepositional phrases. Also remember always to follow agreement rules that cover contractions, subjects and verbs, and nouns and pronouns.

Discussion Questions

1. Comment on the impact poor grammatical skills can have in a job interview or in a telephone conversation with a customer.
2. Select one of the ten grammatical errors covered in this chapter that you believe communicators must avoid at all times. Describe the best way to learn to eliminate the error in writing and speaking.

Spelling and Word Usage Application

Note the correct spelling of the following words:

bankrupt	beneficial	efficiency	February
maintenance	misspell	occurrence	prevalent

Rewrite the following sentences, correcting all misspelled words.

1. The plan has no benificial attributes.
2. In Febuary in the East, snow is prevelent.
3. The frequent occurence of sandstorms hindered the hikers.
4. Try not to mispell foreign words.
5. Studio and efficiensy apartments are similar in size.
6. The maintanance plan on the equipment is quite costly.

If necessary, refer to Appendix A for the correct usage of the following words:

there/their/they're   cooperation/corporation

Practical Applications

Part A
Select the correct answer in each sentence.

1. Several fattening (food's/foods) have been removed from the menu.
2. (Women's/Womens') tailored suits are appropriate for job interviews.
3. One (bankers/banker's) loan portfolio surpassed all the others.
4. Greta and Tony (have spoke/spoke) to their colleagues.
5. Either we or they (is flying/are flying) to Des Moines.

Part B
Correct all errors in the following sentences.

1. The man and the woman is hosting the annual dinner.
2. The Clarke's seen you before you saw them.

3. Neither Anne nor Ben recommend this route.
4. The chefs in the French restaurant is very experienced.
5. Clara, who is related to them, are proficient in Russian.

Part C
Select the word or words that belong in each blank.

There are   There's/their   his/her   it's/its/me   I/us/we

1. _____ the book I need on the bottom shelf.
2. Each of the sellers presented _____ wares.
3. The library wants _____ reader population to increase.
4. My manager and _____ have worked together for five years.
5. Our spouses and _____ are invited to the retreat.

Editing and Proofreading Application
Correct all errors in word usage and spelling in the following message.

Several supervisors' in the tax division met with me on Wenesday. They're records indicate that several employee's whom report directly to them have been arriving at work late and leaving early. Either the supervisors or the employees is being lax in fullfiling his or her responsibilitys. Every employee who works for this company have to follow regular working hour's on a consistent basis or expect to be docked or terminated.

Here's the two choices availible to all employees: Begin at 8 a.m. and leave at 4 p.m. or begin at 9 a.m. and leave at 5 p.m. Each of the staff members in the tax division which are not punctual are to expect further word from the Office of the President on the very near future.

The president and me look forward to an improved punctuality and attendance record from now on for every one.

Chapter 14

A Grammar Review: Eight Additional Common Errors

OBJECTIVES

After studying this chapter and completing the chapter activities, you will be able to do the following:

1. Use objective case pronouns after *between*, select correct pronouns in statements of comparison and in homonyms, and use possessive case pronouns before gerunds.

2. Use the words *good* and *well* correctly and match *this*, *that*, *these*, and *those* correctly with singular-form and plural-form nouns.

3. Use *were* instead of *was* in statements that indicate a wish or something contrary to fact, and refrain from using the word *like* as a conjunction.

INTRODUCTION TO EIGHT MORE ERRORS

Your grammar review continues as you focus on eight additional common errors that good communicators should avoid. When you complete this chapter, you will have a solid grammar foundation to help you develop error-free messages.

ERRORS IN PRONOUN SELECTION

Four common errors that communicators should avoid pertain to the use of incorrect pronouns after the word *between*, in statements of comparison, in selection of homonyms, and before gerunds. Let's start with Error Number 11.

Error Number 11. Incorrect Pronoun Choice After Between

Remember that an objective case pronoun is used as an object of both verbs and prepositions. Communicators who use the incorrect phrase "between you and I" do so either from habit or from a desire to impress. The nominative case pronoun *I* cannot serve as the object of the preposition *between*. If you remember this, you will always say "between you and *me*," "between you and *her*," "between you and *him*," and "between you and *them*." Also remember to use objective case pronouns as objects of action verbs.

Find the Errors

1. Between you and I, I believe that the budget is inflated.
2. Send copies to Jack and she.
3. Ms. Encino preferred the designs submitted by Karen and they.
4. Our supervisor invited Carla and he to the luncheon.
5. The director wants Ronald and I to go to the meeting.
6. Theresa will send copies for Brian, Renee, and she.

Corrections

1. **Between you and me**, I believe the budget is inflated. (Use objective pronoun *me* as object of preposition *between*.)
2. Send copies **to Jack and her**. (Eliminate *Jack and* to see why objective pronoun *her* is needed to serve as object of preposition *to*.)
3. Ms. Encino preferred the designs submitted **by Karen and them**. (Use objective pronoun *them* as object of preposition *by*.)
4. Our supervisor **invited Carla and him** to the luncheon. (Use objective pronoun *him* as object of verb *invited*.)
5. The director **wants Ronald and me** to go to the meeting. (Use objective pronoun *me* as object of verb *wants*.)

★ If any areas of grammar still present problems, review the specific problem areas in the applicable chapters in Part 2.

★ Do not be one of the many people who consistently misuse nominative and objective case pronouns.

6. Theresa will send copies **for Brian, Renee, and her**. (Use objective pronoun *her* as object of preposition *for*.)

Error Number 12. Incorrect Pronoun Choice in Comparisons

Pronoun choice in comparisons is especially challenging because you often must mentally fill in missing verbs to determine the correct pronoun. In the sentence, "Greg keys much more quickly than I," the nominative pronoun *I* serves as the subject of the omitted verb *key*. Another example is, "Arielle likes this software better than I." The nominative pronoun *I* serves as the subject of the omitted verb *like*. Only by completing the unfinished thought can you be sure to select the correct pronoun in expressions of comparison.

Find the Errors

1. Owen believes that Francine is more experienced than him.
2. Ms. Fergus knows more about computer languages than them.
3. Dani sketches more meticulously than her.
4. Deanna prefers working with Rachel rather than with I.
5. Mr. Hardesty thinks more highly of direct mail advertising than me.
6. Do you think that Raymond likes New York better than them?

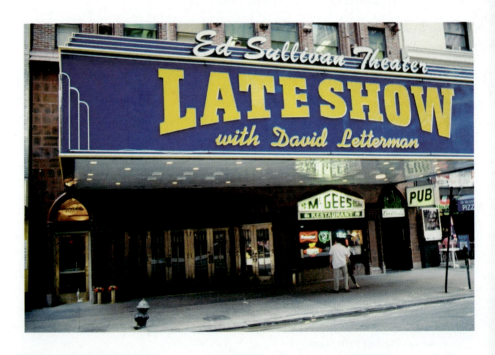

Corrections

1. Owen believes that Francine is more experienced **than he** (is).
2. Ms. Fergus knows more about computer languages **than they** (know).
3. Dani sketches more meticulously **than she** (sketches).
4. Deanna prefers working with Rachel **rather than with me.** (Use objective pronoun *me* as object of preposition *with.*)
5. Mr. Hardesty thinks more highly of direct mail advertising **than I** (do).
6. Do you think that Raymond likes New York **better than they** (like New York)?

CHECKPOINT 1

Pronoun Selection

Select the correct pronoun in each sentence.

1. Perhaps Mr. Seybold would like to discuss this strategy with Adam, Marisa, and (I/me).
2. Because Jeremy and (she/her) had already submitted their budgets, they were scheduled first.
3. All the ads were reviewed and approved by Denise, Marly, and (him/he).
4. The company invited Sophia and (they/them) to present their recommendations.
5. Joy works more overtime than (they/them).
6. Between Garth and (she/her), the research will be completed on time.
7. His brother communicates better than (he/him).

Check your answers in Appendix F.

Error Number 13. Misunderstanding of Homonyms

Try not to overlook homonym errors such as substituting *it's* for *its*, *there's* for *theirs*, and *you're* for *your*. By converting the contraction *it's* to *it is* or *it has*, *there's* to *there is*, and *you're* to *you are*, you can check if your word choice is correct. Remember that possessive personal pronouns never have apostrophes, but contractions always have apostrophes.

Find the Errors

1. The city claims that it's budget statement is correct.
2. Do you think its necessary to include this information?
3. Please let me know as soon as possible when your ready.

★ Review the spelling, pronunciation, and definition of the word *homonym*

4. Do you realize that this is you're copy on the desk?
5. Theirs the key that you need to open the door.
6. Don't take this one; this key is there's.

Corrections

1. The city claims that **its budget statement** is correct. (possessive pronoun needed; *it is* (it's) does not make sense)
2. Do you think **it's necessary** to include this information? (it is)
3. Please let me know as soon as possible **when you're ready**. (you are)
4. Do you realize that this is **your copy** on the desk? (Use possessive pronoun *your* because *you are* (you're) does not make sense.)
5. **There's the key** that you need to open the door. (There is)
6. Don't take this one; **this key is theirs**. (Use possessive pronoun *theirs* because *there is* (there's) does not make sense.)

Error Number 14. Misunderstanding of Gerunds

Remember that gerunds are verb forms that end in *ing* and function as nouns in sentences. Possessive forms of nouns and pronouns should precede gerunds. By preceding a gerund with a possessive form, you accentuate the gerund and deemphasize the noun or pronoun (your *helping*, his *explaining*, Fred's *smoking*, Abby's *writing*).

Find the Errors

1. Shirley appreciated you helping us with this project.
2. We enjoyed him explaining the reasons for the delays.
3. Mr. Saga and I certainly appreciated them sending us all those samples.
4. They enjoyed Tom telling them about the Alaska trip.
5. All of us were grateful for you offering to help us.
6. Quincy and Izumi liked him resolving this issue promptly.

Corrections

1. Shirley appreciated **your helping** us with this project. (Use possessive *your* before gerund *helping*.)
2. We enjoyed **his explaining** the reasons for the delays. (Use possessive *his* before gerund *explaining*.)
3. Mr. Saga and I certainly appreciated **their sending** us all those samples. (Use possessive *their* before gerund *sending*.)
4. They enjoyed **Tom's telling** them about the Alaska trip. (Use possessive *Tom's* before gerund *telling*.)

★ The person doing the acting is not as important as the action itself.

5. All of us were grateful for **your offering** to help us. (Use possessive *your* before gerund *offering*.)
6. Quincy and Izumi liked **his resolving** this issue promptly. (Use possessive *his* before gerund *resolving*.)

CHECKPOINT 2

Pronoun and Noun Possessives

Identify and correct any errors in the following sentences.

1. Jennifer approves of you helping the campers this weekend.
2. Dave writing to us each week has kept us up to date.
3. Rose printing the data helps us to have the statistics by noon.
4. What do you think of Gerald speaking at the conference?
5. One firm claims that it's trademark has been infringed.
6. The new computer furniture is definitely there's.
7. You're check arrived two days after the due date.

Check your answers in Appendix F.

ERRORS USING *GOOD* AND *WELL* AND MATCHING ADJECTIVES WITH NOUNS

Two errors made by communicators concern the incorrect use of *good* and *well* and adjectives that specifically match either singular or plural noun forms. Let's begin with Error Number 15.

Error Number 15. Incorrect Use of Good *and* Well

To communicate well, be sure to distinguish between the adjective *good* and the adverb *well*. Use the word *good* to describe nouns and pronouns (this is a *good* book; they are *good*). Use the word *well* to describe verbs and adjectives (the machine runs *well*; he is *well*-known). However, *well* is used as an adjective when describing health.

★ Remember to use the word *well* (not *good*) to describe one's health, as in "She is *well*."

Find the Errors

1. Leroy sketches and paints pictures good.
2. They worked very good together on the Carey case.
3. She admitted that she has not felt good since Monday.
4. The trainee was advised to do the job as good as he can.

5. The soldiers look well in their summer uniforms.

6. Malcolm feels well about the company's new project.

Corrections

1. Leroy **sketches and paints pictures well**. (Use adverb *well* to describe verbs *sketches* and *paints*.)

2. They **worked very well** together on the Carey case. (Use adverb *well* to describe verb *worked*.)

3. She admitted that she **has not felt well** since Monday. (Use adverb *well* to describe health.)

4. The trainee was advised to do the job **as well as he can**. (Use adverb *well* to describe the infinitive verb phrase *to do the job*.)

5. The soldiers **look good** in their summer uniforms. (Use adjective *good* to describe noun *soldiers*.)

6. Malcolm **feels good** about the company's new project. (Use adjective *good* to describe *feelings*.)

Error Number 16. Misuse of Adjectives with the Noun Kind

Use the adjectives *this* and *that* with the singular noun *kind* or a similar word; use the adjectives *these* and *those* with the plural noun *kinds* or similar words. On a related issue, do not use *them* as an adjective because *them* is an objective case pronoun. For example, do not say "Them apples are delicious."

Find the Errors

1. We have no more of those kind of manuals.
2. Do you enjoy these kind of mystery stories?
3. Please do not order them sizes any more this winter.
4. These kind of books do not belong in a children's library.
5. Those kinds of movie win awards for the director and the stars.
6. Do not hesitate to borrow them videotapes for review.

Corrections

1. We have no more of **those kinds of manuals**. (plural)
2. Do you enjoy **these kinds of mystery stories**? (plural)
3. Please do not **order those sizes** any more this winter. (Do not use objective pronoun *them* as an adjective.)
4. **These kinds of books** do not belong in a children's library. (plural)
5. **That kind of movie wins** awards for the director and the stars. (singular)

★ These principles are based on logic; therefore, they should be easy to remember.

6. Do not hesitate **to borrow those videotapes** for review. (Do not use objective pronoun *them* as an adjective.)

Adjectives and Good and Well

Select the correct answer in each sentence.

1. The teenager dresses (good/well) for her age.
2. His proofreading skills are (well/good) at all times.
3. I do believe you are feeling (good/well) these days.
4. Where can I find more of (them/those) kinds of book covers?
5. (That/Those) shoes are attractive, and they look very comfortable.
6. (This/These) kind of responsibility can be easily handled.
7. Be certain to store (those/them) cartons in a waterproof locker.

Check your answers in Appendix F.

ERRORS USING *WERE, WAS,* AND *LIKE*

Two common errors involve the use of *like* as a conjunction and the use of *was* in a sentence that states a wish or something contrary to fact. Let's begin with Error Number 17.

Error Number 17. Incorrect Use of Like *as a Conjunction*

In spoken English, the word *like* is gaining gradual acceptance as a conjunction. In business writing and speaking, however, its use as a conjunction is still unacceptable. Avoid using *like* as a conjunction that means *as* or *as if.* ("*As* Gail suggested, we will stay" instead of "*Like* Gail suggested, we will stay.") Use *like* either as a verb (we *like* the idea) or as a preposition (we need more books *like* them).

Find the Errors

1. Like my manager said, we should revise this old manual.
2. She acts like she doesn't even work here.
3. Like Ben remarked, we must be sure to cut spending.
4. Do you believe this equipment is inexpensive, like they indicated?
5. They pretended like we weren't in the room.
6. He monopolizes the office computer like he owns it.

Corrections

1. **As my manager said**, we should revise this old manual. (Use conjunction *as* instead of *like*.)
2. She acts **as if** she doesn't even work here. (Use conjunction *as if* instead of *like*.)
3. **As Ben remarked**, we must be sure to cut spending. (Use conjunction *as* instead of *like*.)
4. Do you believe this equipment is inexpensive, **as they indicated**? (Use conjunction *as* instead of *like*.)
5. They pretended **as if we weren't** in the room. (Use conjunction *as if* instead of *like*.)
6. He monopolizes the office computer **as if he owns it**. (Use conjunction *as if* instead of *like*.)

Error Number 18. Incorrect Verb Use in Sentences That State a Wish

Always use **were** instead of **was** when a sentence states either a wish or something contrary to fact. For example, the sentence "I often wish I *were* living in the country rather than in this crowded city," states a wish. The sentence "If she *were* the supervisor, she would surely change these policies," states a statement contrary to fact, as she is not the supervisor. A clause that begins with the word *if* frequently states a wish or something contrary to fact, as in "If I were talented, I would try out for the starring role."

Find the Errors

1. If I was Mr. Long, I would not approve these expenses.
2. We believe that if she was in charge, she would cancel the project.
3. Sometimes I wish I was the president of this company.
4. If she was a soprano instead of an alto, the choir could use her talent.
5. If only I was younger, I could climb the mountain with you.
6. If Alfredo was here, you would have to answer to him.

Corrections

1. **If I were Mr. Long**, I would not approve these expenses. (statement contrary to fact)
2. We believe that **if she were in charge**, she would cancel the project. (statement contrary to fact)
3. Sometimes **I wish I were the president** of this company. (states a wish)
4. **If she were a soprano** instead of an alto, the choir could use her talent. (she is an alto not a soprano)

★ As the name of the error implies, the person is not the president; therefore, *were* replaces the word *was* in situations that represent wishful thinking.

5. **If only I were younger**, I could climb the mountain with you. (he/she is not younger)
6. **If Alfredo were here**, you would have to answer to him. (Alfredo is not here)

Were, Was, and Like

Identify and correct any errors in the following sentences.

1. Sanford acted like he was an expert on the subject.
2. Like I said earlier, today is hot and humid with no sun.
3. I prefer working with designers as Carol and Steven.
4. I wish Rover was a cat; he wouldn't eat as much.
5. If I was a lottery winner, I would take my mother on a Caribbean cruise.
6. The unemployed teenager would buy that car if he was still employed.
7. Scott pretended like he had already won the election.

Check your answers in Appendix F.

Summary

This chapter covers eight additional grammar errors that communicators should avoid. First, remember to use an objective case pronoun after the word *between* and a possessive case pronoun before a gerund. Also, select a correct pronoun after *than* in statements of comparison, and do not interchange personal possessive case pronouns and contractions that contain pronouns.

Remember to use the words *good* and *well* correctly, and match *this* and *that* with singular nouns and *these* and *those* with plural nouns. Lastly, use *were* instead of *was* in statements that indicate a wish or something contrary to fact, and refrain from using the word *like* as a conjunction that means *as* or *as if*.

The eight errors presented in Chapter 14 end the discussion of grammar principles and the review in Part 2.

Discussion Questions

1. Some people say that confusing homonyms such as *there's* with *theirs* and *you're* with *your* is unimportant. After all, in oral communications, both words in the pairs sound the same. Do you agree with these people? Explain your response.

2. Grammarians contend that a study of grammar and adherence to its principles have a definite impact on the effectiveness of written and spoken communications. Do you support their belief? Explain your response.

Spelling and Word Usage Application

Note the correct spelling of the following words:

census	courteous	guarantee	hindrance
language	minimum	physician	preference
experienced	receive		

Rewrite the following sentences, correcting all misspelled words.

1. The expereinced survey taker signed up to work on the United States censes.
2. A curteous physisian puts patience at ease.
3. What guarente did you recieve on the used part you purchased?
4. His poor health is an hindrence in following his exercise schedule.
5. What is your preferrence in a foreign langage—Spanish or French?
6. The miminum number of days you have to stay at the resort is two.

If necessary, refer to Appendix A for the correct usage of the following words:

    envelope/envelop   to/too/two

Practical Applications

Part A
Select the correct answer in each sentence.

1. Be sure to fax copies of the report to Jay and (I/me).
2. They gave Cara and (her/she) new responsibilities.
3. The student writes as well as (them/they).
4. He cares for the leased car (as if/like) he owns it.
5. The squirrel hid (it's/its) collection of seed and other food.

Part B

Correct all errors in the following sentences.

1. Theirs no point in you staying; there not coming until tomorrow.
2. The young children read good for there age.
3. He doesn't know what's wrong with him; he doesn't feel good.
4. These kind of concerts are much to expensive for me.
5. Anna said him taking care of her sons enabled her to prepare for the insurance examination.

Part C

Select the correct word(s) for each blank.

were	was	well	good	There's
Theirs	me	I	like	as if

1. If I _____ able, I would visit you more often.
2. My grandfather is not feeling _____ these days.
3. _____ a good suggestion for you in today's paper.
4. Between you and _____, I think the victims should sue.
5. They proceeded with the meeting _____ we were present.

Editing and Proofreading Application

Correct all errors in word usage and spelling in the following message.

Between you and I, you taking me to the stake and seafood restaurant on the water front was the very best experience I has had in a long, long time. No one have had a better birthday celebration than me. Like I said on Saturday, theirs no better restaurant in the city, and the food lived up to it's reputation in everyway.

Birthday celebrations always made my parents and I very happy when I were young, and now that I'm a adult, these kind of dinner outings make me even happier. I am glad that you was feeling good enough to go on Saturday, and I apologize for me taking so many words to tell you what a good friend you are. If I was in a better financial situation, I would plan now to take you and you're mother to New York for dinner and a Broad Way show on you next birthday.

Mechanics of Writing

Now that you have completed Part 2 and have reviewed parts of speech and important grammar guidelines, you are ready for the next step that will improve your skill in the writing of business communications. This step includes a thorough review of punctuation, abbreviations, capitalization, and number expression.

Chapters 15 through 21 give you an opportunity to sharpen your skills and acquire precision in the use of correct punctuation and abbreviations. These chapters also cover the guidelines for capitalization and number expression and provide ample opportunities to apply these guidelines in writing and proofreading exercises.

Your skill in the mechanical aspects of communication, which can be significantly improved by studying and applying the contents of Part 3, will have a definite impact on receivers of your communications. You determine whether the impact is positive or negative. Keep in mind as you study this part that both accuracy in grammar and precision in mechanics enhance your credibility and ultimately help you fulfill your communication objectives in your business career.

Part 3

Chapter 15

Periods, Question Marks, and Exclamation Points

OBJECTIVES

After studying this chapter and completing the chapter activities, you will be able to do the following:

1. Use punctuation correctly to help readers interpret your ideas and inquiries precisely as you intend.

2. Determine when to use periods, question marks, and exclamation points in your writing.

INTRODUCTION

In order for readers to interpret your ideas and inquiries precisely as you intend, you need to use correct punctuation in every message you write. Punctuation may include external marks such as periods, question marks, and exclamation points. Punctuation also may include internal marks such as commas, semicolons, colons, quotation marks, parentheses, dashes, apostrophes, and hyphens. All these punctuation marks are discussed in Part 3 to provide a comprehensive review of punctuation.

A good place to begin is with a discussion of the guidelines that cover the usage of external punctuation marks. Let's start with periods.

PERIODS

A **period** can be used to indicate the end of a sentence, to indicate the end of an abbreviation, and to accompany an enumeration. The guidelines and examples in this section fully explain the usage of periods.

Using Periods at the End of Sentences

A period is used at the end of a declarative sentence, a mild command, an indirect question, and a courteous request.

Declarative Sentence

A **declarative sentence** makes a statement. Here are some examples:

Gloria and Ralph are competing for the treasurer's position.

The accountants and attorneys met in the president's office last Tuesday.

The choir members will sing in Italy during the holiday season.

Mild Command

A **mild command** is a stern request from the writer to the reader. The words give a sense of urgency, but the command is not strong enough to require an exclamation point. Note these examples:

You should watch your step or you will fall.

Make arrangements to attend the company holiday party on December 16.

Return the defective merchandise to the plant today.

★ Although most people understand how to use the period correctly, it is an important mark of punctuation and merits a brief review.

★ Find the definition of the noun *command* in a dictionary.

Indirect Question

An **indirect question** is a statement that contains a reference to a question. For example:

> They inquired how your parents are feeling since their accident.

> The judge asked if the prosecutor had any more questions for the witness.

> The only question he had is whether you will join him at the conference in Miami in January.

Courteous Request

A **courteous request** is a polite way to ask for action on the part of the reader; it does not ask for a *yes* or *no* answer. Use a period after a courteous request phrased as a question. Here are examples of courteous requests sometimes included in business writing:

> May I have an interview when convenient.

> Would you be kind enough to revise the proposal and return the corrected copy to me as soon as possible.

> May I hear from you by next Thursday.

EXTRA, EXTRA!

★ A courteous request is really a statement converted to a question form to present a polite way of communicating.

---

1 CHECKPOINT

Using Periods

Identify each sentence as a declarative sentence, a mild command, an indirect question, or a courteous request.

1. Watch what you say around the office.
2. Would you grant me an interview.
3. Economics 101 is my favorite course this semester.
4. They asked if you would be available to join their team.
5. Please plan to work overtime to complete the project.
6. May I hear from you as soon as possible.
7. John questioned why you accepted the first offer.

Check your answers in Appendix F.

Using Periods with Abbreviations

Periods are placed after many commonly used abbreviations to indicate that the words are shortened forms of longer words. Here are some examples:

Mr. (Mister)   **Jr. (Junior)**   **Dr. (Doctor)**
Ltd. (Limited)   **Inc. (Incorporated)**   **Sr. (Senior)**

Chapter 19 provides a further discussion of abbreviations.

Using Periods in Enumerations

When numbers or letters are used in a vertical list, periods are placed after each number or letter. For example:

Your child will need the following items for the outing:

1. one change of clothing
2. bathing suit, swim cap, sandals, towel, and sunscreen lotion
3. snack money

Submit the following by July 11:

a. the topic you have chosen for your research
b. the names of five primary sources
c. the names of five secondary sources

QUESTION MARKS

A **question mark** is used after a direct question and after each part in a series of questions. The guidelines and examples in this section fully explain the usage of question marks.

Using Question Marks After Direct Questions

Use a question mark after a complete or incomplete sentence that asks a direct question. For example:

Do you agree that summer seems to pass more quickly than winter?

Have you considered relocating to find suitable employment?

What? He won the lottery again?

ACROSS
CULTURES

- The names of many firms in Great Britain include the abbreviation *Ltd.*; the names of many firms in the United States include the abbreviation *Inc.*

★ If a sentence requires a *yes* or *no* response, then the sentence is a direct question.

★ By ending each part in a
series of questions with a
question mark, the writer
captures the reader's
attention.

Using Question Marks in a Series

Occasionally, a series of questions may be useful in your writing. For emphasis, follow each segment in the series with a question mark. Note these examples:

> Were all the votes counted? all the winners notified? all the losers contacted?

> Did she apply to Temple University? to Boston College? to Florida International University? to Miami Dade Community College?

> Let's see, should we go? should we stay? should we forget about it altogether?

CHECKPOINT 2 — *Periods and Question Marks*

Indicate whether a period or a question mark should be used at the end of each sentence.

1. The service agent asked when the equipment was last serviced (./?)
2. Would you please give me an opportunity to display my portfolio and to speak with you about my qualifications (./?)

(Continued on next page)

3. Do you know that a big price difference exists between London broil and flank steak at the supermarket (./?)
4. Where is your partner now? in Florida? in Alabama? in Puerto Rico (./?)
5. I would appreciate your not asking me that question (./?)
6. May I request that you call me before the week is over (./?)
7. Do you really think this topic is appropriate for our audience (./?)

Check your answers in Appendix F.

EXCLAMATION POINTS

An **exclamation point** is a mark of punctuation that follows a word, a group of words, or a sentence that shows strong emotion. When an expression shows excitement, urgency, or anger, the exclamation point, together with the words, conveys the strong emotion intended by the writer. Here are some examples that show the use of exclamation points:

Quick! Here's an opportunity to make money!

I'll never do that again!

Be quiet! They are recording.

Use exclamations and exclamation points sparingly in all writing, but especially in business communications. Because exclamations signify strong emotion, they lose their impact if overused.

In business writing, exclamation points primarily appear in sales and promotional communications and in informal memos.

Selecting Punctuation

Select the correct punctuation choice in each sentence.

1. Watch it (./!) Here comes a foul ball (./!)
2. What do you mean by that statement (!/?)
3. Stop it (!/.) Don't ever do that again (./!)
4. The vice president asked why you were late for the meeting (?/.)
5. Do not answer the telephone after ten o'clock (!/.)
6. May I visit your office at a time convenient to you (?/.)
7. Is your appointment at eight or at nine (./?)

Check your answers in Appendix F.

Summary

A good way to begin a review of punctuation is to take a careful look at external marks; namely, the *period*, the *question mark*, and the *exclamation point*.

The period is used at the end of sentences, with abbreviations, and in enumerations. The question mark is used after direct questions and after each part in a series of questions. The exclamation point follows a word, a group of words, or a sentence that shows strong emotion.

Use periods and question marks as often as needed, but use exclamations and exclamation marks sparingly in business communications.

Discussion Questions

1. Discuss the guidelines for using periods and give several examples.
2. Explain the role of punctuation in written communication.

Spelling and Word Usage Application

Note the correct spelling of the following words:

strategy	strength	superintendent	symptom
transferred	unanimous	usually	vacuum
achieve	mosquito		

Rewrite the following sentences, correcting all misspelled words.

1. An unamimous decision by lodge members provides strentgh to the organization.
2. They will be very happy when they're new superintendant is transfered to the other plant.
3. We usualy work on stratigy before listing the outcomes we wish to acheive.
4. What did you say the sympton is for a infected musquito bite?
5. Youngsters dont mine emptying the dishwasher but usually do not like to sweep and vacumm.

If necessary, refer to Appendix A for the correct usage of the following words:

complement/compliment   farther/further

Practical Applications

Part A

Select the correct external punctuation for each sentence.

1. Why continue with this line of discussion at this time (!/?/.)
2. The teacher asked the class what year the Concorde had its first flight (!/?/.)
3. May I hear from you without delay (!/?/.)
4. The systems analyst praised the new software (!/?/.)
5. Yea! We won the World Series (!/?/.)

Part B

Select the correct answer to fill in the blank in each sentence.

period	question mark	exclamation point	mild command
declarative	sentence	indirect question	direct question

1. A(n) _____ accompanies many abbreviations to show that they are shortened forms.
2. The sentence "Carla and Howard have successfully completed the assignment" is a(n)_____.
3. A statement that contains a reference to a question is a(n) _____.
4. Use a(n) _____ after an expression that expresses excitement or anger.
5. A(n) _____ is needed after each part of the following series: "Were the minutes read Was the treasurer's report given Was any new business discussed"

Part C
Correct all errors in external punctuation, word usage, and spelling.

1. Has you finished painting the powder room and laundry room.
2. We're felling pretty good! Thanks for asking us!
3. The attorney's had ask if we wanted to observe the trial?
4. Would you please call my assistent as soon as you have the answer?
5. Yes, Joe and me seen the fire the second it started!

Editing and Proofreading Application

Insert all external punctuation where needed, capitalize the first word of each sentence, and correct all errors in word usage and spelling in the following message.

As you are aware, the city counsel meet last night to discussed zoning we are interested in the result's of the meeting because we want to built are new offices at Main and Shunk Streets we recieved the support of the counsel would you beleive that the vote was unaminous The zoning classification for that location caused no arguements.

Now you can procede with you're plans as quick as possible as we need them office's by the end of the year would you please call me at the first oportunity so that we can discuss our building plans' wow what a great break

Commas

OBJECTIVES

After studying this chapter and completing the chapter activities, you will be able to do the following:

1. Use commas correctly with introductory elements in sentences and with independent clauses.
2. Apply comma guidelines with nonessential elements, with direct address, in a series, with a measurement or weight, between adjectives, with omission of words, and in numbers.
3. Use commas for clarity, with abbreviations, and between repeated words.
4. Avoid comma pitfalls in your writing.

USES OF THE COMMA

External punctuation marks tell the reader whether a sentence is a statement, question, or exclamation. Internal punctuation marks clarify the message intended by the writer. Of all the internal punctuation marks discussed in Chapters 16, 17, and 18, the comma is without a doubt the most frequently used and misused. Because it has such a vital role in written communications, we have devoted this entire chapter to its more important uses.

Commas are used with introductory elements, independent clauses, nonessential elements, direct addresses, numbers, abbreviations, and repeated words. Commas also are inserted in a series and between adjectives. In addition, commas are used to indicate the omission of words and to promote clarity in sentences. This chapter will fully explain and illustrate the guidelines that pertain to comma usage.

With Introductory Elements in Sentences

Insert a comma after an introductory word, phrase, or clause. For example:

Introductory word

Meanwhile, I will begin the next phase of the project. Nevertheless, I think we can attend the meeting.

Introductory phrase

Before running, the teenager warms up the leg muscles.

In the long run, the cutback will be beneficial.

Introductory clause

Because we have no record of the sale, we cannot help you.

Although he was not present, his influence was evident.

With Independent Clauses in Compound Sentences

When independent clauses in a compound sentence are joined by a coordinate conjunction such as *for, and, nor, but, or,* or *yet,* precede the conjunction with a comma. Here are some examples:

I will go to the hockey game on Friday, or I will babysit for my niece.

The new order forms are on legal-size paper, and the quantity we bought should last us a while.

We thought he was guilty at first, but now we have changed our minds.

When each independent clause in a compound sentence has less than four words, no comma is needed. Note these:

Yoshi spoke and they responded.

I rode but he walked.

The wind blew and the rain fell.

★ Placing the comma *after* the coordinate conjunction instead of *before* the conjunction is incorrect.

Introductory Elements and Compound Sentences

Insert commas where needed; delete unnecessary commas.

1. I will go to the store, and buy the food.
2. While waiting for the train she thought about the job offer.
3. Yes I will consider attending the seminar.
4. Zelda and Laurie write well and they also have had success in having their articles published.
5. Personally I believe that we should wait at least two weeks.
6. Listening carefully, is important in this situation.
7. They say that they are interested yet their actions speak differently.

Check your answers in Appendix F.

With Nonessential Elements

Nonessential elements are set off from the rest of a sentence with commas. Examples of **nonessential elements** are interrupting expressions, nonrestrictive elements, and appositives. Nonessential elements include information that may be interesting but is not necessary to the meaning or the structure of a sentence.

To determine if the information is essential, temporarily omit it. If the meaning of the sentence stays the same, set off the nonessential word, phrase, or clause with commas.

★ Nonessential elements add interest and creativity to a sentence; but because they are not needed, they must be set off from the rest of a sentence.

Interrupting Expression

Any expression that is nonessential and interrupts the flow of a sentence is set off with commas. For example:

> The most interesting part of the movie, I believe, is the entrance of the ex-wife. (The expression *I believe* is not needed.)

> He should, on the other hand, separate the items in the box. (The expression *on the other hand* is not needed.)

Nonrestrictive Element

A **nonrestrictive phrase** or **clause** adds additional information that is not essential to the meaning of the sentence. Some that begin with *who* or *which* clauses are not essential. For example:

> Jeffrey Chang, who graduated from Loyola, is my neighbor. (The clause that begins with *who* is not needed.)

> We plan to order Part 643, which Steve recommended. (The clause that begins with *which* is not needed.)

A phrase or clause that is essential to the meaning of a sentence is called a **restrictive phrase** or a **restrictive clause** and is not set off with commas. Here are two examples:

> Ask the nurse who was on duty that night.

> The man who was just hired is part of my team.

★ In these sentences, the *who* clauses tell information that is needed; commas are omitted.

Appositive

An **appositive** is a noun or noun substitute that renames and refers to a preceding noun. An appositive provides additional information that is not necessary to the meaning of a sentence. They are set off from the rest of the sentence with commas. Note these sentences:

> Dr. Mary Towne, the eminent surgeon from Cleveland, Ohio, was the principal speaker. (*Eminent surgeon from Cleveland, Ohio* tells which Dr. Mary Towne; *Ohio* tells which Cleveland.)

> The paper contained the forecasts for the next quarter, July through September. (*July through September* tells which quarter.)

> Ruby Munoz, the councilwoman, is soliciting suggestions to bring up in council. (The phrase *the councilwoman* refers to and renames *Ruby Munoz*.)

An appositive that is only one word is not set off with commas. For example:

My brother Mario is touring the factory.

Her supervisor Gina is receiving a promotion.

With Direct Address

In order to personalize a message, a writer may use **direct address** by mentioning the reader's first or last name in the beginning, middle, or end of a sentence. Because the name is not needed to convey the meaning of the sentence, it is set off with commas. Here are examples:

Dr. Oakes, you have been exceedingly helpful to my family.

Have I told you, Gwen, that we appreciate your purchase?

The equipment is ready for you to see, Ms. Garton.

★ Readers will be more receptive to your ideas and inquiries if you mention their names in your communications.

In a Series

Use a comma to separate three or more items in a series of words, phrases, or clauses. Although some experts omit the comma before a conjunction in a series, we recommend that you include the comma to avoid confusion. Note these examples:

The flag of the United States is red, white, and blue.

I will be going to the movies, to the mall, or to my grandparents' home Saturday evening.

Wake up early, prepare and serve breakfast, and take the children to the school bus.

With Parts of One Measurement or Weight

Do not use commas to separate the parts of one measurement or weight. For example:

The trip took 1 hour 40 minutes and 15 seconds.

The measurement you asked for is 1 yard 2 feet and 4 inches.

Comma Usage

CHECKPOINT 2

Insert commas where needed; delete unnecessary commas.

1. Next winter regardless of my schedule we will go skiing.
2. Kim who is a newscaster thoroughly enjoyed her work.
3. My attorney, George, congratulated us on our success.
4. Your earning a scholarship Maria is a credit to your family.
5. The couch is modern comfortable and attractively covered.
6. She moved to 10 State Road Dayton Ohio last Saturday.
7. The train moved 2 miles, 875 feet, and 4 inches between the signal towers.

Check your answers in Appendix F.

★ The adjectives should be parallel; they must modify the same noun to the same degree.

Between Adjectives

Use a comma between two adjectives that modify the same noun when the coordinate conjunction *and* is omitted. If the word *and* wouldn't make sense between the adjectives, do not insert a comma. Here are some examples:

The short, thin teenager envied the tall, husky football players. (*Short and thin* and *tall and husky* make sense; insert a comma between each set of adjectives to show that *and* is omitted.)

Their kind, considerate neighbor drives them to the train. (*Kind and considerate* makes sense; insert a comma between the adjectives.)

Janet's royal blue suit is inappropriate attire for a job interview. (*Royal and blue* does not make sense; do not insert a comma.)

With Omission of Words

Occasionally, a writer may omit words that are understood by the reader. Inserting a comma at the point of omission helps to provide clarity. Note these examples:

The treasurer is Johnetta; the secretary, Garth; and the vice president, Warren. (The word *is* is omitted twice in the sentence; commas are inserted at the points of omission.)

We buy our produce at Apex; our meat, Jones Market; and our dairy products, Barden's Dairyland. (The word *at* is omitted twice in the sentence; commas are inserted at the points of omission.)

In Numbers

Use commas to indicate a whole number in units of three whether in money or items. Here are some examples:

$1,000	$16,245	$235,110.32	$2,000.25
2,468 tablets	34,235 hot dogs	526,230 pins	278,249

EXTRA, EXTRA!

★ Commas are not inserted in the decimal part of a number—.505643.

Identifying Comma Use

Identify the specific comma use in each sentence.

1. We have no place to stock 1,000 soft pretzels for the fair.
2. They sold Matt the vase; Hertha, the set of tables; and Antique Masters, the twin lamps.
3. The well-educated, enthusiastic applicant was hired.

(Continued on next page)

4. My supervisor, Barnett Davis, has good management skills.
5. Jan and Gary served a salad, lasagna, and iced tea.
6. We can't thank you enough, Mr. Cohen, for your assistance.
7. The students, along with their parents, attended the orientation meeting.

Check your answers in Appendix F.

For Clarity

Occasionally, a sentence requires a comma for no reason other than to ensure clarity. In constructions such as the following, notice the important role of the comma to clarify the writer's meaning.

Not Clear	Shortly after the teacher left the classroom.
Clear	Shortly after, the teacher left the classroom.
Not Clear	Zachary implied Samuel was untrustworthy.
Clear	Zachary, implied Samuel, was untrustworthy.

With Abbreviations

Writers who use abbreviations such as *etc., Jr., Sr.,* and *Inc.* should be familiar with the following comma rules that concern these abbreviations, as described in the rules below.

Rule 1. In a series, insert a comma before *etc.* when it appears at the end of a sentence, and use commas before and after *etc.* when it appears in the middle of a sentence. For example:

We will be taking camping clothes: shorts, hiking boots, swimwear, etc.

The first day on the job may be stressful, uncomfortable, and scary, etc., but all the negative feelings disappear within a day or two.

Rule 2. Generally, place a comma before *Jr., Sr.,* and *Inc.* when the abbreviations appear in a name, and also insert commas after the abbreviations in the middle of a sentence. For example:

His name is Jay Lloyd, Sr.

Harry Larkin, Jr., was elected to the presidency.

Able, Inc., is owned by a conglomerate in New York.

Some people who have *Jr.* in their names omit the commas. Some companies that have Inc. in their names also omit the commas. Follow the wishes of the people or companies in these matters. See Chapter 19 for additional information about abbreviations.

Refer to a company's letterhead or business card to verify the use of a comma before Inc. in a business name.

Between Repeated Words

To impress and emphasize, writers sometimes repeat identical words. Separate the words with a comma. For example:

Well, well—look who's here!

They are the *greediest, greediest* retailers on the block.

After that trip, I will not fly again for a *long, long* time.

Clarity, Abbreviations, and Repeated Words

Insert commas where needed; delete commas that are incorrectly placed.

1. Way before he stated, that he wanted to go.
2. The interviewer judges the personality, appearance etc. of each candidate.
3. That restaurant serves a big big breakfast on Sunday.
4. They must have 1000 bags of used clothes stored in the warehouse.
5. Down under you will find the box of files you requested.
6. That was a hard hard test for everyone in the room.
7. Jill is not sure Dr. Thomas when she can meet with you.

Check your answers in Appendix F.

COMMA PITFALLS

Avoid misusing commas with conjunctions in a series, between subjects and verbs, between two words or phrases, between two independent clauses, and with incomplete dates. The following guidelines explain comma pitfalls to avoid.

With Conjunctions in a Series

If coordinate conjunctions precede each item in a series, omit commas. For example:

> My day includes exercise and work and good eating practices.

> Do you want eggs or cereal or pancakes for breakfast?

Between Subjects and Verbs

Never separate subjects and verbs with commas. Note these two sentences in which commas are unnecessary:

> Working at the supermarket is a difficult job. (A comma does not separate the complete subject *Working at the supermarket* from the verb *is.*)

> Spelling accurately is one of his skills. (A comma does not separate the complete subject *Spelling accurately* from the verb *is.*)

★ Locate the subject and verb first to be sure that you do not incorrectly insert a comma that will separate them.

With Two Words or Phrases

Sometimes, two words are joined by a coordinate conjunction or two phrases are joined by a coordinate conjunction. A comma is not used to separate two items. For example:

> The officers are knowledgeable and enthusiastic. (No comma is needed to separate the two words *knowledgeable* and *enthusiastic.*)

> They plan to swim first and to hike later. (No comma is needed to separate the two phrases *to swim first* and *to hike later.*)

Between Two Independent Clauses

Separate two independent clauses that are not joined by a coordinate conjunction with a semicolon or a period. A comma inserted between two independent clauses results in a *comma splice.* For example:

Incorrect	Bert refused to work overtime on Friday, he was available for extra hours on Monday.
Correct	Bert refused to work overtime on Friday; he was available for extra hours on Monday.
Incorrect	Give me the papers, I will deliver them on the way home.
Correct	Give me the papers. I will deliver them on the way home.

With Incomplete Dates

A comma is not inserted in an incomplete date. For example:

> He was born early in January 1994.

> Our next conference in Boston is in May 1997.

★ Commas, which are temporary rests, never take the place of external punctuation at the end of complete sentences.

5 Comma Pitfalls

CHECKPOINT

Delete incorrect commas and insert needed commas in each sentence.

1. For his new position, he will need new suits, and a new brief case, and a laptop computer.
2. A dark, blue casual dress is suitable for a meeting.
3. Their driving her to the train, helped her to leave early.
4. You are to research the topic, and prepare an outline.
5. The day is overcast and chilly, rain is forecasted.
6. The best joint meeting of all was in February, 1994.
7. Gloria James the receptionist saw him enter the office.

Check your answers in Appendix F.

Summary

The comma is used more frequently than any other internal mark of punctuation. It has many uses, twelve of which are discussed in this chapter. This chapter examines comma use with introductory elements, independent clauses, nonessential elements, direct address, a series, measurements and weights, adjectives, omission of words, numbers, abbreviations, and repeated words. Commas also are used to promote clarity.

The chapter emphasizes specific pitfalls that arise in comma use. These pitfalls include using commas in a series with conjunctions in the series, between subjects and verbs, with two words or phrases, between two independent clauses, and with incomplete dates.

Learning the guidelines that cover comma usage and applying them in your writing will provide clarity to your communications.

Discussion Questions

1. Some writers contend that comma usage has too many guidelines to remember and apply; these writers prefer to follow one or two rules and ignore the rest. What would you tell these people about the importance of correct comma placement?
2. What use is the comma to readers of written communications, articles, and books?

Spelling and Word Usage Applications

Note the correct spelling of the following words:

separate	similar	sufficient	syllable
treasurer	truly	pronounce	withholding

Rewrite the following sentences, correcting all misspelled words.

1. The treasuerer will seperate the expense sheets today.
2. Our past's are similiar in respect to family life.
3. I truley beleive that I took sufficeint steps in this case.
4. Weather they strike is up to there officers.
5. Which sylable is accented when you pronounce his last name?
6. The new employee was given an witholding tax form.

If necessary, refer to Appendix A for the correct usage of the following words:

loose/lose   passed/past

Practical Applications

Part A
Insert commas in the following sentences.

1. Therefore we will not meet until the end of the year.
2. I think however that she will accept the equipment proposal.
3. He wanted to be a doctor but his grades were not high enough.
4. Clara who is a computer whiz is upgrading her equipment.
5. After we left work we went directly to the restaurant.

Part B
Delete unnecessary commas in the following sentences.

1. George, the teller, closed his window, and counted his money.

2. If I were going on vacation, I could get ready to leave, now.
3. She bakes, and cooks, and sews during her spare time.
4. For the spring, I plan to buy a new, navy, blue suit.
5. Speaking out of turn, is a rude way to participate.

Part C
Correct all errors in comma usage, word usage, and spelling.

1. The boys romped, and the girls giggle.
2. The bill as you can well imagine is extreme over due.
3. That point however has no baring on they're currant problem.
4. The women, who has just entered, is my sister.
5. Herman attending you're tutoring session's is a pleasure.

Editing and Proofreading Application

Insert commas and periods where needed, delete unnecessary commas and periods, and correct errors in word usage and spelling.

Now, that I have calm down I am writing to tell you that I believe I was justify in the matter we discussed on Friday, being penalized for not working overtime last weekend, does not seem like a fare penalty.

I do understand, that I had agreed to put in over time hours, when they were needed but last weekend my twin son's where three years old and they expected me to attend they're birthday party, if I had known several weeks' ago that I had to work on June 7 I would have arrange for a substitute, or changed the party date. With such little notice I were unable to make any last minute arrangements

I know I was wrong when I went over your head to talk with Howard your supervisor and apologize for doing so. Can we discuss this farther?

Chapter 17

Semicolons, Colons, Dashes, and Hyphens

OBJECTIVES

After studying this chapter and completing the chapter activities, you will be able to do the following:

1. Use semicolons correctly in your writing.
2. Apply the guidelines for using colons.
3. Enliven sentences by using dashes where appropriate.
4. Use hyphens accurately.

SEMICOLONS

A **semicolon** is a form of punctuation used to denote a pause. Semicolons are stronger than commas but weaker than periods. In certain situations, use semicolons between independent clauses, before conjunctive adverbs, with enumerating words such as *for example*, in compound sentences that have internal commas, and in a series. The following guidelines and examples will explain when you should insert semicolons in your writing.

Between Independent Clauses

Use a semicolon between two related independent clauses instead of using a comma and a coordinate conjunction. Note these:

> George is studying economics; his brother Dave is majoring in accounting.

> Elaine will attend the July convention in Memphis; she then will vacation in Lofton.

Before Conjunctive Adverbs

Use a semicolon before a conjunctive adverb (*moreover, nevertheless, however, consequently*) that joins two independent clauses. Conjunctive adverbs, which function as transitional expressions, introduce the second clause. Note these examples:

> His report is too long; therefore, he cannot submit it until he revises it.

> Getting information from Amtrak can be easy; however, the voice mail system tends to confuse some callers.

In a Series

Use a semicolon before expressions such as *for example* (e.g.), *that is* (i.e.), and *for instance* when they introduce a list of examples. Note these sentences:

> You can attend some interesting functions; for example, an art show, a dance performance, or a special film screening.

> They must follow smart money management principles; that is, save part of their income, make purchases they can afford, and avoid buying inferior goods.

★ Independent clauses should be related in thought; if this is not the case, a period should follow the first clause when a conjunction is not used.

★ Note the comma after the conjunctive adverb. The comma after *however* is required; the comma after all other conjunctive adverbs is optional.

ACROSS CULTURES

• The abbreviation *e.g.* is Latin from *exempli gratia*, meaning *for example*. You may use either the abbreviation or the English words.

★ Note the comma after *for example, that is, e.g.,* and *i.e.* This comma is required.

Semicolons

Add or delete semicolons in each sentence.

1. The staff members profited by attending the in-service session however, it set them back one week in meeting their quota.
2. Accountants are busy in April for example, they prepare income tax reports, they counsel their clients for next year, and they work on their own income tax payments.
3. The computer is in the second floor office the answering machine is in the reception area.
4. People who own cars should have auto insurance; and should always carry their owner's card with them.
5. Children should not talk to strangers in fact, they should immediately report any questionable encounter to their parents.
6. You, Gina, should dress conservatively for an interview for instance, wear a tailored suit, a long-sleeved white blouse, and mid-heel pumps.
7. The World Cup soccer games in 1994 were played in the United States Brazil was the winner.

Check your answers in Appendix F.

In Compound Sentences

Use a semicolon before a coordinate conjunction in a compound sentence when either or both of the clauses have internal commas and the sentence might be misread if a comma is inserted before the conjunction. The semicolon promotes clarity in sentences such as these:

> I requested a return call, information about a particular check, and the teller's extension number; but instead I received a past-due notice, a reference to the wrong check, and an incorrect telephone number.

> On Wednesday, March 12, 1997, the group will meet; but Florio will not officiate.

In a Series Containing Commas

Use semicolons to separate items in a series when an item or items contain commas. For example:

The mortgage company has branches in Newport, Rhode Island; Atlanta, Georgia; and Chicago, Illinois.

In attendance were Acklin, the chairman; Ikuko, the treasurer; Maria, the corresponding secretary; and Sean, the parliamentarian.

Inserting Semicolons

Insert semicolons where needed in these sentences. You may need to delete misplaced commas.

1. San-li faxed the order to the restaurant it was never received.
2. My itinerary includes places such as Key West, Florida, New Orleans, Louisiana, and Dallas, Texas.
3. The very talented young lady, I believe, is his sister Meredith, and, without a doubt, I recommend her for the job.
4. The PBS concert with the three famous tenors is used for fund-raising, moreover, the concert helps acquaint thousands with opera music.
5. Beth and Cory suggested some convenient dates to consider, for example, January 2, February 28, or April 15.
6. Feel free to contact me, I am always happy to supply you with the names you need.
7. The first people to arrive were Jay Chan, the sales manager, his wife, Sara Chan, Gilbert Dumas, the department head, and his wife, Glenda Dumas.

Check your answers in Appendix F.

COLONS

A **colon** is a form of punctuation that directs the reader's attention to the material that follows it. The material that follows the colon completes or explains the information that precedes the colon. The following guidelines and examples show the specific uses of a colon.

Before a Series

Use a colon when the words *the following*, *as follows*, and *are these* are near the end or at the end of a sentence that introduces a series of items. For example:

★ A colon may also be used to separate a report title from a subtitle. (*Banking: The Role of the Teller*)

★ If the lead-in statement before a list is long, with the words *the following* near the beginning of the statement, follow the statement with a period instead of a colon.

Each person will need the following at the meeting: a computer, a printer, a set of instructions, and a writing tablet.

The new automobile's special features are as follows: anti-lock brakes, a built-in CD player, and leather upholstery.

Before a List

Use a colon before a vertical, itemized list. As with a series, the words *the following*, *as follows*, or *are these* may precede the colon. For example:

She submitted the following items last week:

1. A monthly report

2. A request for additional supplies

3. Copies of three faxes received from the branch

Your instructions for Sunday are these:

1. Open the office at 9 a.m.

2. Check Saturday's mail, and call me if Pinder's check arrived.

3. Answer the telephone until noon.

4. Close the office no later than 1 p.m.

★ If items in an enumerated list are not complete sentences, omit ending periods.

Before a Long Quotation

Use a colon to introduce a long quotation of more than two lines. Here are two examples that require a colon:

Chien remarked: "When I think of my home in Beijing, I can just picture the hundreds of people riding their bicycles to work early in the morning and returning from work late in the evening."

The administrative assistant said: "Your travel plans include one week at a hotel in downtown Phoenix, three days visiting clients in Sedona, two days staying in the outskirts of Tucson, and an overnight stay in Scottsdale before you fly home."

Between Special Independent Clauses

Use a colon to separate two independent clauses when the second clause explains the first. In the following situations, a colon replaces a semicolon:

> Lucia is a skilled artist: She won an award for sketching animals, received the honor of having three of her paintings hanging in the art museum, and lectures to community artists several times a year.

> Here is one way to improve your sense of humor: Recall experiences that seemed serious at the time, and realize how funny they actually were.

To use mixed punctuation in a business letter, follow the salutation with a colon and the complimentary close with a comma.

After a Salutation

When using mixed punctuation in a letter, use a colon after a salutation. For example:

Dear Sir: **Dear Dr. Santiago:**   **Dear Ms. Linden:**

In Time Designations

Use a colon between the hour and the minutes when the time is expressed in numerals. For example:

Let's meet at 11:30 a.m. in the lobby of the office building.

The mail is distributed daily at 2:45 p.m.

---

3 CHECKPOINT

Colons

Insert colons where needed in each sentence.

1. The skills needed for model railroading are these working with electricity, building models, and using small tools.
2. Bonita awakens at 630 to take the 730 train to work.
3. In the article, the author stated "It is a wonder that a small town just ten years ago has become such a thriving and successful medium-size city because of the entertainment and casino business."
4. The garden is beautiful The flowers are abundant, the grass is lush and bright green, and the bushes are trimmed to perfection.
5. The list of items includes the following
   1. Paper plates and napkins
   2. Paper cups and ten two-liter bottles of soda
   3. Three paper tablecloths and six packages of ice

Check your answers in Appendix F.

DASHES

A **dash**, formed by keying two unspaced hyphens, is an informal punctuation mark. It is used sparingly to enliven sentences and make them forceful. A dash is used with appositives or other nonessential elements that contain commas, before a summarizing statement, with a sudden change of thought, or before a detailed listing. The following guidelines and examples will help you to understand the use of the dash.

With Nonessential Elements

For emphasis, use a dash to set off appositives and other nonessential elements from the rest of the sentence. Some of the nonessential elements may have internal commas. Note these:

He waited on the stage—poised, confident, and well-prepared—ready to begin at the signal.

The stockbroker's office—the newly equipped, modernly decorated, and spacious room in the corner—is perfect for the hospitality reception.

The annual Fine Arts Fund drive was a success because of all the friends of the fine arts—civic leaders, professional and business people, and concerned citizens.

Before a Summarizing Statement

Use a dash after a listing at the beginning of a sentence that is followed by a summarizing statement. Summarizing statements usually begin with the words *all* or *these*. Here are two examples:

A nurturing manner, a love of people, and an unselfish attitude—these are three traits school counselors need.

Precision in mechanics, vocabulary, and facts—all these are necessary for effective communications.

With a Sudden Change of Thought

Use a dash to indicate a sudden change of thought or a sudden break in a sentence. Note these examples:

Here is the perfect suit for work—and it's on sale, too!

"Then we both agree that—oh no, now what's wrong?" asked Amy.

★ A dash is used instead of a comma, semicolon, or colon to emphasize the content.

★ Remember the two other nonessential elements are classified as interrupting and nonrestrictive elements.

Before a Detailed Listing

Use a dash to set off a listing or an explanation that provides details or examples. The dash can give a creative flair to your writing. Note these:

> The restaurant features exotic desserts—Polynesian pudding, Hawaiian coconut sherbet, and Samoan almond supreme cake.

> Do your graduates have employable skills—excellent oral communications, typing speeds that exceed 70 wpm, and desktop publishing experience?

★ The abbreviation *wpm* refers to *words per minute*.

4 | CHECKPOINT | *Dashes*

Insert dashes where needed in each sentence.

1. Amanda has ambition, intelligence, and maturity three traits that contribute to her success.
2. Do you believe that yes, I guess you do.
3. Good management skills, effective listening habits, and patience these are the qualities of a good manager.
4. Three of our brightest graduates Zoe, Manuel, and Jeffrey will address their classmates.
5. Bob Flaherty he's the one who moved from Boise is our ace.
6. Renee disapproves of the change but, of course, Renee always disagrees with us.

Check your answers in Appendix F.

HYPHENS

A **hyphen** is a punctuation mark used in word division, in the formation of compound hyphenated words, and after some prefixes. The following guidelines and examples will help you to understand the use of the hyphen.

Use hyphens sparingly because reading hyphenated words is more difficult than reading unhyphenated words.

In Word Division

Use a hyphen between syllables to indicate word division at the end of a line. If you are not sure if a word can be divided or at what point a word may be divided, consult a dictionary. The purpose of word division is to maintain a reasonably straight right margin.

With the advent of word processing, both margins may be even (justified) without hyphenation. However, some experts do not recommend justification of the right margin for letters or business reports. Therefore you should be familiar with these few word-division guidelines:

1. Do not divide words with only one syllable.
2. Do not hyphenate more than two word endings in a row.
3. Do not divide the last word on a page.
4. Divide hyphenated compound words only at the hyphen.
5. Use word division sparingly.

After Prefixes

Use a hyphen after prefixes in some words. When you are unsure if a word needs a hyphen, consult a dictionary. Note these examples:

ex-president	pro-American	semi-invalid
de-emphasize	co-coordinator	

★ Some prefixes that previously required a hyphen no longer do so; consult a dictionary if you are unsure about current usage.

In Compound Words

Use a hyphen in some compound words. In the English language some compound words are written as one word, others are written as two words, and

others are hyphenated. Because spelling changes, refer to a dictionary if you are in doubt. Here are some examples of hyphenated compound words:

up-to-date reports	*self-confident* speaker
well-informed reporter	*two-year-old* child
Abe's *mother-in-law*	*one-half* the members
her *attorneys-at-law*	*run-on* sentences

Some compound adjectives, such as *up to date*, *well informed*, and *two year old*, are hyphenated if they precede the noun they modify, but they are not hyphenated if they follow the noun. For example:

The report is *up to date*.

Mae is a typical *two year old*.

Our *up-to-date* equipment improves productivity.

5 Hyphens

CHECKPOINT

Insert hyphens where needed in the following sentences.

1. Her attorney at law is Sarah Duncan, a graduate of Harvard.
2. He is thrilled to be selected as president elect of the organization.
3. That medicine is certainly not a cure all for AIDS.
4. Ken's father in law was the founder of the company.
5. Please explain your up to date software to the students.
6. She is the ex president of the local auxiliary.
7. The self made entrepreneur is proud of his success.

Check your answers in Appendix F.

Summary

The punctuation marks discussed in this chapter—semicolons, colons, dashes, and hyphens—can add clarity, emphasis, and effectiveness to your writing.

A semicolon is used with independent clauses, conjunctive adverbs, enumerating words, compound sentences, and a series. A colon introduces a series, a list, and a long quotation. Colons also are used with special independent clauses, salutations, and time designations. A dash is used with a nonessential element, a summarizing statement, a sudden change of thought, or a listing. A hyphen denotes word division, follows some prefixes, or separates some compound words.

Mastering the use of these punctuation marks will improve your precision in the mechanics of writing.

Discussion Questions

1. Because dashes frequently take the place of commas, semicolons, and colons, many writers do not bother to use them in their communications. What special role do dashes play in the English language?
2. Some students use colons when they need semicolons or use semicolons when they need colons. How would you explain the difference in the functions of these punctuation marks to these students?

Spelling and Word Usage Application

Note the correct spelling of the following words:

accidentally	achievement	eighth	guidance
length	mischief	procedure	scissors

Rewrite the following sentences, correcting all misspelled words.

1. Take a pair of scissers and fix the lenghth of your over long jeans.
2. We accidently called his home number and woke up his family.
3. This is the eigth time you're mischeif has backfired.
4. Carys achievment in math has earned him recognition in the field.
5. Do you know the proceedure to follow to change the belt on the vacumm cleaner?
6. All Gretchen need's is a little guidence at this time.

If necessary, refer to Appendix A for the correct usage of the following words:

altogether/all together   capital/capitol

Practical Applications

Part A

Insert semicolons and colons in the following sentences.

1. Meetings are scheduled in Dayton, Ohio Wilkes Barre, Pennsylvania and Trenton, New Jersey.
2. I will be on the 830 morning train to New York.
3. Help us to move these boxes we have to get ready to take inventory.
4. Quincy stated "My ancestors are reputed to have come over with the early settlers in Massachusetts and eventually moved westward to settle in what is now California, Oregon, and Washington."

5. I am saving 10 percent of my income for the future furthermore, I am doubling my mortgage payments each month.

Part B

Insert dashes and hyphens in the following sentences.

1. The beds were unmade, the dirty dishes were in the sink, and the stereo was blasting the teenagers' parents were away.
2. The township's crime fighters spot checked the area every hour.
3. Morris the cat that appeared from nowhere disappeared the other night.
4. They are interested in investing in a time share resort in St. Thomas.
5. Certainly we agree well, some of us do.

Part C

Use hyphens to indicate possible division points in each word. You may use a dictionary.

1. beneficiary
2. jurisdiction
3. recycle
4. hypothesis
5. accountability

Editing and Proofreading Application

Revise the following message by adding semicolons, colons, dashes, hyphens, and external punctuation where needed. Also correct any misspelled words.

Charlotte, this note is to apolagize for not forewarding your tax bill in fact, I sincerly want to make it up to you Could you meet me in my office at 1015 on Tuesday I will have it ready for you then

I think that I must be getting forgetful or is it that I'm just over worked I promise that next year I will send your bill on time furthermore, I will send you two copies for your personal record's

When I spoke with my assistant about the error, she implied that she had double checked to see that all bills had been mailed I guess that she only spot checked her records. Please let me know if Tuesday, August 10, is conveneint for you my assistant, Gladys Small my secretary, Gerard Alvarez and I will give you the tax bill and go over all your records for the last twelve month's.

Chapter 18

Quotation Marks, Parentheses, Underscores, and Apostrophes

OBJECTIVES

After studying this chapter and completing the chapter activities, you will be able to do the following:

1. Apply the guidelines for using quotation marks.
2. Use parentheses correctly in your writing.
3. Use underscores where appropriate.
4. Use the apostrophe accurately in your communications.

QUOTATION MARKS

Quotation marks indicate a direct quotation, a definition, nonstandard English, a word or phrase used in an unusual way, and a title. This section explains each of these uses in detail.

With Direct Quotations

When stating someone's exact words, enclose the words within opening and closing quotation marks. For example:

Betty exclaimed, "It's getting late; let's go!"

"We still have a few minutes," replied Jeff.

"We'll leave now," answered Betty. "We don't want to miss the train."

Within Quotations

Use single quotation marks to enclose a quotation within a quotation. Here are examples:

Amanda stated, "They listened carefully to the president when he said, 'Our competition is getting ahead of us.'"

When citing a quotation within a quotation within a quotation, follow the order of double, single, double quotation marks. For example:

Roberta stated, "I cannot agree because our accountant said, 'We should abide by the words of Jon Grawley, "Tax-free bonds are a sound investment." ' "

With Other Punctuation Marks

When placing ending quotation marks, follow the guidelines below.

Rule 1. Place periods and commas within ending quotation marks. For example:

"I concur," said the investor, "with your suggestion."

Rule 2. Place semicolons and colons outside ending quotation marks. For example:

His best lecture is called "Psychoanalysis in the 1990s"; have you had an opportunity to hear it?

★ Notice how other punctuation marks are used with quotation marks in these sentences.

★ When a quotation is interrupted by a phrase such as *answered Betty*, one set of quotation marks encloses the quotation before the interruption and a second set encloses the quotation after the interruption.

This is the "beauty of San Diego": ideal temperatures and clear skies.

Rule 3. Place question marks and exclamations points inside the ending quotation marks when the quoted material is a question or an exclamation. For example:

She shouted, "Watch out!"

He replied, "What's happening?"

★ If both the sentence and the quotation are questions, place the question mark inside the ending quotation mark.

Rule 4. Place question marks and exclamation points outside the ending quotation marks when the sentence, but not the quoted material, is a question or an exclamation. For example:

Did Lydia actually say, "I will attend the seminar"?

What a deplorable situation; he's just "goofing off"!

CHECKPOINT 1 — *Inserting Punctuation*

Insert quotation marks, commas, and ending punctuation in each sentence where needed.

1. They each get an allowance said Meg He spends it wisely, but she squanders it
2. Clancy stated The firefighters had yelled Leave the yard at once
3. The poet remarked I cannot participate in the English Literature Conference in May.
4. We believe said Ann and Charles that the college should be co-ed
5. After scanning the article on testing, did they say, This will never work
6. Genevieve inquired Are you going on safari in Kenya
7. They exclaimed Bring our military home

Check your answers in Appendix F.

★ A definition is usually followed by the words *is/are*, *means*, or *is/are known as*.

With Definitions and Nonstandard English

Use quotation marks to designate a term that is defined in the same sentence in which the term appears. For example:

A "couch potato" is someone who watches television all day and all evening.

A "saint" is a kind person who does no wrong.

Use quotation marks to enclose slang words or expressions to indicate that the words or expressions have substandard status. For example:

She said, "We just 'ain't' going to do it."

He referred to his car as a "dumb bunny."

With Special or Unconventional Words

Use quotation marks around words used in a special or an unconventional manner. Here are examples:

By adopting a "must-do" approach, the residents grew market-quality produce in their gardens.

The minister praised her as a "woman of valor."

With Titles

Use quotation marks to enclose the titles of parts of whole works such as magazine articles and chapters. Quotation marks also are used to enclose titles of lectures, songs, sermons, and short poems. Here are examples:

I read the article "The New Subcompact Cars" in *Consumer's Digest*. [or: Consumer's Digest.]

Gregory's lecture "E-Mail Versus Voice-Mail" created a stir in the audience.

The third chapter titled "The Sunflower Seed Foreign Market" enlightened the agricultural economist.

★ Although the title of a magazine article is enclosed in quotation marks, the title of the magazine represents a complete work and is printed in italics or is underscored.

Quotation Marks

Insert quotation marks in each sentence.

1. After a losing streak, last year's champions were down in the dumps.
2. Most of those surveyed answered affirmatively in the article titled Software Use in Small Offices.

(Continued on the next page)

3. The poet sold his poem You Are My Destiny to *Cosmopolitan.*
4. A master chef is one who cooks delicate, delicious, and sought-after fish entrees and veal specialties.
5. Brenda, you are a sight for sore eyes.
6. The author of the magazine article Sunscreen for Children is appearing on television today.
7. Tony Bennett made the song I Left My Heart in San Francisco famous for many years.

Check your answers in Appendix F.

PARENTHESES

A **parenthesis** is used in pairs to set off nonessential words, phrases, or clauses. The pair is called *parentheses.* Parentheses also are used with monetary designations, abbreviations that follow names, references and directions, and numerals and letters accompanying a list.

★ Words set off with parentheses could be omitted entirely, but words set off with commas or dashes add interest and provide needed information.

With Nonessential Elements

De-emphasize nonessential elements by placing them in parentheses. For example:

A high percentage of the alumni (73 percent of those surveyed) opposed changing the name of the college.

Some runners (Susie Appleton is one) never give up in marathon races.

When the items in parentheses appear at the end of a sentence, place the external punctuation mark after the ending parenthesis. For example:

We received a visit from our ex-president (1991–1992).

The winter conference is in Orlando (January 3–6).

★ Parentheses may enclose just a few words in a sentence or an entire sentence.

When an item in parentheses is *intentionally* a complete sentence, capitalize the first word and end the item with an internal punctuation mark. Here are two examples:

My brother-in-law received a promotion. (Jay is younger than I.)

Luis and Ramona relocated to Brooklyn. (Didn't you meet them in San Juan?)

When a dependent clause is followed by an item or items within parentheses, place the comma after the ending parenthesis. For example:

When they arrive at the airport (around 6 p.m.), George will meet them.

With Monetary Designations and Abbreviations

Primarily in legal documents, parentheses are used to enclose a numerical designation ($500) following a verbal designation of money (five hundred dollars). For example:

Mr. Chin has deposited the sum of five hundred dollars ($500) in your escrow account.

In addition, parentheses are used with abbreviations that follow names. For example:

The Association for Business Communication (ABC) had selected Robert Myers as its Interim Executive Director.

With References and Directions

Use parentheses to set off both references and directions to minimize their importance in a sentence. For example:

You may consult the appendix (page 345) for the correct format.

This trip (see the enclosed brochure) is a once-in-a-lifetime opportunity.

With Numerals and Letters Accompanying a List

When numerals or letters are used to list items in a sentence, parentheses may be used to enclose the numerals or letters. Here are two examples:

We plan to (1) fly to San Diego, (2) drive up the coast, and (3) spend three days in San Francisco before flying home.

Please include (a) your date of birth, (b) your social security number, and (c) your mother's maiden name.

★ Omit parentheses around the numerals or letters if the enumerations are in a vertical listing.

3 *Parentheses*

Insert parentheses where needed in each sentence.

1. Isabel or Mario one or the other will most likely be selected.
2. We saw many couples six we knew on the boardwalk.
3. In the article on photography May issue of *Photography Digest,* our new camera was featured.
4. Add *'s* to a singular noun to create a singular possessive form girl's.
(Continued on the next page)

5. My nephew the black sheep of our family dropped out of school on his sixteenth birthday.
6. The price of General Motors GM stock is attractive to investors.
7. Refer to Chapter 3 pages 11–21 if you want a more detailed explanation.

Check your answers in Appendix F.

UNDERSCORES

The **underscore**, also known as the *underline*, calls attention to a word or expression. The underscore is used with the title of complete works or with foreign expressions. With the use of word-processing software, italics are used in print instead of the underscore. This section provides guidelines for underscore usage.

With Titles

If you do not utilize italics, use an underscore with titles of complete works that are published as individual items. Examples of complete works include books, magazines, newspapers, and plays. In addition, use an underscore with the name of a film, television program, aircraft, cruise ship, sculpture, or painting. Note these examples:

Will television programs such as All in the Family and Cheers ever be forgotten?

The stockbroker reads The Wall Street Journal every morning before the market opens.

Their cruise on the Royal Princess took them through the Panama Canal.

With Foreign Expressions

Use an underscore or italics to distinguish foreign expressions from standard English vocabulary. For example:

Her baked goods are par excellence; no better pastries exist.

The whole group traveled en masse through the park.

ON THE JOB

When you are not sure if you should underscore the word *The* in a newspaper name, check the newspaper itself to determine its official name.

APOSTROPHES

The **apostrophe** is used primarily to indicate the omission of one or more letters or numbers in a contraction, to indicate possession in nouns and indefinite pronouns, or to denote time and money. The apostrophe also has a minor role in forming plurals of lowercase letters.

In Contractions

Contractions, although considered by some to be overly informal, are accepted in today's business world by many communicators. We recommend, however, using contractions sparingly. To indicate a contraction, insert an apostrophe in the space where the missing letter or letters belong. For example:

don't (do not)	didn't (did not)	we'll (we will)
you're (you are)	it's (it is)	they're (they are)

To indicate an omission in a number, insert an apostrophe in the space where the missing number or numbers belong. Note these:

Martin graduated in '94. (1994)

The reunion was planned for this year but rescheduled for '97. (1997)

EXTRA, EXTRA!

★ A contraction is created by merging two words and omitting one or more letters, thereby creating a shortened word form.

---

4 CHECKPOINT

Apostrophes and Underscores

Insert an apostrophe or an underscore where needed in each sentence.

1. The Hebrew word for *hello* and *goodbye* is shalom.
2. Its a very long commute to the office by train.
3. While sitting in the lobby, I read an interesting article in Newsweek.
4. Ralph and Theresa should work overtime, but they cant because of personal problems.
5. The manual Tips for Word Processors contains many helpful hints.
6. Because he left college to play professional football, he did not graduate in the class of 93.
7. The applicant sensed that the job interviewer implied, "Dont call us; well call you."

Check your answers in Appendix F.

In Possession

Apostrophes are used in the possessive case in nouns, discussed in Chapter 4, to indicate possession. Note these examples:

The *boy's* suit needs pressing. (singular possessive)

The *boys'* suits need pressing. (plural possessive)

The *children's* toys are new. (irregular noun—plural possessive)

Add an *'s* to an indefinite pronoun such as *someone* or *everyone* to show possession. For example:

Someone's television has been left on.

One's thoughts should be shared in an emergency.

In compound words, add the apostrophe to the last word to indicate possession. For example:

Her *mother-in-law's* house will be used for the party.

My *brother-in-law's* education prepared him for his career.

★ Remember that possessive case pronouns (*its, ours*) do not need apostrophes because they are already in the possessive form.

In Time and Money

Add an *'* or *'s* to *dollar, day, week, month,* and *year* to indicate each word's relationship with the noun that follows it. For example:

A *week's* salary is needed to pay the rent.

Two *hours'* time is not sufficient to complete the project.

Today's class was very interesting.

Buy ten *dollars'* worth of produce at the farmer's market.

In Plurals

Add an *'s* to lowercase letters and to some abbreviations to form the plural. For example:

We sometimes find it difficult to distinguish her *a's* from her *o's.*

In your letter, you omitted the periods with the *a.m.'s.*

Do not include so many *etc.'s* in your listings.

I have no problem rolling my *r's* when I speak that language.

5 **CHECKPOINT** *Apostrophes*

Insert apostrophes where needed in each sentence.

1. The building project represents three years labor.
2. "The ts are purposely left uncrossed," said Bette.
3. Their companys profits went up during the first quarter of 94.
4. Pronouncing ths may be difficult for a young child just learning to speak.
5. Aida and Miguel are looking forward to next weeks game.
6. Buying a dollars worth of gum seems extravagant to me.
7. His father-in-laws loan subsidized his car purchase.

Check your answer in Appendix F.

Summary

Chapter 18 concludes the coverage of both external and internal punctuation. In this chapter, the review of the use of quotation marks, parentheses, underscores, and apostrophes provides guidelines for using these punctuation marks wisely in your writing.

Quotation marks are used with direct quotations, definitions, nonstandard English, special or unconventional words, and titles. Parentheses are used with nonessential elements, monetary designations, names, references, directions, and numerals and letters. The underscore or italics are used to emphasize titles of complete works and foreign expressions. Lastly, the apostrophe is used with contractions, possession, time and money, and plurals of lowercase letters.

By studying and applying the guidelines for the internal and external punctuation introduced in Chapters 15, 16, 17, and 18, you are one step closer to producing error-free written communications.

Discussion Questions

1. State the guidelines for the use of parentheses and provide several sentences that contain parentheses.
2. Discuss the importance of either quotation marks or apostrophes in producing clarity and effectiveness in written communications.

Spelling and Word Usage Application

Note the correct spelling of the following words:

acquaintance	analysis	extension	familiar
manufacture	mathematics	religious	remembrance
equipment	competitive		

Rewrite the following sentences, correcting all misspelled words.

1. I met an aquaintance at her place of worship on a religous holiday.
2. We have begun to manfacture competetive automobile part's.
3. Their analysus of the situation does'nt make any sense.
4. Tex teaches mathmatics at the extention branch of the university.
5. Are you familar with the new software that was recently installed on this equiptment?
6. Jason and Mildred sent him a remembrence on behalf of his son.

If necessary, refer to Appendix A for the correct usage of the following words:

continual/continuous   decent/descent/dissent

Practical Applications

Part A

Insert quotation marks and parentheses in the following sentences.

1. Did she say, The trainees have finished their program?
2. The plaintiff in the case is owed the sum of five thousand dollars $5,000.
3. The author stated, After I wrote the book, my daughter said, Dad, I am proud of you.
4. The consultant said, Act on the policy now or forget about the policy altogether.
5. Most of the baseball players 83 percent of them favored going on strike August 19.

Part B
Insert underscores and apostrophes in the following sentences.

1. You inserted Ibid. in your footnotes in the wrong place.
2. John Grisham's book The Chamber is about a convict on death row.
3. He doesnt print correctly; the bs look like ds.
4. The Hamiltons cars are both in the garage.
5. Leave the rough draft of your revised will in the attorney-at-laws office in center city.

Part C
Insert all missing internal and external punctuation.

1. The trip starts in Osaka said the travel agent You are then taken to the cruise ship in Kobe
2. They have an impossible commute every day 80 miles
3. The mens suits womens dresses and childrens snowsuits are ready to be inventoried
4. A weeks wages are needed to pay for the Encyclopedia Atlas and Illustrations
5. Before you traveled to Korea did you read her most recent article What Present Day South Koreans Think About America

Editing and Proofreading Application

Revise the following message by adding quotation marks, parentheses, underscores, apostrophes, and external punctuation where needed. In addition, correct all misspelled words and incorrect word usage.

Because my husband and me both have IRA accounts in your fund, I thought you would be interest to know that we are becoming increasing displeased with one fase of your operation. When I had spoke with one of your representives, she said, All you half to do to have your funds transfer to your bank is to have the bank send an IRA Transfer Form to us. The directions are clearly outlined in our booklet How to Transfer Funds.

I read the booklet and had the bank Fidelity Fiduciary Bank mailed the correctly filled-in form to your company The fund's still have'nt been transferred. Another one of your representatives told me on the telephone, Because a bank administrater did'nt sign the form, we have to return it to your bank for a signature. This stipulation did not appear in the book let I was told to read.

Aparent, your company makes it easy to deposit money in your IRA funds, but makes it difficult for customers when they want to transfer money out of one of the funds When my friends ask me if I would reccommend your company, I would have to tell them, Not at the present time

Abbreviations

OBJECTIVES

After studying this chapter and completing the chapter activities, you will be able to do the following:

1. Select and use acceptable abbreviations in business correspondence.
2. Apply the guidelines for abbreviations used in technical materials.
3. Use familiar acronyms in your communications.

Chapter 19

ABBREVIATIONS USED IN BUSINESS CORRESPONDENCE

An **abbreviation** is a shortened form of a word or a group of words. Shortened forms are used sparingly in business letters as they sometimes obscure the writer's meaning and also present an informality that may offend the reader. Abbreviations do have a role in communications, however, and the following guidelines clearly explain their uses. Notice that although many abbreviations are followed by periods, some abbreviations are not.

Shortened forms that apply to business writing include courtesy titles, Jr. and Sr. designations, and initials; professional titles and academic degrees; addresses and states; and names of companies, organizations, and government departments. In addition, abbreviations such as *a.m.*, *p.m.*, *Co.*, *Inc.*, *Corp.*, and *Ltd.* appear in business communications. This section presents acceptable abbreviations and illustrates their use.

Courtesy Titles and Family Designations

Abbreviate a personal title that precedes a person's name. For example:

> *Messrs.* White and Rome represent our firm at the negotiations. (The title *Messrs.* is the plural of the title *Mr.*)

> We will interview *Ms.* Violeta Ruiz. (*Ms.* is a title for a woman that omits reference to marital status.)

> *Mr.* George Abbott will be joining our company.

Abbreviate family designations such as *junior* and *senior* that appear after a person's name. Commas usually set off the family designations unless the people themselves omit the punctuation. For example:

> Carl Brockman, *Jr.*, is the first speaker on the program.

> Her father, Louis Greene, *Sr.*, was a famous athlete.

Sometimes people use an **initial** to indicate the first letter of their first name or middle name. Note these examples:

> *I. H.* Roth uses his first and middle initials, not his first name, in all business and personal correspondence.

> Gladys *S.* Blackwood insists that her middle initial, which stands for her maiden name, appear on all correspondence and legal documents.

★ Through the years, many abbreviations that previously required periods no longer need them—CPA, YMCA. Refer to a dictionary if you are not sure.

★ Notice that a.m. and p.m. are both in lowercase letters with periods but no spaces.

Professional Titles

Some professional titles are abbreviated in business writing. Note these examples:

> *Dr.* Sergio Silva is an internist in private practice.

> The company lawyer, Sonia Ramos, *Esq.*, has an office on the eleventh floor. (The title *Esq.* is set off with commas.)

Sometimes a professional title may be abbreviated if both the first and last name of a person is used. For example:

> *Sen.* Clara Bryson represents our state in Congress.

If just the last name had been used, the word *Senator* would have been spelled out. For example:

> *Senator* Bryson represents our state in Congress.

Many professional titles are spelled out, not abbreviated. Note these examples:

> My teacher for French is *Professor* Evans.

> The minister who will give the invocation is *Reverend* Clarence Tully.

> *Dean* Gutekunst from the community college will join the panel.

> *Honorable* Yoko Akita will be on the bench.

> *Governor* Casey is not running for office a second time.

★ Frequently, professional titles are spelled out to show respect for the person who has the title.

Academic and Professional Degrees

Abbreviate academic and professional degrees that follow a person's name. Here are some examples:

> Luisa Barnes, *Ed.D.*

> Steven Joffe, *Ph.D.*

> Letitia Anderson, *M.D.*

> Edwin Jeffreys, *D.D.S.*

> Alice State, *D.V.M.*

★ Ed.D. and Ph.D. are examples of academic degrees; M.D., D.D.S., and D.V.M. are examples of medical degrees.

Do not precede a name with *Dr.* if an academic or medical degree is indicated after the name. In other words, do not write *Dr. Luisa Barnes, Ed.D.* or *Dr. Letitia Anderson, M.D.*

The American Medical Association and the American Osteopathic Association prefer not to use periods in medical abbreviations. Within the medical profession, titles such as MD, DO, and RN often are written without periods.

The abbreviation *CPA* stands for Certified Public Accountant. It, like other familiar abbreviations, no longer requires periods. Note this example:

Nora L. Fried, *CPA*, is glad when tax season is over.

Usually, commas set off degrees that follow people's names. For example:

Alexandra Jackson, *J.D.*, is a recent graduate of Temple University Law School.

Kenneth Pitcairn, *Th. D.*, addressed the seminary students.

Abbreviations

Follow the guidelines by inserting or deleting abbreviations where needed in each sentence.

1. Miss Greta Brightson and Mister Raymond Key will be our delegates.
2. Missus Jenkins and her husband own this property.
3. Doctor Douglas Fox is a noted cardiologist in Land City.
4. The attorney, Wanda Chase, Esquire, will relocate.
5. Lana Grayson, Certified Public Accountant, is auditing the books this week.
6. Because I love cats, I would like to be a D.V.M.
7. The judge to hear the case is the Hon. Chi Liang.

Check your answers in Appendix F.

Addresses

In business correspondence, do not abbreviate words such as *street, avenue, boulevard, road, north, south, east,* and *west.* For example:

Our new address is 123 *South* Main *Street.*

★ Abbreviating *street, avenue, east,* and *west* is acceptable in addresses in <u>personal</u> correspondence.

The meeting will take place at 4 Spring *Boulevard*.

Abbreviate compass designations after street names. For example:

Our president lives at 1605 Bird Lane, *NW.*

She is moving to 134 Second Avenue, *SE.*

Although the Postal Service will accept a five-digit ZIP code, it prefers a nine-digit code.

•

Try to memorize the two-letter postal abbreviations for the states to which you usually send mail. Keep the postal abbreviation list handy when sending mail to other states.

States

Two-letter postal abbreviations appear in all capital letters without punctuation. Refer to the list of postal abbreviations in Appendix B that are accepted by the U.S. Postal Service. Use these abbreviations with the appropriate nine-digit ZIP codes in your correspondence.

Two-letter postal abbreviations are used in full addresses within the text of a letter but are not used when a state name appears in a sentence by itself. Note these examples:

Please send the product to Ms. Lucy Sands, 1004 Clemens Avenue, Roslyn, *PA* 19001-4356.

The product will have to be shipped directly to *Pennsylvania*.

---

2 CHECKPOINT

Addresses and States

Insert abbreviations where needed and spell out words that should not be abbreviated in each sentence.

1. On what ave. did you say the doctor lives?
2. Her new office address is 16 Pine Blvd., Northwest.
3. Does she live on Tustin St. or Tustin Rd.?
4. The receptionist comes from either WY or WV; I can't remember which one.
5. My mailing address is Ms. C. A. Grange, 15 Aruba Drive, Lafayette, Louisiana 70507-3142.
6. San Juan in PR is very hot during the summer months.
7. The hwy. she uses has a lot of busy traffic during peak hrs.

Check your answers in Appendix F.

Companies, Organizations, and Government Departments

You may abbreviate the names of some well-known companies and organizations if the institutions themselves use the abbreviations. This policy also applies to U.S. government departments. Here are some examples:

ABC	American Broadcasting Company
AMA	American Medical Association (or American Management Association)
FBI	Federal Bureau of Investigation
IBM	International Business Machines
IRS	Internal Revenue Service
YWCA	Young Women's Christian Association

Notice that each of these abbreviations is in all capital letters without punctuation. Here are some additional examples that may be familiar to you:

FDIC	Federal Deposit Insurance Corporation	UAW	United Automobile Workers
MADD	Mothers Against Drunk Driving	UN	United Nations
SBA	Small Business Administration	UPS	United Parcel Service
SEC	Securities and Exchange Commission		

★ Do not create your own abbreviations for companies that use their full names at all times.

Company, Incorporated, Corporation, Limited

The abbreviations *Co.*, *Inc.*, *Corp.*, or *Ltd.* may be used in a company name if the company uses it as part of its official name. Always check a company's letterhead to see if the company uses an abbreviation. Note these examples:

The Moseley *Co.* is located west of the river.

The china replacement company is China Distributors, *Inc.*

Our accountant previously worked for Mobil Oil *Corp.*

The British firm Lourdes, *Ltd.*, distributes this product.

Do not abbreviate *company, incorporated, corporation,* or *limited* when it appears in lowercase letters in a sentence; instead, spell out the entire word. For example:

One firm has *incorporated* into the other.

Does he work for a large *corporation*?

We are *limited* to hiring only one new computer operator.

She now owns her own *company.*

Expressions of Time

The abbreviations *a.m.* and *p.m.* may be used to designate time when they accompany numerals. The abbreviation *a.m.* comes from Latin **ante meridiem**, which means *before noon*, and *p.m.* comes from Latin **post meridiem**, which means *after noon*. Note these examples:

The next meeting is called for 8 *a.m.* on Tuesday.

You can call Jane until 6:30 *p.m.* any weekday.

To avoid confusion, writers usually use *midnight* rather than 12 a.m. and *noon* rather than 12 p.m.

Familiar Business Abbreviations

Here are more examples of abbreviations, some of which tend to be used in informal business communications such as memos:

A.I.A.	Associate of the Institute of Actuaries
ASAP	as soon as possible
CEO	chief executive officer
C.O.D.	cash on delivery (c.o.d. and COD also are used)
EST	Eastern Standard Time
FYI	for your information
GNP	Gross National Product
PE	price to earnings ratio
P.O. Box	Post Office Box
vs.	versus

★ Use abbreviations such as FYI and ASAP only when you know the recipient; these abbreviations are very informal and may offend some readers.

Applying Abbreviation Guidelines

Apply abbreviation guidelines to fix any errors in each sentence.

1. We do not look forward to an IRS audit.
2. The office of the orgn. is across the street from the YWCA.
3. Did you purchase an I.B.M. computer and printer?
4. We are waiting for the U.P.S. truck before we leave.
5. The firm that hired her is a major corp.
6. The breakfast meeting will begin at 7 A.M.
7. Edward Jacino is the c.e.o. of the co.

Check your answers in Appendix F.

ABBREVIATIONS USED IN TECHNICAL COMMUNICATIONS

Many abbreviations are used in technical material such as tables, charts, business forms, and statistical documents. Using abbreviations offers advantages because the shortened forms take up less room on lines and in columns. Business expressions, units of measure, days of the week, and months of the year frequently appear in their shortened forms in technical documents. This section provides a close look at these abbreviations.

The lack of space on many technical forms may require you to use abbreviations whether you prefer it or not.

Miscellaneous Abbreviations

Some abbreviations used in statistical documents should not be used in business letters. They include the following:

mfg.	manufacturing	reg.	registered
bal.	balance	mdse.	merchandise
pd.	paid	whlse.	wholesale

Other abbreviations such as *No.* (Number) and *Acct.* (Account) may be used in technical documents and also in business correspondence when they are followed by numerals. For example:

Please refer to our check *No.* 654.

This information pertains to *Acct.* 6J843.

Units of Measure

The following abbreviations, though not acceptable in standard business correspondence, are widely used in technical documents:

★ Abbreviations such as *lb., yd., in.,* and *cm.* can be used as singular or plural (1 lb. or 16 lb.).

mph	miles per hour	in.	inches
oz.	ounce	ft.	feet
lb.	pound	kg.	kilogram
cm.	centimeter	yd.	yard

Days and Months

In lists and business forms, the abbreviations for days and for months are acceptable; however, these abbreviations are not acceptable in general business correspondence. Here are the abbreviated forms:

Monday	Mon.	Tuesday	Tues.	Wednesday	Wed.
Thursday	Thurs.	Friday	Fri.	Saturday	Sat.
Sunday	Sun.				
January	Jan.	February	Feb.	March	Mar.
April	Apr.	August	Aug.	September	Sept.
October	Oct.	November	Nov.	December	Dec.

The months of May, June, and July do not have abbreviated forms.

ACRONYMS

An **acronym** is a special type of abbreviation that is formed from the first letter or letters of a series of words. The letters form a pronounceable word. Here are examples:

EPCOT	Experimental Prototype Community of Tomorrow
NASA	National Aeronautics and Space Administration
NATO	North Atlantic Treaty Organization
OPEC	Organization for Petroleum Exporting Countries
radar	radio detecting and ranging

CHECKPOINT 4

Technical Communications and Acronyms

Correct any misuse of abbreviations in each sentence.

1. The co. she works for specializes in mfg. auto parts.
2. He still hasn't pd. for the mdse. he bought last mo.
3. How many lb. and ozs. did her baby weigh?
4. We plan to vacation in Disney World and visit E.P.C.O.T.
5. The conference call will take place either Mon. or Tues. at 8:45 AM EST.
6. May I be interviewed on Fri., Oct. 9.
7. Reports about N.A.S.A.'s activities appear in the newspaper.

Check your answers in Appendix F.

Summary

Abbreviations, which have an important role in technical communications, have a comparatively small role in business correspondence. Some abbreviations used in general business correspondence include courtesy titles, family designations, and initials; professional titles and academic degrees; addresses and states; names of companies, organizations, and government departments; time designations; and abbreviations such as *Co.*, *Inc.*, *Corp.*, and *Ltd.*

Technical materials such as tables, charts, business forms, and statistical documents often have limited space available and are ideal for abbreviated business terms, units of measure, days of the week, and months of the year.

The use of familiar acronyms is also acceptable in business communications.

Discussion Questions

1. Many communicators use abbreviations frequently, while others stay away from them as much as possible. Present reasons for or against using abbreviations in business.
2. What, if any, is the value of acronyms to companies, organizations, government departments, and the general public?

Spelling and Word Usage Application

Note the correct spelling of the following states:

Colorado	Connecticut	Hawaii	Illinois
Louisiana	Massachusetts	Tennessee	Minnesota

Rewrite the following sentences, correcting all misspelled words.

1. The regional conferences are in San Juan, Puerto Rico; Denver, Colarado; and Oahu, Hawaai.
2. The personal department's new computer had to be returned to Minesota.
3. What is the occassion that brings you to Massachusets in the winter?
4. The star's arrivel at the airport in New Orleans, Louisana, caused quite a commotion.
5. Representives from Tenessee and Ilinois are staying at the Hilton Hotel.
6. For little children who live in that state, Conneticut is dificult to spell.

If necessary, refer to Appendix A for the correct usage of the following words:

desert/dessert   disburse/disperse

Practical Applications

Part A

Correct any misuse of abbreviations in the following sentences.

1. My sister who lives in SC and my brother who lives in NC try to visit each other once a yr.
2. The Y.M.C.A. is sponsoring a trip to NY for local orgns.
3. The U.S. government office is closed Sat. afternoon and all day Sun.
4. We will check your Jan. acct. bal. for you as you requested.
5. Doctor Lloyd Servino and Mister Ian Johnson are the first two people on the waiting list.

Part B
Correct errors in word usage and abbreviations.

1. Sen. George Clapton from GA had address the members of the grp.
2. Dr. Ellen G. Eaton, M.D., is hosting the reception on the hospital.
3. The winter mos. of Jan. through Mar. tends to be cold, snowy, and icy in the East.
4. My savings are insure at the bank by the F.D.I.C.
5. Have you ever visited the u.n. bldg. in NY?

Part C
Correct errors in spelling, word usage, and abbreviations.

1. Which co. in Virgina handles the antique funiture I collect?
2. The firm I left in Nov. was sold to a largest major corp.
3. The reputible company, C. Foxwood, Limited, distribute fine glasswear.
4. Hannah previously work for Broadway Tickets, Incorporated.
5. Three wks. from now we will get to gether for about two hrs.

Editing and Proofreading Application

Proofread the following message. Eliminate errors in abbreviations and spelling, and insert external punctuation. Prepare a corrected copy.

On Mon., Aug. 1, I sent you a letter asking for the procedures' to follow to pay off my mtge. loan You sent me a reply on Fri. of the same week, telling me that the bal. due on the loan was $2,003.94 minus $694 left in my escrow acct.

I dont want to be a nusance, but I still have these few unanswered questions,

1. Should I deduct the escrow acct. bal. from the mtge. loan bal. and send you a chk. for the diference

2. Should I mail my pymt. to this address or to the NJ address were I usually send my mtge. pymt.

3. Will you mail the evidents of my mtge. satisfaction pymt. directly to my county seat to be registered, or will you send the evidents to me to take to the office of the county seat

Please call me at 555-0234 or respond to my question's ASAP so that I can pay off this loan to your satisfaction and to mine FYI, I have had nothing but coperation from your bank in the passed, and I am sure that this matter can be taken care of by Fri., Aug. 20 at the lattest

Capitalization

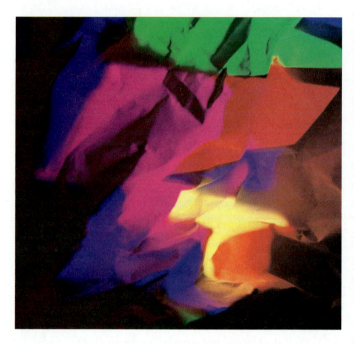

OBJECTIVES

After studying this chapter and completing the chapter activities, you will be able to do the following:

1. Use capital letters correctly with first words of sentences, quotations, salutations, complimentary closings, poems, and outlines.
2. Use capital letters correctly with titles of persons and written works.
3. Capitalize all proper nouns and other words and abbreviations that require capitals.

USING CAPITALIZATION WITH FIRST WORDS

A capital letter is used in the first word of a sentence, quotation, salutation, complimentary close, poem, and outline. This section explains and illustrates each of these uses.

To Begin a Sentence

To indicate the beginning of a sentence, capitalize the first letter of the first word. For example:

> *The* tax collector is at the door.

> *When* did this problem begin?

> *I* cannot work overtime on Friday. (The pronoun *I* is always capitalized.)

When a complete sentence that states a rule or emphasizes a statement is preceded by a colon, capitalize the first letter of the first word. Note these examples:

> It is a perfect beach day: *The* sun is out, the breeze is warm, and the temperature is balmy.

> Remember to follow our policy: *Greet* customers at the door and volunteer assistance, but do not pressure them.

★ Capitalize the first word in an expression that substitutes for a sentence. (Sure! Okay!)

To Begin a Quotation

Capitalize the first word of a direct quotation. For example:

> He said, "*Let* me help you perform the end-of-month audit."

> "*That* would be very helpful," she replied.

Do not capitalize the second part of an interrupted direct quotation. Note these examples:

> "We should congratulate Gail," James stated, "*on* her recent promotion."

> "Marathon running is healthy for you," said the aerobics instructor, "*if* you have the stamina."

★ Remember that the first word in an indirect quotation is not capitalized. (She said that *she* would go.)

In a Salutation and Complimentary Close

In a business letter, capitalize the first letter of the first word, the person's title, and the proper name in a salutation. Also capitalize the first word in a complimentary close. Examples are shown on the next page.

| Dear Sir | Ladies and Gentlemen | Dear Ms. Morales |
| Yours very truly | Very truly yours | Sincerely |

In a Poem

Unless the poet uses a different form, capitalize the first word of each line of a poem. Note these examples:

Persistent achievers are hard to find

Thus some people think he's one of a kind

But first let me take you down memory lane

To show you why his energy refuses to wane

CHECKPOINT 1

Capitalizing First Words

Correct all errors in capitalization in each sentence.

1. Tyrone and i are serving as delegates to the convention.
2. They appear to be ready for the next assignment; Their pencils are down, and they turned over their papers.
3. let me express my thoughts to you.
4. Begin your letter with Dear sir, and end it with Yours Very Truly.
5. Raymond asked, "when will the meeting end?"
6. "The meeting should be over by 5 p.m.," responded Cynthia, "But you can never be sure."
7. The project was a success: all project members contributed, everyone cooperated, and the assignment was completed before the due date.

Check your answers in Appendix F.

USING CAPITALIZATION WITH TITLES

This section presents guidelines that apply to the use of capital letters with titles of persons and titles of written works.

Titles of Persons

Capitalize professional titles that precede proper names. For example:

Dr. Nancy Musi   *Governor* Louis Ramos

Capitalize professional titles that do not precede proper names but that refer to specific, well-known individuals. For example:

The *President* is concerned with the uprising in Europe. (refers to the President of the United States)

Generally, do not capitalize a job title that follows a name. For example:

Tanya Blank is the *marketing manager* for our company.

★ Titles can be courtesy titles (Mrs.) or professional titles (Dr.).

Titles of Written Works

Capitalize all words in report headings and the titles of books, magazines, newspapers, articles, movie films, television programs, songs, poems, reports, and chapters except for the following:

1. the articles *the*, *a*, or *an*
2. short conjunctions—three or fewer letters
3. short prepositions (even the word *to* in an infinitive)—three or fewer letters

Here are some examples:

War and Peace (book)

U.S. News and World Report (magazine)

How to Succeed in Business Without Really Trying (film)

Communication for Management and Business (book)

Capitalize an article, a short conjunction, or a short preposition when it is the first or last word in a heading or title. For example:

The Far Pavilions

As You Like It

To the Manor Born

A Concise Manual for Writers

★ Capitalize the first word that follows a colon or a dash in a title (Banking: *The* Role of the Loan Officer).

Capitalizing Titles

CHECKPOINT 2

Identify and correct all errors in capitalization in each sentence.

1. My favorite film was *Gone With The Wind.*
2. The movie *the Creature From the Deep* is too scary for children.
3. Stan, dr. Post, and I play golf on Wednesday afternoons.
4. Did you see the Mayor at city hall?
5. The president's residence at the White House is luxurious.
6. The chapter titled "a Thought For Youth" interests adolescents.
7. An article in the magazine *Business And Computing* discussed the report "the Value Of A Modem For All."

Check your answers in Appendix F.

★ If you are not familiar with the word *deities*, check the definition in a dictionary.

USING CAPITALIZATION WITH NAMES

This section explains guidelines pertaining to capitalization with proper nouns, commercial products, and points of the compass. This section also discusses capital letters that introduce months, days, holidays, and seasons of the year; nationalities, races, religions, and languages; deities; academic degrees; and hyphenated names and words.

Proper Nouns

Capitalize the names of specific people, places, and things in written communications.

Capitalize Names of People

Capitalize all proper names and nicknames. For examples:

> *Yoko Tanaka* is a professor at the university.

> The baseball player is called *Crime Dog.*

Capitalize all titles of family members when the titles are used as proper nouns and are not preceded by a possessive noun or pronoun.

> Let's visit *Grandmother* this morning.

> Are you accompanying *Mother* and *Father* on the trip?

Do not capitalize titles for family members, however, if they are preceded by a possessive noun or pronoun.

Bertha's *sister* is about to be hired.

My *grandfather* started this business.

Capitalize Names of Places

Capitalize the names of streets, parks, buildings, bodies of water, cities, states, and countries. For example:

He lives at 106 *Green Street.* (street)

We use the jogging track at *Mondauk Commons.* (park)

The *Ledger Building* was destroyed in the fire. (building)

Have you crossed the *Atlantic Ocean* on the cruise ship? (body of water)

I have not visited *Jackson, Mississippi.* (city and state)

Steve travels to *Zimbabwe* three times a year. (country)

Capitalize Names of Things

Capitalize the proper names of historical events, companies, documents, organizations, institutions, government departments, periods in history, course titles, and automobiles. For example:

She is a veteran of *World War II.* (historical event)

Walt is a systems analyst for the *General Electric Company.* (company)

Have you studied the *Constitution* of the United States? (document)

Her mother is active in the *Daughters of the American Revolution.* (organization)

I graduated from *Furness Junior High School* in 1985. (institution)

She is a member of the *House of Representatives.* (government department)

Studying about the *Stone Age* bores me. (period in history)

Glenda enrolled in *Physics 103.* (course title)

Suzannne's new car is a *Ford Taurus.* (automobile)

★ Capitalize family names used as titles before proper names (*Uncle* George and *Aunt* Lillian).

★ Common nouns such as *war*, *company*, and so forth are not capitalized (He fought in the last *war*.).

Capitalize some adjectives that are derived from proper nouns. If you are uncertain if an adjective requires capitalization, refer to your dictionary. Note these examples:

> Several excellent *Spanish* students are enrolled in my class.

> Do I detect a *Bostonian* accent?

Capitalize most nouns that precede numbers or letters. For example:

Flight 643	Chapter VI	Vitamin C
Chart 6J	Invoice 1675	Check 563

Exceptions to this guideline include *line, paragraph, verse, size, page,* and *note* when they precede numbers or letters. For example:

line 4	paragraph 2	verse 16-5
size 10	page 24	note 14

★ Distinguish between the brand name, which is capitalized, and the uncapitalized common noun that follows it (IBM printer).

Commercial Products

Do not capitalize common nouns that refer to, but are not part of, a proper noun. For example:

Bic pen	Maytag dishwasher	Olympia camera
Folgers coffee	Lipton tea	Breyers ice cream

Points of the Compass

Capitalize compass points (*north*, *south*, *east*, and *west*) when they refer to a geographical area or a definite region. For example:

> The corporate office is in the *South*.

> Many prestigious universities are located in the *Northeast*.

Do not capitalize compass points, however, when they indicate a direction or a nonspecific location. For example:

> Travel *east* to the river and then drive *south* to the farm.

> Did you say that they work in the *western* section of the city?

Months, Days, and Holidays

Capitalize the months of the year, the days of the week, and the names of holidays. Note these examples:

> In *December*, we are having a company party.

> The sales meeting will take place either *Monday* or *Tuesday*.

> Where are you having your *Fourth of July* picnic?

Seasons of the Year

Do not capitalize summer, fall (autumn), winter, or spring unless a specific designation accompanies the season. For example:

> Our *Spring Blockbuster Sale* begins March 21. (name of sale)

> The *Autumn Victorian Fair* attracts many tourists. (name of fair)

> *Old Man Winter* is just around the corner.

> After this icy *winter*, we are looking forward to *spring*.

> The leaves turn beautiful colors in the *fall*.

★ A poet may personify a season of the year and capitalize it (Oh *Spring*, glorious *Spring*!), but business writers follow different guidelines.

CHECKPOINT 4

Capitalizing Names

Correct all errors in capitalization in each sentence.

1. My headache is awful; may I have the Tylenol Headache Medicine?
2. Did you see my new cross Pen and Pencil Set?
3. Take 1-95 South to the Bridge, and wait for us in the Recreational area.
4. Visiting an Indian Reservation in the southwest is an enlightening experience.
5. Plan to attend tuesday's Labor Negotiations meeting.
6. Our family always dines together on thanksgiving.
7. The winter ice carnival in Minnesota is a crowd-pleaser.

Check your answer in Appendix F.

Nationalities, Races, Religions, and Languages

Capitalize the names of nationalities (American), races (Caucasian), religions (Catholicism), and languages (Latin). Note these sentences:

> Many *Mexican* tourists visit San Diego.

> Black History Month attracts noted *African-American* speakers.

> Students learned about *Judaism*, *Christianity*, and *Buddhism* in Comparative Religion 101.

> Her job at the World Bank requires her to learn both *French* and *Russian*.

Deities

Capitalize nouns that refer to a deity. For example:

> God   the Almighty   Lord   Allah   Buddha

Academic Degrees

Because academic degrees such as Doctor of Philosophy and Doctor of Education are capitalized, also capitalize the abbreviated degrees. For example:

> Maria Sanchez, *Ph.D.*, will address the seminar class.

> Leonard, a consultant, has *Ed.D.* printed on his business stationery.

Hyphenated Names and Words

Apply the guidelines for capitalizing single names and words to hyphenated names and words. Capitalize elements of hyphenated words if they are proper nouns (Leonard Cross-Townsend) or proper adjectives (Atlanta-Chicago train). Do not capitalize prefixes or suffixes added to proper words (mid-Atlantic flight). Note these examples:

President-elect Corcoran is responsible for the agenda.

The *French-Canadian* residents are very cordial to visitors.

He fought in the *Spanish-American* War.

Up-to-date proposals are due this Friday.

★ Note that only the first element in the hyphenated adjective *Up-to-date* is capitalized because it is the first word in a sentence, but it is not a proper adjective.

Capitalizing Names

Correct all errors in capitalization in each sentence.

1. My favorite Building is the empire state building in new york.
2. She earned a ph.d. degree from brandeis university.
3. We want a chinese counselor to work with the chinese orphans.
4. The panel is composed of a catholic priest, a jewish rabbi, and a protestant minister.
5. Did you see the picture of the indian, african-american, asian-american, and caucasian children in the nursery?
6. We take part in the parade on memorial day every year.
7. She is a linguist; she speaks spanish, italian, and german fluently.

Check your answers in Appendix F.

Summary

By mastering the use of capitalization in your writing, you will be able to place emphasis where it is needed. Readers will know where your sentences and quotations begin, which nouns are proper nouns, and which nouns are common nouns. The guidelines in this section will help you correctly capitalize salutations and complimentary closings and present the titles of persons and works in the correct form.

Follow the guidelines to ensure you use capitals correctly with proper nouns; commercial products; points of the compass; months, days, and holidays; seasons; nationalities, races, religions, and languages; deities; academic degrees; and hyphenated names and words. In addition, you will avoid overusing and misusing capitalization by following the guidelines in this chapter.

Refer to a dictionary if you have questions pertaining to capitalization use in a specific situation.

Discussion Questions

1. What guidelines pertain to capitalizing personal and professional titles and titles of written works?
2. What impact, if any, might capitalization errors in proper names have on the receiver of business correspondence?

Spelling and Word Usage Application

Note the correct spelling of the following words:

Indiana	Wednesday	sophomore	legitimate
bureau	conscientious	ninety	exaggerate
committee	February	itinerary	Missouri

Rewrite the following sentences, correcting all misspelled words.

1. The sophmore prom comittee is meeting in Febuary.
2. The buereau that matches your bedroom set will be delivered on Wedesday at 10 a.m.
3. The most consientious student in my Advanced Physics' class is Rosemarie Eto.
4. Did you exagerate when you said that ninty couples attended the reunion?
5. He wants to make alot of money in a legitemate business.
6. Our itinery includes Indiania, Missourri, and West Virgina.

If necessary, refer to Appendix A for the correct usage of the following words:

hoard/horde   medal/metal/meddle

Practical Applications

Part A

Correct errors in capitalization and insert external punctuation in the following sentences.

1. do you know that the Second annual office equipment association conference will meet in Oakland, california, the third week of April
2. The spiegel Catalog is worth every penny it costs
3. When you go to Washington, dc, visit the air and space museum and the national gallery of art
4. The national spelling bee champion was told, "you are a true scholar"
5. Some native floridians prefer Skiing in colorado to Surfing in miami

Part B

Correct errors in capitalization, word usage, and spelling in the following sentences:

1. Bob Clancy, a Colonel in the U.S. army, spend his leave suning on the beaches of hawaii.
2. We has reached our Maximum Potential with the new generic medicine available to high blood pressure patience.
3. Chrysler Automobiles are poplar with peoples of all age.
4. My uncle Harry willingness to rebuild the engine saved us quiet a bit of money.
5. Be sure to bought some irish linen and english bone china on you're trip abroad.

Part C

Correct all errors in capitalization, and insert all missing punctuation in the following sentences.

1. Although he is the Minister of the Church he is the best friend of many congregants.
2. When you visit the Free Library of oshkosh take out a copy of *adventures in the south pacific*
3. The phillies who were the 1993 national league Champions had many injuries in the 1994 season.
4. Some sights in california such as yosemite national park alcatraz and the hearst estate are worth seeing.
5. A tour of Washington, dc which included the lincoln memorial brought tears to the eyes of the tourists.

Editing and Proofreading Application

Eliminate errors in capitalization and spelling in the following letter and write a corrected copy.

Dear ms. MacFarland:

Your Name was recomended to me by your friends who are my aunt Miriam and uncle Theodore, residence of annapolis. When I mentioned that I needed infomation quickly about several Companies and Organizations to use in my economics 2 class and my ethics 1B class, they suggested that I write to you.

The Companies I'am interested in our international business machines, AT&T Corp., PECO energy, and potomac electric company. The Organizations include the wildlife foundation, united way, metropolitan opera guild, and unicef.

ms. MacFarland, would you or you're Assistant call me at my home in rockville or at my School, montgomery county high school. The number's are printed on the enclosed Business Card.

Because writting directly to the Companies and Organizations will take more time then we have availible, may I here from you by thursday or friday. Student's in my classes will profit from your help on there Spring Assignment.

Very Truly Yours,

xxx

Enclosure

Chapter 21

Number Expression

OBJECTIVES

After studying this chapter and completing the chapter activities, you will be able to do the following:

1. Use numbers correctly in business communications.
2. Follow the ten-and-under/eleven-and-over rule with the exceptions.
3. Express numbers correctly when beginning sentences and writing dates.
4. Express numbers correctly in addresses and with money.
5. Use the correct numerical form to express percentages, decimals, fractions, and time.
6. Express numbers correctly with weights and measures, distance, age, financial quotations, and governmental units.

WORD STYLE OR NUMERAL STYLE

Because numbers are used in most business communications, writers must present them accurately and clearly to the reader. In correspondence, writers commonly refer to quantities, dollar amounts, percentages, dates, addresses, time, invoice numbers, and similar items. In reports and proposals, tables, charts, and graphs frequently accompany statistics. In all situations, the writer must follow recommended guidelines to decide whether to use words or numerals to present the numbers to the reader.

Numbers generally are written in *word style* in more formal and literary communications. *Numeral style* generally is used for routine business and personal writing. A few situations, however, require words to represent numbers even when numeral style seems preferable. By heeding the guidelines presented in this chapter, writers will be able to avoid errors that may lead to embarrassment, time consumption, and lost money.

Errors in number expression costs companies billions of dollars each year and cost employees their jobs.

★ Word style means that certain numbers are written in words; certain others are written in numerals.

TEN-AND-UNDER/ELEVEN-AND-OVER RULE

Write quantities of ten and under in words. For example:

Mail *three* copies of the proposal to us.

We rented a *four*-bedroom house in the mountains.

Write quantities of eleven and over in numerals. For example:

Would you buy *25* yellow-lined writing tablets for them?

Charles received *16* inquiries the first day of the session.

One exception to the ten-and-under/eleven-and-over rule involves indefinite or approximate numbers. Use words to express these numbers in a sentence. For example:

Several *thousand* people attended the concert.

Around *thirty-five* students complained to the department head.

Use words for numbers in a sentence that includes two or more related numbers all ten and under. If the numbers are all eleven and over, use numerals. Note these examples:

Daniel has written *five* articles, *one* anthology, and *three* textbook chapters since 1993.

Please bring to the meeting *15* copies of the report, *20* copies of the names and addresses, and *25* copies of the newsletter.

When two or more related numbers are included in a sentence—some of which are ten and under and some of which are eleven and over—use numerals for all numbers. For example:

Our inventory list of paint shows *18* cans of white, *24* cans of eggshell, and *9* cans of light blue.

The child carried *2* books, *4* dolls, and *12* pieces of doll clothing to her grandmother's house.

★ The word *shorter* refers to the number of letters required to spell out the number.

Consecutive Numbers

When two related numbers appear next to each other in a sentence, write the shorter number in words and the other in numerals. For example:

Ms. Chan received *160 two*-inch samples.

Oscar brought *twelve 36*-inch pieces to the classroom.

Consecutive Unrelated Numbers

If two unrelated numbers appear next to each other in a sentence, separate them with a comma to avoid confusion. For example:

In *1994, 18* of the girls made the All-State Team.

On February *2, 25* sales representatives will be meeting at the Wynette Hotel.

On page *254, 16* authors of psychology articles are listed.

1

CHECKPOINT

Ten and Under/Eleven and Over

Select the correct number expression in each sentence.

1. Eva usually travels to New York (4/four) times a year.
2. We were told that (16/sixteen) applicants are being considered.
3. Approximately (200/two hundred) letters were sent out.
4. Order five sodas, eight cups of iced tea, and (9/nine) muffins.

(Continued on the next page)

5. A total of 12 marketing majors, 15 computer science majors, and (8/eight) accounting majors will be at the orientation.
6. Please bring (57/fifty-seven) twelve-foot boards to the site.
7. As many as (12/twelve) 25-year-old men are being tested.

Check your answers in Appendix F.

NUMBERS TO BEGIN SENTENCES

Use words to express a number at the beginning of a sentence. If a number is very long, rewrite the sentence. Note these examples:

> *Eighty-one* questionnaires were returned.

> A total of *5,243* employees applied for the new health-care benefit. (Avoid spelling out 5,243 at the beginning of a sentence because of the length of the number.)

EXTRA, EXTRA!

★ If a number, when spelled out, is more than two words, consider it to be very long (five thousand, three hundred and twenty-seven).

NUMBERS IN DATES

When the day follows the month, express the day in numerals. For example:

> Kim's presentation is *March 26*.

Use ordinals (*d* or *th*) with the day when the day precedes the month and when the month and the year are omitted. Write out ordinal (*first*) or use numerals (*1st*) if the month is omitted. Use numerals if the month is not omitted. Note these sentences:

> The *26th of March* is her graduation date.

> Your letter of the *26th* arrived today.

> Your letter of the *twenty-sixth* arrived today.

Write the year in numerals, but spell out the month. For example:

> **INCORRECT:** Let's meet at City Hall Annex on Aug. 3, 1996.

> **CORRECT:** Let's meet at City Hall Annex on August 3, 1996.

When writing formal invitations, spell out the year (Nineteen hundred ninety-five).

To avoid confusion in business correspondence, do not use a numeral to express the month. Residents of other countries may interpret 3/2/95 as February 3,

1996, using the second number as the month and the first number as the day. For example:

INCORRECT: 2/3/96

CORRECT: February 3, 1996

2 CHECKPOINT

To Begin Sentences and Express Dates

Select the correct number expression in each sentence.

1. (16/Sixteen) suggestions are being considered.
2. (50/Fifty) miles is a long distance to commute.
3. Antonia completed her chapter on (1/23/95/January 23, 1995).
4. Our next reunion will be in (1996/nineteen ninety-six).
5. Please mail your check by April (4/4th).
6. Your order of the (first/1st) will be mailed out today.
7. The (10/10th) of September is the deadline.

Check your answers in Appendix F.

NUMBERS IN ADDRESSES

In ordinary text, use numerals to express house and building numbers except for the number *one*. For example:

One East Grayson Place

6743 North Market Road

In envelope addresses, all numbers are written in figures. For example:

MR C JOHNSON

1 EAST GRAYSON PLACE

PHILADELPHIA PA 19052-1235

Follow the ten-and-under/eleven-and-over rule for numbered streets. Use words for streets numbered first through tenth and numerals with ordinals for streets numbered 11th and over. For example:

210 West *Fifth* Avenue

634 South *21st* Street

To avoid confusion, if a street name is written in numerals and a direction such as West or East does not separate the house number from the street name, insert a dash between them. For example:

123–19th Avenue

3032–120th Court

Use numerals for ZIP codes, post office box numbers, and room numbers. For example:

The medical offices are in *Suite 310* in the new building.

Send your payment to P.O. *Box 4750,* Dresher, PA 19125-3466.

NUMBERS WITH MONEY

Write sums of $1 or more in numerals preceded by a dollar sign ($). Eliminate decimals with even or round dollar amounts ($20, $1,500) unless other amounts with cents are in the same sentence ($15.35, $2,300.95). For example:

The baseball game program costs *$5.*

Our total expenses are *$5.00* for the program and *$3.50* for a soda and a snack. (Insert a decimal and zeros after *$5* for consistency within the sentence.)

For sums less than one dollar, use numerals followed by the word *cents.* For example:

The small tablet costs *75 cents.*

She bought a candy bar for *50 cents* and a pencil for *45 cents.*

In a series of amounts in the same sentence, use a consistent format. For example:

Be sure to budget *$17.00* for the textbook, *$3.50* for the pens and marker, and *$0.99* for the paper clips. (All amounts must use the same format.)

Write approximate amounts in words. For example:

A few *hundred dollars* should cover the cost of the trip.

Use a combination of words and numerals to express very large amounts of money ($1 billion). Here are some examples:

> They won a *$20 million* state lottery last Tuesday.

> The building is selling for over *$2 million.*

★ Repeat words like *billion* after each amount ("The project will cost either $3 billion or $4 billion.")

CHECKPOINT 3

Addresses and Money

Select the correct number expression in each sentence.

1. The sales meeting will take place in our (7th/Seventh) Avenue branch office.
2. On the island, I stayed at (One/1) Sunburst Place.
3. Kay and Victor are relocating to 33–(Seventy-fifth/75th) Street.
4. Mrs. Aguilar paid ($350.00/$350) for the 26-inch television set.
5. The decorative bow costs (($.89/89 cents) on sale.
6. If I had ($1,000,000/$1 million), I would share it with you.
7. Spend $2.25 for milk, $3.00 for fruit, and (25 cents/$.25) for the newspaper.

Check your answers in Appendix F.

NUMBERS WITH PERCENTAGES, DECIMALS, AND FRACTIONS

Use numerals followed by the word *percent* (not %) to express percentages. For example:

> The department store is offering a *40 percent* discount during the end-of-season sale.

Always express decimals in numerals. If no number is at the left of the decimal point, place a zero there unless a zero immediately follows the decimal point (.0457). A zero placed at the left of a decimal point prevents the reader from overlooking the decimal point. For example:

0.364   0.457   .064

Express simple fractions in words. For example:

> A *one-half*-inch length is more than adequate.

> We will need *three-quarters* of an hour to travel.

To indicate percent, use the symbol % in statistical writing (such as tables, graphs, and charts), not in business correspondence.

Express mixed numbers in either a fraction or a decimal unless they appear first in a sentence. Note these examples:

The job will take *2.5* hours to complete.

The corridor is *45 1/2* feet long.

Two and one-half pounds of coffee are enough for the group.

NUMBERS WITH TIME

Use numerals before *a.m.* and *p.m.*, but use words before *o'clock*. To express the time on the hour, omit the colon and two zeros before a.m. or p.m. For example:

One session begins at *9 a.m.*; the other begins at *1 p.m.*

A *ten o'clock* meeting could extend past noon.

If a sentence contains two references to time, one on the hour and the other not on the hour, then be consistent—use a colon and figures in both. For example:

One session begins at *9:00 a.m.*; the other begins at *1:30 p.m.*

Use words to express time on the hour without a.m., p.m., or o'clock. For example:

Dinner will be served at *eight*.

★ Use a.m. or p.m. with times on and off the hour (8 p.m. or 8:30 a.m.), but *use o'clock* only with times on the hour (eight o'clock).

4 Percentages, Decimals, Fractions, and Time

CHECKPOINT

Select the correct number expressions in each sentence.

1. Over (two-thirds/2/3) of the sales agents will attend the national sales meeting.
2. At (ten o'clock p.m./ten o'clock) my lights are out, and the telephone ringer is shut off.
3. The program will begin at (eleven-thirty o'clock/11:30) a.m.
4. (6 3/4/Six and three-quarter) pounds of chicken are ready for the barbecue.
5. Stipulate the decimal (.1532/0.1532) clearly in your letter.
6. Her schedule is free at 11:15 a.m. or (2 p.m./2:00 p.m.).
7. Tea at the British hotel will be served at (4/four).

Check your answers in Appendix F.

NUMBERS IN MISCELLANEOUS SITUATIONS

Use numerals to express *weights, measures,* and *distances.* Note these examples:

> The farm produced *150 bushels* per acre.

> The models are *6 feet tall* and weigh less than *130 pounds.*

> The closest seashore resort is *60 miles.*

Use words to express a distance that is a fraction of a mile. For example:

> The college is less than *one-half mile* from the station.

To express *age,* use numerals unless the age is approximate. For example:

> My grandparents are both *72 years old.*

> She is in her early *sixties* or late *fifties.*

To express *financial quotations,* use numerals (with fractions if applicable). You can use a hyphen between whole numbers and fractions to help readability. For example:

> The stock is selling at *53-5/8.*

★ Look for financial quotations in the business section of your daily newspaper.

Some utilities that were trading at *36-1/4* are down to *21-1/2.*

Use words to express numbers in *governmental units.* For example:

The candidate ran for office in the *Eleventh Ward.*

She served as a Representative in the *Ninety-First Congress.*

Miscellaneous Situations

Select the correct number expression in each sentence.

1. Travel (ten/10) miles south, and then look for the station.
2. The office is only (two-thirds/2/3) of a mile from my home.
3. Do you know that (20/twenty) yards and (20/twenty) meters are not the same?
4. The recipe calls for (one/1) teaspoon of minced onion.
5. My great aunt lived in the senior citizen home when she was in her (80s/eighties).
6. I remember when IBM stock was selling at (one hundred and thirty-five/135).
7. He hopes to represent the (23d/Twenty-third) Congressional District by this time next year.

Check your answers in Appendix F.

Numbers are used in all forms of business communications. Because numbers reflect quantities, dollar amounts, percentages, dates, addresses, time, invoice numbers, and so forth, they must be accurate and clear. Guidelines introduced in this chapter specify when to present numbers in numerals and when to present them in words.

Following the ten-and-under/eleven-and-over rule with its exceptions is generally an acceptable practice in business. In addition, improve your ability to write effective communications by paying particular attention to numbers beginning sentences; expressing dates and addresses; expressing money, percentages, decimals, fractions, and time; and providing weights, measures, distance, age, financial quotations, and governmental units.

Discussion Questions

1. Are the guidelines for numbers that begin sentences and numbers that express dates exceptions to the ten- and-under/eleven-and-over rule? Explain.
2. What are the guidelines for number expression in addresses and in money?

Spelling and Word Usage Application

Note the correct spelling of the following words:

accurately	correspondence	percentage	proposals
statistics	accompany	situation	numerals
equipment	beginning		

Rewrite the following sentences, correcting all misspelled words.

1. Take time to compute the percentige acuratly right from the begining.
2. Develop skill in writing business correspondance and business proposels.
3. The statistic's course that John took was very dificult for him.
4. A cover letter should acompany your resume when you apply for a job openning.
5. You may express a number in words or in nummerals, depending on the sitiation.
6. Sharing computer equiptment can be a hinderance if all party's want to use it at once.

If necessary, refer to Appendix A for the correct usage of the following words:

personal/personnel   taut/taught

Practical Applications

Part A

Identify errors in number expression and word usage in the following sentences, and write the corrected sentences on a sheet of paper.

1. Yesterday, they order four alternators and 8 snow tires.
2. Approximately 200 people responded at the help-wanted advertisement.
3. 11 of the athletes will sit on the bench or return to the minor leagues.
4. The Cromwell Company shipped 8 two-hundred-volt batteries tomorrow.
5. We still has 13 reams of letterhead paper, six large boxes of printed envelopes, and 15 reams of copy paper.

Part B

Identify errors in number expression, capitalization, and word usage in the following sentences. Write the corrected sentences on a sheet of paper.

1. In 1997 100 of are middle managers will work out of our indianapolis office.
2. Responds to this inquiry by september 12th to earn the 1% discount.
3. The new office at 1 East munroe street will accommodates our present staff.
4. The united states Navy have a budget of well over 7,000,000 dollars.
5. He said, "representative Baldwin of the Twenty 2nd Congressional district support this bill."

Part C
Select the correct number expressions in the following sentences

1. Sell your pharmaceutical stock when it goes to (63/sixty- three).
2. Henrietta's project is already (one-half/1/2) finished, and she has another week to work on it.
3. The Real Estate Fund increased its dividend by ($.75/75 cents).
4. The company received ($300.00/$300) for the used equipment.
5. The Texan's oil well produced (250/two hundred fifty) barrels per day.

Editing and Proofreading Application

Proofread and correct all errors in number expression, word usage, and spelling in the following message. Prepare a revised copy.

On Saturday the 10 of August, I visit your fashion consultant and ordered 2 pairs of jeans, three blouse's, 1 fall dress, and two professional outfits for work. She promised me that I would recieve the clothes from the distributor at September eighth. This is the 2nd time that a order have gone to a wrong address.

I live at 1 Oak Drive in Tarrytown. When the cloths finally arrive on the 18, I noticed that they had been sent to Ten Ox Drive in Tarrytown and then forwarded to me. In nineteen ninety-four, 11 items was ordered from the same consultant, and a mixup in my address occurred at that time. 2 errors in shipments is too many for me.

If you do not apologize by 10/1/95, you may have to cross my name of you're list of customers. Because it appears that my purchase of five hundred and thirty-five dollars is not important enough for you to get my address strait, I am thinking of going elsewhere to get the same two percent discount and recieve my clothes in 1/2 the number of days. Please consider my position in this matter and also help yourself by eliminating this one weakness in you operation.

Basics of Effective Writing

In today's business world, you need more than good job qualifications and a business wardrobe to be successful in many careers. You also need the ability to write compelling business communications. That ability can launch your career if your cover letter convinces a company to invite you for a job interview. When you get a job, you will probably need to write effectively to keep it because most jobs require writing to keep work flowing. Good writing skills almost always are a prerequisite for promotion.

The information in Part 4 will help you set sail on the seven Cs of powerful writing. You will learn to write business communications that are courteous, considerate, concise, clear, concrete, correct, and complete.

Chapter 22

Planning and Organizing Messages

OBJECTIVES

After studying this chapter and completing the chapter exercises, you will be able to do the following:

1. Plan messages by first identifying the objective of each message.
2. Determine the main idea of messages.
3. Choose supporting information in messages.
4. Adjust messages for the receiver and write considerate receiver-oriented messages.
5. Organize messages.

PLANNING MESSAGES

Have you ever sent a message that you wished you had not sent? Have you ever wished you had stated your ideas differently? If you have experienced an uneasy feeling about your written communications, the problem may be that you did not plan before you wrote. Planning a message involves four steps: (1) identify the objective, (2) determine the main idea, (3) choose supporting information, and (4) adjust the message for the receiver.

Identify the Objective

The **objective** is what you want to achieve through a message. The objective may be (1) to promote goodwill, (2) to inform, (3) to request, (4) to record, or (5) to persuade.

Every business message should promote goodwill. *Goodwill* is the expression of good wishes, warm feelings, and concern for the receiver. It contributes to the success of the company you work for and the stability of your job because it strengthens business relationships. Goodwill helps attract and keep customers and encourages good working relationships among company employees.

You can determine the objective of a message by asking yourself what you hope to accomplish with the communication. When a message tells a customer when a shipment of flea collars for cats will be delivered, it *informs*. When a message asks the prices of office furniture at a furniture outlet, it *requests*. When a message restates the time and place of a meeting that was agreed upon in a telephone conversation, it *records*. When a message is designed to sell a new kitchen appliance, it *persuades*. Figure 22–1 lists the objectives of a business message.

★ "To fail to plan is a plan to fail." (Author unknown) Be sure you plan your written business messages before you write them.

Bill Marriott, founder of Marriott Hotels, said the following about the value of goodwill: "We know that if we treat our employees correctly, they'll treat the customers right, and if the customers are treated right, they'll come back."

Objectives of a Business Message

1. Promote Goodwill
2. Inform
3. Request
4. Record
5. Persuade

Figure 22–1 Objectives of a business message

Identify the Objective of a Message

CHECKPOINT **1**

Identify the objective of messages that begin with the following sentences.

1. Bret's Gas 'N Go free calendars will be available on June 1.
2. We are out of the winter gray stock you ordered for your letterhead. We hope you will accept our popular, metallic mist, as a substitute.
3. Please send me your latest catalogue.
4. The following are highlights of the interview I conducted with Juan Rios.
5. Your report was very helpful, and we will call you when we need this service again.

Check your answers in Appendix F.

Determine the Main Idea

After determining the objective of a message, the next step is to identify the main idea. The **main idea** is the central theme or most important thought. In a message informing your customer about the delivery of flea collars for cats, the main idea is the time the delivery will arrive. In a request for furniture prices, the main idea is which pieces of furniture are being priced. The main idea of a record of a telephone conversation is the topic discussed. In a message to persuade receivers to buy a kitchen appliance, the main idea is the benefits they will receive.

EXTRA, EXTRA!

★ Johann Wolfgang Von Goethe believed that clear thinking creates clear, effective messages, stating the following: "If any man wishes to write in a clear style, let him first be clear in his thoughts."

Choose Supporting Information

Supporting information includes essential facts that explain, reinforce, or justify the main idea in terms receivers can understand and from which they can benefit. To select supporting information, answer these basic questions:

1. What does the receiver need to know about the main idea to respond to my message?
2. How will the message benefit the receiver?

For example, when you inform your supervisor that you will be absent from work next Wednesday, the supporting information could be:

1. The frequent headaches I have had lately might be caused by my glasses prescription.

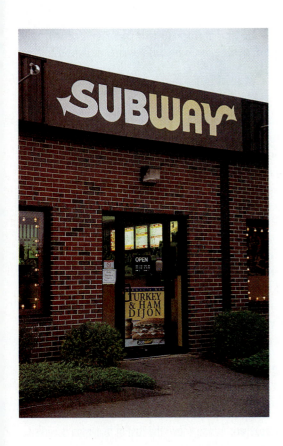

2. I had to make the appointment during work hours because my doctor does not have evening or weekend hours.

Make sure receivers have all the information they need to respond to your message. For example, if you are the purchasing agent for a fast food restaurant and write an order for employee uniforms, the objective of your message is to request, and the main idea is to order uniforms. Make sure you include essential supporting information so that the uniform supply company can send exactly what you want. Supporting information would include quantity, sizes, colors, style numbers, prices, and the address to which the shipment and the bill should be sent.

Adjust the Message for the Receiver

Practice empathy—put yourself in the place of the receiver—when adjusting the content of a message to your receiver. Through empathy, you can see the situation from the receiver's perspective and compose the message accordingly. When you adjust the content of your messages, you will write considerate, receiver-oriented messages.

Write Considerate Messages

Considerate messages address the receiver's level of interest, involvement, knowledge, or opinions regarding the subject. Writing considerate messages is the first of seven Cs of effective business communications described in Part 4 of this text. (The remaining six are courteous, correct, concise, concrete, complete, and clear.) Considerate messages use supporting information that receivers will benefit from, understand, and appreciate. A checklist for writing receiver-oriented messages is shown in Figure 22–2.

The following message is written in two ways to reach two different receivers. The first message is written to a small business manager who does not know about the subject of the message. The second message is written to an advertising executive who knows a great deal about the subject. The objective of both messages is to persuade. The main idea is to promote television advertising as the most effective and economical way to increase business.

Message to a business manager: Television advertising can increase your business substantially by reaching more prospective buyers more times and for fewer dollars per thousand viewers than any other advertising medium.

Message to an advertising executive: As you know, the cost of television advertising is justified on the basis of reach, frequency, and CPT.

Write Receiver-Oriented Messages

Another way to be considerate of your receivers is to address them directly. Use second-person pronouns *you* and *your* instead of first-person pronouns *I* or *we* as

Checklist for Writing Receiver-Oriented Messages

❑ 1. How much knowledge, experience, background, and education does the receiver have about the subject of your message?
❑ 2. What does the receiver need to know about the subject?
❑ 3. What opinions or attitudes might your receiver have about your subject?
❑ 4. How does the receiver feel about you, your department, your company, or your products?
❑ 5. How can your message benefit the receiver?

Figure 22-2 Checklist for writing receiver-oriented messages

the subject of your sentences. The following sentences show the differences between the writer-oriented approach and the receiver-oriented approach.

SENDER-ORIENTED	RECEIVER-ORIENTED
We made all employees eligible for profit-sharing this year.	You are part of our profit-sharing plan this year.
We will make up a schedule for you when you give us your vacation dates.	If you give us your preferred dates now, you can take your vacation when you wish.

Planning the Message for the Receiver

A. Choose the letter that corresponds to the main idea of each message.

1. As the bookkeeper for A-Jay Company, you must inform one of your customers, Z-Slats Company, that the 2 percent discount they deducted from their payment is not allowed.
    a. Thank you for your payment.
    b. You have been a steady customer.
    c. Unfortunately, a 2 percent discount cannot be deducted from your bill.
2. You send a cover letter with your resume in response to a newspaper advertisement for an entry-level sales position.
    a. I am sending you my resume to be considered for the sales position.
    b. I read your advertisement in the paper.
    c. I am qualified for the job.

B. Choose the letters that describes the essential supporting information for the main idea in each sentence.

1. Main Idea: Please consider me for the position of administrative assistant.
    a. My education and experience qualify me for the job.
    b. I have always liked hard work.
    c. My mother was an administrative assistant.
2. Main Idea: You are invited to a party for departmental staff.
    a. It will be great fun.
    b. The department head will be there.
    c. It will be held in the 4th floor conference room on Friday at 5 p.m.

(Continued on the next page)

C. Write the number of the message that is receiver-oriented.

1. Our company requires all employees to show their ID cards to the guard at the entrance of the building.
2. Have your ID card ready to show the guard at the entrance of the building, and you will be admitted quickly.

Check your answers in Appendix F.

ORGANIZING MESSAGES

After identifying the content of the message, the next step is to determine the order in which to present the information so that the message will achieve its objective. The order depends on how you expect the receiver to react (favorably or unfavorably) to the message. Most business messages are organized using direct, indirect, or direct-indirect order.

Direct Order

The **direct order** presents the main idea first and follows it with the supporting information. Favorable (good news) and neutral (routine) messages are organized in the direct order. Beginning with the good news enables the sender to establish a positive tone immediately. Routine messages also are organized in the direct order. The assumption is that the receiver will respond in a positive or neutral manner.

Main Idea	Enclosed are the brochures you requested on the educational version of WordMagic.
Supporting Information	WordMagic incorporates many of the desktop publishing features users have been requesting. For example, WordMagic will format columns that extend beyond a page and produce documents in different type sizes and fonts.
Goodwill Closing	Thank you for your interest.

Use the direct order to relate good news and routine messages.

Indirect Order

The **indirect order** presents the supporting information before the main idea. Unfavorable (bad news) messages and persuasive messages are organized using the indirect order. Receivers usually are disappointed by bad news messages or suspicious of persuasive messages; therefore, provide an explanation before presenting the main idea. In the following bad news message, the receiver is being told that the request for two computers cannot be filled by the manufacturer.

Neutral Beginning	Thank you for your order for two Fastwriter computers.
Supporting Information	Fastwriter is a manufacturing company only. Our products are sold directly through authorized dealers.
Main Idea	The authorized Fastwriter dealer in your area is Jewel's Business Equipment. That dealer will be able to provide you with excellent service and training support.
Goodwill Closing	We appreciate your interest. If you have any questions, please call Joe Miller at 555-1234.

Even though this message conveys a negative response, it is not unpleasant or insulting to the receiver. By first explaining why a sale cannot be made, the sender has prepared the receiver for the bad news. Therefore, the receiver probably will not lose his or her interest in buying the product.

Direct-Indirect Order

The **direct-indirect order** is used when the sender has both good news and bad news for the receiver. In these situations, present the good news first using the direct order. Second, follow the indirect order by providing the reasons for the bad news and then stating the bad news itself. The following example illustrates the direct-indirect order.

Good News Main Idea	The brochures and supporting information that you requested are enclosed. Fastwriter International, Inc., is pleased to provide this information for you.
Supporting Information	Because we are manufacturers only, we sell our products directly through authorized dealers. The Fastwriter dealer in your area is Jewel's Business Equipment. That dealer will be able to provide you with excellent service and training support.

Continued on next page.

Bad News **Main Idea**	We have forwarded your order for the two Fastwriter computers to Jewel's Business Equipment for fast processing.
Goodwill **Closing**	Thank you for your interest. If you have any questions, please call Joe Miller at 555-1234.

Use of the direct-indirect approach increases the chance that the receiver will understand the message and accept its outcome. Figure 22–3 indicates the different ways to organize a message.

Organizing Messages

DIRECT ORDER	INDIRECT ORDER	DIRECT-INDIRECT ORDER
1. Main Idea	1. Neutral Beginning	1. Good News Main Idea
2. Supporting Information	2. Supporting Information	2. Supporting Information for bad news
3. Goodwill Closing	3. Main Idea	3. Bad News Main Idea
	4. Goodwill Closing	4. Goodwill Closing

Figure 22–3 Organizing messages

3 CHECKPOINT *Organizing Messages*

Indicate whether each paragraph is organized in the direct or indirect order.

1. June and Debra have similar personalities. Both are willing to work long hours and in an industrious manner. Also, they are very organized.
2. A new building is needed. In the old building, the wood is deteriorating and will need to be replaced. The floors are rotten and cannot be refinished. In fact, fixing the existing structure will cost just over 30 percent more than building a new structure.
3. The president's duties include representing the company to the media, welcoming visiting dignitaries, working with the board of directors to develop policies and procedures, and so forth. The duties seem endless.
4. John always gets to work on time, and he is never late for an appointment. He is very punctual.

Check your answers in Appendix F.

All messages require planning and organization before they are written. Planning a message involves (1) identifying the objective of the message, (2) determining the main idea of the message, (3) choosing supporting information, and (4) adjusting the message to ensure it is considerate and receiver oriented. Every business message should promote goodwill. Additional objectives of messages are to inform, request, record, or persuade. Each message should have a main idea or central theme and contain information that supports the main idea. All ideas and information in a message should be presented in a receiver-oriented manner that emphasizes the benefits to the receiver. Messages can be organized in the direct, indirect, or direct-indirect order.

Discussion Questions

1. List five objectives a business message may have. Why is goodwill the objective of every business message?
2. How is the main idea different from the objective of a message?
3. List three ways to organize messages.

Practical Applications

Part A

Identify the objective of the message in each sentence.

1. My recommendation that the Accounting Department buy five ASTRO computers was approved at the planning meeting Thursday.
2. The new travel expense reimbursement policy requires approval of expenses before they are incurred.
3. Would you please send me the productivity charts for April?
4. I think you will like your desk chair. It is designed to relieve tension in the lower back.

Part B

Identify the sentence in each message that contains the main idea (MI), and identify the sentences that contain the supporting information (SI).

1. (a) My presentation will include slides; will a screen be available? (b) The title of my presentation will be "Surviving Office Politics." (c) Yes, I am available to speak at your meeting on the 23rd; thank you for the invitation.
2. (a) For each new item, please provide the release date, the packaging requirements, and the units available. (b) May I expect to receive this information within three weeks? (c) To coordinate our local advertising campaign with the release of the new cosmetic line, we will need additional information.
3. (a) I will be wearing a blue coat with a red carnation in the lapel, so you will know who I am. (b) I will be happy to pick you up at the Newark airport at 5:30 p.m. on December 16th.

Part C

Write two sentences to support each main idea with receiver-oriented information.

1. Congratulations! Company profits doubled last year.
2. Please hire me as your administrative assistant.

Part D
Arrange each group of thoughts in the direct order.

1. (a) In May I will graduate from Ultra University with my bachelor of science degree in Management Information Systems. (b) I read your advertisement in the local paper. (c) The two years I managed a computer department have helped me understand a manager's role and challenges. (d) I believe I would be an asset to your organization.

2. (a) Fill out the form and return Copy A to her by the next day. (b) Keep Copy B for your records. (c) Failure to fill out the form or to return Copy A to her could result in not being paid for the days of sick leave taken. (d) Michelle Hollis has the new forms for sick leave reimbursement. (e) She will give you a "Report of Sick Leave," Form 19634.

Part E
Arrange the following message in indirect order.

(1) Small businesses promise the most growth in creating jobs in the future. (2) When your company has been operating for at least six months and can show steady growth, please contact us again. (3) We regret that we cannot approve your loan at this time. (4) The Bank of Roanoke appreciates your interest in obtaining a small business loan for your new venture. (5) Our loan officers receive many requests for loans from small business owners, and we are glad to help them.

Editing and Proofreading Application

Edit and proofread the following message. Rewrite it in direct order.

> We also want to expand our operations to foriegn countries. At that time, we will beginning interviewing consultents. Hour firm is interested in hiring a managment consultant to help increase proffits through more efficeint operating policies. Send the information know later than too weeks from this date. Please send me information about your services and costs, and include a list of your clients. We are a privatly owned company with 200 employes.

Chapter 23

Choosing Words

OBJECTIVES

After studying this chapter and completing the chapter exercises, you will be able to do the following:

1. Write courteous messages.
2. Create a positive tone.
3. Choose bias-free language.
4. Write communications that have correct words.
5. Use the dictionary and thesaurus to write precise communications.

COURTEOUS WORDS

Courteous words are polite, considerate, positive, and bias-free. Courteous business communications address receivers by their proper titles, capture the receivers' attention, and encourage a positive response to your message.

Polite Words

Polite words show receivers that you appreciate them. The following sentences begin or end with words of appreciation for the receiver:

LESS THAN COURTEOUS	COURTEOUS
You inquired about . . .	Thank you for inquiring about . . .
Send me . . .	Please send me . . .
I know you are willing to . . .	Your willingness to . . . is appreciated.

Positive Words

As you learned in Chapter 22, the purpose of every business communication is to promote goodwill. Never just say "no" or express anger or other strong emotions in a business communication. Always keep a courteous, positive, and professional tone even when your message is negative. The statements below show how positive words make negative messages polite and businesslike:

NEGATIVE WORDS	POSITIVE WORDS
You cannot have a refund because you failed to bring a receipt.	You will receive a refund when you send the receipt.
I paid the bill two months ago, and you have not credited my account yet.	My records show that I paid my bill two months ago, but the credit has not appeared on my statement. Has a mistake been made?

Proper Titles

Show receivers respect by using their proper titles. The following guidelines will help you use titles correctly.

When to Use Titles

Use the titles *Mr.*, *Mrs.*, *Ms.*, or *Miss* before last names if the receivers have no professional title. If the receiver has a professional title such as *doctor*, *reverend*,

★ The word *courtesy*, derived from medieval French, originally meant befitting the court of a prince, graciously polite, or respectful.
—*The Oxford Dictionary of English Etymology*

professor, governor, superintendent, senator, representative, or *judge,* you can use the title abbreviations before the last name. Chapter 19 provides more information on titles and their abbreviations.

When to Use Last Names

Generally, use last names in the following cases:

1. When you have not met the receiver.
2. When you wish to show respect.
3. When the receiver is older than you.
4. When responding to a letter in which the sender used his or her title and/or last name.

When to Use First Names

Use first names in the following cases:

1. When you have met the receiver more than once and feel he or she would not be offended.
2. When the reader's age is about the same as or less than yours.
3. When the receiver has asked you to use his or her first name or has identified himself or herself to you by his or her first name previously in person, on the telephone, or in writing.

Many dictionaries and style manuals have a section on abbreviations that includes titles. Use these sections to be sure your title abbreviations are correct.

Bias-Free Words

Courteous business communications do not offend the receiver by showing biases and making the receiver feel singled out in a negative way. Biases to avoid in communications are those of gender, race, age, and disability.

Gender Bias

Men and women can be hired for any job for which they are qualified in today's workplace. Women are pilots, police officers, engineers, doctors, and lawyers. Men are nurses, secretaries, elementary school teachers, and the principal caretakers of small children. The words used for today's workers should be free of gender bias to reflect the genderless work force. Use neutral words like the ones listed below to identify employees:

GENDER-BIASED WORDS	NEUTRAL WORDS
actress, female vocalist	actor, vocalist

cleaning man/woman	cleaner
foreman	supervisor
office girls, businessman	office workers, businessperson
waiter/waitress, stewardess	server, flight attendant
salesman, policeman	salesperson, police officer
mankind, man-hour	people, working hours/staff hours
manmade, manpower	manufactured, synthetic, employees
executives and their wives	executives and their spouses
congressman	member of congress/congressperson

Neutral nouns need neutral pronouns. If you use a singular neutral noun, the pronoun will need to include both masculine and feminine forms to be neutral, such as *him or her* or *his or hers*. You can avoid using two pronouns by using a plural noun. Pronouns that represent plural nouns are neutral, such as *them* or *theirs*. The sentences below show how to eliminate double pronouns by using neutral nouns:

SINGULAR NOUN	PLURAL NOUN (NEUTRAL)
Each member of congress sat in his or her chair.	The members of congress sat in their chairs.
A doctor uses his or her expertise with every patient.	Doctors use their expertise with every patient.

Race and Age Bias

A simple way to avoid race and age (young and old) biases is to avoid mentioning race or age unless it is essential to your meaning. The following sentences show how to avoid race and age biases:

BIASED WORDS	NON-BIASED WORDS
We hired an African-American lawyer.	We hired a lawyer.
Have you met the little old man?	Have you met the man?

Disability Bias

Avoid disability bias by avoiding reference to a disabling condition. If you must mention the condition, use non-offensive words as shown in the following examples:

BIASED WORDS	NON-BIASED WORDS
afflicted with, suffering from,	has
crippled by defect, disease	condition

Courteous Words

Rewrite these sentences to make them courteous.

1. Bring me the report.
2. Ms. Jennifer Chang, Minister, will conduct the session.
3. The old Indian attorney was an expert trial lawyer.
4. The lady professor is afflicted by Lymes Disease.
5. Mankind thinks, therefore mankind worries.

Check your answers in Appendix F.

CORRECT WORDS

Correct words for business communications are precise, familiar, up-to-date, and concise. Correct messages have no errors in meaning or spelling. A dictionary and a thesaurus can help you write correct communications.

Precise Words

Precise words are exact and specific. They let you say exactly what you mean in specific, vivid, and informative language. For example, instead of using *concerned*, you might really mean *anxious*. Instead of using the word *store*, you can specify which store and write *Hatcher's Jewelry Store*. Instead of using the phrase *appropriate time*, use a phrase such as *within ten days* to show the precise time. The sentences below are more interesting and informative when rewritten in precise language:

Imprecise	He presented a *bad* report about the new *product*.
Precise	He presented an *inaccurate* report about the new *stove*.
Imprecise	Did you *send* the copy to Tom yesterday?
Precise	Did you *fax* the copy to Tom yesterday?
Imprecise	Sales have increased *substantially* this year.
Precise	Sales have increased *75 percent* this year.
Imprecise	Our new telephone system has *great* sound quality.
Precise	Our new telephone system has *clear* sound quality.

★ "The difference between the right word and the almost right word is the difference between lightning and the lightning bug."
—Mark Twain

Familiar Words

Skillful communicators select **familiar words** that their receivers use and understand. Receivers understand messages more easily if the language is familiar. Familiar words are substituted for unfamiliar words below:

UNFAMILIAR WORDS	FAMILIAR WORDS
ascertain	find out
cognizant	aware
endeavor	try
expedite	rush, speed up
facilitate	help

Up-to-Date Words

Use **up-to-date** words, and avoid using outdated words and phrases. A way to identify out-of-date expressions in your writing is to ask yourself, "Would I say this if I were talking with the receiver?" If the answer is no, then do not use the dated language in your writing. For example, if you acknowledge an inquiry from a customer, would you say, "As per your request"? No. You would probably say, "As you requested." The lists below include some outdated words and expressions and their up-to-date alternatives:

OUTDATED WORDS AND EXPRESSIONS	UPDATED WORDS AND EXPRESSIONS
acknowledge receipt of	received
enclosed please find	enclosed
at our earliest convenience	as soon as possible
in due course	eventually
in the event that	if
due to the fact that	because

Concise Words

Good business communications use **concise words**. **Concise** means brief, to the point, or short. Concise words, nonetheless, are comprehensive. To write concise messages, eliminate redundant expressions. **Redundant** expressions include excessive, unnecessary, repetitive words. The lists below include some redundant expressions to avoid and concise word replacements:

REDUNDANT EXPRESSIONS	CONCISE WORDS
free gift	gift
but nevertheless	but
consensus of opinion	consensus
end result	result
for the purpose of	to
in all probability	probably
whether or not	if
past history	history

Correct Words

Rewrite the following sentences, substituting precise, familiar, concise, or updated words for the words in italics.

1. Topek Motor Scooters get *good gas mileage*.
2. Please *ascertain* if Bill can reserve the hotel for our conference.
3. I do not know *whether or not* I will apply for that job.
4. *In the event that* we have to recall the product, compile a customer list.
5. Customers who place their orders by November 30 will receive a *free* gift.

Check your answers in Appendix F.

Dictionary

A **dictionary** is a book containing the words of a language, arranged in alphabetical order, with definitions. Most dictionaries contain other information about each word, such as spelling, pronunciation, word division, parts of speech, synonyms, and antonyms. Larger dictionaries contain additional information such as prefixes, suffixes, and word origins. A sample dictionary entry for the word *courtesy* is shown in Figure 23–1.

Spelling

The preferred spelling of a word appears first, followed by other acceptable spellings, if any. The spelling shows capitalization. Dictionaries also show the spelling of plural, verb, adverb, and adjective forms of a word.

Use the spelling function on your word-processing software to check the spelling of most words.

¹cour·te·sy \'kərt-ə-sē, *esp Brit* 'kȯrt-\ *n, pl* **-sies** [ME *corteisie,* fr. OF, fr. *corteis*] **1 a :** courteous behavior **b :** a courteous act or expression **2 a :** general allowance despite facts : INDULGENCE <hills called mountains by ~ only> **b :** consideration, cooperation, and generosity in providing; *also*: AGENCY, MEANS
²courtesy *adj* : granted, provided, or performed as a courtesy or by way of courtesy <made a ~ call on the ambassador>

Figure 23–1 Sample word entry from a dictionary

Electronic word division, or hyphenation, is available on most word-processing software programs. When using this feature, make sure the hyphenation follows accepted rules of word division found in a dictionary.

Pronunciation

Pronunciation is shown as a phonetic spelling. The most common pronunciation appears first, followed by any alternate pronunciations. Make sure you understand how to interpret pronunciation symbols. Because dictionaries can use different symbols, refer to the guides for pronunciation symbols in the front of the dictionary you are using.

Word Division

Word division is shown in the pronunciation. The dots between syllables in a word indicate places where the word can be divided when it does not fit on one line.

Parts of Speech

The part of speech is given before the definition and can help you use a word correctly.

Definitions

Definitions are listed in historical or most frequently used order. For example, a label of *Archaic* means a particular definition is used rarely in modern communication. A label of *Obsolete* means the particular definition is no longer used.

Synonyms

Synonyms are words that have the same meaning. Synonyms allow you to avoid using the same word repeatedly and add variety and interest to your writing.

Antonyms

Antonyms are words that have the opposite meaning. Using the correct antonym for a word can give contrast and depth to your writing.

Other Word Information

Other information on words includes the way a word is used in a sentence, its origin, prefixes and suffixes, antonyms, the word's specialized meaning in a particular field of knowledge, related words and their grammatical functions, idioms, and commonly used phrases in which the word appears. In addition, many good unabridged dictionaries contain special sections. These sections include signs and symbols used in different fields of knowledge, biographical data of famous people, geographical data about important places, and a handbook of style.

Types and Sizes of Dictionaries

Dictionaries are available in three types and sizes—pocket, abridged, and unabridged.

A **pocket dictionary** is the smallest dictionary. It is easy to carry but contains fewer words and less information than other types of dictionaries.

An **abridged dictionary** contains nearly as many words and some of the information found in unabridged dictionaries. It contains introductory pages that describe how to use a dictionary; gives the spelling, pronunciation, word division, parts of speech, definitions, synonyms of words; and contains special sections. It is the best dictionary for business writers.

An **unabridged dictionary** is the most complete and detailed dictionary. Usually printed in many volumes, it contains thousands of words as well as illustrations and graphics. This large dictionary is found most often in libraries and used for reference.

★ Check compound words in a dictionary. They can be written three ways—as one word (postmark), as two words (post office), or as hyphenated words (part-time).

An electronic thesaurus is available on most word-processing software programs.

Thesaurus

A **thesaurus** is a book of words that are classified by meaning. It contains synonyms and antonyms for every word. Using a thesaurus, you can find the precise word you need, avoid using any one word repeatedly, and substitute an abstract or obscure word with a concrete and vivid one. Excerpts from an entry for *courtesy from Roget's International Thesaurus*, 5th Edition, are shown in Figure 23–2.

504 COURTESY

NOUNS **1 courtesy,** courteousness, common courtesy, **politeness, civility,** graciousness, thoughtfulness, considerateness, tactfulness, respect, respectfulness
2 gallantry, gallantness, **chivalry,** mannerliness
VERBS **11 mind one's manners,** observe etiquette, extend courtesy, pay attention to, give one's best regards.
ADJS **14 courteous, polite, civil, gracious,** agreeable, affable, fair, thoughtful, considerate, tactful, respectful, mannerly, well-mannered, correct
ADVS **19 courteously, politely, civilly,** mannerly, gallantly, graciously, gracefully, obligingly, accommodatingly, respectfully

Figure 23–2 Excerpt from a thesaurus

CHECKPOINT 3

Dictionary and Thesaurus

Fill in the blanks.

1. A dictionary is a ———— containing the ———— of a language, arranged in ———————— order, with ———————— .
2. Definitions are listed in ———— or ————————————
   order.
3. The three types of dictionaries are ————————, ————————,
   and ———————— .
4. A thesaurus is a book of ———————— that are classified by
   ———————— .
5. A thesaurus contains ———————— and ———————— for every
   word.

Check your answers in Appendix F.

Summary

Effective business communications use courteous and correct words. Courteous words are polite and positive; they address receivers by their proper titles and show no biases. Correct words for business communications are precise, familiar, up-to-date, and concise. Careful business communicators use a dictionary to be sure the meaning and spelling of the words are correct. They use a thesaurus to find the precise word to convey their meaning.

Discussion Questions

1. Why are courteous words effective in business communications?
2. How do polite words affect your receiver?
3. What is the value of positive words in effective business communications?
4. Why should you use proper titles and bias-free words in communications?
5. What are two main ways a dictionary is used to make business communications correct?
6. Name five ways a thesaurus can help business communicators.
7. Name four types of words that are appropriate for business communications.
8. What are concise words?
9. What are redundant expressions?

Practical Applications

Part A

Write a courteous message for the following situation.

As an administrative assistant for a business publication, you are compiling statistics on salaries, positions, and benefits for men and women of all ages and with all types of disabilities in your city. Write a message to the vice president of the human resources department of a large publishing company to ask for these statistics. Make sure the message is polite and positive, is properly addressed, and is bias-free.

Part B

Write a correct message for the following situation.

You own a small bicycle shop. Recently, five customers have complained about the Speedo brand bicycles sold in your shop. The seats shifted positions and caused three customers to fall off their bikes and sustain minor injuries. Although you have tried to fix the seats, they still shift. As a service to your customers, you told them you would contact Speedo about the matter. Ask Speedo Company to refund your customers' money or to send them new bicycles with reliable seats. Write a message that uses precise, familiar, up-to-date, and concise words.

Editing and Proofreading Application

Part A
Edit and rewrite the following sentences to make them courteous.

1. I received your first report; when will you finish the second.
2. Maria Garcia, M.D., will address the staff on the effects of poor eating habits on job performance.
3. Foremen, office girls, and actresses may apply for jobs at the employment agency.
4. I want to introduce our new female supervisor, Helen McIntyre. She is 35 and Hispanic. She also has been in charge of a large personnel department for ten years.
5. Please leave the door to the access ramp unlocked so that people afflicted with motor disabilities or confined to a wheelchair can get in.

Part B
Edit and rewrite the following sentences, substituting precise, familiar, up-to-date, or concise words where needed.

1. The new microcomputer purchased for Sol's office cost a lot of money.
2. Our new time/motion study shows that collating, folding, and inserting 5,000 two-page letters manually takes a long time.
3. Much of the equipment in our satellite office is inoperative.
4. I would like to acknowledge receipt of your letter.
5. Tom is tired because he is very weary.

Creating Vigorous Sentences

OBJECTIVES

After studying this chapter and completing the chapter exercises, you will be able to do the following:

1. Write concise and concrete sentences.
2. Eliminate unnecessary sentence elements.
3. Use a conversational tone.
4. Clarify vague adjectives and adverbs.
5. Include important facts and sensory details.

Chapter 24

CONCISE SENTENCES

You learned in Chapter 23 that the word *concise* means brief, to the point, or short. A concise sentence is unified. **Sentence unity** occurs when the words in a sentence express one clear thought. Concise sentences are effective in business because they are emphatic and easy to remember. They can capture and hold the attention of receivers who are too busy to read long, complicated messages.

This first section describes two basic techniques to help you write concise, unified business sentences: (1) eliminate unnecessary elements and (2) use a conversational tone.

Eliminate Unnecessary Elements

Business communications are weakened by unnecessary sentence elements such as redundancies, empty and wordy phrases, needlessly long phrases and clauses, and irrelevant information. The following paragraphs show how to avoid using these unnecessary elements.

Eliminate Redundancies

In Chapter 23, you learned about some common redundant phrases that express the same idea twice. The following sentences illustrate how to make sentences concise by avoiding redundancies:

Wordy	During *the month of January,* our store, Jansens, will give a *full and complete refund* for *items returned to us.*
Concise	During January, Jansens will give full refunds for returned items.
Wordy	The *free gift* is *cash money.*
Concise	The gift is money.

Eliminate Empty and Wordy Phrases

"I believe," "in my opinion," "there is," "there are," and "here is" are examples of empty phrases that clutter sentences without adding meaning. These phrases are usually implied and do not need to be stated. The following sentences show how to make sentences concise by eliminating empty and wordy phrases:

Wordy	*In my opinion,* you should not compromise on document appearance.
Concise	You should not compromise on document appearance.
Wordy	*There are* several ways to solve the problem.
Concise	You can solve the problem in several ways.

A national business consulting firm recommends that sentences in business communications contain no more than 15 to 20 words.

★ Watch for redundant verbs such as *turn around, lunge forward,* and *speed ahead.* These verbs do not need modifiers.

Condense Words

Substitute a word for a phrase or clause or shorten a clause to a phrase when possible. The following examples show how to make sentences concise by condensing sentence elements:

Wordy	A suit jacket *that is completely lined* will keep its shape.
Concise	A lined suit jacket will keep its shape.
Wordy	When you present complex information, *you need to ask yourself if a graphic illustration would make it easier to understand your message.*
Concise	Graphic illustrations can clarify the presentation of complex information.

Eliminate Irrelevant Information

Irrelevant information is data that are not needed to understand a message. Concise sentences contain only information that clarifies the main idea. The following sentences show how to make sentences concise by eliminating irrelevant information:

Wordy	Your order #3452 *for 50 pairs of rollerblades in different sizes and colors for both men and women* will be sent *to you by the shipping department, which has been reorganized during the last month, sometime in the* next week.
Concise	Your order #3452 will be sent next week.
Wordy	I received your impressive resume for the position of office manager *that we advertised in many local newspapers for the last month* and would like you to come in for an interview.
Concise	I am impressed by your resume for the position of office manager and would like you to come in for an interview.

CHECKPOINT 1

Unnecessary Elements

Identify the unnecessary elements to eliminate in each sentence.

1. Overall, in my opinion, Ralph Rodriguez is by far the best qualified candidate for the job that is open.

(Continued on the next page)

Unnecessary Elements, Continued

2. The race car that was painted a nice blue was the preferred visual of the client for the ad.
3. The many helpful new office supplies you will need for work are in the supply cabinet at the end of the hall.
4. Let it be known that I believe the new yellow leather cafeteria chairs, which were recently reupholstered at great expense by the Save-A-Chair Company, that are in the cafeteria are very attractive.
5. The house that was built during the Victorian era was renovated for office space.

Check your answers in Appendix F.

Use a Conversational Tone

Sentences written in a conversational tone are written the way they would be spoken. Conversational sentences are concise because spoken sentences are usually to-the-point and simple. The following sections show how to make sentences conversational.

Use an Approach That is To-the-Point

When you speak to someone, you usually get to the point by beginning your sentences with the subject first, followed by the predicate, then the object. You usually do not relate a thought backwards by telling the end of each sentence first. The following examples show how to write direct sentences:

★ Take Mark Twain's advice and use conversational words. He said, "I never write *metropolis* for seven cents because I can get the same price for *city*. . . ."

Indirect	After eating breakfast, personnel who have been invited will convene at the site of the meeting in the board room at 9:30 a.m.
Direct	You are invited to have breakfast in the cafeteria before meeting in the board room.
Indirect	It is with pleasure that we advise you that your application for credit with The Bank of Money, Unlimited, has been granted by the credit committee with the proviso that a credit limit of $5,000 not be exceeded and that a low interest rate of 12 percent be paid on any monthly balance.
Direct	Your request for a $5,000 line of credit at our low 12-percent interest rate was approved.

Write Simple Sentences

Good business messages use **simple sentences** because they use a direct conversational tone to convey one idea and only the necessary information. A **simple sentence** contains one independent clause and can include phrases and compound subjects or verbs. The following sentences show how to change wordy sentences to simple, emphatic ones:

Wordy	The president of the company was jogging with some friends this morning and twisted an ankle on the driveway near her house.
Emphatic	The president of the company twisted her ankle this morning.
Wordy	Please send the order for a dozen toy fire trucks as soon as possible, and we can discuss the invoice for the Kung Fu dolls later.
Emphatic	Please send a dozen toy fire trucks as soon as possible.

Conversational Tone

Rewrite the following sentences to make them conversational.

1. For our employees, to reward their hard work, there will be an across-the-board 5-percent raise for everybody.
2. When writing the memo to copywriters on finding a name for the new dog food, Ms. Lewis asked for suggestions.
3. To order 30 pairs of red gloves for the Christmas season is the purpose of this letter.
4. You made errors in the correspondence.
5. Chien, the new sales manager, likes to play squash, riding unicycles, and he flies light airplanes.

Check your answers in Appendix F.

CONCRETE SENTENCES

Concrete words are specific and precise. They clarify the meaning of sentences and provide necessary information. Concrete words are especially effective in business writing. Research indicates that receivers understand concrete language more easily and remember it longer than they do broad, general words. The following sections describe how concrete language improves sentences.

Clarify Meaning

Concrete language clarifies the meaning of sentences by eliminating vague adjective and adverb modifiers.

Eliminate Vague Adjectives

Vague adjectives include words such as *many, better, bigger, some,* and *few.* The following examples show how to clarify sentences by replacing vague adjectives with specific and precise language:

Vague	This CD player is better than the other.
Clear	Mary's CD player is better than Jeff's because it has a non-skip feature.
Vague	The dog was a perfect companion for Jenny.
Clear	Fetchet, the Golden Retriever, was a gentle, loyal, and fun-loving companion for Jenny.

Use standard English for business communication. Standard English does not include jargon, buzzwords, legalese, foreign words, or slang.

Eliminate Vague Adverbs

Adverbs modify adjectives, verbs, or other adverbs. Words such as *clearly, perfectly, adequately, fast, later,* and *soonest* are vague adverbs. The following examples show how to use specific language to eliminate vague adverbs:

Vague	Will they be there soon?
Clear	Will they be at the hotel by 5 p.m.?
Vague	Jose and Harry addressed the envelope clearly.
Clear	Jose and Harry addressed the envelope to the attention of the department heads.

Include Necessary Information

Good writing is concise but does not leave out necessary facts and details. The following sections show how concrete language adds vital information to business messages.

Include Important Facts

When you order flowers for a client, you need to tell the florist more than, "Please send flowers to Jane Barlow." You must provide important information like the kind of flowers to send, the amount you wish to spend, the date you want the flowers to arrive, and the place where you want them sent. The following examples show how adding important facts improves sentences:

Incomplete	Please send pizzas to the news building.
Complete	Please send three onion pizzas to J. Smith, 3458 Main Street, Room 203.
Incomplete	Gerald will arrive on the 8:00 train.
Complete	Gerald will arrive at Grand Central Station on the 8 a.m. train from Cincinnati on Tuesday, May 15.

Add Sensory Details

Receivers become involved when language stimulates their five senses—seeing, smelling, touching, tasting, or hearing. Abstract words such as *honesty, truth, justice, utilization,* and *fabrication* do not involve receivers so they will understand

★ Travel writers use details to make their writing come alive for readers. One successful travel writer said not to write, "There is a funny guy outside the museum." She wrote instead, "We saw a man dressed in a tuxedo jacket and jeans singing on the doorstep of the Vatican Museum."

and remember your message. The following sentences show how to use sensory language:

Abstract	The beautification of the lobby has been completed.
Graphic	The lobby is decorated with two dozen wooden tubs of flowering pink and white azalea bushes.
Abstract	Who knows the truth about the car?
Graphic	Which mechanic at Al's Service Station knows what is causing the ticking sound in the engine of Aunt Pauline's pickup truck?

3 Concrete Sentences

CHECKPOINT

Specify how these sentences or the situations they describe could be made concrete.

1. Breakfast today is better than the one I had yesterday.
2. Tom clearly had the experience for the job.
3. The brownies in the cafeteria are great.
4. Please meet Mr. Rios tomorrow when he arrives on the sleeper.
5. Amy was a good employee for 15 years.

Check your answers in Appendix F.

Summary

The foundations of effective written business communication are concise and concrete sentences. Concise sentences are unified and contain no unnecessary sentence elements. They are businesslike, yet conversational, with words written in natural speaking order. Concrete sentences contain precise and specific language. They eliminate vague modifiers and include necessary information. Necessary information includes facts needed to understand the message fully. Concrete sentences also include sensory details to involve receivers by stimulating their five senses.

Discussion Questions

1. Define *concise* and describe four ways to create concise sentences.
2. Why are conversational sentences concise?
3. List two types of vague modifiers and discuss why they should not be included in business writing.
4. Define *concrete* as it relates to good writing. List two ways in which concrete language improves sentences.
5. Explain why including necessary information is important in business communications.
6. How do sensory details involve the receiver?

Practical Applications

Part A

Identify the unnecessary elements to eliminate in the sentences below. Write *OK* if a sentence is correct.

1. You, the recipient of this letter, are the lucky winner of the company raffle prize—a fun-filled, sun-drenched, two-week vacation in Hawaii in the Pacific Ocean.
2. The meeting was held in the fourth floor boardroom at 8 a.m., and the president discussed salary increases for all employees.
3. In my humble opinion, cash money is a greater incentive for increased worker productivity than added vacation time.
4. Business communicators who work in the nation's businesses cannot compete competitively without knowing how to operate a computer.
5. Employees who work for the company have been encouraged that they should take the allotted time of one hour for lunch and 15 minutes, a quarter of an hour, for morning and afternoon breaks.

Part B

Identify the vague modifiers in the following sentences. Write *OK* if a sentence is correct.

1. The human resources department is functioning better since the report.
2. Lowenstein, Inc., got the bid to supply the town for the next five years.
3. Maria's dry cleaning store has the lowest prices for shirts.
4. I am sending you the great report.
5. Please reserve 15 terrific rooms for our company representatives next month.

Editing and Proofreading Applications

Part A

Identify unnecessary elements and unclear language in the following sentences and rewrite them so they are concise and concrete.

1. By the way, it would be great if you could please come in Tuesday morning for an interview with me.
2. Allison and Joe were filing until they decided to take a much needed lunch break.
3. I am a young dentist who has recently leased a new compact car, and I need to hire your business consulting firm to help me organize my office and solve my scheduling problems.
4. The truckers who transport our line of office lamps must receive full and complete payment within, but not before, 30 days.
5. The company picnic was more fun this year.

Part B

Proofread the following sentences and correct misspellings, capitalization errors, and punctuation errors. Write *OK* if a sentence is correct.

1. employees must not use Company cars for family purposes?
2. Meat me in st. loois after the conference;
3. The qualifications for a department supervisor include five years' experience and a degree in business management.
4. 10 qualfied people apply four every opening in our advertising department.
5. you're order will be scent on thrusday, september 3.

Building Strong Paragraphs

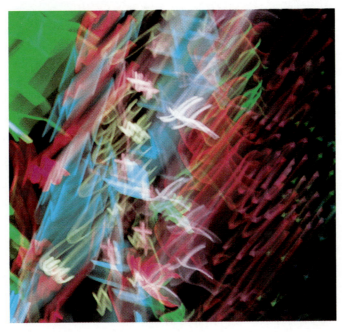

OBJECTIVES

After studying this chapter and completing the chapter exercises, you will be able to do the following:

1. Write complete and clear paragraphs and messages.
2. Describe the sentence structure of paragraphs and the paragraph structure of business messages.
3. Include the five Ws (*who, what, where, when,* and *why*) in paragraphs and messages.
4. Vary sentences and paragraphs.
5. Identify transitions that connect sentences and paragraphs.

COMPLETE PARAGRAPHS

Complete paragraphs create messages that are well structured and contain all the information necessary for the receiver to respond. The following sections will show you how to write complete paragraphs and messages.

Sentence Structure in a Paragraph

A **paragraph** is a group of one or more sentences that expresses one idea in a message. Each sentence in a paragraph should contain one thought that relates to and helps complete the main idea of the paragraph. A paragraph can be as short as one sentence, but most contain at least three. Most paragraphs include a beginning sentence, one or more middle sentences, and an ending sentence. The following sections describe the purpose of each type of sentence.

Beginning Sentence

The *beginning sentence* is the first sentence of a paragraph. Most paragraphs in good business writing begin with the topic sentence because it states the main idea of the paragraph and therefore gets to the point as quickly as possible.

Middle Sentences

The *middle sentences* develop the topic sentence or the main idea of the paragraph. These sentences provide your receiver with a description, an example, or other information to support the main idea of the paragraph.

Ending Sentence

The *ending sentence* brings the paragraph to a close. It is a short summary of the other sentences in the paragraph and sometimes restates the beginning sentence in a different way.

Paragraph Structure in Business Communications

A message can consist of only one paragraph, but most complete business messages have opening, developmental, and closing paragraphs.

Opening Paragraph

The first paragraph in a message is the *opening paragraph*. In business messages, the opening paragraph tells the receiver the subject of the communication. This paragraph should only have two to five typed lines.

Developmental Paragraphs

The middle paragraph(s) are called *developmental paragraphs*. They explain or give important information about the main idea of the message. Developmental paragraphs average four to eight lines. Developmental paragraphs can provide specific facts and details, reasons, steps or stages, or examples.

Specific Facts and Details. Developmental paragraphs can contain facts and details to provide information and prove a point. Suppose you are the administrative assistant to the director of admissions of a two-year career college. The director has asked you to answer a letter inquiring about business management courses at the college. The main idea of your opening paragraph states that your school has a wide selection of courses in business management. You can develop the main idea by presenting details about the types of courses your school offers and facts about the high percentage of graduates who have successful businesses management careers.

Reasons. Another type of developmental paragraph states reasons why something should be done or why something is the way it is. If your first paragraph states the need for a company to provide a gym for employees, your developmental paragraph could give reasons why you think the gym is a good idea. Your reasons might include the fact that healthier employees could lower company health insurance premiums.

Steps or Stages. When your main idea is to show the receiver how to do something, the steps or stages in the process can be explained in developmental paragraphs. If you are an accountant and you are going on vacation, you might leave your replacement a step-by-step list of what to do while you are away.

Examples. Developmental paragraphs also can provide examples of the main idea. Imagine that you have been asked to write a letter of recommendation for a friend who wants to attend a police academy. If you want to impress the admissions committee with your friend's bravery, use an example such as the time she saved a five-year-old boy from drowning.

Closing Paragraph

The *closing paragraph* ends a communication with a summation or reference to the main idea stated in the opening paragraph. The closing paragraph prevents a communication from ending abruptly and gives you an opportunity to thank the reader and make a hopeful statement or plan for the future. The closing paragraph should be as short as the opening paragraph. The following letter shows how the closing paragraph can refer to the opening paragraph:

★ "The paragraph (is) a mini-essay; it is also a maxi-sentence."

Dear Robert:

(First sentence of the opening paragraph) Your pressure-sensitive labels arrived from the mailing list companies today, and your catalogs will be mailed on October 13, as planned.

(First sentence of the closing paragraph) We are pleased to meet your deadline once again and hope we can serve you in the future.

★ Too many long-winded paragraphs? Make your page look better and emphasize key ideas by formatting an unwieldy paragraph that contains a series of items into a numbered list.

Necessary Information—Who, What, Where, When, and Why

Complete business messages often include the five Ws: *Who, what, where, when,* and *why.* A message that contains the five Ws can be as concise as the following sentence: *You are invited to a meeting in the conference room at 2 p.m. Tuesday, August 2, to discuss sales goals.* Many business messages require several paragraphs to answer the five Ws. However, some messages are complete without answering all five Ws. If your receiver does not need to know all five Ws, your message is complete by including only as many as needed. The five Ws are described as follows:

Who:	Subject of the communication, usually the receiver
What:	Purpose of the message
Where:	Location of the event or action
When:	Dates and times of the event or action
Why:	Reason for the communication

The following interoffice memorandum contains all five Ws:

TO:	All Employees
FROM:	Frank Lanford
DATE:	April 30, 19—
SUBJECT:	New Vice President

I am pleased to announce the appointment of Sonya Berkhart as Vice President of Computer Operations effective May 1. She served as Manager of computer systems at Wellco, Inc., for 15 years and was elected President of Computer Operations Executives this year. She graduated from Dillard School of Business. I am sure she will make a valuable contribution to our company.

The preceding memorandum answers the five Ws as follows:

Who:	All employees
What:	Appointment of Sonya Berkhart as Vice President
Where:	Computer Operations
When:	Effective May 1
Why:	She is qualified and will make a valuable contribution.

Variety

Complete messages contain a variety of sentences and paragraphs. Varying the length and types of sentences and paragraphs and sentence structure gives written messages a flow and rhythm that hold the receiver's attention.

Length

You learned in Chapter 24 that the best paragraphs and sentences for business messages are short. While this is true, if every sentence in a paragraph and every paragraph in a written message is the same length, the message becomes choppy and uninteresting. The following sections provide guidelines for varying the length of sentences and paragraphs.

Sentence Length. Vary sentence length within paragraphs. In Chapter 24, you learned that most sentences in business communications should have less than 20 words. Try mixing 10-word sentences with sentences of 15 to 20 words. Sentences should average around 15 or 16 words.

Paragraph Length. Vary paragraph length within business messages. Make introductory and closing paragraphs shorter than developmental paragraphs. Paragraphs in business messages should range from six to eight lines. Vary paragraphs of two or three lines with paragraphs of six to eight lines.

Sentence Structure and Type

For most business messages, the most effective sentence structure is simple; and the best type of sentence is a statement—a sentence that states a fact or an idea. However, varying sentence structures and types makes messages more interesting, epecially if messages are three paragraphs or longer. The following sections describe other sentence structures and types.

Structures. Mix a few compound, complex, and compound-complex sentence structures with simple sentences. A **compound sentence** contains two or more related independent clauses. In the following compound sentence, the subject and verb of each independent clause is italicized:

> The ergonomic *chair was* expensive, but *it provides* good back support.

A **complex sentence** contains one independent clause and one or more dependent clauses. The dependent clause in the following sentence is italicized:

> Your home is probably the largest purchase *that you will ever make.*

A **compound-complex sentence** contains two or more independent clauses and at least one dependent clause. The dependent clauses are italicized in the following sentence:

> The opera season gets under way this month *when the National Opera Company performs,* and I plan to buy season tickets.

Types. Pepper the statements in your business messages with other types of sentences, such as questions, exclamations, commands, or requests. You can also vary the way sentences begin. Instead of always placing the subject

After you write a business communication, review it as though it were a picture with various shapes of blocks. Is it attractive? Are the paragraph shapes varied and interesting? If not, break up some longer paragraphs or combine short ones where possible.

first, sometimes begin with a prepositional or infinitive phrase. The following are examples of sentence types:

Statement:	Thousands of secretaries use computers.
Question:	Do the phones in your office work?
Exclamation:	Congratulations on your promotion!
Command/Request:	Leave the report on my desk by 3 p.m.

Complete Paragraphs

CHECKPOINT 1

Indicate if each sentence is true or false.

1. A complete paragraph expresses many ideas.
2. Most complete paragraphs have beginning, middle, and ending sentences.
3. There are five types of developmental paragraphs.
4. One sentence can contain all five Ws.
5. Varying sentence length and structure and varying paragraph length and type add interest to messages.

Check your answers in Appendix F.

CLEAR PARAGRAPHS

Clear paragraphs create messages that communicate quickly without confusion. Clear paragraphs have unity, coherent sentence arrangement, and transitions that firmly connect sentences and paragraphs.

Unity

You learned in Chapter 24 that a sentence has unity when the words in the sentence express one clear thought. **Paragraph unity** occurs when sentences in a paragraph express one clear idea. Paragraphs express one idea when they contain sentences that provide necessary information in a coherent arrangement.

Coherence

In a **coherent paragraph**, sentences are arranged in a logical order that allows thoughts to flow smoothly. Two types of sentence arrangements are effective for paragraphs in business messages: direct paragraphs and indirect paragraphs. The basic difference between these arrangements is the position of the topic sentence.

Direct Paragraph

A **direct paragraph** begins with the topic sentence. Direct paragraphs are used frequently in business communications because they get to the point quickly. The topic sentence is italicized in the following direct paragraph:

> *We continue to make changes to our new store prototypes.* Last year, we tested a new layout in which we rearranged certain product categories within the store. This arrangement enhanced our merchandise presentation and eased customer shopping. We expect to use this new prototype in the future.

Indirect Paragraph

The topic sentence can appear in the middle or at the end of an **indirect paragraph**. Indirect paragraphs can be used as developmental paragraphs, but direct paragraphs generally are best for business communications. The topic sentence is italicized in the following example of an indirect paragraph:

> Tire rims, handle bars, loose spokes, bells, wire baskets, and seats were scattered all over the floor. New tires and chains were hanging from nails on the walls. We spent all day cleaning it up. *The bicycle shop was a mess.*

Transitions

A **transition** is a word or phrase that connects sentences in paragraphs and connects paragraphs in messages. Transitions clarify paragraphs and messages by emphasizing the relationships between sentences and paragraphs. Transitions let the reader move easily from one sentence to the next and from one paragraph to another without misunderstanding the message or losing the main ideas. The four types of transitions include (1) repeating key words or ideas, (2) using pronouns, (3) using transitional words and phrases, and (4) using parallel structure.

Key Words or Ideas

Repeating key words or ideas from a preceding sentence in the same paragraph or repeating the last sentence of the previous paragraph reinforces an idea and leads the reader from sentence to sentence or paragraph to paragraph without confusion. The following sentences show how repeating key words can clarify ideas:

★ James Joyce produced a 14-page paragraph in *Ulysses;* John Barth ends *The End of the Road* with a one-word paragraph: "Terminal."

The company experienced *sales growth* for the last three years. *This growth* is caused by the company's 136 new stores.

Pronouns

Pronouns that refer to key words in the previous sentence make effective transitions. Use a pronoun as an adjective to modify its antecedent. The following sentences show how to use pronouns as transitions:

The school library recently started a computer service with 30 software programs. *This new service* can be used by every student.

Transitional Words and Phrases

Transitional words and phrases are an effective and commonly used device to connect sentences and paragraphs. They also show the relationship between sentences and paragraphs. Figure 25–1 contains a list of transitional words and the types of relationships they reinforce.

RELATIONSHIP	WORD OR PHRASE
Contrast	but
	however
	in contrast
	in spite of
	on the contrary
	on the other hand
	nevertheless
Cause-Result	because of
	consequently
	for this reason
	hence
	therefore
	thus
Explanation	also
	for example
	for instance
	to illustrate
	too

(Continued on the next page)

Figure 25–1 Transitional words and phrases

RELATIONSHIP	WORD OR PHRASE
Likeness	in a like manner
	likewise
	similarly
Listing	besides
	first, second, third, etc.
	in addition
	moreover
Time	since
	finally
	first, second, third, . . . last

Figure 25–1 Transitional Words and Phrases - *continued*

Parallel Structure

Parallel structure can be used to connect sentences and paragraphs and to emphasize important ideas. The following paragraph is an example of parallel structure:

> *The lawyers asked to see* the company's tax returns. *They asked to see* the company's stock portfolio. *They even asked to see* the architect's plans for the new office building.

2 CHECKPOINT

Clear Paragraphs

Indicate the type of developmental paragraph and identify the types of transitions connecting and within the numbered sentences.

We start by respecting our people and their contributions. (1) This, our most fundamental value, is reflected in the growth of our variable compensation and recognition programs. (2) Since 1992, we have introduced seven new programs, and annual awards have grown from $2.5 to more than $10 million.

Check your answers in Appendix F.

Summary

Effective business communications depend on complete and clear paragraphs. Most complete paragraphs in business messages contain a beginning sentence, middle sentences, and an ending sentence and answer the five Ws—*who, what, where, when,* and *why.* The five Ws can be answered in introductory, developmental, and closing paragraphs. Complete messages contain sentences and paragraphs that have a variety of lengths and sentences of different structures and types. Clear paragraphs have unity and contain coherent sentences arranged in direct or indirect order. Clear messages contain sentences and paragraphs that are connected by transitions that reinforce their relationships.

Discussion Questions

1. Describe the characteristics of a complete business message.
2. How are clear messages created?
3. List the five Ws.
4. List the four types of sentence and paragraph transitions.

Practical Applications

Part A

Arrange the following sentences to create a direct-order paragraph with opening, middle, and ending sentences.

1. An associates degree in horticulture from City University and three workshops taken at Western College in flower arrangement helped to prepare me for this position.
2. Please consider me for the position of Director of Floral Arrangement at your nursery.
3. Also, I have been director of floral arrangement at Pine Front Nurseries for the last five years.
4. As my resume shows, my educational background and professional experience fit your job description.
5. I believe I can make a significant contribution to your nursery and look forward to hearing from you.

Part B

Identify which sentence contains all five Ws.

1. Please attend the expansion planning meeting in the board room on the third floor at 3 p.m., Thursday, October 8.
2. Our new president will address all employees on Tuesday.
3. Send copies of your reports to the advertising staff.
4. The Personnel Department will be closed.
5. Representatives from our London office will visit.

Part C

Identify the type of paragraph—opening, developmental, or closing—each sentence represents.

1. Again, thank you for your interest in our company.
2. Our advertising team made the decision based on the results of consumer research that included direct mail questionnaires, telephone interviews, and focus groups.
3. I have enclosed a check for $1,150 for the flowers.

Part D

Indicate the type of developmental paragraph that could contain each of the following sentences.

1. Sixty percent of our graduates started their own businesses; over half of these graduates used the business incubator on campus.
2. He directed the sales team that sold more than $3 million last year.
3. We cannot process your order because the items are temporarily out of stock.
4. To get to the personnel office, use the side entrance of Building 8, and take the elevator to the 2nd floor to Room 210.

Part E

Indicate the correct order of the following sentences to form a complete three-sentence paragraph.

1. These annual sales meetings stimulate our sales representatives to attain greater sales every year.
2. You are invited to attend our annual sales meeting on June 18 at the conference center at 9 a.m.
3. I look forward to seeing you there.

Part F

Write a sentence in each of the four structures—simple, compound, complex, and compound-complex.

Part G

Write a message that has at least three paragraphs. Your message should contain an opening, a middle, and a closing paragraph. Each paragraph should contain a beginning, a middle, and an ending sentence. Vary the structure, type, and length of the sentences. Vary the length and sentence arrangement of the paragraphs. Include the five Ws, if necessary.

Part H

Write a paragraph on a topic that interests you. Use three types of transitions. Underline each transition and indicate the relationship it describes. Figure 25-1 may help you.

Editing and Proofreading Applications

Part A

Rewrite the following paragraph so that it has sentence variety and effective transitions.

COMMUNICATION ACTIVITIES

Electronically prepared letters are becoming more common in today's society. Electronically prepared communications are an expected part of today's society. A major challenge for communicators will be to make these electronically prepared communications successful. They can make them effective by using the same skills as those needed for preparing communications in the traditional manner.

Part B

Indicate the missing information in the following sentences.

1. Please reserve a room on Friday.
2. Return your registration early to receive a $50 discount.
3. Send the shipment to Fitness, Little Rock, AR.
4. Please reserve a large meeting room for the conference.
5. Please send me a pair of Comfort shoes, No. R106, in white.

Editing and Proofreading Messages

OBJECTIVES

After studying this chapter and completing the chapter exercises you will be able to do the following:

1. Edit writing to ensure it incorporates the seven Cs of effective business writing.
2. Edit and revise on a word processor or a computer.
3. Proofread for content and mechanical errors.
4. Use different methods of proofreading.
5. Use proofreader's marks.

EDITING

Editing is the process of reviewing and revising a piece of writing to improve it. When editing messages, review and revise to incorporate the seven Cs of effective business writing (considerate, courteous, correct, concise, concrete, complete, and clear). Editing is so important to good writing that you should spend at least half of your writing time on the editing process. Review the seven Cs of effective writing in Figure 26–1 and ensure you include them in your writing.

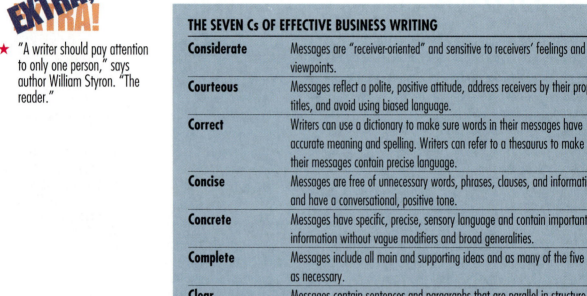

THE SEVEN Cs OF EFFECTIVE BUSINESS WRITING

Considerate	Messages are "receiver-oriented" and sensitive to receivers' feelings and viewpoints.
Courteous	Messages reflect a polite, positive attitude, address receivers by their proper titles, and avoid using biased language.
Correct	Writers can use a dictionary to make sure words in their messages have accurate meaning and spelling. Writers can refer to a thesaurus to make sure their messages contain precise language.
Concise	Messages are free of unnecessary words, phrases, clauses, and information and have a conversational, positive tone.
Concrete	Messages have specific, precise, sensory language and contain important information without vague modifiers and broad generalities.
Complete	Messages include all main and supporting ideas and as many of the five Ws as necessary.
Clear	Messages contain sentences and paragraphs that are parallel in structure and connected logically with key words, pronouns, and transitional words and phrases.

Figure 26–1 Revise all business communications to include the seven Cs of effective business writing.

1 CHECKPOINT

Editing Communications

Edit and revise the following sentences to reflect the seven Cs of effective business communication.

1. I welcome you as a new staffer and give you the pass to the cafeteria, which I highly recommend for lunch.

(Continued on the next page)

2. The movers will move some of your office equipment tomorrow afternoon.
3. Please have Mrs. Lewis, reverend of our church, speak at the dinner.
4. Meet my train.
5. As you know, according to the rules stated in the company handbook, all people who are not employed by the company must have a visitor's pass to get into the building.

Check your answers in Appendix F.

REVISING

After messages have been edited, they must be revised to incorporate the edits. Revisions can be performed more quickly through the use of a word processor or word-processing software on a computer.

The Process of Revising

Revise means to change or modify. When you revise a communication, you review and rewrite it to improve it or bring it up to date. Good writing often requires more than one revision. After revising your first draft, determine if additional editing could improve it. Repeat this process until you feel your message is as clear and complete as possible. If your communication has two or more pages, put it away for several hours or until the next day. Spending time away from your writing allows you to view it more critically later.

Revising on a Word Processor or a Computer

Most business messages need to be written, edited, proofread, and sent to receivers quickly. Using a word processor or computer to write and edit allows business writers to produce edited messages quickly. Word-processing software programs can help you revise business messages in many ways, as described in the paragraphs below.

Insert Text

The insert text function allows you to add material without rekeying an entire document. When words are inserted, the lines adjust automatically to include them.

To avoid confusing the draft copy of a document with the final copy, label every page of the draft copy with the word *DRAFT*. If you are using a word processor or a computer, you can create a header or a footer that will print the word *DRAFT* automatically.

Delete Text

The delete text function lets you remove portions of text and keep other parts. Some word-processing software will store deleted text in temporary memory for future use. If your software program does not have temporary memory, you will have to rekey deleted material if you want to use it again.

Move Text

The move text function lets you select a portion of text and move it to another part of a document. Moving text allows you to experiment with different organizations without rekeying the entire document. You can save versions of the text under separate filenames, print the versions, and compare them in hard copy.

Revise Words

A thesaurus software program can help you sharpen your writing skills by helping you choose precise or concise words to replace nondescriptive or lengthy words. When you select the thesaurus feature, a list of words appears. These words are similar to or are synonyms for the word you want to replace. The word you select replaces the current word automatically.

Revise from Hard Copy

Word processors or computers allow you to edit and print a revision of text in double spacing to make editing easier. You can make additional edits on a clean hard copy, make corrections on the word processor or computer, and print an updated copy.

CHECKPOINT 2

Revising on a Word Processor or a Computer

Choose the correct answer from the column on the right and write it in the space provided.

_____ 1. Revise text	a. Print double-spaced versions
_____ 2. Revise words	b. Add material without rekeying
_____ 3. Insert text	c. Eliminate part of text
_____ 4. Move text	d. Try different organizations
_____ 5. Delete text	e. Use thesaurus software
_____ 6. Revise from hard copy	f. Change or modify text

Check your answers in Appendix F.

PROOFREADING

Proofreading is the process of reviewing and correcting the final draft of a communication. It is the last step and one of the most important stages of editing because errors in business communications give a bad impression of the writer and his or her company. Errors can cause confusion and loss of time and money. The following paragraphs discuss proofreading for common errors, using proofreading methods, performing proofreading functions on a word processor, and using proofreading marks.

Proofreading Checklist—Common Errors

Two types of errors to look for when proofreading are general content errors and mechanical errors. An efficient way to find these errors is to proofread a communication twice—once for each type of error.

General Content Errors

Begin proofreading for general content errors such as missing information, missing words, and number and name errors. The following examples are common general content errors:

1. One small word substituted for another. For example:

Error:	*You* order is in the mail.
Correction:	*Your* order is in the mail.

2. One or more missing, repeated, or additional words. For example:

Error:	You will be reimbursed for *travel and travel expenses.*
Correction:	You will be reimbursed for *travel and entertainment expenses.*

3. Transposed words. For example:

Error:	The meeting *held is* in room 312.
Correction:	The meeting *is held* in room 312.

4. Incorrect proper name. For example:

Error:	Helen *Reid,* founder of Reed Ltd. . .
Correction:	Helen *Reed,* founder of Reed Ltd. . .

5. Incorrect use of homonyms. For example:

Error:	It was a golden *error.*
Correction:	It was a golden *era.*

★ Take a look now at the proofreader's marks shown in Appendix D. Practice using them the next time you edit one of your drafts for a letter or a report.

The most common errors found when proofreading are (1) word/letter omission or addition, (2) transposed letters or numbers, and (3) misspelling.

6. Revisions made on previous drafts that have not been incorporated into the final draft.

7. Errors in headings and footnotes. For example:

Error:	Eric Walsh	*?2-*	*Septembre 3, 19—*
Correction:	Eric Walsh	*-2-*	*September 3, 19—*

8. Errors near the beginnings and ends of lines. For example:

Error:	Have you made reservations for the *confrence*?
Correction:	Have you made reservations for the *conference*?

Mechanical Errors

Proofread the second time for mechanical errors such as incorrect spelling, punctuation, grammar, and format. The following examples are common mechanical errors:

1. Incorrect paragraph indentions, uneven margins, or off-center items.
2. Missing letter parts such as the date, a line of an address, an enclosure notation, or a copy notation.
3. Salutation and address that do not match.
4. Page numbers or numbered items that are not consecutive.
5. Additional letters in a word such as *occassional* for *occasional*.
6. Transposed letters in a word such as *storng* for *strong*.
7. Transposed digits in a number such as *1,203* for *1,230*.
8. Incorrect punctuation, capitalization, or spelling.
9. Incorrect word division.
10. One line of a paragraph left at the end of a page or at the beginning of the next page.

★ Most mechanical errors are found in (1) additional occurrences of a misspelled word, (2) long words, (3) capitalized words such as names of people or places, (4) numbers, and (5) material that has been revised.

EXTRA, EXTRA!

CHECKPOINT 3

Proofreading Checklist

Proofread and correct the general content and mechanical errors in each sentence.

1. The key to the supply cabinet if in the desk drawer.
2. dr. Helen Wong will introduce the the speaker.
3. New salery levels be will announced
4. The latest model truck has improved breaks.
5. Proper busniess dress is required.

Check your answers in Appendix F.

Proofreading Methods

The following list describes seven of the most effective proofreading methods:

1. *Scroll the screen.* Move the cursor down the screen on the word processor or computer, and proofread each line. You also can move a piece of paper down the screen and proofread each line above the edge of the paper. These methods allow you to make changes before you print.

2. *Read aloud.* Read each word aloud or say it quietly to yourself. Reading forces you to slow down and examine words more carefully. When you hear the words, omissions and word substitutes become more obvious.

3. *Compare drafts.* Check the final copy against the edited copy. This method safeguards against omitting edits on the final draft. Lay a ruler across both copies to ensure you do not skip lines.

4. *Proofread the printed page.* Always proofread the printed copy, even after you have proofread the document or message on the screen. By reviewing the printed copy, you may discover overlooked errors or reveal hidden codes that changed the desired format when the document was printed.

5. *Follow the paper bail.* If you are producing a document on a typewriter, roll the paper back so that the first line is just above the paper bail. Proofread one line at a time. Because the paper is still in the typewriter, it stays in alignment, making corrections easier.

★ A good proofreading environment includes adequate nonglare lighting; a quiet, clear, and clean workspace; and a comfortable chair.

6. *Proofread backwards.* Proofread from right to left. This method works best for detecting spelling or typographical errors.
7. *Use two proofreaders.* This proofreading method is the most effective and should be used for very important documents. One proofreader reads aloud from the edited copy while the other checks the final copy. The reader spells out proper names and numbers.

Proofreading on a Word Processor or a Computer

Word-processing software programs allow you to perform many proofreading functions. These programs include spelling functions, search-and-replace functions, and text-analysis functions.

Spelling Functions

The spelling function compares words in a document against words stored in the software program's dictionary. If a word such as a proper name or a technical term is not in the dictionary, the spelling function gives you several options: keep the word, delete it, or change it. The spelling function only checks spelling. It will not identify a word spelled correctly but used incorrectly such as *there* for *their.*

Search-and-Replace Function

The search function allows you to identify a character or string of characters such as a word, words, punctuation, or formatting codes in text and view it every time it appears. The replace function can change items identified during a search. For example, if you have capitalized the word *South* throughout your document and want to make the first letter lowercase, use the search-and-replace function to replace *South* with *south* automatically throughout the document.

Text-Analysis Function

Text-analysis programs also are called *grammar and style checkers.* They are designed to identify patterns in writing style and readability. They provide a file of comments and suggestions for improvement on the following elements in a document:

1. punctuation errors
2. average number of words in each sentence
3. wordy or vague sentences
4. sentence fragments
5. use of jargon
6. passive voice constructions
7. repetitive use of particular words or phrases
8. reading grade level
9. number of long and short words in each sentence
10. subject-verb disagreement

★ The tools of proofreading include a current dictionary, a style manual, a ruler, pens, pencils, erasers, and a list of proofreading symbols.

Proofreading on a Word Processor or a Computer

Identify the proofreading function described in each sentence. Write *SF* for spelling function, *SRF* for search-and-replace function, and *TAF* for text-analysis function in the space provided.

_____1. Allows writers to view specific words in a document and replace them.
_____2. Corrects the spelling of words.
_____3. Calculates the reading grade level of a document.
_____4. Identifies subject-verb disagreement in a document.
_____5. Locates passive voice constructions in a document.

Check your answers in Appendix F.

Proofreaders' Marks

Proofreaders' marks are an editor's shorthand. They are symbols that can be written and read quickly and that use very little space on a page. You will need to be able to write and read proofreaders' marks when you edit or revise business communications. Remember to use the proofreaders' marks shown in Appendix D.

6 Using Proofreaders' Marks

Find the errors in each sentence and use the appropriate proofreaders' mark to show what changes to make.

1. he memo has ben sent.

2. The meeting will held be in the board.

3. Mr. Sanchiz of Sanchis and Sanchis, Ltd. speaking is.

4. Dear Dr. Lei, Ph.D: Please have patients with our billign department.

5. company Sales have increases; but profits have declined.

Check your answers in Appendix F.

Summary

Editing is the process of reviewing and revising a piece of writing to improve it. When you edit business communications, you review and revise them to ensure they include the seven Cs of effective writing. Revising involves changing and modifying to make your writing more clear and correct. Word-processing programs allow you to revise by inserting, deleting, and moving text; using a thesaurus; and printing hard copies of your revisions. Proofreading is the part of editing concerned with reviewing and correcting general content and mechanical errors in the final draft. Using several proofreading techniques and a word-processing program can help the process. Most word-processing programs include a spelling function, a search-and-replace function, and a text-analysis function.

Discussion Questions

1. Briefly describe the seven Cs of effective business writing.
2. What is the relationship between editing, revising, and proofreading?
3. What types of errors do proofreaders discover? List the seven proofreading methods and explain when to use each one.
4. What do text-analysis programs analyze?
5. Why is proofreading important?

Practical Applications

Part A

Write a paragraph detailing your career plans. Edit, proofread, and rewrite the paragraph to achieve a final draft.

Part B

Write a paragraph on your plans for your next vacation. Edit, proofread, and rewrite the paragraph to achieve a final draft.

Editing and Proofreading Applications

Part A

Edit the following message to ensure it includes the seven Cs of effective business communications.

> We have found the photos of your Arizona trip that you claim we lost. You overexposed the photos of the youngish man standing beside the cactis. The other photos look good. If you are so inclined, send 20 dollars to the adres below and we will send the photos shortly.

Part B

Proofread the following message to correct general content and mechanical errors. Work in teams of two. One person should proofread the message using proofreaders' marks to indicate changes. The second person should read the proofreaders' marks, make the changes on the computer, print a copy, and mark other changes, if necessary. The first person should make those changes on the computer. Teammates should exchange the revision until both feel the document is correct.

> Welcomed to Acme Motrgage company. for you're infromatoin and knowlege we have inclosed herewith a brochure to answer any questions I think you might have about you new mortgage laon. You loan number is located in the the uper left left hand cornor of the payment coupon. payment coupons will be be maled to You under separate cover and must acompany all payments?

Writing Memos

The memo, sometimes called a memorandum, *is the most common business document; it is a written medium used for internal communication. Effectively written memos are a necessity for effective communication within an organization.*

Chapter 27 explains traditional and simplified memo formatting. Chapter 28 focuses on the uses and abuses of memos. Memos are used to inform, to direct, to provide a record, and/or to promote goodwill. When used in an abusive manner, memos damage the sender's image and the effectiveness of an organization.

Chapter 29 concentrates on writing effective memos. Guidelines for planning, organizing, and writing effective memos are given. A checklist for writing effective memos is also included.

Formatting Memos

OBJECTIVES

After studying this chapter and completing the chapter exercises, you will be able to do the following:

1. Explain how memos are used in internal communication.
2. Identify the parts of a memo.
3. Write memos using the traditional and the simplified memo formats.

Chapter 27

USING BUSINESS MEMOS

Memorandums (*memos* for short) are informal messages sent to persons within an organization. A memo is a quick, easy way to communicate in writing with a colleague or a supervisor in your own department, in another department, or in another company office.

Memos usually are more concise and less formal than the messages you would write to someone outside your organization. Memos do not include the receiver's complete address or other elements that are needed when communicating with someone outside the company. Consequently, the memo is a streamlined, efficient way to send a message to an internal audience.

More and more companies are using *electronic mail (e-mail)*, a computerized communication system for sending and receiving memos and other messages. To use e-mail, the sender types the memo onto a special screen, such as the one shown in Figure 27–1. With the touch of a few keys, the message is sent instantly to the receiver's *electronic mailbox*, a computer file that holds messages sent to a particular person. The receiver can view the memo on the screen and respond using e-mail.

A sender can broadcast one e-mail message to all computers in a company whether in the same building, in the same state, in the same country, or world wide.

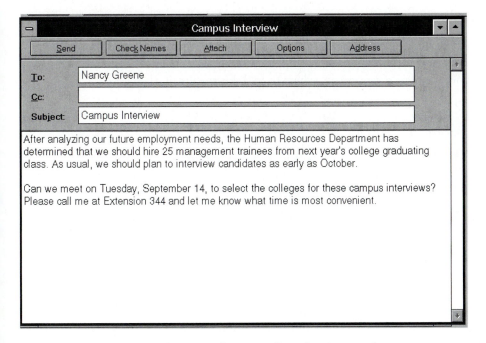

Figure 27–1 In many companies, employees can send memos to colleagues by using an e-mail system.

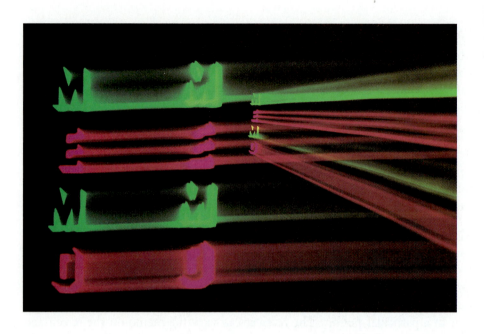

PARTS OF A MEMO

Most memos contain a heading, a body, and one or more notations. These memo components present important information in an organized way, and they show receivers exactly where to look for the details they need.

Memo Heading

The four standard components in a memo heading are *TO, FROM, DATE,* and *SUBJECT.* Each component guides the writing process by prompting the writer to include the needed information. As shown in Figure 27–2, headings components usually appear in capital letters. Use double-spacing to separate heading components. The information following each component appears in uppercase and lowercase.

The TO Line

This line contains the name of the person or people who will receive the memo. Depending on the style preferred by your company, you can write only the receiver's full name, add an appropriate courtesy title, add the receiver's title, or add the receiver's department name:

The capital letters in the memo headings contrast with the uppercase and lowercase letters in the details provided on the TO, FROM, DATE, and SUBJECT lines. This contrast draws the receiver's attention to this important information.

TO: All Mountain Light & Power Employees

FROM: Sergio Reyes, General Manager

DATE: September 4, 19—

SUBJECT: Storm Emergency Brochure

Our Public Relations office has prepared a new brochure outlining storm
emergency guidelines for household and industrial customers in our service
area. Although such emergencies are rare, we want to help our customers
and employees prepare for any problems that may arise during the winter
storm season.

The attached informative 20-page brochure is free. If you need additional
copies, please call Kimberly Albano at Extension 56.

js

Attachment

Figure 27–2 Memo in traditional format on plain paper.

TO: Fred Eckstrom

TO: Mr. Fred Eckstrom

TO: Fred Eckstrom, Benefits Manager

TO: Fred Eckstrom, Human Resources Department

When sending a memo to everyone who holds a particular job, you can omit individual names and address the memo to those who hold that particular job title:

TO: Service Managers

When sending a memo to everyone in a particular department or location, you can omit individual names and address the memo to everyone in that department or in that location:

TO: All Customer Service Personnel

When sending a memo to many people, you can avoid listing all the addresses on the TO line by referring to a distribution list positioned at the end of the memo:

TO: Committee Members—Distribution Below

The FROM Line

The sender's name appears on this line. Generally, you should not use a courtesy title with your own name, unless that is your company's style. However, you may need to include one or more pieces of information such as a job title, a department, a location, or a telephone extension:

FROM: Denise Slattery, Security Manager, Extension 505

The sender should sign his or her initials beside the printed name on the FROM line or at the end of the memo.

The DATE Line

Put the date that you write the memo on this line, showing the full name of the month, the day, and the year.

DATE: October 25, 19—

The SUBJECT Line

This line shows the topic of the memo. Word the subject as a phrase instead of a complete sentence. Make the subject brief and to the point so that your receiver can quickly identify the purpose of the memo. For example, if the memo concerns the company health insurance program, you might write:

SUBJECT: Health Insurance Program

Do not provide too much information in your SUBJECT line; save the details for the body of the memo. All capital letters may be used to catch the reader's eye.

Memo Body

Communicate your message in the body of the memo. Memos need no salutation; simply double-space after the heading and start the body of the memo. The body is usually single-spaced; however, the body of a very short memo may be double-spaced.

ON THE JOB

Signing your initials beside your printed name helps personalize the memos you write. It also shows that you have reviewed the memo and verified its accuracy before sending it.

Memo Notations

Place the keyboard operator's reference initials below the body of the memo and add any notations below the initials. For example, if a document is attached to the memo with a staple or a paper clip, note this below the reference initials.

The distribution list, if any, appears below any notations. Most of the time, the names on this list should be alphabetized. However, some companies prefer to organize distribution lists according to rank. Thus, the name of the highest-ranking person would appear first, followed by other names in descending order of rank in the company.

When sending a copy of a memo to another person place a notation such as *c Gerald Harrigan* below the reference initials.

Using Memos

Indicate if each statement is true or false.

1. Interoffice memos are used to communicate with people in the same organization.
2. Memos usually are more concise and formal than messages sent outside the organization.
3. Alphabetize the distribution list in all memos.
4. Use the SUBJECT line to give a detailed description of the subject of the memo.
5. Unlike letters, memos never use a salutation.

Check your answers in Appendix F.

FORMATTING MEMOS

Memorandum formats can follow one of two styles: traditional or simplified. In the *traditional* style, the heading appears at the top of the page. In the *simplified* style, the heading is omitted. The simplified style is produced more easily on a computer or a word processor because of its uncomplicated format.

The Traditional Memo Format

You can use the traditional memo format with letterhead stationery or plain paper. Figure 27–3 shows an example of a traditional memo on letterhead. When a company uses e-mail, its computer system often includes a preformatted memo screen for the writer's convenience.

An example of a traditional memo on plain paper is shown in Figure 27–2.

The following guidelines will help you prepare a memo using the traditional format:

1. Use a 1½-inch top margin on a plain sheet or two lines below the letterhead.
2. Use 1-inch side margins.
3. Type *TO:, FROM:, DATE:,* and *SUBJECT:* in capital letters vertically down the left margin.
4. Key all heading information 10 spaces from the left margin.
5. Double-space between the TO, FROM, DATE, and SUBJECT lines, between the heading and the body of the memo, and between paragraphs in the body.
6. Start all paragraphs at the left margin; do not indent text.
7. Type the keyboard operator's reference initials two lines below the body of the memo and key any additional notations below these initials.
8. Try to limit a memo to one page.

The Simplified Memo Format

Because of the widespread use of personal computers and word-processing equipment, the simplified memo format is becoming increasingly popular. This format, shown in Figure 27–4, can be produced easily on automated equipment using either letterhead stationery or plain paper.

The following guidelines will help you prepare a memo using the simplified format:

1. Use block format (all lines, including paragraphs, begin at the left margin) with 1-inch side margins.
2. Omit *TO, FROM, DATE,* and *SUBJECT.*
3. Place the date two lines below the letterhead or 1½ inches from the top (line 10) of a plain sheet.
4. Show the receiver's name four lines below the date.
5. Place the subject line in all uppercase letters or in uppercase and lowercase letters two lines below the receiver's name.
6. Begin the body of the memo two lines below the subject line.
7. Place the name of the sender four lines below the body.
8. Place the keyboard operator's reference initials a double space below the printed signature line.

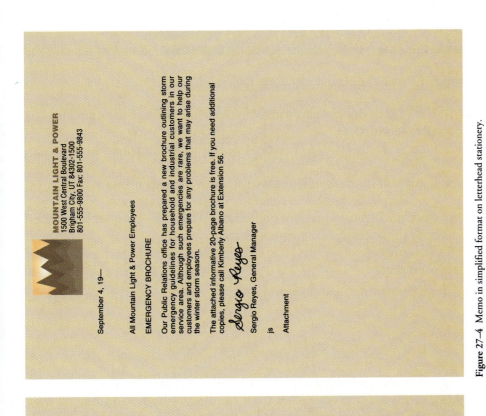

MOUNTAIN LIGHT & POWER
1500 West Central Boulevard
Brigham City, UT 84302-1500
801-555-9800 Fax: 801-555-9843

TO: Board Members—Distribution Below

FROM: Sergio Reyes, General Manager *SR*.

DATE: September 4, 19—

SUBJECT: Storm Emergency Brochure

Our Public Relations office has prepared a new brochure outlining storm emergency guidelines for household and industrial customers in our service area. Although such emergencies are rare, we want to help our customers and employees prepare for any problems that may arise during the winter storm season.

The attached informative 20-page brochure is free. If you need additional copies, please call Kimberly Albano at Extension 56.

js

Attachment

Distribution: Sandra Chasen
             Peter Donnelly
             Leon Garcia
             Michelle Stanton
             Virginia West

Figure 27–3 Memo in traditional format on letterhead stationery.

MOUNTAIN LIGHT & POWER
1500 West Central Boulevard
Brigham City, UT 84302-1500
801-555-9800 Fax: 801-555-9843

September 4, 19—

All Mountain Light & Power Employees

EMERGENCY BROCHURE

Our Public Relations office has prepared a new brochure outlining storm emergency guidelines for household and industrial customers in our service area. Although such emergencies are rare, we want to help our customers and employees prepare for any problems that may arise during the winter storm season.

The attached informative 20-page brochure is free. If you need additional copies, please call Kimberly Albano at Extension 56.

Sergio Reyes
Sergio Reyes, General Manager

js

Attachment

Figure 27–4 Memo in simplified format on letterhead stationery.

2 *Traditional and Simplified Memo Formats*

CHECKPOINT

Indicate if each statement is true or false.

1. Use 1½-inch side margins with both the traditional and the simplified memo format.
2. Omit *TO*, *FROM*, *DATE*, and *SUBJECT* in the simplified memo format.
3. Because of its uncomplicated format, the traditional memo style is produced more easily on a computer or word processor.
4. Place the keyboard operator's reference initials a double space below the body in the traditional memo format.
5. The date appears on line 10 in the simplified memo format when using plain paper.

Check your answers in Appendix F.

Summary

Interoffice memorandums are informal messages sent to persons within an organization. Most memos contain a heading, a body, and one or more notations. Memos can be formatted in the traditional or simplified style. The traditional memo format can be used with letterhead stationery or plain paper. The simplified format, which is easily produced on computers or word processors, also can be used with letterhead stationery or plain paper.

Discussion Questions

1. How are memos used for internal communication?
2. Describe the parts of a memo.
3. Explain how the traditional memo format differs from the simplified memo format.

Practical Applications

Part A

As a member of your company's legal department, you review all advertisements before they are used. The marketing department recently sent you some new food advertising materials. Because the federal guidelines covering food advertising recently changed, you asked an expert if the materials comply with these guidelines. Explain the situation in a simplified memo to Lu-yin Sheng of the marketing department, and tell her that you will call her when you receive the expert's report.

Part B

Draft a memo to the manager of your college cafeteria or food service department. Discuss what foods you would like added to the lunch menu and what foods you would like removed. Indicate that you are sending a copy of the memo to the college president.

Editing and Proofreading Applications

Part A

Edit and rewrite the following memo using the (1) traditional format and then the (2) simplified format.

TO: All Central Region Technicians FROM: Heather A. Goodwin, Des Moines Office DATE: December 19, 19— SUBJECT: New Service Guarantee Offered by Central Region Repair Centers

A new service guarantee will apply to all computer repars made after January 1. This guarantee covers both parts and labour for 90 days. Following a repair made in any central region repair center. If the repaired computer develops a similar problem, we will service the unit again without charge. If any part we install proves defective, we will replace it without charge.

We need your help tracking the results of this new program. Use this new form to report how many customer request's for free parts or free service are received during January February and March. Please return the completed form to me by April 10.

Part B

Find the spelling errors in the following memo body. List the words, correctly spelled, on a separate sheet of paper.

The meddical records department will be closed on Monday, October 10. You can get a copy of any pashient's record on that day by using the central computer sistem or by calling the shift superviser on extention 29. The depaartment will reopen at 6 a.m. on Tusday, October 11.

Uses and Abuses of Memos

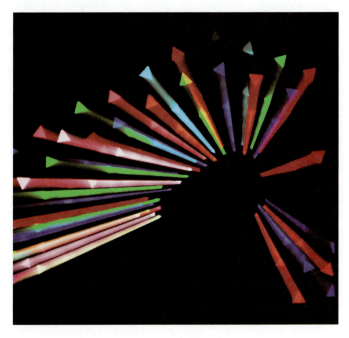

OBJECTIVES

After studying this chapter and completing the chapter exercises, you will be able to do the following:

1. Describe the uses of memos.
2. Identify and describe the abuses of memos.

USES OF MEMOS—WHEN TO USE THEM

Memos are used for internal business communications. They are an efficient medium for several reasons:

- Memos can be sent to more than one receiver.
- Memos take less time to format and key than letters.
- Memos are less expensive, time-consuming, and complex than conference calls or meetings.

Memos are internal messages that supervisors and peers will use to judge your on-the-job performance; therefore, use them with care. Also, choose the people to whom you send these internal documents carefully. The content and tone of your memos **must** not be offensive to anyone. Knowing how to use and when not to use memos is critical to success in your career.

Memos are used to (1) provide a record; (2) advise, direct, or state policy; (3) inform; and (4) promote goodwill.

Provide a Record

Memos often are used to record certain events that occurred or specific things people said. For example, suppose that you took part in an explicit discussion of a particular topic. You might send a memo to your supervisor containing the ideas discussed and any recommendations made. After this memo was filed, it could be retrieved and used as a record if needed. (See Figure 28–1.)

ACROSS
CULTURES

- The business world of every culture uses a message format for internal written communications. Most of these formats are similar to the memo format. Did North Americans borrow the idea for the memo from another culture or did other cultures take it from the North American culture?

SUBJECT: Proposed Changes in Computer File Security

Opening access to computer files would be a serious mistake. If the company loosened its access to computer files, it would be more susceptible to corporate espionage. Presently, this type of espionage is one of the biggest problems we have in our industry. Thank you for allowing me to provide input into the discussion on computer file security.

Figure 28–1 A message that provides a record.

Advise, Direct, or State Policy

Memos also are used to advise, direct, or state policy. Employees often write memos to advise supervisors or peers on particular topics or procedures. For example, suppose the supervisor of your department has requested your advice on the selection of an integrated software package for the department. After your investigation, you send your supervisor a memo recommending a new package. Figure 28–2 is an example of what this memo might contain.

SUBJECT: Recommendation for Integrated Software

Last week you asked me to examine and recommend a new integrated software package for the department. I recommend Writeworks. This flexible inexpensive package provides the capabilities that we need. If you have any questions, please call me at Extension 72.

Figure 28–2 A message that advises.

Supervisors commonly use memos to direct. For example, as a supervisor, you might write a message like the one in Figure 28–3 to direct the purchasing agent of your company to acquire a new integrated software package.

SUBJECT: Writeworks for the Administrative Services Department

Please deliver five copies of Writeworks to our department as soon as possible. Donna Dunlop, Vice President of Administrative Services, has given her permission to purchase copies of Writeworks for each employee in our department. Purchase order #25930 is attached.

Thank you.

Figure 28–3 A message that directs.

Memos also are used to state policy and explain procedures. Claudia, a supervisor, might write a memo that explains to employees that they should use Writeworks for all their computerized communications after September 1. (See Figure 28-4.)

USE WRITEWORKS AFTER SEPTEMBER 1

After September 1, all department documents should be produced using Writeworks. You may use WordDone, our present program, until September 1. Thank you for providing input in the selection of Writeworks. It will help us produce better looking documents in less time.

Figure 28–4 A message that states policy.

Use a memo as the main written medium for providing information to co-workers.

Inform

Memos frequently are used to inform. For example, assume that your supervisor will take maternity leave for two months. The message in Figure 28–5 informs department members of the situation and states who will replace her during her absence.

SUBJECT: Maternity Leave for Lucia Roberts

On September 1, my maternity leave will start. I will return on November 1. While I am on leave, John Dennison will take my place.

I appreciate all the help you have given me while I have been your supervisor. Please provide the same level of support to John. Thanks!

Figure 28–5 A message that informs.

Promote Goodwill

Another use of memos is to promote goodwill. Send a goodwill message to congratulate someone who has accomplished something outstanding or to tell someone "thanks." Figure 28–6 shows the subject and body of a congratulatory goodwill memo.

Use goodwill memos to promote good interpersonal relationships with co-workers. For example, send an occasional memo to acknowledge birthdays, anniversaries, and other special occasions.

SUBJECT: Your Promotion

Allison, congratulations on your recent promotion! You truly deserve it. Your hard work and loyalty to the company have finally paid off. Keep up the excellent work.

Figure 28–6 A message that promotes goodwill.

Uses of Memos

Identify the purpose of the memo in each situation.

1. A memo to provide employees with a new set of directions for obtaining reimbursement for medical expenses.
2. A memo to employees in the Accounting Department telling them the new departmental supervisor is Jane Boyle.
3. A memo to a co-worker thanking her for her support on an important project.
4. A memo to your supervisor stating your belief that the workload should be more evenly distributed. You have expressed your feelings on this topic before. Nevertheless, you want to write a memo to ensure that your supervisor understands your position.

Check your answers in Appendix F.

ABUSES OF MEMOS—WHEN NOT TO USE THEM

Even though memos are the most frequently used form of written business communication, people sometimes abuse them. Abuse occurs when memos are (1) written too frequently, (2) written to gain attention, (3) written by a committee, and (4) rewritten for each level of management.

Written Too Frequently

Although memos are the best medium for written communications within an organization, they can be overused. The convenience of e-mail sometimes results in problems such as writing too many with copies to too many others.

Senders can grow too comfortable when writing e-mail memos. They get careless with word choice, content, and proofreading. Sometimes they also become more aggressive or even abusive with their language. These senders fail to realize that e-mail memos are frequently sent on by the receiver to others. To remedy these abuses, give e-mail memos the same careful attention given to traditional memos.

When memos, whether e-mail or hard copy, are overused, the organization may suffer from communication overload. Communication overload is a mental condition that occurs when a person receives so many messages that he or she fails to take the time necessary to read or comprehend them. When overload occurs, communication within an organization breaks down.

When people receive too many memos, they either skim them quickly and react and make judgments too quickly (which often results in errors) or set them aside to read later. By the time people read these memos, if they read them at all, they often have missed important deadlines.

Supervisors often make the mistake of sending a memo a second time because employees have ignored the first. If the second memo communicates successfully with subordinates, the supervisor may assume that he or she needs to send two memos to get a message across—an attitude that may result in communication overload. The solution to communication overload is fewer communications, not more.

Written to Gain Attention

Too often, an ambitious person will view memos as a way to call attention to what he or she is doing for the company or as a way to receive recognition from his or her supervisor. As a result of such usage, supervisors can become disgruntled with the sender—the employee. In his or her attempt to gain recognition, the worker can be viewed as a problem rather than an asset. A memo to gain attention often includes numerous *I's*, *me's*, and *my's*; see the message in Figure 28–7.

Avoid communication overload by discussing and planning social and sports activities with colleagues during lunch or over the telephone; do not send a memo.

LEGAL/Ethical

- Sometimes workers use memos to raise their status above others—especially when seeking promotions. They hope to achieve this status by writing memos that use a condescending tone or that discuss the actions or attitudes of fellow workers.

SUBJECT: A Change in Line Production

I am pleased to say that I have some suggestions that would drastically increase production. I have been with the company about three weeks now and have made several important observations. I think these suggestions could increase production by at least 50 percent. Let me know when we can get together to discuss my ideas.

Figure 28–7 A message that gains attention.

Even though this writer may have some effective suggestions, a memo is not a good medium to use in this situation. Instead, the employee might want to hold a casual discussion with his or her supervisor and then provide specific suggestions later. Avoid using memos to seek attention.

Written by a Committee

Memos written by a committee are often poorly written. Committee members may be competitive or disagree on memo style and content because of egos, not reason. When many people try to write a memo, the memo often becomes uninformative and unfocused, making it difficult for the receiver to understand the purpose and the content.

The memo in Figure 28–8 was written by a committee. The opening paragraph does not state the objective of the memo. Even the subject line provides no indication of the topic. What does the memo really say? Is the committee deadlocked? Will it make a recommendation to Leslie? Is this a final report or is it a report of temporary conditions? While the ideas in the memo are quite clear, its purpose and the committee's plan for the future are unclear. The memo is poorly written. The solution to this problem is to let one person represent the committee and write its memos.

When writers try to be formal, they often shift from the active voice to the passive voice. Remember to use the active voice as much as possible; it is concise and clear.

Rewritten for Each Level of Management

Sometimes messages need to be sent to each employee level of a company—from entry-level workers to the president. In these situations, the sender of the memo may be tempted to rewrite the memo for each level. Such reasoning is faulty.

Any adjustments to the memo should be minor The higher the level of the receivers, the more formal you should make the memo. To make a memo formal, use the traditional format and formal business language. However, the main idea should remain the same.

Figure 28–9 shows a memo rewritten for upper-level management. What is the main idea of the memo? Mr. Powell will probably have a difficult time understanding this memo because it does not have a clear main idea. In fact, the memo includes several main ideas. Many areas are mentioned without supporting information. If you were Mr. Powell, you probably would need to ask June Jacobs for the meaning of the message and what she wants you to do.

Figure 28–8 A memo written by a committee.

TO: Leslie Dubach, Vice President of Human Resources

FROM: Employee Committee on Work Schedules

DATE: October 1, 19—

SUBJECT: Report on Committee Decision

The committee has met several times to discuss the possibility of flexible scheduling. The results of this four-person committee are most interesting.

Al has strong feelings and believes that flexible scheduling would result in a loss in productivity. He feels employees would take advantage of the freedom.

Susan also has strong feelings but feels just the opposite of Al. She thinks flexible scheduling would increase the productivity of the company and states that she has research to back up her views.

Tom and June have listened to the statements of both Al and Susan and see the wisdom of both systems.

dw

Figure 28–9 A memo rewritten for upper-level management.

S·H·M
Smith-Howard Mfg., Inc.
13000 West Walnut Boulevard
Lubbock, TX 79410-1344
806/555-3376 Fax: 806/555-3000

TO: Tony Powell, President

FROM: June Jacobs, Vice President of Systems

DATE: January 12, 19—

SUBJECT: Changes in Computer Information Systems

For some time now, our department has been discussing some changes in our computer information system here at headquarters.

Certain minor changes in procedures may be necessary to enable other departments to facilitate sales and purchasing procedures. A new system would correct the problems we have been having for quite a while. Also new capabilities in accounts receivable and accounts payable would be realized.

kg

When to Use a Memo

Determine if a memo would be appropriate for each situation. If so, indicate how the memo would be used.

1. You are a department head and you sent your employees a memo requesting specific information so that they and their families can participate in the new benefits package. You sent the memo on Monday and asked for the information by Thursday. It is now Friday, and you have received only one of ten replies. This is the first time employees have not quickly responded to a request.
2. As the head of a team project, you have been asked to inform members of your group of complex step-by-step procedures that will enable them to obtain reimbursements for business expenses.
3. Today is Thursday and you want to remind a co-worker of a social gathering at your home Saturday night.
4. A co-worker has just received news of a promotion and transfer to another office. You want to congratulate and wish your colleague well.

Check your answers in Appendix F.

Summary

Memos are used for internal communication within an organization. They have four purposes: (1) to provide a record; (2) to advise, direct, and state policy; (3) to inform; and (4) to promote goodwill. Memos are misused sometimes. Common misuses occur when memos are (1) written too frequently, (2) written to gain attention, (3) written by a committee, and (4) rewritten for each level of management.

Discussion Questions

1. Describe four uses for memos in organizations.
2. Identify and describe common abuses of memos.

Practical Applications

Part A

List the main idea and use for each memo.

1. Congratulations on your promotion. We would like to hold a small celebration in your honor in the marketing conference room on Tuesday at noon.
2. My recommendation was to open a new branch in Landcaster, but I have no problem with your decision to open one in Juniper instead. Juniper also has excellent potential. If I can help in any way, let me know.
3. The annual vacation-leave policy requires employees to apply for leave at least two weeks before the suggested vacation time and to receive preapproval of all annual vacations. Please use Form 908941-B for this approval. If emergencies occur and you cannot provide the two-week notice, use Form 908942 to receive emergency approval.

Part B

Divide into groups of three or four members. Assume that you are departmental supervisors and that you have received the following memo from your supervisor. Rewrite the memo for your subordinates. Each group will revise the memo for a specific purpose, which your instructor will provide. Each group will not know the purpose assigned to other groups.

TO: Janice Davenport, Supervisor

FROM: Stephanie Fergason, Vice President of Human Resources

DATE: July 24, 19—

SUBJECT: New Preferred Providers of Health Care Services

Please write a memo to your subordinates telling them that Green Clinic and Washington General Hospital have recently become Preferred Providers of Health Care Services (PPHCS).

This means that when employees enrolled in our health care plan use Green Clinic and Washington General Hospital, they will receive health care services at a lower cost. Also, it means that all covered employees need to do is show their membership card to the PPHCS organization and all insurance claims will be filed for them. In summary, if our employees use the PPHCSs, they will receive low-cost health care services without worrying about insurance claims.

Part C

Team with a class member to evaluate the following memo written by a subordinate to his supervisor. Evaluate the memo by answering the following questions: Is this a good memo? Why or why not? Does this memo illustrate a good use of memos? Why or why not? Write a memo to your instructor that contains your evaluation.

TO: Carlos Tibbets, Sales Supervisor

FROM: Russell LeBeau, Sales Representative

DATE: September 12, 19—

SUBJECT: Attendance at the San Francisco Trade Show

Thank you for permitting me to attend next week's trade show in San Francisco. I'm sure it will be the most exceptional trade show ever. All of our main competitors will be exhibiting their most advanced technologies. I am very excited!

The knowledge that I gain there will really help me. I sure am happy that the company is paying my expenses—five nights in a $150-a-night room would be too expensive for me.

Part D

Assume that you head the lay-away department in a large retail store. Write a memo to all members of your department. Explain that management has decided that employees cannot take annual vacations during November and December because of the holiday season. Use the indirect order and positive language to write this memo in the simplified memo format.

Part E

Using the situation in Practical Application D, write a memo to the assistant manager of your department. In the memo, tell him or her that you have informed members of your department of the restriction on annual vacations. Use the traditional memo format.

Part F

A salesperson of a small insurance company obtained names, addresses, and telephone numbers of employees in your department. The salesperson calls the employees, implies that he is calling with your approval, and states that his insurance rates are the cheapest—even cheaper than the rates provided in the company's benefit package. Neither of these inferences are true; he does not have your approval, and the insurance rates provided in the company's benefit package are cheaper. Write a memo to your subordinates informing them of the situation and these facts. Use the traditional memo format.

Part G

Using the situation described in Practical Application F, write a memo to the vice president of your department, Shannon Smith. Tell her what the insurance salesperson has done and suggest that this person might be calling employees of other departments. Suggest a course of action she might take to inform other employees. Use the traditional memo format.

Part H

As an employee of Tim's Graphics, Inc., you have earned a two-week vacation. Write a memo to your supervisor requesting your annual vacation for Monday, June 23, through Tuesday, July 8. Explain that your vacation ends on Tuesday, July 8, because July 4 is a holiday and does not count as a day of annual vacation. Use the simplified memo format.

Editing and Proofreading Applications

Part A

Proofread the following memo and list all errors in formatting, grammar, spelling, and word usage.

Part B

Edit and rewrite the memo to correct all formatting, grammar, spelling, and word usage errors. Use better word choices, correct words, and avoid negative language.

Febuary 15, 19—

Vickie Bradford

HOTEL ACCOMODATIONS FOR SEATTLE
As you know four managers will attend the DAC Conference in Seettle.

You're responsibility is to make reservations for us, the conference material is enclosed. We have three hotels to chose from—the Bilton, the Intercontinental, or the Alcove Inn. We have all ready decided to stay at the Bilton. We don't want to stay in the smoking section—we would like non-smoking rooms only. Your to tell them that we will arrive before 6:00 p.m. on

Thursday, March 3 and remain thier too nights. Ask them to send the reservations and confirmation numbers to both John and I.

Tyler Jones

yw

Writing Effective Memos

Chapter 29

OBJECTIVES

After studying this chapter and completing the chapter exercises, you will be able to do the following:

1. Describe the steps in planning memos.
2. Explain ways to organize memos.
3. List and explain the guidelines for writing effective memos.

GUIDELINES FOR PLANNING EFFECTIVE MEMOS

In most business organizations, memos comprise most written business communications. You must carefully plan, organize, and edit your memos.

Planning a message (discussed in detail in Chapter 22) requires four steps: (1) identify the objective, (2) identify the main idea, (3) determine the supporting information, and (4) adjust the content to the receiver. Planning a memo requires the same four steps.

1. *Identify the Objective.* Messages are used to promote goodwill, inform, request, record, or persuade. Memos have the same four objectives. Ask these questions to identify the objective: Why am I sending this memo and what do I hope to accomplish?

2. *Identify the Main Idea.* The main idea is the theme of the memo, which closely corresponds to the objective or purpose of the memo. However, the main idea is receiver oriented—it states the main idea in such a way that the receiver will do what is asked or will accept the information presented.

3. *Determine the Supporting Information.* Supporting information contributes to the success of a memo. Brainstorm if necessary to make the supporting information as effective as possible. Ask these questions to help determine the supporting information: What does the receiver need to know about the main idea to respond to my message and how will the message benefit the receiver?

4. *Adjust the Content for the Receiver.* Practice empathy by putting yourself in the place of the receiver and trying to see the situation from the receiver's perspective. Ask these questions to help adjust the message to the receiver:
   (a) To whom am I sending the message?
   (b) How much knowledge (experience, background, education) does the receiver have about the subject?
   (c) What does the receiver need to know about the subject?
   (d) What is the receiver's opinion of or interest in the subject?
   (e) How does the receiver feel about me, our department, and our company?
   (f) How can I help the receiver?

CHECKPOINT

1 *Planning Memos*

Identify the objective and the main idea of each memo.

1. A copy of our report and recommendation is attached. Mark will make his recommendations by Thursday. I need any changes by Tuesday morning.

(Continued on the next page)

2. The ad hoc committee in charge of developing procedures for part-time employees recommends the following:
   A. Pay part-time employees every two weeks like full-time employees.
   B. Use an abbreviated pay slip to explain their pay—an example is attached.
   C. Pay part-time employees time-and-a-half or double-time for weekend or holiday work like full-time workers.
3. I still do not have the Jones Report. Please check with your administrative assistant to determine if he forgot to send it. Thanks.

Check your answers in Appendix F.

GUIDELINES FOR ORGANIZING EFFECTIVE MEMOS

After planning, you need to determine how to organize the message to achieve its purpose. A message may be organized in the direct order, the indirect order, or the direct-indirect order. However, the direct-indirect order is not used in memos for two reasons: (1) Memos are internal documents and receivers should be objective, and (2) memos should have only one main idea. Direct-indirect messages have two main ideas—good news and bad news. Figure 29–1 shows how to present information in direct order and indirect order memos.

ACROSS **CULTURES**

- Other cultures use the direct-indirect order in memos, but the North American culture does not. To other cultures, tact is more important than presenting only one main idea.

DIRECT ORDER MEMO	INDIRECT ORDER MEMO
1. Main Idea	1. Neutral Beginning
2. Supporting Information	2. Supporting Information
	3. Main Idea (Bad News)

Figure 29–1 Organizing memos

Direct Order

Use the direct order in a memo that contains good news for the receiver or that makes a routine request. The direct order presents the main idea first, followed by supporting information. In the memo in Figure 29–2, the main idea in the first sentence makes a routine request.

TO: Lolita Hanson, Supplies Clerk

FROM: Richard Byers   *R.B.*

DATE: March 26, 19—

SUBJECT: Supplies Needed by Administrative Services

Please prepare an order of supplies for the Administrative Services Department. The following supplies are needed:

1. Four packages of company letterhead stationery
2. Twelve cartridges for Burnitout Laser Printers (Model 500)
3. Six packages of plain bond stationery
4. Eight boxes of envelopes with the company's return address

I know you are busy and have no assistants to deliver this order; therefore, Thedrick Harris, a department member, will come to the supply room tomorrow at 10 a.m. to pick up the order. Thank you for your help.

ra

Figure 29–2 Memo using the direct order

Indirect Order

Supporting information appears before the main idea in the indirect order. Use the indirect order in memos that contain bad news for the receiver or that try to persuade the receiver. In bad news situations, prepare the receiver for the bad news by giving the reasons for the bad news before presenting the bad news itself—the main idea. In persuasive situations, receivers are more apt to do what you want if they understand the reasons before being asked.

Messages written in the indirect order have three parts and are presented in this sequence: (1) a neutral beginning, (2) supporting information, and (3) main idea (bad news). The neutral beginning should not state or imply the main idea. However, it should introduce the topic of the memo as in the example shown in Figure 29–3.

ACROSS CULTURES

- Because bad news is difficult to relate, North Americans prefer to present reasons for the bad news as quickly as possible. Members of others cultures sometimes consider this attitude abrupt or unsympathetic.

REDUCTION IN PERSONNEL

I certainly appreciate all the input you gave us on the staff-reduction decision we had to make. As you know, headquarters asked us to reduce staff by 10 percent. If we could leave your department status quo, we would. However, two members of your staff must be retired or dismissed. I will meet with you on Monday the 9th to identify specific individuals.

Figure 29–3 Memo using the indirect order.

The message in Figure 29–3 contains the following parts:

Neutral Beginning	I certainly appreciate all the input you gave us on the staff-reduction decision we had to make.
Supporting Information	As you know, headquarters asked us to reduce staff by 10 percent.
Main Idea	If we could leave your department status quo, we would. However, two members of your staff must be retired or dismissed. I will meet with you Monday the 9th to identify specific individuals.

2 CHECKPOINT

Organizing Memos

Indicate the organization for each memo—direct order or indirect order. Justify your answer.

1. Memo to selected subordinates to tell them that they are appointed to a project team.
2. Memo to the Vice President of International Operations to explain why sales in the past fiscal year fell 12 percent.
3. Memo to all employees telling them their part of the health insurance premium will increase $25 a month, and benefits will be reduced. Employees are strongly opposed to this action and have threatened the company with a strike.
4. Memo to the payroll supervisor to explain that the amount of income reported on your W-2 Form is too high. The amounts withheld for federal and state income tax are too low.

Check your answers in Appendix F.

GUIDELINES FOR WRITING EFFECTIVE MEMOS

After planning and organizing a memo, writing and editing become your focus. The following guidelines will help ensure that you write clear, concise memos that receivers understand.

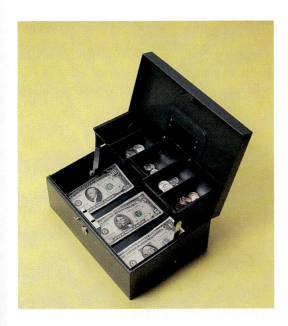

Restrict a Memo to One Main Idea

Because memos often require no feedback from the receiver, the writer some-times does not know if the receiver understood the memo. Therefore, to simplify and help ensure understanding, put only one main idea in each memo. The memo in Figure 29–1 contains only one main idea.

Compose a Short, Clear Subject Line

The subject line of a memo should reflect the main idea. The sentence that contains the main idea and the subject line of the memo should be similar and use the same key words in them. Examples of short, clear subject lines include:

SUBJECT: New Policy for Petty Cash

SUBJECT: Status Report on Cafeteria Remodeling

Make the Body Stand Alone

A memo should be written clearly enough for the receiver to understand it even if the receiver does not read the subject line. Unity, simple language, effective organization, and coherence make the body of a memo stand alone.

LEGAL/Ethical

• Our court system often uses memos as written records. Think of all the cases against people in the federal government in which memos were used as evidence—Watergate, Iran-gate, Whitewater, and so forth.

Use Tables and Visual Aids

When you need to communicate with statistics or other quantitative data, arrange the data in a table or a visual aid. Explain the table or visual aid as in Figure 29–4. Refer to Chapter 36 for detailed information on types of visual aids and their use.

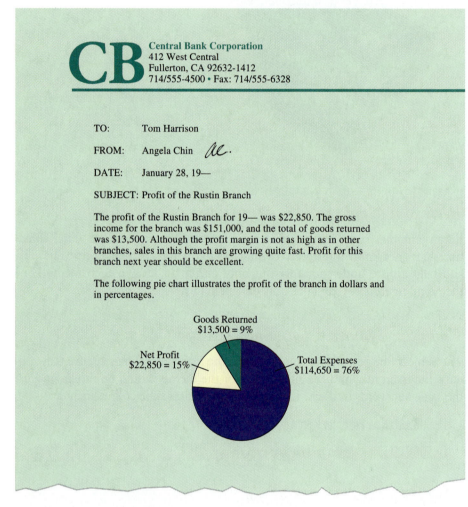

CB **Central Bank Corporation**
412 West Central
Fullerton, CA 92632-1412
714/555-4500 • Fax: 714/555-6328

TO: Tom Harrison

FROM: Angela Chin   *ac.*

DATE: January 28, 19—

SUBJECT: Profit of the Rustin Branch

The profit of the Rustin Branch for 19— was $22,850. The gross income for the branch was $151,000, and the total of goods returned was $13,500. Although the profit margin is not as high as in other branches, sales in this branch are growing quite fast. Profit for this branch next year should be excellent.

The following pie chart illustrates the profit of the branch in dollars and in percentages.

Goods Returned
$13,500 = 9%

Net Profit
$22,850 = 15%

Total Expenses
$114,650 = 76%

Figure 29–4 Memo containing a visual aid

Use Headings in Long Memos

Divide a memo that is longer than one page into sections. Insert headings before each section to guide the receiver.

Some sections of a long memo may be written before others. After writing all sections, arrange them in a logical order and, if necessary, add transitions. If a memo is complex, construct an outline before writing any section; then place the sections in the appropriate order.

Number Items in a List

Use enumerations to separate steps in a process, a list of items, and so forth. Numbering or lettering items helps communication by clarifying where items begin and end.

★ "Write to express, not impress!" (Author Unknown) Effective writing is clear and concise, not long and complex.

Most word-processing software programs allow users to insert bullets (dots, squares, diamonds) before items in a list. Bullets also help separate items.

Guidelines for Writing Effective Memos

Indicate if each statement is true or false as it applies to a two-page memo that contains quantitative data and several lists.

1. This memo should contain enumerations.
2. This memo does not need headings.
3. This memo should have several main ideas.
4. This memo probably should include one or more tables or visual aids.
5. This memo does not need a clear and precise subject line because the contents are too complex.
6. This memo has an adequate subject line, so the body of this memo does not need to stand alone.

Check your answers in Appendix F.

Use the checklist in Figure 29–5 to help you write effective memos.

Planning

_____ 1. I have identified the objective of the memo.

_____ 2. I have identified the main idea of the memo.

_____ 3. I have determined the supporting information for the memo. (Use brainstorming if necessary.)

_____ 4. I have adjusted the memo for its receiver(s).

Organizing

_____ 5. I used the correct order. (Direct or indirect. Direct order most of the time!)

Editing

_____ 6. The memo has only one main idea.

_____ 7. The subject line is short and clear.

_____ 8. The body of the memo stands alone.

_____ 9. I use tables or visual aids when the memo contains considerable quantitative information.

_____ 10. I use headings when a memo is over one page in length.

_____ 11. I use enumerations when a memo contains steps in a process or a list.

Figure 29–5 Checklist for writing effective memos

Summary

When planning memos, use the four-step process for planning all messages: (1) identify the objective, (2) identify the main idea, (3) determine the supporting information, and (4) adjust the content to the receiver(s).

Write memos in the direct order when they contain good news for the receiver or make routine requests. Write memos in the indirect order when they contain bad news for the receiver or try to persuade the receiver.

Guidelines for writing memos include: (1) restrict memos to one main idea; (2) compose a short, clear subject line; (3) make the body stand alone; (4) use tables and visual aids; (5) use headings in long memos; and (6) number items in a list.

Discussion Questions

1. List the steps in planning memos.
2. Explain ways to organize memos.
3. List the guidelines for writing effective memos.

Practical Applications

Part A

Identify the objective of each memo.

1. Congratulations on your 25th wedding anniversary. I know you and your spouse are pleased.
2. Even though my recommendation was to sell the ADC common stock and buy NuLow Company common stock, I have no problem with the decision to retain the ADC stock. Only time will tell which decision is better.
3. The new reimbursement policy for client entertainment requires approval for expenses before they are incurred. Please use Form 5893 to request approval. Unapproved entertainment expenses will not be reimbursed.
4. Sales increased 25 percent last year. Because of this improvement, we need to hire two additional salespersons. These new employees will help us cover our area and serve our customers better.

Part B

Indicate the organization of each memo—direct or indirect.

1. Write your department supervisor and resign. He will be disappointed; he was hoping you would take his place in two years.
2. Write to ask members of a committee on which you serve to delay a presentation scheduled for Wednesday morning until Thursday morning. The visual aids will be ready Wednesday afternoon.
3. A fellow employee has just been elected as an employee representative on the company's executive committee. Write and congratulate your colleague.
4. As department supervisor, write your department members and tell them the recommended pay raise was approved. However, instead of starting on June 1, it will start on September 1.

Part C

In the Unison Construction Company, the Purchasing Department buys supplies for all departments. As head of the Sales and Communication Department, you need to order 24 #2 lead pencils, 2 packages of computerized answer sheets, and 50 copies of the IDC reading comprehension test. Write a memo to order these materials. Send it to Frank Avenelli, supervisor of the Purchasing Department. Use the traditional format.

Part D

Assume that you are Frank Avenelli, supervisor of the Purchasing Department. Send Carla Jamison a memo telling her the supplies she ordered will be delivered in two days. Also, tell Carla you will send the 36 TicTop pens with black ink and 6 three-ring binders from a previous order. Use the simplified format.

Part E

Mrs. Betty Hernandez, a sales representative, has asked permission to miss the annual sales meeting in Boise, Idaho. Many new products are being introduced at this meeting. In addition, you do not want to set a precedent for allowing representatives to miss these meetings. Write and tell her that she cannot be excused.

Part F

You are responsible for reserving meeting rooms, and you often receive requests for their use. The head of the Department of Research, Dr. Rachel Orr, sent you a memo requesting to use Conference Room 215 for a meeting of 30 people on May 5 from 9 a.m. to 12 noon. The conference room is not available; however, Conference Room 415 and Conference Room 515 are available. Both will seat more than 30 people. Write Dr. Orr a memo informing her of this situation. Use the simplified format.

Part G

Mr. Tink Anderson, Vice President of Human Resources, sent you a copy of a proposal for a new company policy that strongly discourages overtime. After discussing the proposal with the leaders in your department, you decide that you disagree with the proposal. It would have a negative impact on employees who are currently earning less than other employees in the region. Send a memo informing Mr. Anderson of your position.

Part H

You are leading a team responsible for examining the system that produces tubing for space vehicles. You want the new engineer in the design department as part of the team because of her expertise. Write a memo to Joe Guard, head of the Design Department, seeking permission to ask Anita Bennett to join the team.

Part I

You work in the Accounting Department of Harrison and Son, Inc. The accounting system is part manual and part automated. After talking with friends who work for other companies, you are convinced that Harrison and Son could save money and time by automating the entire accounting system. Write your supervisor, Rosemary Hill, and suggest that a committee look into the possibility of automating the accounting system. Tell her that you would like to chair the committee.

Editing and Proofreading Application

Edit and proofread the following memo. Rewrite it and choose better words, use correct words, and avoid negative language.

> Recently you offerred some suggestions on ways to make our grevience procedures more accommodating. The suggestions and the council you gave was excellant. However, we can not implement them this calendar year. If you have any farther suggestions, don't hesitate to send them to me. They would be appreciated.

Writing Letters

Members of organizations use letters for external communication. A letter is representative of both the sender and his or her organization. To enhance your image and the image of your employer, your letters must look professional and be accurate.

Chapter 30 presents the formatting used for letters—block, modified block, and simplified block. Using these formats will help to ensure attractive, professional-looking letters.

Chapters 31 through 33, provide instruction for the planning, organizing, and writing of routine, good news, goodwill, bad news, and persuasive letters. A checklist to assist in writing each type of letter is presented.

Chapter 30

Formatting Letters

OBJECTIVES

After studying this chapter and completing the chapter exercises, you will be able to do the following:

1. Explain how the business letter is used in external communication.
2. Describe the standard and optional parts of a business letter.
3. Use the block, modified block, and simplified block letter formats.
4. Prepare a business envelope.

BUSINESS LETTERS

The basic written communication sent by someone in one organization to someone in another organization is the *business letter*. Because business letters are addressed to persons outside an organization rather than to persons within an organization, they are more formal documents than memos.

Business letters are printed on **letterhead stationery**, which includes the company name, address, telephone number, and logo. In addition, a letterhead sometimes shows the company facsimile (fax) number, the company slogan, or the names of company officials and departments. The letterhead is important because a receiver starts to form an opinion of the sender and the company by looking at the stationery.

LETTER PARTS

The standard parts of a business letter are the dateline, letter address, salutation, body, complimentary close, writer's name and title, reference initials, and copy notation. A business letter also may include these optional parts: attention line, subject line, enclosure notation, copy notation, postscript, and second-page heading. Refer to Figure 30–1 as you read about these letter parts.

Dateline

The **dateline** is the line that shows the date of the letter. Position the dateline about two inches from the top of the page or at least two lines below the letterhead. The exact placement depends on the letter length. The horizontal placement of the dateline depends on the letter format used.

Letter Address

The **letter address** is the part of the letter that shows the complete name and address of the receiver. Position the letter address four lines below the dateline. Place each part of the letter address on a separate line, beginning at the left margin.

Include the receiver's personal or professional title (*Mr., Ms., Dr., Mrs.*) in the letter address. The job title can appear either on the same line with the name or on the line below, whichever gives better balance. Allow one space between the two-letter postal abbreviation and the ZIP code. Use the ZIP+4 code if you know the last four digits. Look at the example at the top of page 383.

If you are writing to a woman and you do not know the personal title she prefers, use *Ms.*

Good Taste Cookbooks

300 Broadway, Evanston, IL 60204-2301 • (701) 555-1200 • Fax (708) 555-1256

Dateline	April 28, 19—
Letter Address	Mr. Thomas R. Morton 91 East Elm Street Lawton, OK 73501-6432
Salutation	Dear Mr. Morton
Body of Letter	If you enjoy cooking, then you will want a copy of <u>Lighter Cooking.</u> This new cookbook features step-by-step instructions for preparing more than 250 appetizer, main dish, and dessert recipes. By sending in the enclosed card, you can receive this colorful, spiral-bound book free for 30 days. If at the end of 30 days you are not completely satisfied with this book, return it at no charge. We believe, Mr. Morton, that you will find <u>Lighter Cooking</u> to be one of the best cookbooks you have ever used.
Complimentary Close	Sincerely yours *Charles Fountain*
Name and Title	Charles Fountain President
Reference Initials Enclosure	ep Enclosure
Copy Notation	c Gregory Smith

Figure 30–1 Letter in block format, open punctuation

Ms. Maureen Saunders, Treasurer
Central Tennessee Bank
396 Stewart Avenue
Franklin, TN 37064-7109

The ALL CAPS format may be used for the letter address if the letter is sent in a window envelope or if form letters are merged with mailing addresses using computerized equipment. This format uses no punctuation. For example:

MS MAUREEN SAUNDERS TREASURER
CENTRAL TENNESSEE BANK
396 STEWART AVENUE
FRANKLIN TN 37064-7109

Attention Line

The **attention line** is the part of the letter address that directs the correspondence to a particular individual when the letter is addressed to an organization. Begin the attention line at the left margin on the second line of the letter address. For example:

Central Tennessee Bank
Attention Ms. Maureen Saunders
396 Stewart Avenue
Franklin, TN 37064-7109

Salutation

The **salutation** acts as the greeting to the receiver. Position it two lines below the letter address. (The simplified letter format omits the salutation.) The salutation should agree with the first line of the letter address. If the first line of the address does not contain a person's name, use the neutral salutation *Ladies and Gentlemen*. If the letter is addressed to a job title, use that title, such as *Dear Service Manager*, or the neutral salutation *Dear Sir or Madam*.

Use a first name in the salutation only when you are certain that the receiver believes that you have a personal relationship.

When you prepare a letter with **mixed punctuation**, key a colon after the salutation. When you prepare a letter with **open punctuation**, use no punctuation after the salutation. The example below shows two letter addresses and salutations:

Brennan's Supermarket	Produce Manager
1018 Eighth Street	Brennan's Supermarket
Monroe, WI 53566-0011	1018 Eighth Street
DS	Monroe, WI 53566-0011
Ladies and Gentlemen:	DS
	Dear Sir or Madam

Subject Line

The optional **subject line** contains the topic of the letter. Key the subject line in all capital letters two lines below the salutation at the left margin. Omit the word SUBJECT. For example:

Mr. Mario Petrocelli
570 Orchard Boulevard
Northbrook, IL 60062-4110
DS
Dear Mr. Petrocelli:
DS
OVERSEAS TRAVEL REGULATIONS

Body

The **body** contains the message of the letter. Single-space the body of the letter and double-space between paragraphs. Place the letter attractively on the page using side margins of 1, 1½, or 2 inches, depending on the length of the letter.

Complimentary Close

The **complimentary close** is the formal closing or the "goodbye." Place the complimentary close two lines below the body of the letter. (The complimentary close is not used in the simplified format.) Capitalize only the first word of the complimentary close. Use a comma after the complimentary close with mixed punctuation; omit the comma with open punctuation.

Writer's Name and Title

Position the writer's name four lines (a quadruple space) below the complimentary close. Omit the title *Mr.* before a man's name, unless the name can be confused with a female name. *Miss, Mrs.,* or *Ms.* may be used before a woman's name, depending on the writer's preference. Place the writer's official title on the line below his or her name.

Reference Initials

The operator's **reference initials** indicate who keyed the letter. Key the initials in lowercase and position them at the left margin two lines below the printed signature line. If the initials of the person writing or dictating the letter also are included, key them in capital letters and separate them from the operator's initials with a colon (GK:er).

Enclosure Notation

An **enclosure notation** indicates that an additional item is included with a letter. Type the word *Enclosure* (or its abbreviation, *Enc.*) two lines below the reference initials when including an item.

Copy Notation

A **copy notation** indicates that someone else is to receive a copy of the letter. Key the copy notation two lines below the reference initials or enclosure notation. Where appropriate, use the following abbreviations and the name of the person receiving the copy: *c* for *copy* (also shown as *pc* for *photocopy*) and *bc* for *blind copy*. A *blind copy* notation appears on the copy (but not on the original) when you do not want the receiver to know that you sent a copy to someone else. For example:

    bc Carolyn A. Northcott

Postscript

For emphasis, you may add a **postscript**, a sentence or paragraph at the end of the letter that reinforces the message in the body. New information should not be included in a postscript. Position the postscript two lines below the last notation. The letters *P.S.* may be omitted.

Second-Page Heading

Use a *second-page heading* when the letter continues onto a second page. This heading consists of the addressee's name, the page number, and the date. Use plain paper of the same quality as the letterhead, and single space all three elements at the left margin. The second-page heading also can be keyed on the same line—name at left margin, page number at center, and date at right margin. Continue keying the body two lines below the heading. For example:

    Miss Matilde Delgado
    Page 2
    June 2, 19—

or

Name	page #	date

Letter Parts

Identify each letter part.

1. FEBRUARY ORDER
2. Enclosure
3. Dear Mr. Yamagishi
4. c Josephine Ray
5. Sincerely

Check your answers in Appendix F.

BUSINESS LETTER FORMATS

Like memos, business letters may be prepared in different formats. The three basic letter formats are block, modified block, and simplified block.

Block Format

In the **block format**, all lines begin at the left margin. Refer to Figure 30–1, page 382, for an example of the block format. (The figure also identifies the letter parts.)

Modified Block Format

In the **modified block format**, all lines begin at the left margin except for the dateline, the complimentary close, and the writer's name and title, which begin at the center of the page. This format is fairly efficient because only one tab setting at center is required. Paragraphs may begin at the left margin or be indented five spaces. As shown in Figure 30-2, the indention is optional because paragraphs are separated by double spacing.

Simplified Block Format

The **simplified block format** omits the salutation and the complimentary close. Designed for efficient processing, the simplified block format often is used when preparing letters by merging addresses from a database with a form letter. As in the block format, all lines begin at the left margin; the spacing between letter

★ Regardless of the kind of equipment used to prepare the letter, the block format is fast and simple to use because you do not need to set tabs.

Main Street CLOTHIERS

15 Main Street, Arlington, VA, 22210-3428,
(703) 555-3200, Fax (703) 555-3392

June 29, 19—

Mr. Robert DeSousa
89 Gateway Street
Arlington, VA 22210-1452

Dear Mr. DeSousa:

We are delighted to enclose your new Main Street Clothiers
credit card. You may use this card in both the Arlington and
Crystal City locations.

Because of your fine credit record, you will be able to charge as
much as $3,500 in clothing and accessories. Simply present your
credit card to any salesperson at the time of purchase.

Our annual summer clearance sale starts on July 1, and we hope
you will stop in early for the best selection. Thank you for doing
business with Main Street Clothiers.

Sincerely,

Mary Ann Loudon

Mary Ann Loudon
Credit Manager

MAL:jp

Enclosure

Figure 30–2 Letter in modified block format, mixed punctuation

parts is the same as that in block or modified block format. Also, it is a good format to use if you know the name of the receiver but cannot determine his or her sex (Pat Thomas).

Refer to Figure 30–3 as you read these guidelines for preparing letters in simplified block format:

1. Place the dateline on line 13 (2 inches from the top of the page) so that the letter address is positioned for use with a window envelope.
2. Do not include a salutation and a complimentary close.
3. Place a subject line keyed in ALL CAPS or in uppercase and lowercase letters two lines below the letter address.
4. Position the writer's name and title four lines below the body in either ALL CAPS or in uppercase and lowercase, depending on the writer's preference.
5. When writing a letter, personalize it by incorporating the receiver's name within the body of the letter.

BUSINESS ENVELOPES

When preparing a business envelope, key the receiver's personal or professional title and the job title as they appear in the letter address. If the letter address contains an attention line, type this information on the line below the receiver's company name on the envelope.

Type the address on the envelope using all the information in the letter address. The address should be keyed in all capital letters to comply with the official U.S. Postal Service format. Include the ZIP code or the ZIP+4 code on every envelope.

With a standard business envelope ($9\frac{1}{2}''$ by $4\frac{1}{8}''$), the receiver's name and address should begin on line 14. Key all information single-spaced in block style, four inches from the left edge of the envelope, as shown in Figure 30–4.

EXTRA, EXTRA!

★ The standard-sized business envelope is commonly known as a Number 10 envelope.

Letter Formats and Business Envelopes

Indicate if each statement is true or false.

1. In the block format, all lines begin at the left margin.
2. Paragraphs in the modified block format are always indented.

(Continued on page 391)

Main Street CLOTHIERS

15 Main Street, Arlington, VA, 22210-3428,
(703) 555-3200, Fax (703) 555-3392

June 29, 19—

MR. ROBERT DESOUSA
89 GATEWAY STREET
ARLINGTON VA 22210-1452

NEW CREDIT CARD

We are delighted to enclose your new Main Street Clothiers credit card. You may use this card in both the Arlington and Crystal City locations.

Because of your fine credit record, you will be able to charge as much as $3,500 in clothing and accessories. Simply present your credit card to any salesperson at the time of purchase.

Our annual summer clearance sale starts on July 1, and we hope you will stop in early for the best selection. Thank you, Mr. DeSousa, for doing business with Main Street Clothiers.

Mary Ann Loudon

Mary Ann Loudon
Credit Manager

MAL:jp

Enclosure

Figure 30–3 Letter in simplified block format (to fit window envelope)

3. Paragraphs in the simplified block format are always indented.
4. The salutation and complimentary close are omitted in the simplified block format.
5. Each line in the envelope address is separated by one double space.

Check your answers in Appendix F.

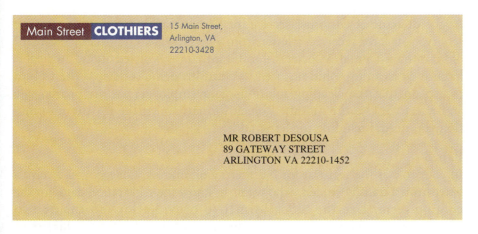

Main Street **CLOTHIERS** 15 Main Street,
Arlington, VA
22210-3428

MR ROBERT DESOUSA
89 GATEWAY STREET
ARLINGTON VA 22210-1452

Figure 30–4 Business envelope

People use business letters to send a written communication to a person in another organization. The standard parts of a business letter are the dateline, letter address, salutation, body, complimentary close, writer's name and title, and reference initials. Optional parts of a business letter include the attention line, subject line, enclosure notation, copy notation, postscript, and second-page headings. Business letters may be prepared in three formats: block, modified block, and simplified block. Envelope addresses are keyed using the title and address information contained in the letter address.

Discussion Questions

1. List the standard and optional parts of a business letter.
2. Describe the block, modified block, and simplified block letter formats.
3. How is the information in the letter address used when preparing the business envelope?

Practical Applications

Part A

As the director of customer service for Clean Machine, an office cleaning service, you have received a letter from Dr. Howard Grantham, President of Grantham Dental Associates. Dr. Grantham is worried about the health hazards of cleaning solutions used to clean his dental office. Write to him to explain that the cleaning solutions your employees use are proven safe and effective. Use the modified block format, and make up any information you need, including the letter address.

Part B

In your role as the registrar for Northern Community College, you receive a letter from a transfer student who wants to know the registration dates for the coming term. Use the block format to provide this information in a letter to the student. Make up any information you need to write this letter.

Editing and Proofreading Application

Edit and rewrite the following letter in (1) block format with open punctuation and (2) modified block format with mixed punctuation and paragraphs beginning at the left margin.

April 14, 19—/Mr. Marvin Fontana/98 Barfield Road/Atlanta, GA 30328-5187/Dear Mr. Fontana

Welcome to First Bank. We have enclosed herewith a brochure that will answer any question's about your new checking account.

In addition to that brochure, enclosed you will find your "Everywhere" automated teller machine card with this letter. Let us point out that you can use your "Everywhere" card at any First Valley Bank branches. In addition, you can use it at any other teller machines anywhere that displays the "Everywhere" logo.

Thank you once more for choosing First Bank. We are pleased to be able to serve your banking need.

Sincerely/Nancy Tallman/Customer Service Representative/cp/Enclosures

Routine, Good News, and Goodwill

OBJECTIVES

After studying this chapter and completing the chapter exercises, you will be able to do the following:

1. Plan routine, good news, and goodwill letters.
2. Organize routine, good news, and goodwill letters.
3. Write routine, good news, and goodwill letters.

Chapter 31

PLANNING AND ORGANIZING ROUTINE, GOOD NEWS, AND GOODWILL LETTERS

Communication is receiver oriented; therefore, senders should view messages from the receiver's perspective. This perspective helps the sender obtain the desired response from the receiver. The four steps in planning routine, good news, and goodwill letters are to identify the objective, identify the main idea, determine the supporting information, and adjust the content to the receiver. These steps are applied in the following example:

Identify the Objective	To make an offer of employment
Identify the Main Idea	Offer the applicant a position as a training director in the Office Services Department
Determine the Supporting Information	Impressed with the applicant's knowledge of company and good work attitude; annual salary of $28,000; paid semimonthly; starting date is July 1; conditions of employment; decision needed within one week
Adjust the Content to the Receiver	Applicant is knowledgeable about the job requirements and the company. Applicant will be eager to hear from us.

Routine, good news, and goodwill letters are organized in the direct order—the main idea is presented immediately, followed by the supporting information.

Main Idea

In an effective routine, good news, or goodwill letter, the main idea appears clearly and concisely in the first or second sentence. Emphasize good news by keeping introductory paragraphs short—one or two sentences (usually no longer than four lines).

ACROSS CULTURES

- In the North American business culture, writing in a clear and concise manner is very important. This concept is especially true when writing main ideas.

CHECKPOINT 1

Main Idea

Indicate if each sentence would be a good or poor opening for a response to a request for customer credit information.

1. We appreciate your confidence in our credit information.
(Continued on the next page)

Supporting Information

After conveying the good news or main idea in the first paragraph, the next step is to provide information that will clarify the main idea and help the receiver. Supporting information should furnish necessary explanations, state conditions of the good news, or answer questions.

This section may have one or more paragraphs. For clarity, make sure each paragraph has a central idea, repeat key words, and enumerate important points. For psychological appeal, make these middle paragraphs no longer than eight lines.

★ Receivers usually scan letters before reading them more carefully. Keep paragraphs relatively short so that receivers develop a positive attitude toward your letters.

Goodwill Closing

The closing of a letter provides an excellent opportunity to build goodwill. The closing should be friendly and courteous and leave a favorable impression with the receiver. In addition, it should identify any required action. Using the receiver's name adds a personal touch. Figure 31–1 shows a good news letter in the direct order.

Correspondence from a company that sells products or services may include a soft sale in the closing. A soft sale is an attempt to sell a product or service but is not strong or pushy. The following is an example of a goodwill closing that contains a soft sale:

> Thank you, Mr. Ruiz, for your order. By the way, you may want to visit our store during our Anniversary Sale between the 15th and 29th of May. All personal computers and word processors will be reduced 25 percent.

Letterhead: **Microcomputer Services Company, Inc.**
13450 Grant Boulevard
Greensville, SC 50298-1345

September 10, 19—

Ms. Elizabeth Shiflett
4103 East Waketon Avenue
Greensville, SC 50293-4303

Dear Elizabeth:

Main Idea   Congratulations! You have been selected for the position of training director in the Office Services Department.

Supporting Information   During your visit, we were impressed with your knowledge of our company and of the management techniques that we use. Your positive attitude is very apparent.

Your starting date is July 1. If this date is inconvenient, please let us know—there is some flexibility. Your annual salary will be $28,000, and you will be paid $1,250 semimonthly.

Please let us know your decision in writing by Wednesday, June 8.

Goodwill Closing   Elizabeth, we eagerly await your reply and hope that you will accept our offer. If you have any questions, please call me at (318) 555-5800.

Sincerely,

Harry James

Harry James
Vice President of
Administrative Services

rk

Figure 31–1   Good news letter in direct order

Goodwill Closings

Indicate if each sentence would be a good or poor closing for a letter that supplies requested credit information.

1. The next time I need credit information from your agency, you'll certainly hear from us.
2. If you need additional information, please ask.
3. Please ask if you need more information on John Rogers.
4. We appreciate your request.
5. John Rogers will be an excellent credit customer.

Check your answers in Appendix F.

ROUTINE LETTERS

A **routine letter** makes no demands the receiver will view as a burden. Thus, *the receiver does not need to be persuaded to do something.* Examples of routine letters are routine requests and claims.

Routine Requests

A **routine request** is a request for an action that will be done willingly. "Will you . . ." is the main idea of a routine request. To aid the receiver in the response, the writer must provide sufficient detail for the receiver to understand the request and respond easily. Providing details means anticipating the receiver's questions and responding to them. For example, if you asked someone to speak, you would need to provide the receiver with answers to the following questions:

1. What is the topic?
2. What is the background, knowledge, and expected size of the audience?
3. What is the date, time, and location of the presentation?
4. Will the speaker receive remuneration? If so, how much?
5. If travel is involved, who will arrange and pay for accommodations?

In a routine request, reveal the main idea quickly, provide necessary supporting information concisely, and close in a polite, helpful manner. This routine request is organized in the direct order:

Receiver-oriented supporting information in a request helps the receiver judge the sender in a favorable light.

Main Idea	States the request politely and directly and provides a reason for the request, if appropriate.
Supporting Information	Specifies information required to obtain a complete response, such as times, dates, benefits to the receiver, and terms of payment.
Goodwill Closing	Ends pleasantly and indicates the action the receiver should take.

The following routine request is in the direct order:

Main Idea	On March 3, our sales representatives will attend a seminar on improving oral presentations. Would you give a 45-minute presentation on the effective use of visual aids?
Supporting Information	Our representatives are receiving an increasing number of requests for presentations. Any techniques and hints you could give them would be helpful. The seminar will be held on the 15th floor in the conference room. If you accept our invitation, you will speak to about 15 representatives from 10:00 a.m. to 10:45 a.m.
Goodwill Closing	We would greatly appreciate your speaking at the seminar. Please let me know your decision by February 20 so that we can finalize plans for the seminar.

Claims

A **claim** is a special request for a refund, an exchange, or a discount on merchandise or services. Customers and clients use the direct order in claim letters to communicate to the receiver that they expect an **adjustment**—a positive settlement to a claim. A claim letter should have a positive but firm tone, as shown here:

Main Idea	Asks for an adjustment.
Supporting Information	Explains the problem or the reason for the request and identifies the damage (if damage occurred).
Goodwill Closing	Ends with a positive statement and indicates how to correct the situation.

The following letter requests an adjustment to an account:

★ In positive responses to claims, tone is extremely important. It tells the receiver how willingly the sender made the requested adjustment.

Main Idea	Please adjust my account for $16.
Supporting Information	Last month I placed an order with Lehi and Alma's. As usual, you filled the order quickly and completely. Upon checking my invoice against my purchase order, however, I realized I was charged $6.95 per copy for *The Tunnel and the Pathway* instead of the list price of $4.95. Because I received the eight copies requested, I am asking that my account be adjusted for $16.
Goodwill Closing	Please either credit my account for $16 or send me a refund. I look forward to receiving the adjustment.

GOOD NEWS LETTERS

A **good news letter** contains good news for the receiver. Therefore, the receiver's reaction to the letter is positive. Examples of good news messages are orders and positive responses to requests. Orders for merchandise, claims, and credit applications receive positive responses. Good news letters use the direct order:

Main Idea	Says "yes" to the receiver.
Supporting Information	Provides any details the receiver needs to carry out specific instructions.
Goodwill Closing	Ends with a helpful, positive closing. If the sender sells goods or services, the closing should contain a soft sale.

Orders

Companies usually place orders by using a form called a *purchase order*. Occasionally, a small company or an individual will use a letter to place an order. "Please send me . . ." is the main idea of an order letter. Provide complete supporting information to ensure an order will be filled correctly and to avoid wasting time and money. Formatting the middle paragraph as a table provides clarity and completeness. An order letter is organized in the direct order, as shown below:

Main Idea	Asks the receiver to fill the order.
Supporting Information	Supplies specific details needed by the receiver. For each item ordered, indicate the stock number or catalog number, a description including the size and color where applicable, quantity ordered, unit cost, total cost, method of shipment and shipping address, and method of payment.
Goodwill Closing	Ends with a statement indicating the action the receiver should take.

Forms for purchase orders and procedures for completing them usually are included in an organization's operations manuals.

The following letter shows a table that lists items ordered:

Main Idea	Please send the following items by Quick Express to the address shown above.				
Supporting Information	Item No.	Description	Quantity	Unit Cost	Total Cost
	#2986-A	Long-sleeve blouses (3 each of sizes 6–10, 12, and 14)	21	$9.99	$209.79
	#9041-M	Wool scarves	36	5.99	215.64
	#8695	Winter socks (6 each of sizes 7, 10, 11, and 13)	24	3.49	83.76
		TOTAL			$509.19

Goodwill Closing If you need additional information about this order, please call our toll-free number 1-800-555-0178 and ask for Sumi.

Positive Responses

A positive response tells the receiver the sender is saying "yes" to a request. The direct order is used for positive responses, as shown below:

Main Idea	Gives a positive response to the request.
Supporting Information	Provides necessary information so that the receiver knows what the sender is offering and expects. Also makes necessary requests.
Goodwill Closing	Ends with a courteous, positive statement and possibly a reminder of any action the sender wants the receiver to take. If the sender is a profit-seeking organization, the closing should include a soft sale.

The following example is a positive response to a request for someone to speak at a conference. Note that the supporting information confirms such details as the date, time, and place and makes a request of the receiver.

Main Idea	I will be pleased to speak in Seattle at the National Conference for Human Resources Directors.
Supporting Information	The honorarium you offer is fine, as are the time and date of the presentation—November 6 from 11:00 to 11:45 a.m. As you requested, I have made my travel arrangements. I will arrive on Delta Flight #1363 at 4 p.m. on November 5. Because I will have no transportation available, could you have someone pick me up at the airport.
Goodwill Closing	Thank you for the opportunity to speak at this conference and to visit your beautiful city. I look forward to meeting you and meeting someone at the airport.

A positive response to a credit request is good news to the receiver. In the following response, the supporting information includes a description of restrictions on the account and the payment terms. The closing includes a soft sale.

Main Idea	Your McFarland's charge account is ready for you. Thank you for your interest in our products.
Supporting Information	For new accounts, the terms are 2/10, net/30. Because your credit rating and references are excellent, the limit for your account is $15,000.
Goodwill Closing	Enclosed are catalogs of our products. If you have questions about our products, call 1-800-555-0300. Our trained salespersons will be happy to help you.

★ A soft sale is an easy way to remind a customer of a company's products or services.

GOODWILL LETTERS

A **goodwill letter** is a friendship message designed to build relationships. Effectively written goodwill letters help increase the receiver's goodwill toward the sender. Goodwill letters may express congratulations, sympathy, welcome, or appreciation. They may also extend invitations. The expression is the main idea of a goodwill message.

A goodwill message may or may not need supporting information. For example, when expressing sympathy, details are inappropriate. Yet, details in an invitation are critical because the receiver needs to know who is invited, when and where the occasion will be held, and how to dress.

The following congratulatory letter needs no supporting information:

Main Idea	Congratulations on your recent promotion to Supervisor of Office Services.
Goodwill Closing	You truly deserve this promotion, and those who will work for you will be fortunate to have you as their supervisor.

The following invitation includes necessary supporting information:

Main Idea	You are invited to a small surprise party celebrating Mark Mortonsen's recent promotion.
Supporting Information	It will be held on the third floor in the cafeteria at 4:15 p.m. on Wednesday, August 25.
Goodwill Closing	Come and help us congratulate Mark. RSVP by Monday, August 23, ext. 5068.

An **acknowledgment** tells a sender that a message has been received. The main purpose of an acknowledgment is to maintain or build goodwill. An acknowledgment also may be used to inform the receiver that a request cannot be filled right away. These messages often are used to acknowledge orders and credit applications. The supporting information usually reveals the reasons for the delay, and the goodwill closing contains a soft sale, as shown on page 403.

Main Idea	Thank you for your order. We are pleased to have you as one of our customers.
Supporting Information	The demand for the earthenware plant holders has far exceeded our supply. Your order will be sent May 15, the day we expect our shipment.
Goodwill Closing	In the meantime, look over the enclosed flier announcing our "Spring Fling Sale." Place your order now to enjoy 50 percent savings on several items.

Figure 31–2 provides a checklist to help you compose effective routine, good news, and goodwill letters. Questions in the planning stage will help you determine the content of the message and adjust it to your receiver. The writing stage will help you to organize and present the message in a complete, considerate manner. The editing stage will help you make your writing correct and concise.

Routine, Good News, and Goodwill Letters

Indicate if each statement is true or false.

1. Use the direct order for all routine, good news, and goodwill letters.
2. In routine, good news, and goodwill messages, the receiver views the main idea of the letter neutrally or positively.
3. All goodwill letters require supporting information.
4. In an order letter, supporting information should be placed in tables.
5. A claim should be written in the indirect order when the sender asks for a refund.

Check your answers in Appendix F.

Place a check mark in the blank when you can respond "yes" to the question.

Planning Stage

_____ 1. Have I identified the objective of the message?
_____ 2. Have I identified the main idea of the message?
_____ 3. Have I identified the supporting information needed by the receiver?
_____ 4. Have I adjusted the main idea and supporting information to the needs and background of my receiver?

Writing Stage

_____ 5. Have I presented the main idea in the first or second sentence of the first paragraph?
_____ 6. Have I presented all supporting information the receiver will need in order to do what I want?
_____ 7. Have I presented the supporting information after the main idea?
_____ 8. Is the ending friendly, courteous, and personable?

Editing Stage

_____ 9. Is the language clear and concise, and is the message in the appropriate tone?
_____ 10. Are format, grammar, punctuation, and spelling correct?
_____ 11. Are the first and last paragraphs no longer than four lines each?
_____ 12. Are other paragraphs no longer than eight lines?

Figure 31–2 Checklist for routine, good news, and goodwill letters

Summary

Routine, good news, and goodwill letters should be planned and organized to include the main idea, supporting information, and a goodwill closing in the direct order. Routine letters include routine requests and claims. Good news letters include orders and positive responses. Goodwill letters may express congratulations, sympathy, welcome, or appreciation. They also may extend invitations.

Discussion Questions

1. Where is the main idea placed in routine, good news, and goodwill messages? Why?
2. What supporting information should be included in (a) an order? (b) a request? (c) a positive response? (d) a goodwill letter?
3. Why is a goodwill closing important?

Practical Applications

Part A

Indicate the type of letter each sentence might open. Choose from these types of letters:

order	acknowledgment	positive response
request	claim	

1. Please replace this faulty lock.
2. I would like to open a charge account with your company.
3. Your account has been adjusted as you requested.
4. Here are the prints you ordered.
5. Your order for 12 two-drawer Ez-Clos file cabinets has been received.
6. Please credit my account for the cost of one 16-oz. container of Restoration Carpet Cleaner.

Use Figure 31–2 to help you write the following letters.

Part B

Compose a letter congratulating a friend on a recent promotion, anniversary, birthday, or other event. Supply all necessary information.

Part C

Assume that you are a loan officer for Stonehead First National Bank. You have received a request for a $25,000 home improvement loan from Mr. and Mrs. James Kennedy of 973 East Ashbrooke Drive, Tennison, VA 22812-3735. Write Mr. and Mrs. Kennedy, acknowledge receipt of their application, and explain that processing will take about ten days.

Part D

Write Mr. and Mrs. Kennedy—address shown in Practical Application Part C—and tell them their loan has been approved. Advise them that they must sign the loan agreement within 14 days. Because they are such a good credit risk, tell them of other loans available to them, such as car loans, small investment loans, and boat loans.

Part E

Ms. Wilson Washington, 4091 South Pearl Drive, Thomasville, SD 57245-1642, purchased an electric stove Model 76931-el. After two months, one of the small burners stopped working. The stove is still under warranty. Write and request that the Thomasville Mercantile and Appliance Shop, 496 Woodward Street, Watertown, SD 57201-1574, repair or replace the stove.

Part F

Anita Bennett has written you, the manager of Katina's Fashions, and requested a charge account. Write Ms. Bennett and ask her to complete and return the enclosed credit application. Explain that application processing takes about two weeks. Ms. Bennett lives at 4391 North Plum Tree Avenue, Apartment #6, Cuidad de Vacas, CA 92383-0413.

Part G

Write Ms. Bennett—address shown in Practical Application Part F—and tell her the credit application with Katina's Fashions, 391 East Kamala Lane, San Jacinto, CA 92383-0413, has been approved. Her account will have a $500 limit. The interest rate on the unpaid balance at the end of each billing period—30 days—is 18 percent a year.

Part H

Write to the university of your choice and request admission forms, scholarship information, and on-campus housing information.

Part I

Assume that you are James Fitzgerald who lives at 3920 Benson Avenue, in your city. Last year on July 1, the city informed you that your street would be repaved and that each homeowner would be assessed $150 in three monthly payments of $50 due August 1, September 1, and October 1. You have made these payments. However, as of July 1 of this year, the street still has not been repaved. Write Kyle J. Torbusch, City Engineer, City Government Offices, 4973 South Glen Ellyn Drive, your city and ZIP code, and ask for an explanation or for a refund.

Part J

Assume that you are Kyle J. Torbusch, City Engineer of your city. Respond to the request in Practical Application I. Tell Mr. Fitzgerald that some homeowners were slow to pay their assessments. Consequently, the repaving, scheduled to start last May, was posponed until August 15.

Editing and Proofreading Application

Edit, proofread, and rewrite the following message.

> Yesterdays' announcment of a more restrictive budget was a definite suprise. It is to supercede other budgetary information received. This extraordinary action will require alot of corporation among department supervisors.

Bad News Letters

OBJECTIVES

After studying this chapter and completing the chapter exercises, you will be able to do the following:

1. Plan bad news letters.
2. Organize bad news letters.
3. Write bad news letters.

PLANNING THE BAD NEWS LETTER

A **bad news letter** conveys news that will disappoint the receiver. Letters that deny requests, decline to supply information, refuse credit, or reject a proposal are examples of bad news letters. Careful planning and organizing are required to convey the disappointing news and yet maintain goodwill.

The tone of a bad news letter should reflect a sincere concern for the receiver's interests. Your aim is to present the unfavorable news positively and in a manner the receiver will view as fair and, if possible, in the receiver's best interests.

The steps in planning a bad news message are to identify the objective, identify the main idea, determine the supporting information, and adjust the content to the receiver, as shown below:

LEGAL/Ethical

- Laws guide society through tough times. Well-written bad news letters are like laws— they get businesses through tough times, yet maintain goodwill.

Identify the Objective	Convey the unfavorable news and maintain goodwill.
Identify the Main Idea	State the refusal in a positive way that reflects the receiver's best interests. The refusal should include valid supporting information.
Determine the Supporting Information	Determine what, if any, additional background information the receiver may need; determine logical reasons for the refusal; and determine possible benefits to the receiver.
Adjust the Content to the Receiver	Determine the receiver's values and concerns. Adjust the supporting information accordingly.

ACROSS **CULTURES**

- In Latin American cultures, writers do not use the direct order for bad news letters. To state the bad news before explaining the reasons behind the news is considered extremely offensive.

ORGANIZING THE BAD NEWS LETTER

Letters that convey unfavorable news are organized in the indirect order. The indirect order presents the reasons or details that explain the unfavorable news *before* stating the bad news itself. The reasons are presented first to prepare the receiver for the unfavorable news. The direct order is used in bad news messages *only when the sender knows the receiver prefers the direct order.*

When organizing a letter in indirect order to convey unfavorable news, follow these steps:

1. Begin with a neutral opener.
2. Explain the reasons for the bad news.
3. State or imply the bad news.
4. Close on a positive note; if possible, offer an alternative.

Neutral Opening

The objectives of the opening are to establish rapport and to focus the receiver's attention on the topic of the letter. To establish rapport, the opening paragraph should be neutral, implying neither a positive nor a negative response. A neutral opener does not mislead the receiver into thinking the response is positive or discourage the receiver by revealing the bad news right away.

Assume that the sender is writing to refuse a request to serve on a committee. A message that opens with a statement that, "Serving on such an important committee would be a real pleasure," or "The Improvements Committee is an important committee on which to serve," implies that the sender will accept the offer. Such opening statements are misleading. If the sender opens the message by stating, "I wish I could serve on the Improvements Committee," on the other hand, he or she would reveal the negative response too soon.

Maintain a positive tone in the opening by avoiding the use of negative words or phrases such as, "unable," "regret to tell you," "problem exists," or "unfortunately." Instead, use positive, neutral words and phrases such as "appreciate," "agree with you," and "thank you."

Avoid opening a letter by referring to the date of the receiver's communication. "Thank you for your letter of August 10" is an example of this overused opening. This opening does not introduce the topic of the message. The following opening introduces the topic: "Your application for a charge account received our immediate attention."

EXTRA, EXTRA!

★ If you state your negative response or imply it in the opening, the receiver may become so upset that he or she stops reading.

CHECKPOINT 1

Neutral Openings

Rate each neutral opening as good or poor for the following situation. Explain all ratings.

Situation: You are a manager for a company that gives seminars on effective business communication. Dr. Reid Carlisle, a professor at Northern State University, has requested techniques for writing bad news memorandums. Because your business depends on teaching such information, you cannot share the techniques.

1. I have been asked to respond to your letter of May 15.
2. Writing effective bad news memorandums is a demanding task.
3. GoodCom Seminars, Inc., always gives consumers what they want.

(Continued on the next page)

CHECKPOINT 1

Neutral Openings Continued

4. Writing effective bad news memorandums is an interesting challenge.
5. I wish I could send you the techniques you requested.

Check your answers in Appendix F.

★ The most important elements in a bad news letter are the reasons for the negative response. If done well, the receiver will accept the bad news; if done poorly, the letter will damage goodwill.

Reasons for the Bad News

The supporting information provides the reasons for the bad news. This section may have one or two paragraphs, depending on the complexity of the letter. Present the receiver with a logical explanation of the reasons why you cannot grant the request. Keep the letter unified by concentrating on one or two main reasons. If possible, emphasize how the decision ultimately will benefit the receiver. The following example is receiver oriented:

> Providing free repair of telephones out of warranty would add greatly to the retail price of our telephones. For example, our improved cordless telephone, now selling for $79, would have to be priced at $159. Comparable price increases would be necessary for all our models.

The following response to a request for a refund on merchandise damaged in shipment is not acceptable. The reasons given are not receiver oriented. Such messages can damage goodwill between a company and its customers.

> *Weak Reasons:*
>
> If we replaced your sprinkler or refunded your money, we would be doing the work of the shipping company, which is responsible for the damage. Write to them and ask them to refund your money. They have insurance to cover their costs.

The following refusal is receiver oriented because it explains how the company's policy assures the customer that the shipping company will treat him or her appropriately.

> *Improved Reasons:*
>
> We chose the company that ships our merchandise carefully. This shipper guarantees its service yet keeps our costs and therefore your costs low. The shipping invoice on your sprinkler indicates that it was in working condition when shipped. Consequently, you will need to contact the shipping company to request a replacement or refund.

Do not use company policy as a basis for denying a request. Although citing company policy may be appropriate in some cases, always explain how this policy benefits the receiver.

CHECKPOINT 2

Reasons for the Bad News

Rate each reason for the bad news as good or poor for the following situation. Explain all ratings.

Situation: You are a manager for a company that gives seminars on effective business communication. Dr. Reid Carlisle, a professor at Northern State University, has requested techniques for writing bad news memorandums. Because your business depends on teaching such information, you cannot share the techniques.

1. We receive many requests for the techniques used in our seminars. When we supplied them, seminar fees increased.
2. GoodCom Seminars, Inc., is dedicated to helping customers improve their communications. Customers attend our seminars to increase their efficiency and to gain a competitive edge.
3. Giving you our techniques would decrease our potential profits.
4. The policy of GoodCom Seminars, Inc., prohibits sharing techniques.
5. We appreciate your interest in our presentation materials. They were developed over many years and are the primary reason executives want to attend our seminars.

Check your answers in Appendix F.

The Bad News

After learning the reasons for the bad news, the receiver should be mentally prepared to receive the actual refusal. If the reasons are logical, the refusal will evolve almost naturally. Soften the bad news by implying it rather than stating it directly. Convey the message quickly using positive language.

To imply the bad news and to avoid using negative words, (1) use an "if" clause, (2) use the passive voice, and/or (3) focus on what you can do rather than what you cannot do. For example:

"If" clause: If I could, I would send your order today.

Passive Voice: Your order will be sent just as soon as our shipment is received.

Emphasize What You Can Do: Your order will be sent just as soon as we receive the shipment from our supplier.

Avoid using the personal pronouns *I, me, my, mine, we, our, ours, us, you, your,* and *yours* when using negative language. Personal pronouns combined with negative language can insult the receiver. Saying, "Because the camera is no longer under warranty, the request must be denied," has a better tone than saying, "I have to deny your request because your camera is not under warranty."

CHECKPOINT 3

The Bad News

Rate each sentence conveying the bad news as good or poor for the following situation. Explain all ratings.

Situation: You are a manager for a company that gives seminars on effective business communication. Dr. Reid Carlisle, a professor at Northern State University, has requested techniques for writing bad news memorandums. Because your business depends on teaching such information, you cannot share the techniques.

1. If the techniques had been requested before our research, we would have been able to share them with you.
2. I cannot grant your request.
3. If you attend one of our seminars, you will learn our techniques for writing effective good news memorandums.
4. We cannot send our techniques for writing good news memorandums to you.
5. If we felt we could share our techniques, we would.

Check your answers in Appendix F.

The Closing

The closing of a bad news message should be courteous and helpful. The purpose of the closing is to maintain or rebuild goodwill with the sender. After refusing the receiver's request (the bad news), change the emphasis and close on a positive note.

To maintain a positive tone, (1) do not mention or remind the receiver of the bad news again and (2) do not apologize because you cannot accommodate the receiver. If a mistake has not been made, an apology is not appropriate. If you did make a mistake, you owe the receiver an apology. However, place the apology in the middle paragraphs—not in the closing.

The closing also should have a sincere tone. Avoid overused closings such as, "If you have any questions, please don't hesitate to call." You can use a similar statement but with a positive tone; "If you have any questions, please call." Avoid using conditional words such as *hope, think,* and *maybe.* Analyze these poor closings:

> *Reminder of the Negative News:* Even though we cannot fill your order, we have enclosed our newest catalog.

> *Apology:* I'm sorry that we cannot fill your order, but we have enclosed our newest catalog.

> *Overused Expression:* Even though we cannot fill your order, if there is anything I can do, please let me know.

To be as helpful as possible, offer the receiver another option. Most problem situations have more than one solution. Presenting another option shifts the emphasis from the bad news to a positive solution. For example:

> Because part No. 1403 is no longer being manufactured, part No. 1402 is being used as a substitute. The substitute is only $15 and functions just as well as part No. 1403. If you would like to order part No. 1402, just call me at 1-800-284-9021. The day you place your order is the day your order will be shipped to you.

If the receiver is a customer, you may close the message with a soft sale by mentioning a related product, a discount, or some other relevant item that would interest the receiver. A soft sale closing might say, "Our latest sales brochure is enclosed. Note that some of our materials are reduced by as much as 50 percent. Come in and see them soon."

★ Goodwill is the one and only asset that competition cannot undersell or destroy. Only you can let goodwill slip away.

4 | The Closing

Rate each closing as good or poor for the following situation. Explain all ratings.

Situation: Once again, you are a manager for a company that gives seminars on effective business communication. Dr. Reid Carlisle, a professor at Northern State University, has requested techniques for writing bad news memorandums. Because your business depends on teaching such information, you cannot share the techniques.

1. My sincere hope is that this response meets with your satisfaction.
2. As you may know, our seminars are very effective. Attend one and you not only will learn the techniques but also will gain insights into the techniques themselves. A list of the times and places of the seminars, an enrollment card, and a coupon for a 20 percent discount on enrollment are enclosed.
3. Dr. Carlisle, several other companies might share their techniques. Have you tried SITCOM Co. or LITCOM, Inc.? Their addresses are enclosed.
4. I am sorry I cannot grant your request.
5. Our library is extensive, and we often allow researchers to use it. If you are interested, please call to arrange a time convenient for you.

Check your answers in Appendix F.

WRITING THE BAD NEWS LETTER

Typical bad news messages that need special attention are messages that (1) decline a request and (2) refuse credit.

★ Initially, writing effective bad news letters will take more time than writing other letters. As you write more and more of them, however, the process will become easier and less time consuming.

Declining a Request

The reasons for declining a request are the most important aspect of these letters. The success of the message depends on whether the receiver judges these reasons as valid. Based on the situation explained in earlier checkpoints, the following letter is an example of an effective message that denies a request. The letter says *no* to Dr. Carlisle, but does not damage the goodwill between Dr. Carlisle and the company.

Neutral Opening	Writing effective bad news memorandums can be a demanding task.
Reasons for the Bad News and the Bad News	Requests for techniques on writing effectively are frequently sent to us. Therefore, we conducted a study to determine if sharing these techniques with the public affected attendance at our seminars. We found that it did. Attendance at the seminars is important because it provides the income that we need to pay our employees. If these techniques had been requested before our research, we might have been able to share them with you.
Closing (Soft Sale)	Dr. Carlisle, as you may know, our seminars are very effective. Attend one and you not only will learn the techniques but also will gain insights into the techniques themselves. A list of the times and places of our seminars, an enrollment card, and a coupon for a 20 percent discount on enrollment are enclosed.

Refusing Credit

Credit may be refused for several reasons. The credit application may contain incomplete information or insufficient credit references. The references may not be verifiable or they may be negative. The employment record may not be strong enough or verifiable. The applicant may have excessive debt obligations, delinquent credit obligations, or insufficient income.

If credit must be refused, the receiver has a right to know why. The sender's responsibility is to explain the reasons tactfully. The goal is to refuse credit but maintain the person as a cash customer. Study the following example:

LEGAL/Ethical

- Credit laws require credit lenders to inform receivers of their rights when they have been refused credit. If these rights are explained in legalistic language and are not clear, help the receiver by writing the refusal letter in clear, easy-to-understand language; then, enclose the required statements on a card.

Neutral Opening	Thank you for your order for Stonecut Flooring. You certainly have selected a quality product that is extremely durable.
Reasons for the Bad News, the Bad News, and an Alternative	Your credit application has been reviewed. As you probably know, financial experts suggest that individuals maintain an income-to-debt ratio of about 3 to 1. Because your obligations extend beyond one third of your income, we suggest that a cash purchase be made.
Helpful Closing	Please let us know if you wish to place a cash order now. In addition to flooring, we have many other quality products for your home at low, discounted prices. As a cash customer, you will receive the same quality merchandise, courtesy, and low prices.

The following rejection of a request for credit could offend some people:

Neutral Opening	Your application for credit has been considered.
Reasons for the Bad News	Upon examining your credit situation, we found that you have extended your credit to the limit. Therefore, we must reject your application. To give you credit at this time would be unwise.
Closing	I'm sorry we have to refuse your request, but we must. Our most recent catalogue is enclosed. We hope you would like to purchase some of these products with cash.

Although the opening is neutral, the reasons for the bad news are not presented tactfully. The message uses negative language (the words *reject* and *unwise*) to say *no*. The closing should not include an apology. Even though the closing offers an alternative, the words "we hope" make it very weak.

The checklist in Figure 32–1 will help you to compose effective bad news messages. The planning stage will help you identify the appropriate content of the message. The writing stage will help you select effective language for the message and place the content in an appropriate order. The editing stage will help you detect any errors when writing.

Place a check mark in the blank when you can respond yes to the question.

Planning Stage

_____ 1. Have I identified the objective of the message?

_____ 2. Have I identified the main idea of the message?

_____ 3. Have I identified the supporting information needed by the receiver?

_____ 4. Have I adjusted the main idea and supporting information to the receiver?

Writing Stage

_____ 5. Is the opening neutral and does it introduce the topic of the message?

_____ 6. Does the supporting information focus on one or two receiver-oriented reasons for the bad news?

_____ 7. When giving the bad news, have I used positive language?

_____ 8. When giving the bad news, have I used an "if" clause or the passive voice (if possible)?

_____ 9. When giving the bad news, have I told the receiver what could be done rather than what couldn't?

_____ 10. Is the closing helpful and courteous? (Including a soft sale is appropriate in a letter to a customer.)

_____ 11. Does the closing offer an alternative if possible, contain no apology, and avoid reminders of the bad news?

Editing Stage

_____ 12. Is the language clear and concise? Is the tone positive?

_____ 13. Are the format, grammar, punctuation, and spelling correct?

Figure 32–1 Checklist for bad news messages

Summary

Effective bad news messages convey disappointing news without losing the receiver's goodwill. These messages are written in the indirect order. The opening paragraph introduces the topic of the message in a neutral manner. The next part of the message gives the reasons for the bad news and prepares the receiver for the coming bad news. The bad news itself should be presented using positive language, if possible. The closing of a bad news message should be helpful and friendly, aiming to rebuild or maintain goodwill.

Discussion Questions

1. What are the steps in planning a bad news letter?
2. Why is the indirect order used in most bad news letters?
3. Explain the purpose of the opening, supporting information, and closing of a bad news message.

Practical Applications

Part A

Mays Printing Service prepared and printed a resume for Ms. Pam Donaldson. The resume was printed exactly as she specified. She proofread the resume but overlooked a mistake in the spelling of a previous employer's name. The resume was printed with the mistake, and she has asked for a refund. As manager of Mays Printing Service, write Ms. Donaldson, 1607 North Benard Avenue, River City, TN 37415-0551, and refuse her request.

Part B

Mr. Steve Chandler, Route 4, Box 51, Rock Canyon, WY 82901-0021, purchased a SilverMaster toaster 13 months ago. He has written you, the manager of the store where he made the purchase, to say that the toaster is not working properly and to ask for a replacement. The toaster is no longer under warranty. Write Mr. Chandler and refuse the request. Suggest that he send in the toaster for repairs.

Part C

Dr. Toni Powell, a researcher at the Utopia Research Institution, 2501 Western Junction, Sioux Cliffs, SD 57078-0135, has asked for the names and addresses of 250 of our stockholders. Company policy forbids releasing the names and addresses of our stockholders because revealing such information could result in a lawsuit against the company. Write Dr. Powell and refuse her request. You know Dr. Powell very well and know that she prefers the direct order.

Part D

Mrs. Susan McCurdy of 869 South Cactus Boulevard, Camelback View, AZ 85635-0095, has written you to order a book entitled *Computers and You.* She has enclosed a check for $24.95. Write the customer and tell her the book is out of stock until your next shipment arrives on July 14. You will hold her check until you ship the book.

Part E

As credit manager for Best Foods, Inc., write Ms. Chantel Washington, 445 Ocean View Lane, New Beach, CT 06513-1413, and refuse her request for credit. At present, she has many charge accounts that are charged to their limits. She might not be able to make the payments if you allowed her additional credit.

Part F

Stanley Thomas used the placement office at his school in an effort to obtain a job. He indicated on each reference request form that the reference would remain confidential. This confidentiality was evident to everyone who completed a reference form for Stanley. Now Stanley has written to the placement office asking for a complete copy of his file, including the completed reference forms. As director of the placement office, write to Stanley and explain that you will send him a copy of all material in his file except the reference forms. Releasing the completed forms to Stan would disclose confidential information. Stanley lives at 396 Turk Bluffs Avenue, River Crest, OR 97360-0442.

Part G

Ms. Kathy O'Neal, 2903 North Woodhaven, Mount Whitney, WA 98273-9998, bought a dress from your department at Elaine's Dress Shoppe. All dresses are altered to fit the customer. After Ms. O'Neal had the dress altered, she decided it was the wrong color. She has returned the dress and has asked for a refund. As manager of Elaine's, write to her and refuse the request.

Part H

Ashad Mostika of 2148 Western Golf Avenue, Chicago, IL 60505-6131, a recent immigrant to this country, has sent you a credit application. Write Mr. Mostika and refuse his request because of his lack of credit references.

Editing and Proofreading Application

Edit, proofread, and rewrite the following paragraph.

> If your interested in an obivous oppertunity, consider the restuarant business in Dayton. Questionaires completed by residents of that city indicated a real need for restuarants. Enthusiastic, efficient individuals could take advantage of this situation and open there own business.

Persuasive Letters

OBJECTIVES

After studying this chapter and completing the chapter exercises, you will be able to do the following:

1. List the steps in planning persuasive letters.
2. Explain each section in the organization of persuasive letters.
3. List and define three types of persuasive letters.
4. Write persuasive letters.

PLANNING PERSUASIVE LETTERS

A persuasive letter motivates the receiver to act. A persuasive message may try to convince the receiver to buy a product or a service, to do a favor, or to change an opinion. Sales letters, persuasive requests, and collection letters are examples of persuasive letters.

Some experts estimate that selling consists of 90 percent planning and 10 percent presentation. Constructing persuasive messages is similar to selling. At the planning stage, assume that the receiver will lack interest in or resist the persuasive message. Why? Because most businesspeople are extremely busy and have limited resources of time, money, and energy. The challenge of a persuasive letter is to overcome barriers caused by the lack of resources, resistance to change, or satisfaction with present conditions.

People are not persuaded to buy a product or accept an idea just because it has several good features. People are persuaded because they feel a need for the product or idea. Although needs vary among people, needs often are linked to achievement, recognition, comfort, convenience, physical well-being, or money.

Identify the Objective and the Main Idea

The objective and main idea of a persuasive letter are closely related. For example, the objective may be to motivate the receiver to buy a product or service, to share information, to help with a project, to contribute money, or to cooperate with a decision. This objective becomes the main idea. The main idea in a persuasive letter usually appears in the closing.

Determine the Supporting Information

To persuade the receiver successfully, the sender must analyze the receiver to determine the person's needs or viewpoints. Keeping the receiver in mind, the sender then determines the main feature of the product or idea that will appeal to the receiver. Finally, and most important, the sender must then convert the main idea into benefits for the receiver.

Adjust the Content to the Receiver

People are motivated when a product or an idea meets a need. Discovering the receiver's specific needs and the benefits the receiver hopes to obtain from your idea or product requires empathy. You must be sincerely concerned about the interests and needs of the receiver.

Analyze the receiver and determine as best you can the characteristics or values important to him or her. Is the receiver interested in status? comfort? convenience? What benefits will appeal to the receiver? price? quality? speed? Is the receiver concerned about income? education? security? The more you can learn about the receiver, the better you can translate the features of the product or idea into benefits for the receiver.

Select the Primary Appeal

Identify the main idea by determining what will appeal most to the receiver. Although several appeals can be used, determine the one that will attract the receiver's attention and motivate the receiver to act. In a sales letter, the primary appeal is often called the *main selling point.* The primary appeal is the focus of a persuasive letter.

If the objective of the letter is to convince the receiver to pay an overdue account, the primary appeal might be maintaining the receiver's excellent credit rating. If you know that the receiver always waits until the last minute to re-order merchandise, the primary appeal could be fast delivery.

Provide Supporting Information

Once you have established the primary appeal, identify the information necessary to explain or reinforce this appeal. Determine how to express the features as benefits to the receiver. For example, if the primary appeal is the receiver's interest in quality merchandise, the supporting information should provide convincing details that will influence the receiver to buy the product because of its high quality. Adjust supporting information to the receiver to create interest and desire for the product or idea.

ORGANIZING PERSUASIVE LETTERS

Persuasive letters use the indirect order. The supporting information appears before the main idea—the action you want the receiver to take. By using the indirect approach, you prepare the receiver for the main message before presenting it.

Follow these steps when presenting persuasive messages:

1. Gain the receiver's attention.
2. Present the supporting information.
3. Close by presenting the main idea—the desired action.

★ When a persuasive letter has multiple receivers, determining the primary appeal is much more complex. Divide the receivers into groups by probable appeal.

ACROSS CULTURES

- Most Latin Americans always use the indirect order for persuasive letters. These cultures are more receiver-oriented than the North American business culture.

Attention-Getting Opening

The purpose of the opening is to grab the receiver's attention so that he or she will read the rest of the letter. The opening paragraph should introduce the topic of the letter in an interesting, original, and relevant manner. Make the tone positive, sincere, honest, and receiver oriented.

Gain attention by using one of the following types of openings:

> Propose a solution to the receiver's problem.
> Provide a bargain.
> Present an important fact.
> Quote a famous or respected person.
> Make an analogy.
> Present a "what if" situation.
> List an outstanding feature of the product or service.

Compare the following attention-getting openings for a letter that asks a prominent person to speak at a conference:

Weak Opening	I am looking for someone to address the Association of Small Businesses next month. I know you are busy, but would you be our speaker?
Improved Opening	The Secretary of Commerce has said, "Without small businesses, America would be out of work. Nearly half of all new jobs are created by businesses with fewer than 100 employees."

The first opening is weak because it reflects the sender's needs rather than the receiver's interests and uses a negative tone. The second opening uses a quote to gain the receiver's attention and introduces the topic in an interesting, original manner.

This discussion of openings assumes that the persuasive message is unsolicited. An **unsolicited persuasive message** is a persuasive message the receiver has not requested. A **solicited persuasive message** is a persuasive message the receiver has requested. If the message is solicited, the interest of the receiver has already been established; therefore, attention-getting techniques are not critical. The opening of a solicited persuasive message should simply introduce the topic of the letter.

Attention-Getting Opening

Rate each attention-getter as good or poor for a letter to someone who wants to enter the College of Business Administration. Explain all ratings.

1. Our business programs at Morganton University are fantastic.
2. The College of Business Administration at Morganton University is ranked number one in the state.
3. Dr. Shonda Grant said, "My undergraduate degree in the College of Business Administration at Morganton University prepared me well for my graduate degrees at Harvard."
4. Two phrases describe the College of Business Administration at Morganton University—fully accredited and highly respected.
5. Thank you for your letter of May 19. I sincerely appreciate it.

Check your answers in Appendix F.

Supporting Information

The next part of the message should create an interest in the main idea. The sender must convince the receiver that the product or service satisfies the receiver's particular needs. The main selling point determined during the planning stage becomes the focus of the supporting information.

Interest and Desire

Persuasion is not possible unless the receiver is interested in the product or idea. Once interested, the receiver must have or develop a desire for the product or idea. In a business letter, little distinction is made between interest and desire. The sender merely focuses on what the receiver considers important to determine how to meet the receiver's needs.

To create interest and desire, explain how the product or idea will benefit the receiver. Perhaps it will save the receiver money, increase the receiver's self-esteem, or help the receiver gain the approval of his or her peers. The supporting paragraphs should be receiver oriented and positive. Note how the following paragraph appeals to the receiver's need for professionalism and distinction. If the receiver views this speaking opportunity as beneficial, he or she will be motivated to accept the offer.

Each year about 250 professionals from all over the world attend the Conference of Small Businesses. This conference is recognized for its prominent speakers in the areas of small business management, creative financing, and computer technology. Speakers obtain international exposure and have an opportunity to share their knowledge with those who benefit most from it. Because of your expertise in the use of computer applications for the small business, we would like you to be one of our speakers.

One way to create desire is to involve the receiver's senses. For example, real estate agents may suggest that sellers bake an apple pie or warm some vanilla extract and water in the oven before a prospective buyer arrives. These pleasant aromas appeal to a buyer's desire for a homey atmosphere. Writers of persuasive messages must depend on words to excite the senses. Active verbs, specific details, and descriptive modifiers excite the senses and show enthusiasm, as shown in the following example.

As you walk into the store, you will see signs telling you of discounts ranging from 50 to 75 percent off all spring and summer suits. Imagine yourself in that cool, comfortable summer suit with that complementary tie—the only way to go to work on these hot summer days. Both can easily be yours for less than 90 cents a summer day.

A persuasive message is the one business communication in which you should use modifiers— adjectives and adverbs.

To create interest and desire, the sender must remove obstacles or objections the receiver may have. This principle is often applied to amounts of money. Research shows that people are more likely to buy a product if its price is stated as pennies a day rather than $1 a week, $1 a day rather than $30 a month, or $30 a month rather than $365 a year. Why? The lesser amounts sound easier to manage. In the previous example, the suit and tie sell for $85, but "less than 90 cents a summer day" makes payment sound easy.

Conviction

Often an explanation of the benefits will convince the receiver to act. In other situations, however, proving the benefits of your idea or product may provide advantages and add credibility. Research findings, statements of satisfaction from customers, names of prominent persons or institutions that use the product, and free samples are examples of proof. To add credibility, proof must be specific and concrete.

Supporting Information

Rate each paragraph as good or poor for creating interest or desire. Explain all ratings.

1. Would you speak on the tremendous experiences you had on your first and only tour of Iran? We would like to invite you, a real, up-to-date expert, to speak to our social studies class at Lorenzo Snow High School.
2. The Santa Barbara Beach Hotel is the place to be during your spring break. Even while in your room you will hear the ocean waves breaking on the beach. For pennies a night, you can stay in luxury within steps of the beach.
3. Free and young as the wind blows through your hair—what a great feeling! You could be driving that convertible for under $10 a day.
4. Because of your varied experience as an elementary school administrator, we would like you to address the district's annual meeting of school principals.
5. Pure reading excitement! Only $36 dollars a year! The cost of your subscription to *Comics Wholesale* is now lower than ever before. Order now!

Check your answers in Appendix F.

Action Closing

The next step is to persuade the receiver to act. The closing should clearly state the main idea (or benefit) by indicating the action the receiver should take. The action requested should be simple and easy to accomplish. Common ways to request action are to ask the receiver to call or to return a form.

If the receiver must order by telephone, be sure to include the correct area code and number. If the receiver must return a form, make the form accessible, make it easy to fill out, and enclose it with the message. Provide a form that folds into a pre-addressed envelope, with return postage prepaid, or provide a separate envelope if possible. The following message provides the receiver with a choice—telephoning or returning the order form:

> To order your Label Quality leather jogging shoes for only $24.75 a pair, either call 1-800-555-0156 or fill in and return the enclosed form. You could be wearing your new shoes in less than a week.

3 Action Closing

CHECKPOINT

Rate each closing as good or poor. Explain all ratings.

1. Fill out the enclosed, addressed, postage-paid form. You could be sitting in your cool, open-air cabana in three days.
2. We hope to receive your order soon. Take advantage of this great sale.
3. Call 1-800-555-0163 to give us the size and color you want, and we will ship your blouses to you today.
4. As soon as you send us a pre-addressed envelope with the total payment, we will send your order immediately.
5. Maria, I would love to have you deliver the main address at our banquet, but I know how busy you are. However, could you do it?

Check your answers in Appendix F.

WRITING PERSUASIVE LETTERS

After planning and organizing your thoughts carefully, the next step is to write the letter. Examples of persuasive letters are sales letters, persuasive requests, and collection letters.

Sales Letters

A **sales letter** tries to persuade a receiver to purchase a product or service. To organize a persuasive letter, (1) gain attention in the opener, (2) create interest and desire and convince the receiver with supporting details, and (3) provide an easy way for the receiver to act.

The objective of the following persuasive letter is to motivate the receiver to purchase shoes. The main idea or primary benefit emphasized is comfort. The letter includes research findings to convince the receiver of the value of these shoes. In addition, the closing makes ordering the shoes easy for the receiver.

Attention-Getting Opening	On your feet for eight hours but not foot-weary . . . what a great way to end the day!!! Isn't this how you'd like to feel at the end of your workday?
Supporting Information	Through research and exacting development, a shoe with shock-absorbing features has been developed and tested. Surveys were conducted with doctors and nurses who were continually on their feet during their workdays. After wearing our shoes for one month, over 80 percent of those doctors and nurses surveyed stated that, at the end of their workdays, they were not foot-weary.
Action Closing	As an introductory offer, these Quality Label leather shoes are priced at only $24.95 a pair. To order your shoes, just call toll free at 1-800-555-0153 or fill in the enclosed, addressed, and postage-prepaid form. You will be wearing your new shoes within a week and enjoying new freedom from tired feet.

How important is the appeal in a sales letter? If your job required a lot of walking and your feet hurt at the end of each day, would this product appeal to you? If you sat at your desk all day, would it appeal to you?

Persuasive Requests

A persuasive request tries to persuade the receiver to do something. Examples of persuasive requests include requests for donations, requests to serve on a time-consuming committee, and claims that must be justified. The following is a well-written request for a claim. Notice that the sender builds a case through supporting information.

Attention-Getting Opening	*Stay Well Medicine* is an excellent magazine that provides practical tips on preventive medicine.
Supporting Information	After reading *Stay Well Medicine* at our library, I realized that I wanted my own copy. I immediately subscribed because the advertising literature stated that two months should be allowed for the subscription to start. I purchased the May and June issues locally. Needless to say, I was surprised when the May and June issues arrived with the July issue.
Action Closing	The May and June issues that you sent are enclosed. Please adjust the time period of my subscription to cover July through June of next year.

Collection Letters

The purpose of a **collection letter** is to persuade the receiver to pay a past-due bill. Collection letters have four stages: (1) the reminder stage, (2) the strong reminder stage, (3) the discussion stage, and (4) the urgency stage.

The purpose of the *reminder stage* is to help the receiver remember to make a payment. The sender, therefore, assumes that the receiver has just forgotten to make a payment. A message, written in the direct order, is sent as a routine reminder. The following is a good reminder stage collection letter:

Opening	Your prompt payments for all of 19— are greatly appreciated.
Main Idea	A copy of your January statement is enclosed. Did you overlook your February 10 payment?
Closing	An addressed, postage-paid envelope is enclosed for your convenience in sending your payment.

A *strong reminder* is sent when the customer has, for some reason, failed to respond to the first reminder. The tone of this collection letter is direct and firm—send the payment due right away. For example:

Main Idea	A copy of your January statement is enclosed. Your February 10 payment is overdue.
Supporting Information	By sending us a check for $350, you will bring your account up to date, and you will preserve your credit rating.
Closing	A postage-paid return envelope is enclosed. Please use it and clear your account today.

The purpose of the *discussion stage* collection letter is to obtain full payment, partial payment as a temporary measure, or an explanation of why the customer has not made the appropriate payments. For example:

Attention-Getting Opening	Your home loan with First Western Bank has been beneficial to both of us. In the past, your payments have been prompt and consistent. In fact, you have been one of our best customers.
Supporting Information	Two months have passed, however, since your last payment. Although we have sent you two reminders, we have not received a reply. Is there some reason why you cannot make a payment?
Action Closing	Preserve your credit rating by following one of these suggestions: 1. Make your past-due payments totaling $700 within ten days. 2. Send one payment of $350 immediately and send the other payment by March 30. 3. Let us know why you have not made your last two payments, and explain your plans for correcting the situation. Please let me have your response within one week.

★ In large companies, most collection letters for the first two stages are form letters. Companies use personal letters for the last two stages.

The purpose of the *urgency stage* collection letter is to obtain payment and advise the receiver of the consequences if payment is not made immediately. The tone should be strong and firm. For example:

Attention-Getting Opening	I wish this letter were not necessary, but it is. Previous messages and efforts to obtain past-due payments have failed.
Supporting Information	The enclosed statement explains the exact amount due. Unless full payment is received by April 30, your account will be turned over to the Edwards Credit Agency, a collection company.
Action Closing	To prevent this negative situation, send us your full payment immediately.

Writing persuasive letters is a common business activity that takes time and care. Use the checklist in Figure 33–1 to create effective persuasive letters.

Place a check mark in the blank when you can respond "yes" to the question.

Planning Stage

_____ 1. Have I identified the objective of the message?
_____ 2. Have I identified the primary appeal (main idea) of the message?
_____ 3. Have I identified the supporting information?
_____ 4. Have I adjusted the main idea and supporting information to the receiver?

Writing Stage

5. Is the opener
_____ a. sincere?
_____ b. relevant to the receiver?
_____ c. original?
_____ d. pertinent to the message?
_____ e. positive?
_____ 6. Is the supporting information based on the needs of the receiver? "you" oriented? Does the supporting information motivate the receiver?
_____ 7. If action is required, does the closing explain that action clearly? Is it simple to execute?

Editing Stage

_____ 8. Is the language clear and concise, and is the letter positive and "you" oriented?
_____ 9. Are the format, grammar, punctuation, and spelling correct?
_____ 10. Does the message have unity, coherence, and proper emphasis?

Figure 33–1 Checklist for persuasive letters

Letters designed to motivate the receiver to act in a certain way are persuasive messages. Persuasive messages are organized in the indirect order to motivate the receiver to take the desired action. Examples of persuasive letters include sales letters, persuasive requests, and collection messages.

A persuasive message has three parts: (1) an attention-getting opening, (2) supporting information, and (3) the main idea—the action closing. The objective of the opening is to gain the interest of the receiver. The next section of the message tries to create desire and convince the receiver that the product or idea has value. The action closing states the main idea by requesting action from the receiver. The action the receiver should take should be easy to understand and execute.

Discussion Questions

1. List the steps used when planning a persuasive letter.
2. Explain each section in the organization of a persuasive letter.
3. List and define three types of persuasive letters.

Practical Applications

Part A

Visit a local car dealer and obtain brochures or pamphlets on one of your favorite automobiles. Study the material and write a sales letter to the dealer's customers. Enclose one of the brochures or pamphlets with the letter.

Part B

Assume that you are a student at Scottsbluff University. As you walked around the city where the university is located, you noticed that many home and business lawns are not well kept. Thus, you have decided to start a lawn-care service that includes mowing, trimming, weeding, fertilizing, and grooming lawns. Write a sales letter to prospective customers.

Part C

Assume that you are president of the business student organization at your college. Write a letter to the Chief Executive Officer of Jason Products inviting her to make a presentation on April 6, from 10 to 11 a.m., to explain the importance of computer skills. About 45 people will attend the presentation. Write Ms. Juanita Anderson, CEO, Jason Products, 4592 South Hundred Oaks, Henderson, TX 75652-0931. Because Ms. Anderson is so busy, you feel that you will have to persuade her to speak.

Part D

Assume that you are the credit manager for Ed's Shop for Men. Write Steve Brown, P. O. Box 3923, College Station, Missoula State College, Missoula, MT 63901-0001. Remind him that payment on his account was due March 5. The amount of payment is $75.50. This is the first reminder of the overdue account.

Part E

Steve Brown still has not made his March payment. Three weeks have passed since you sent him the reminder, and now the April payment is due. Send him a second stage reminder.

Part F

Six weeks have passed since you sent Steve Brown the first reminder and three weeks have passed since you sent him the second reminder. Both March and April payments are past due, and in two days another payment will be due. Write Steve another collection letter—the discussion stage message.

Part G

Three months have passed since you wrote the first reminder to Steve Brown about his overdue March payment. He has not responded to any of the three letters sent to him. Now the full amount of the account is overdue. Write him an urgency stage collection letter. Tell him that if you do not hear from him by June 25, you will turn his account over to Tolbert's Collection Agency.

Part H

One month ago, Kristine Lee purchased a jogging suit at a 25 percent discount. The tag on the suit indicated that the suit was guaranteed for one year. The seams started to split after being worn only two times. When Kristine returned the suit to the store, the clerk explained that the suit was a model sold the fall before. Therefore, it was discounted 25 percent, and no refund or exchange was possible. Kristine has decided to write the manufacturer and ask for a replacement or a refund. The manufacturer is Sport Clothing, Inc., 903 East Industrial Drive, Commerce City, CA 90022-0001. Write Kristine's letter.

Part I

Visit a local travel agency and obtain one or two brochures on a foreign city you would like to visit. Develop a one-week tour package to that city. Write a one-page sales letter to persuade customers of the agency to take the tour.

Part J

You purchased a one-gallon Green Thumb garden sprayer 13 months ago. You used the sprayer twice last spring and summer and once this spring. When you tried to spray fertilizer on your garden last week, the sprayer would not work. The sprayer is guaranteed for one year from the date of purchase. Write the manufacturer of the sprayer, Green Thumb Products, 983 West Haven Avenue, Clearfield, UT 84015-5920, and ask for replacement or repair of the sprayer even though the warranty expired last month.

Part K

Assume that you are in charge of recruiting for the college you are attending. Write a recruitment letter (a sales letter) to send to all graduating high school students in your state.

Editing and Proofreading Application

Edit, proofread, and rewrite the following message.

> Occassionally, our comittee is asked to select a cite for a new business. After a site is evaluated and selected, attornies are employed to obtain the property from the owners. When selecting the property convenience, enviroment, visibility, and weather are considered.

Reports and Other Business Documents

Report writing serves an important function in the workplace. Reports can vary from a memo advising a supervisor of progress achieved by a project team to annual reports to stockholders. Part 7 concentrates on common types of formal and informal reports and their correct formatting. The Part emphasizes the importance of paying careful attention to planning and outlining a report before beginning the writing process. It also discusses direct and indirect order used in report writing.

Visual aids and their use in reports are emphasized. With the use of computers, accurate and attractive visual aids can be created and inserted into reports at the appropriate places.

Specialized documents prepared in the workplace, including news releases, agendas, and minutes, are disucssed, and their correct formatting is illustrated.

Part 7

Chapter 34

Planning Reports

OBJECTIVES

After studying this chapter and completing the chapter exercises, you will be able to do the following:

1. Explain how to classify reports according to their style, purpose, and format.
2. Identify the steps in planning a report.
3. Contrast topical and discussion outline formats.

TYPES OF REPORTS

A *report* is a document that provides the facts about a specific situation or problem for consideration by a specific group of people. Reports are business tools that enable managers to make decisions or solve problems. Reports can be classified according to their style, purpose, and format.

Style

The two styles of reports are formal and informal. **Formal reports** generally are long, analytical, and impersonal. A formal report often contains preliminary parts such as a title page, an executive summary, and a table of contents, as well as supplementary parts such as a bibliography and an index.

An example of a formal report is a company's annual report to stockholders or a report to a government regulatory agency. Another example is an *external proposal*, a report that analyzes a problem and recommends a solution to people outside the writer's company.

Informal reports are shorter than formal reports and are written in a less formal style. Unlike formal reports, informal reports generally have no preliminary or supplementary parts because they are usually concerned with everyday matters that require little background. In addition, its organization differs from that of the formal report.

A sales report is an example of an informal report. In a sales report, the writer summarizes sales for a specific period, such as the number of cars sold by an automobile dealership during the previous month. Another type of informal report, an *internal proposal* (also known as a *justification report*), is used to analyze an internal problem and recommend a solution. For example, a shift supervisor might write an internal proposal to convince a factory manager to buy new equipment.

Purpose

Reports can be either informational or analytical. **Informational reports** present information (facts), so they include very little analysis. For example, a bank manager may ask the head cashier to prepare an informational report about the average number and value of money orders sold each day. The components of an informational report are the **topics** (subjects) or the areas investigated.

Some reports you write will be for managers only one level above you; others will be for managers two or three levels above you.

Analytical reports analyze a problem, and they include the presentation of the facts, conclusions, and recommendations. In contrast to an informational report, which just presents the facts, an analytical report also suggests what might be done to solve the problem. The components of an analytical report are the problem's probable causes and solutions.

When you write a brief, informal report for a manager in your organization, use one of the memo formats shown in Chapter 27 unless the organization uses its own format.

Format

Informal reports can be written in several different formats, or arrangements, including *memo*, *letter*, and *manuscript* formats. Formal reports are longer and more complex than informal reports, so they are written in manuscript format.

STEPS IN PLANNING A REPORT

Before writing a report, you must do some preliminary work. Even if you are simply reporting facts, you must gather those facts and then arrange them in a logical sequence that is easy for the reader to follow. When planning a report, you should (1) identify the problem; (2) decide what to investigate; (3) develop a preliminary outline; (4) collect the data; and (5) analyze the data, draw conclusions, and make recommendations.

Identify the Problem

The first step is to identify the problem to be studied and the objective of the report. As in planning letters and memos, determine why you are writing the report and what you hope to accomplish.

Prepare a written statement of the problem you will analyze in your report. Depending on the preferences of your company and your supervisor, this statement may be expressed as an infinitive phrase, as a question, or as a statement.

Infinitive Phrase	The purpose of this report is to determine if the accounting department needs to buy new computers.
Question	This report will answer the question, "Does the accounting department need to buy new computers?"
Statement	This report will determine if the accounting department needs to buy new computers.

★ You should be able to express any problem statement in a single sentence. If you cannot, try to simplify the problem until you can state it in one sentence.

Decide What to Investigate

Your next step is to decide exactly what to investigate. Only after you understand the problem and the scope of the investigation can you plan your research.

Determine the Scope

Scope refers to the boundaries of the report—what will be included and what will be excluded. For example, a report about the use of computers in all departments will require more research and have a wider scope than a report that examines computer use in just two departments.

Plan the Research

Once you know the scope of your report, develop a plan for getting the facts you need. List the questions that need answers and execute the steps you need to find those answers. Also consider how much time and money you have. Then develop a schedule for collecting the data, analyzing the results, and writing and finishing the report on time.

★ You can ask "*who, what, when, where,* and *why*" to stimulate ideas about what to research.

Develop a Preliminary Outline

Now you are ready to prepare a preliminary outline to organize the facts you uncover in your research. This preliminary outline will likely differ from the final outline you will use to write your report. The preliminary outline is simply a means for organizing the topic you decided to investigate.

Outlines for Informational Reports

The outline for an informational report can be arranged in one of five ways:

1. *Chronological Order.* Organize the facts in relation to time; that is, what happened first, next, and so on.
2. *Order of Importance.* Arrange the facts in order of importance, from the most to the least important or vice versa.
3. *Logical Sequence.* Group the facts according to the logical order of steps—first, second, third, and so on.
4. *Category.* Separate the facts into categories; for example, stocks, bonds, and certificates of deposit.
5. *Geographical Order.* Organize the facts by location, if appropriate.

Outlines for Analytical Reports

When outlining analytical reports, you can organize the facts in one of two ways. One method is to use a **hypothesis,** a possible cause or explanation of the problem. The second method is to use **alternatives.**

Hypotheses. In this method, phrase each possible cause as a hypothesis in your outline. The following outline shows two *hypotheses* (the plural of hypothesis) for a drop in auto sales. Under each hypothesis are the questions that must be answered to prove or disprove the hypothesis.

I. Our prices are too high. (Hypothesis)
   A. What are our prices?
   B. What are our competitors' prices?
   C. How important is price to our customers?

II. The quality of our product is low. (Hypothesis)
   A. What is our repair record?
   B. How does our repair record compare with that of competitors?
   C. What are the results of product evaluation?

Alternatives. When you evaluate alternative solutions to a problem, you can arrange your preliminary outline according to the relative merits of each alternative. For example, if you want to determine where in your school building to install new computers, one alternative is to research the number of courses in each subject that use computers. Another alternative is to research the number of students enrolled in each course that uses computers. The following example shows how to outline these alternatives:

I. Number of Classes Taught Using Computers
   A. Paralegal Courses
   B. Business Courses
   C. Health Courses

II. Number of Students Enrolled
   A. Paralegal Courses
   B. Business Courses
   C. Health Courses

Figure 34–1 shows two frequently used outline systems—the alphanumeric system and the decimal system. Use the system best suited to the problem or preferred by your company.

Outline Formats

The preliminary outline follows either the topical format or the discussion format. In a **topical outline,** *headings*—the words that start each section—describe in a few words the topics you have investigated. A **discussion outline,** on the other hand, provides more information about the topics and the *subtopics,* the individual parts of the topic that are included under each heading. The discussion outline takes longer to write but is often more helpful to the report writer. These formats are shown in the following examples:

To determine which outline format to use, you can check your company's style manual or look at outlines in other reports written by other employees.

TOPICAL OUTLINE	DISCUSSION OUTLINE
I. Characteristics of Voice Mail	I. Voice mail offers the latest technology for sending messages.
A. Speed	A. It offers rapid speed.
B. Cost	B. It costs no more than a telephone call.
C. Equipment	C. Special equipment is needed.

ALPHANUMERIC

I. xxxxxx
   A.   xxxxxx
   B.   xxxxxx
       1.   xxxxxx
       2.   xxxxxx
          a.   xxxxxx
          b.   xxxxxx
             (1)   xxxxxx
             (2)   xxxxxx

II. xxxxxx
   A.   xxxxxx
   B.   xxxxxx
   C.   xxxxxx
       1.   xxxxxx
       2.   xxxxxx

DECIMAL

1.0 xxxxxx
   1.1   xxxxxx
   1.2   xxxxxx
      1.2.1   xxxxxx
      1.2.2   xxxxxx
         1.2.2.1   xxxxxx
         1.2.2.2   xxxxxx
            1.2.2.2.1   xxxxxx
            1.2.2.2.2   xxxxxx

2.0 xxxxxx
   2.1   xxxxxx
   2.2   xxxxxx
   2.3   xxxxxx
      2.3.1   xxxxxx
      2.3.2   xxxxxx

Figure 34–1 Outline systems

Planning a Report

Indicate if each statement is true or false.

1. The first step in writing a report is to develop a preliminary outline.
2. Identifying the scope enables the report writer to determine how much money to spend on gathering facts.
3. When outlining an informational report, always arrange the facts in chronological order.
4. A hypothesis is a possible cause or explanation for a problem.
5. When planning an analytical report, organize the preliminary outline according to hypotheses or alternatives.

Check your answers in Appendix F.

Collect the Data

The next step in planning a report is to perform *research* by collecting appropriate data. Two sources of data are available—primary and secondary. **Primary research** involves gathering fresh, new data, whereas **secondary research** involves locating data that already has been gathered and reported.

Primary Research

If the facts you need are not available in books, magazines, or other sources, you may need to conduct primary research. To conduct this type of research, you might talk with experts, customers, or suppliers; observe what happens in a particular situation; or experiment to see what works.

Secondary Research

Research completed by others also can be useful. Consult books, periodicals, and other reports to gather information. Computer database services, which you can use at many libraries, often offer a more thorough search of the literature than may be available in printed form in the library.

Look for information on business and specific organizations in the *Business Periodicals Index*, the *Reader's Guide to Periodical Literature*, *The Wall Street Journal Index*, as well as other books, directories, catalogs, and indexes. The U.S. Government publishes reports on a variety of subjects. In addition, some of the most useful sources of information are found inside a company, including reports, memos, and reports to stockholders.

ON THE JOB

Some companies maintain a library where you can look at important documents and reference materials from every department.

Bibliography Cards

As you conduct your research, you will need a method of identifying your sources. You can do this by preparing a *bibliography card* for every source. These cards provide the details for the bibliography that the formal report will include.

For each source that you use, prepare a bibliography card similar to the one shown in Figure 34–2. For books, list the author's full name (last name first), the book title (underlined), the publication date, and the publisher's name and location. For example:

Bolles, Richard Nelson. What Color Is Your Parachute? Berkeley, Calif.: Ten Speed Press, 1993.

When you use information from a magazine article, list the author's full name (last name first), the article title (in quotation marks), the magazine title (underlined), the publication date (shown in parentheses), and the page numbers:

Lesly, Elizabeth. "Polygram Turns Up the Volume." Business Week (April 25, 1994): 112–113.

BIBLIOGRAPHY CARD

Richard Nelson Bolles. What Color Is Your Parachute?

Berkeley, Calif.: Ten Speed Press, 1993.

NOTE CARD

Bolles   Working at home

What Color Is Your Parachute?

According to surveys, nearly 7 million people in the United States work from home on a full-time basis; roughly 20 million work from home on a part-time basis. P. 126.

Figure 34–2 Sample bibliography card and sample note card

Note Cards

Prepare a separate *note card* for each point you plan to mention in your report. In most cases, you will summarize the information you locate in a secondary source, as was illustrated in Figure 34–2. When you want to use material directly from the source, **paraphrase**—change the words—and give credit to the author. Avoid **plagiarism,** which is presenting another person's work as your own, by clearly identifying your sources.

Analyze Data, Draw Conclusions, and Make Recommendations

Unless you have been asked to provide only an informational report, the last step in preparing to write a report is to analyze the results, draw conclusions, and make recommendations.

Analyze Data

Once you have your research results, see how the information fits together. Look for logical links between facts and figures. If you are working with numerical data, use mathematical methods to compare and contrast figures. Then organize the material in a way that helps the reader. For example, if you researched the high turnover rate of production supervisors in your manufacturing company, you might put the data into three categories: salaries of different supervisory jobs in the company, salaries offered by competing manufacturers, and the number and kinds of promotions supervisors have received at each job level.

Draw Conclusions

After you have analyzed the data through mathematical interpretation and logical thought, you may arrive at a **conclusion,** an opinion based on interpretation of data. An example of a conclusion for the study of high turnover among production supervisors might be:

> Production supervisors in our company have limited advancement opportunities.

Make Recommendations

Include recommendations in a report if you have been asked to do so. A **recommendation** offers suggestions of what should be done. Recommendations should be related to conclusions, as is the following recommendation for the supervisory study:

I recommend that supervisory positions within our company be reorganized to provide opportunities for career advancement.

CHECKPOINT 2

Collecting and Analyzing Data

Indicate if each statement is true or false.

1. Primary research involves gathering fresh data.
2. Secondary research involves locating data that already has been gathered and reported.
3. A recommendation is an order to make the changes you suggest in an analytical report.
4. You can avoid plagiarism by carefully noting the source of information that you quote in a report.
5. When you paraphrase, you use phrases exactly as they appear in the original research material.

Check your answers in Appendix F.

Summary

Business reports help management make decisions and solve problems. Reports can be classified according to their style, purpose, and format. When planning a report, first identify the problem and write a problem statement. Second, decide what to investigate and develop a preliminary outline to guide your research using either the topical or discussion outline format. Third, collect data by conducting primary or secondary research. Finally, analyze the data, draw conclusions, and make recommendations.

Discussion Questions

1. How can reports be classified according to their style, purpose, and format?
2. What are the steps in planning a report?

Practical Applications

Part A

Select a topic for a short analytical report. Start planning the report by identifying the problem and writing a statement of the problem. Next, define the scope and prepare a preliminary topical outline for organizing your research. Should you arrange the material according to hypotheses or alternatives? Why?

Part B

Conduct secondary research for the problem identified in Practical Application Part A using no fewer than five sources. Prepare bibliography cards and note cards as you conduct this research.

Part C

Using the research you have conducted for the problem identified in Practical Application Part A, analyze the data, draw conclusions, and make recommendations. Save all your work for use in Chapter 35.

Part D

Develop a preliminary discussion outline for a report on the reasons for lower holiday sales at downtown stores. Organize the report around these hypotheses:

1. The weather kept people from shopping downtown. Possibly the snow on December 20 and again on December 22 discouraged shoppers. Another possibility is that the frigid temperatures during the first two weeks of December hurt sales.
2. The downtown stores closed too early. Other retailers may have stayed open later, drawing customers from our stores. Also, our downtown locations were not open as late as our mall stores.
3. Our staffing was inadequate. We should check if our downtown stores hired extra help for the holiday season. We should also investigate if we had enough staff during the busiest times of the day and during the busiest days of the week.
4. We needed more merchandise. For example, we should check our stock of best-selling books to see if we sold out before the end of December. Did we order extra quantities of gift books in time for the holidays?

Editing and Proofreading Application

Edit, proofread, and rewrite the following short report.

Hear is the report you requested on recomendd electronic mesage systems ofr your organization. After surveying the number and types of messages your company snds I recomend that you consider adding e-mail and fax machines.

Becuase your organization sends many memos among 8 branch offices e-mail would speed up communiction. Additionaly, it would be inespenxive and conveneint.

You're offices often send ilustrations and graphics to each other. Faacsimile machines would speed up the prosess provide high quality imaging, and keep costs low.

Writing Informal Reports

OBJECTIVES

After studying this chapter and completing the chapter exercises, you will be able to do the following:

1. Explain when to use direct or indirect order to organize an informal report.
2. Modify the preliminary outline to create an outline for writing an informal report.
3. Discuss the use of personal and impersonal writing styles in informal reports.
4. List the parts of an informal report.
5. Describe when to use the letter, memo, and manuscript formats for informal reports.

ORGANIZING INFORMAL REPORTS

Most business reports are informal reports and have one of two purposes. They present information that has been requested, or they analyze a problem and report the findings. The organization and the format of these reports vary depending on the nature of the message and the people who will receive it.

Like business letters and memos, informal reports are organized around a main idea and supporting information. If the report is an informational report, the main idea is the information that has been requested. If the report is an analytical report, the main idea is a summary of the conclusions and recommendations. The supporting information of either an informational report or an analytical report explains or details the main idea.

Informal reports may be organized in either the direct order or the indirect order. The organization you choose depends on how receptive you expect your reader to be.

Direct Order

If the report is a routine report (weekly sales report) or if you expect the reader to respond favorably to what you are writing, use the direct order and present the main idea first. Busy managers prefer reading reports written in direct order because the main ideas appear at the beginning.

Informational reports such as progress reports commonly use the direct order. In these reports, the results (or main ideas) appear at the beginning. Analytical reports that are expected to have a favorable response also are organized in the direct order. The main ideas (conclusions and recommendations) appear first, followed by the supporting information.

Indirect Order

Use the indirect order when you expect an unfavorable response or when the receiver may need persuasion to accept the main idea. You can buffer the main idea by presenting the data and the reasons first.

Use the indirect order in an internal proposal when management is likely to be hesitant about approving the project or the budget. You might also use the indirect order for a *troubleshooting report*, an analytical report in which you investigate a problem and propose a solution. Imagine, for example, that your recommendation is to close a company operation, and that you do not expect management to be receptive to the idea. In this case, you would use the indirect order, placing your recommendation—to close the operation—at the end of the report.

OUTLINING AND WRITING INFORMAL REPORTS

Once you have decided how to organize your report, you are ready to outline it. Outlining helps you identify and position the topics and subtopics you will include. After you have placed the main idea and the supporting information in a logical sequence, you can start to write the report.

Report Outlines

As you start to outline an informal report, use the preliminary outline you developed to guide your research. More than likely, the outline will need some revision because of what you learned from collecting and analyzing the research data. Once you have revised the outline, you can use it as a guide for writing the final report.

Outlines for informal reports organized in direct or indirect order are shown in Figures 35–1, 35–2, and 35–3. Most informal reports can be written using one of these outline methods.

Figure 35-1 is an outline for an informational report organized in direct order. Notice that the introduction and the main idea come first, followed by the research findings.

I. Introduction

II. Main Idea: Unisoft, Preferred Word-Processing Software

III. Findings: Word-Processing Needs for Our Office
    A. Lengthy document production
    B. Frequent revisions
    C. Special features needed (mailmerge, macros, sorting)
    D. High-speed, letter-quality print (laser printer)

IV. Findings: Comparison of Four Word-Processing Packages
    A. Word-processing software package A
    B. Word-processing software package B
    C. Word-processing software package C
    D. Word processing software package D

V. Closing

Figure 35–1 Outline of an informational report in direct order

★ Remember that a discussion outline provides more detail than a topical outline and can help you actually write the report.

Figure 35-2 is an outline for an analytical report organized in direct order. The main idea consists of conclusions and recommendations followed by findings and supporting details.

Figure 35-3 is an outline for an analytical report organized in indirect order. The findings and supporting details precede the conclusion and recommendation, which together make up the main idea.

I. Introduction

II. Main Idea
   A. Conclusion: Production supervisors in our company have limited advancement opportunities.
   B. Recommendation: Supervisory positions should be revamped to provide opportunities for career advancement.

III. Findings and Supporting Details
   A. Production supervisors' salaries compare favorably with those of competing organizations.
   B. Fringe benefits are satisfactory.
   C. Opportunities for advancement are limited.

IV. Closing

Figure 35–2 Outline of an analytical report in direct order

I. Introduction

II. Findings and Supporting Details
   A. The company's third- and fourth-quarter sales are down.
   B. Projections for the coming year show slower sales.
   C. The company has too much inventory in stock.

III. Main Idea
   A. Conclusion: We are overproducing cars in our Lakeview plant.
   B. Recommendation: Close the Lakeview plant and lay off plant workers.

IV. Closing

Figure 35–3 Outline of an analytical report in indirect order

Writing Style

Informal reports usually are written in a relatively personal style, using the personal pronouns *I* and *you*. If your report is about a serious problem or if it is going to a senior manager, you may want to use a degree of formality. In this case, you would write your report in an impersonal style, without personal pronouns.

The impersonal style keeps a report from sounding like one person's opinion because it does not refer to *I, me,* or *you.* By avoiding personal references, a report written in the impersonal style emphasizes the facts rather than the writer. This makes the report sound more objective than a report written in the personal style.

When you write each section of your report, you must decide whether to write in the present or past tense. In most cases, use the past tense when writing about events in the past and the present tense for events that are still occurring. Avoid switching back and forth between tenses in a single section. Switching can confuse your readers, who may have difficulty following the timing or sequence of events in that section.

CHECKPOINT 1

Organizing and Writing Informal Reports

Indicate if each statement is true or false.

1. Use the direct order when you expect your reader to be receptive to your report.
2. Use a personal writing style to emphasize the facts rather than the report writer.
3. Write informal reports in either the present or the past tense and avoid switching between tenses.
4. An informational report in direct order starts with the main idea, followed by supporting information.
5. An analytical report in direct order starts with the introduction, followed by findings and then the main idea.
6. Use the indirect order when you think your reader will not want to accept your conclusions.

Check your answers in Appendix F.

FORMATTING INFORMAL REPORTS

Informal reports may be formatted like letters, memos, or manuscripts. The format depends on the receiver and the length of the report.

Parts of an Informal Report

Regardless of the format used, informal reports have three main parts:

1. Opening (the introduction)
2. Body (findings and supporting details)
3. Closing

The length of the opening will vary according to the purpose of the report. For a brief memo report, the opening might be only a subject line. For other informal short reports, the opening may include the following information: the subject of the report, the purpose of the report (the reason why the report is important), and a preview of the main ideas of the report. If you use direct order, include the summary of findings or conclusions and recommendations in the opening.

The body of a report includes the findings and supporting details that resulted from the research conducted. Your revised outline will provide the main organizational plan for this section. This section is usually the longest and must be well organized to make the report easy to understand.

The closing of a report is important because it is the final opportunity to leave an impression on the reader. If you are writing a report in direct order, you should reemphasize the main ideas in this last section. If you are using indirect order, you should first present the summary of findings (informational reports) or conclusions and recommendations (analytical reports). Make sure that any conclusions or recommendations follow from a logical presentation of the data in the report body. If the report includes several conclusions or recommendations, use a list format for simplicity.

★ The closing is your last chance to make a positive, lasting impression on the reader, so choose your final words with care.

Letter Reports

External reports, those written for people outside the organization, often are written in letter format. (See Chapter 30 for details on formatting letters.) In general, an informal report written in letter format should have no more than five pages. If you need more than five pages, use the manuscript format. Manuscript format allows you to separate the various parts of the report so readers can follow the organization of your material.

The opening may mention who asked for the report and the date the report was assigned. The report body is the report itself. This middle section includes findings and supporting details and may include an analysis of the situation being studied and any recommendations. The ending is similar to the closing in any letter. If possible, the ending should mention some expected action on the part of the reader or writer. See Figure 35–4 for an example of a letter report.

Memo Reports

Short internal reports, which are sent to others within the organization, usually are written in memo format. These reports are informal primarily because of their format, not necessarily because of their content.

Use the memo format for routine internal reports that have no more than five pages. (See Chapter 27 for detailed information on formatting memos.) If your report needs to be longer, use the manuscript format. An example of a memo report is shown in Figure 35–5.

Manuscript Reports

Short reports written in manuscript format usually are longer than memo or letter reports but not as long as formal reports. Internal proposals, for example, frequently are formatted as manuscript reports. In addition, the manuscript format often is used instead of the letter format for external reports longer than five pages.

The opening may include the following information: the subject of the report, the purpose of the report (the reason why the subject is important), and a preview of the main ideas of the report. If you are writing in direct order, include the summary of findings or conclusions and recommendations in the opening. See Figure 35–6 for an example of a manuscript report.

Figure 35-4 Letter report

RCG Raleigh Consulting Group
216 North Main Street
Raleigh, NC 27612-7643

December 14, 19—

Mr. Donald A. Stevens
Human Resources Manager
Southern Textiles
6 Elm Street
Kinston, NC 28501-1463

Dear Mr. Stevens

Opening Here is the report you requested on recommended training programs for new shift supervisors. After talking with your plant manager and with one dozen newly promoted supervisors, I recommend that you consider a two-day management and communication course.

Management Training

Body Because new shift supervisors have no management background, an intensive one-day training program would provide management ideas that they can apply immediately. This program would cover basic management functions and information on managing for quality improvement.

Communication Training

New shift supervisors must be able to communicate with workers, peers, top management, and union representatives. A one-day training program would give these supervisors the speaking and writing skills they need to be effective. This program would cover oral and written communication, listening, and feedback.

Closing Our manufacturing clients have found that two consecutive days of training immediately after a promotion can provide the tools that new supervisors need to be productive right away. Please call me at (919) 555-2580 so that we can discuss how to tailor this course to your mill's specific needs. Thank you for giving us the opportunity to work with you.

Sincerely

Dr. Joan Carter, President

wa

Figure 35-4 Letter report

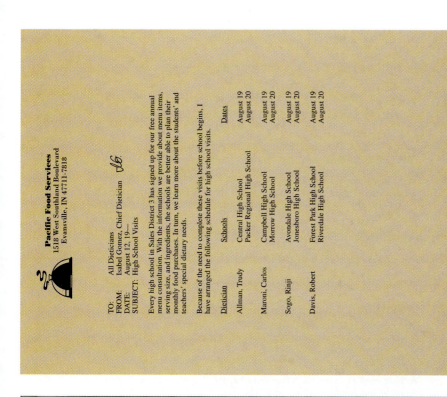

Figure 35-5 Memo report

Pacific Food Services
1518 West Southland Boulevard
Evansville, IN 47711-7818

TO: All Dieticians
FROM: Isabel Gomez, Chief Dietician
DATE: August 12, 19—
SUBJECT: High School Visits

Every high school in Sales District 3 has signed up for our free annual menu consultation. With the information we provide about menu items, serving size, and ingredients, the schools are better able to plan their monthly food purchases. In turn, we learn more about the students' and teachers' special dietary needs.

Because of the need to complete these visits before school begins, I have arranged the following schedule for high school visits.

Dietician	Schools	Dates
Allman, Trudy	Central High School	August 19
	Packer Regional High School	August 20
Maroni, Carlos	Campbell High School	August 19
	Morrow High School	August 20
Sogo, Rinji	Avondale High School	August 19
	Jonesboro High School	August 20
Davis, Robert	Forest Park High School	August 19
	Riverdale High School	August 20

Figure 35-5 Memo report

SPECIFICATIONS FOR NEW CREDIT RECORD STORAGE FACILITY

Opening To accommodate seasonal variations in credit volume, and to allow for future growth in credit sales, the Credit Department proposes that a new credit record storage facility be constructed in the regional office. This facility would store credit and collection records for up to 1,000 regional customers. The specifications for the proposed storage facility are outlined in this report.

Physical Specifications

Body The proposed storage facility should meet the following specifications:

Space. An area of 700–900 square feet is needed.

Furniture and Equipment. Provide two rectangular workstations with seating for two at each workstation. Workstations should each be equipped with one microfiche reader, one microfiche storage file, one personal computer, and one laser printer. The two computers should be linked with the central credit processing system. Each workstation requires two work chairs. In addition, one 3′ × 6′ table for file preparation is needed.

To hold credit applications that must be retained for two years, provide 10 linear feet of reinforced steel shelving. The shelving should be 8′ high with 16″ between shelves. The lowest shelf must be positioned at least 4″ above floor level.

To hold customer correspondence about credit disputes or collections, provide six 4-drawer letter-size file cabinets. To hold returned mail from credit and collection accounts, provide two rolling storage bins.

One multi-line telephone should be installed at each workstation. These telephones should be linked with the regional office's voice mail system.

Provide one facsimile device for transmission of credit documents. The facsimile must be equipped with a ten-page document feeder and a letter-size tray to hold incoming faxes.

Security. This file storage facility must be secure both day and night. Provide one card-activated locking system with a manual override in case of power failure.

Figure 35–6 Manuscript report

<u>Wiring</u>. Appropriate wiring should be provided for the following equipment:

> Personal computers and printers
> Microfiche readers
> Facsimile equipment

Environmental Factors

The proposed file storage area should meet the following specifications for other environmental factors.

<u>Climate</u>. The heating, ventilation, and air conditioning system must accommodate a temperature range between 68–78 degrees Fahrenheit (20–26 degrees Centigrade), and a humidity level of 40–60 percent.

<u>Flooring</u>. Linoleum or vinyl tile should be provided in the area. All furniture and equipment must be set on two-inch risers to prevent water damage in case of flooding.

<u>Lighting</u>. Indirect, nonglare lighting supplemented by task lighting is needed at the workstation. For all other areas in this facility, provide standard ceiling lighting.

Construction Schedule

Every year, the Credit Department experiences heavier demand for record storage as a result of increased credit and collection activity during the fall and winter months. To accommodate this seasonal demand, the facility should be ready by September 15.

File Transfer Schedule

The Credit Department will require two business days to transfer current customer records from the downtown office to the new storage facility in the regional office. Customer correspondence records and microfiche files will be moved on the first day; customer applications will be moved on the second day.

Summary

Closing   A storage facility constructed according to the specifications described in this report would allow the Credit Department to adequately service 800–1,000 customers. With the availability of this storage facility, the Credit Department could comfortably accommodate both seasonal storage demands and expected growth in future credit sales.

Formatting Informal Reports

Indicate if each statement is true or false.

1. Memo reports can be of any length.
2. Manuscript reports usually are longer than memo or letter reports but not as long as formal reports.
3. Informal reports have three main parts: the opening, the body, and the findings.
4. The ending of a letter report is similar to the closing in any letter.
5. In a report written in direct order, the ending should reemphasize the main ideas.
6. Put the conclusions and recommendations in the opening of a manuscript report written in direct order.

Check your answers in Appendix F.

Summary

Informal reports can be organized in two ways. Use the direct order when a favorable response from the reader is expected. Write in the indirect order when an unfavorable response is expected. The preliminary outline used to guide report research usually needs revision to be useful in writing the report. Informal reports may be written in personal or impersonal style, depending on the degree of formality desired. An informal report has three main parts: the opening, the body, and the closing. Informal reports may be formatted like letters, memos, or manuscripts.

Discussion Questions

1. When should direct order be used in an informal report? Indirect order?
2. What are the three parts of an informal report?

Practical Applications

Part A

Plan a brief informational report to your instructor on one of the following topics:

The price range of meals served on campus

Enrollment trends at your campus

Parking facilities on campus

1. Prepare a preliminary outline to guide your research. Then conduct primary research (by interviewing people on campus) or secondary research (by checking reports and other materials).
2. Decide whether to use direct order or indirect order to organize this report; explain your choice.
3. Modify the preliminary outline if necessary so it can be used to write the report.
4. Determine the main idea that you want to convey in this report.

Part B

Review the preliminary outline, research, and conclusions of the short analytical report you planned in Chapter 34.

1. Decide if the preliminary outline must be modified; make any needed modifications.
2. Will you organize the report in direct or indirect order? Why?
3. Prepare an outline for this report.

Editing and Proofreading Application

Edit the following paragraph from the body of a letter report and change the writing style from personal to impersonal.

Electric heat can be convenient, you can turn the heat on and off in each room, depending on where you might need it. However, you should face the fact that electic heat can also be very, very expensive. During an especially cold winter season, you may find that electric heat costs as much as $400 a month.

Writing Formal Reports

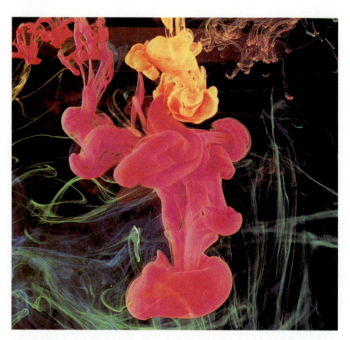

OBJECTIVES

After studying this chapter and completing the chapter exercises, you will be able to do the following:

1. Organize and write a formal report.
2. Identify the three parts of a formal report.
3. Describe the appropriate margins, spacing, and headings for a formal report.
4. Explain how to use visual aids in a report.

ORGANIZING AND WRITING A FORMAL REPORT

Formal reports are more complex and longer than informal reports. Because of this complexity, you may need to allow more time to organize and write a formal report than you would need to prepare an informal report. As with an informal report, the organization and the writing style you choose for a formal report can vary, depending on the nature of the message and the people who will receive it.

Direct and Indirect Order

When you organize your report, you can use either direct or indirect order. Formal informational reports usually follow the direct order because they contain information that readers expect; readers, therefore, should react favorably. Formal analytical reports that probably will receive a favorable response also are organized in the direct order. On the other hand, use the indirect order in a formal report when you expect an unfavorable response or when you may need to persuade the reader to accept the main idea.

Writing Style

Many important business decisions are made on the basis of the information presented in formal reports. With so much at stake, these reports need to sound impartial and professional. Formal reports usually are written in an impersonal style, without personal pronouns such as *I* and *you*. An impersonal writing style focuses attention on the facts rather than on the writer. It also makes the report sound more objective than a report written in the personal style.

EXTRA, EXTRA!

★ Other personal pronouns to avoid when using a formal writing style are *we* and *me*.

FORMATTING A FORMAL REPORT

Both informational and analytical formal reports are longer and more complex than informal reports. As a result, formal reports are formatted differently from shorter, informal reports.

Parts of a Formal Report

A formal report has three major divisions: the preliminary parts, the body or text, and the supplementary parts. Table 36–1 shows the parts of a formal report.

PRELIMINARY PARTS	BODY OR TEXT	SUPPLEMENTARY PARTS
Letter of transmittal	Introduction	Bibliography
Title page	Findings and	Appendix
Table of contents	analysis	
Executive summary	Summary, conclusions,	
	and recommendations	

Table 36–1 Parts of a formal report

Preliminary Parts

The **preliminary parts** are the parts of a formal report that appear first, providing the reader with information about the report body. Preliminary parts include a letter or memo of transmittal, a title page, a table of contents, and an executive summary.

A **letter or memo of transmittal** transmits the report to the reader. This document conveys what you would say if you were giving the report directly to the reader; therefore, it is usually less formal than the report itself. A letter of transmittal would accompany a report to readers outside the organization; a memo of transmittal would accompany a report for internal use. Use the direct order for the letter or memo of transmittal, beginning with a statement such as, "Here is the report you asked me to prepare about . . ." Include a brief statement of the report objective, followed by a short summary of the report. End by thanking the person who requested the report and offering assistance if needed. Figure 36–1 shows a sample memo of transmittal.

A **title page** is the report page that shows the report title; the name, title, and organization of the person for whom the report was written; the writer's name, title, and organization; and the date the report is submitted. Figure 36–2, Part A, shows a sample title page. You may use the title page as the report cover if the report is short or if the report is for internal use. Otherwise, use a cover made of heavier paper or plastic. Label the cover with the report title and, if desired, with the writer's name and the date.

A **table of contents** is a list of the entire report contents. You can prepare the table of contents after the report is written by listing the main headings shown in the report body and indicating the page number where each heading begins. Figure 36–2, Part B, shows a sample table of contents.

Meade Legal Services
1100 Court Street
Cincinnati, OH 45201-1100

TO: Richard Bryce, Senior Vice President
FROM: Katie Goodman, Manager of Office Services
DATE: May 15, 19—
SUBJECT: The Effect of Word Processing

On March 23, 19—, you asked me to prepare a report on the impact of word processing in selected legal offices in the United States. You also asked that my report determine the impact of word processing on business education curricula offered by NABTE institutions.

The completed report, which is attached, shows that word processing has had a significant effect on legal offices and on business education curricula. The report also includes recommendations for ways in which NABTE institutions can match their curricula to the needs of legal offices in their local areas.

Thank you for the chance to study this important issue. If you have any questions about the report, please call me at extension 454.

tr

Attachment

Figure 36–1 Transmittal memorandum

THE IMPACT WORD PROCESSING HAS MADE IN SELECTED
LEGAL OFFICES AND NABTE INSTITUTIONS

Prepared for

Richard Bryce
Senior Vice President
Meade Legal Services

Prepared by

Katie Goodman
Manager of Office Services
Meade Legal Services

May 15, 19—

Figure 36–2, Part A Title page

TABLE OF CONTENTS

ii

Figure 36–2, Part B Table of Contents

The **executive summary**, sometimes called a *synopsis* or an *abstract*, is a brief overview of the report. The purpose of the executive summary is to convey the key points of the report to the reader. The executive summary is especially important when a report is long and technical because it allows busy readers to grasp the main points quickly without reading the entire report. The executive summary should use the indirect approach for reports written in indirect order and the direct approach for reports written in direct order. Figure 36–3, on pages 473 and 474, is an example of an executive summary.

The Report Body

The report body, which contains the actual report, consists of three parts: the introduction; the findings and analysis; and the summary, conclusions, and recommendations.

The **introduction** states the purpose of the report. Figure 36–4 (shown on pages 475 and 476) shows an introduction to the body of the report. The introduction generally discusses several topics, including any or all of the following:

Authorization	Statement of who authorized the report and the time and manner of authorization.
Statement of the Problem	The reasons for writing the report and the goals to be accomplished.
Scope	Information the report covers and does not cover.
Limitations	Factors that affect the scope of the report, such as a limited amount of time or a limited budget.
Definitions	List of unfamiliar terms and their definitions.

The **findings and analysis** section of the report body presents the findings and the supporting details and examines these results. The **summary, conclusions, and recommendations** section summarizes the findings, draws conclusions, and makes recommendations. Figure 36–5 shows a findings and analysis section and a summary, conclusion, and recommendations section. See pages 477 and 478.

Supplementary Parts

A formal report may also contain **supplementary parts** that follow the report body, such as a bibliography or an appendix. The **bibliography** is a list of sources used in preparing the report, shown in alphabetic order by authors' names.

EXECUTIVE SUMMARY

The purpose of the study was to determine the impact that word processing has made in selected legal offices in the United States. Further, the study sought to ascertain the impact that word processing has made on business education curricula offered by selected NABTE institutions.

Methods and Procedures

The participants for the study were secretarial/word-processing specialists employed in legal offices throughout the United States and NABTE representatives from selected collegiate institutions. The legal participants were randomly selected from the Martindale-Hubbell Law Directory, 1983. The NABTE representatives were randomly selected from NABTE institutions located in or near the capital city in each state.

Each legal office participant completed a questionnaire and each NABTE representative completed a business education questionnaire. The t-test, McNemar test, and Stuart-Maxwell test were used to analyze the data.

Results and Conclusions

The results of the study revealed that attorneys hired high school graduates or two-year secretarial graduates who knew how to answer the telephone, operate a word-processing machine, file documents electronically, use various computer software packages, and type straight copy at speeds of 60 to 80 words a minute. The data also revealed that, in general, the firms had not established evaluation standards for secretaries/word-processing specialists and had not increased the number of secretaries/word-processing specialists since purchasing word-processing equipment. The firms also had not increased the salaries of secretaries/word-processing specialists. Further, the findings revealed that the cost of processing information in legal offices had decreased since the implementation of word-processing equipment.

iii

Figure 36–3 Executive summary

Executive Summary, continued   iv

The responses received from the NABTE representatives revealed that
business educators trained office technology and comprehensive business
education majors to operate word-processing equipment, use software
packages, and type documents at production rates. No changes were noted
for teaching basic business or basic English skills.

Figure 36–3 Executive summary, *continued*

INTRODUCTION

Advanced technology has caused many changes in the twentieth century. Typewriting and data processing equipment have changed from manual to electric and, in the eighties, from electric to electronic. Information processing and communication methods have progressed to an extremely high level of sophistication (Simcoe, 1980). Some legal offices have become fully automated while others strive for a similar setting. According to Moody (1978), office automation is an extension of the technologies refined and developed to electronically process data and words.

Statement of the Problem

The problem of this study was to determine the impact word processing has made in selected legal offices in the United States. Further, the study sought to ascertain the impact that word processing has made on business education curricula offered by selected National Association of Business Teacher Educators (NABTE) institutions.

Specifically, the study seeks to determine the training and entry-level skills needed for employment, the functions and operations performed, and the equipment and software used by secretaries in legal offices before and after the implementation of word-processing operations.

Scope

The report will study the impact that word processing has had on the legal office but will not include the impact of other automation technologies on the legal office. Participants identified in the study were from large cities; therefore, this study will not address the impact of word processing on legal firms in small cities.

The study also will determine any changes in secretarial tasks performed before word processing was implemented and after word processing was implemented.

Figure 36–4 Introduction to the body of the report

<u>Limitations of the Study</u>

The limitations of the study are as follows:

<u>Legal Firms</u>. The legal office participants invited to participate in this study were randomly selected from <u>Martindale-Hubbell Law Directory,</u> 1983. Also, the legal firms had to be located in the capital cities in the United States or the largest city in the state where an NABTE institution was located.

<u>NABTE Representatives</u>. The business educators invited to participate in the study were selected from the NABTE Directory. One NABTE institution located in the capital city or a city near the capital per state was identified for the study.

<u>Definitions</u>

These definitions were listed to assist the reader.

1. <u>After word processing</u> means after the implementation of word-processing operations (concepts, equipment, procedures).

2. <u>Before word processing</u> means before the implementation of word-processing operations.

Figure 36–4 Introduction to the body of the report, *continued*

FINDINGS AND ANALYSIS

The responses received from legal office participants relating to the cost of processing information since the implementation of word processing are shown in Table 1. The data presented are classified by National Business Education Association regions. Fifty percent of the legal office respondents indicated a decrease in the cost of processing information, while 28 percent reported no change had occurred in this area.

A summary of the data supplied by legal respondents reported an increase in the number of secretaries employed in 21 percent of the legal offices since implementing word processing, while 23 percent revealed a decrease. Fifty-six percent of the office respondents reported no change in the number of secretaries employed.

Table 1

PERCENTAGE OF LEGAL RESPONDENTS REPORTING THE COST OF
PROCESSING INFORMATION SINCE WORD-PROCESSING
OPERATIONS WERE IMPLEMENTED IN
LEGAL OFFICES

Legal Offices by Regions	Increase in Cost	Decrease in Cost	No Change	Total Percent
Eastern	29%	42%	29%	100%
Mountain Plains	19%	39%	42%	100%
North-Central	25%	63%	12%	100%
Southern	21%	49%	30%	100%
Western	19%	55%	26%	100%
Mean	22%	50%	28%	100%

Figure 36–5 Findings and analysis section

SUMMARY, CONCLUSIONS, AND RECOMMENDATIONS

This study was designed to determine the impact word processing has made in selected legal offices in the United States. Further, the study sought to ascertain the impact that word processing has made on business education curricula offered by selected NABTE institutions.

The conclusions of this study provide the basis for the following recommendations:

1. The NABTE institution representatives participating in this research study and their business education department chairpersons need to study the skills, functions, and operations performed by secretaries in legal offices to determine if the skills, functions, and operations are being taught in business education programs meet the needs of the secretaries employed by legal offices in the local area.

2. The NABTE institution representatives participating in this study and their business education department chairpersons need to analyze the current business education curricula to determine a procedure to eliminate voids in the legal secretarial curricula.

Figure 36–5, *continued* Summary, conclusions, and recommendations section

Figure 36–6, Part A (shown on page 480), shows a sample bibliography. A bibliography shows readers where the information in the report comes from and where to look for additional information.

An **appendix** contains material related to the report but too long to be included in the body. Examples of appendix items include questionnaires or a glossary of terms. Figure 36–6, Part B (see page 481), shows a sample appendix.

The Format of a Formal Report

Formal reports generally follow specific formatting guidelines. A company may develop its own **style manual**, a set of guidelines for formatting documents, to help report writers plan the appropriate margins, spacing, headings, and other details.

Margins

Most formal reports use 1-inch side and bottom margins. However, for a report that is stapled or bound at the left side, use a $1\frac{1}{2}$-inch left margin. The preliminary and supplementary pages and the first page of the body usually have a 2-inch top margin. For all other pages, use a 1-inch top margin.

Spacing

The formal report may be double-spaced or single-spaced, depending on your organization's preference, a preference that will be stated in the style manual. If a report is double-spaced, indent for paragraphs. If the report is single-spaced, double-space between paragraphs; paragraph indentions are not required.

Headings

Use headings to help organize and present data. Headings help the reader follow your line of thought as you move from point to point in the report. A *first-level heading* is a heading that opens a major section; for example, a first-level heading is a heading identified with a roman numeral in your outline. A *second-level heading* is a heading that introduces a subtopic below a first-level heading.

The same-level headings within a section, such as second-level headings at the A and B level in an outline, should be parallel in form. Parallel headings show readers that the ideas are grouped for a reason. If one heading begins with a noun, for

★ When your report relies on primary research such as a survey, your appendix should include a copy of the questionnaire. Including the questionnaire helps readers understand how the data were gathered.

★ Remember to use the appropriate memo or letter margins for the memo or letter of transmittal.

BIBLIOGRAPHY

Anderson, R. I. "Word Processing." <u>National Business Education Yearbook.</u> Reston, Virginia: National Business Education Association, 1980, 55–56.

Bragg, S.M. "A Comparative Study of Major Task Requirements of Word Processing Administrative Support Personnel and the Traditional Secretary." Diss. University of Georgia, 1979.

Breslow, N.E., and Day, N. E. <u>Statistical Methods in Cancer Research, Volume I The Analysis of Case-Control Studies.</u> Lyon: International Agency for Research on Cancer, 1980.

Brostrom, Gail C. "The Importance of Communication Skills in the Business World." <u>National Business Education Yearbook.</u> Reston, Virginia: National Business Education Association, 1988, 1–12.

Chaney, Lillian H., and Otto, Joseph Clair. "Are Schools Meeting Needs of the Business Community?" <u>Business Education Forum</u> (February 1988): 23–24

U.S. Department of Commerce. <u>Statistical Abstract of the United States, 1982-1983.</u> Washington, D.C.: U.S. Government Printing Office, 1982.

Figure 36–6, Part A Bibliography

APPENDIX A

Functions and Operations Performed by Secretaries/ Word-Processing
Specialists in Legal Offices

Please place check marks in the appropriate columns to indicate functions
and operations secretaries/word-processing specialists in your legal office
perform BEFORE WORD-PROCESSING (WP) and AFTER WP.

R = Rarely
O = Occasionally
F = Frequently

BEFORE WP				AFTER WP		
R	O	F		R	O	F
___	___	___	1. Answering the telephone	___	___	___
___	___	___	2. Transcribing handwritten copy	___	___	___
___	___	___	3. Transcribing rough-draft	___	___	___
			4. Transcribing from machine dictation			
___	___	___		___	___	___
___	___	___	5. Transcribing from telephone	___	___	___
___	___	___	6. Receiving oral directions	___	___	___
___	___	___	7. Composing correspondence	___	___	___
			8. Transcribing material received from an attorney			
___	___	___		___	___	___
			9. Transcribing material received from a paralegal			
___	___	___		___	___	___
___	___	___	10. Proofreading others' work	___	___	___
___	___	___	11. Operating a computer	___	___	___
___	___	___	12. Using word-processing software	___	___	___
			13. Using software other than word processing			
___	___	___		___	___	___
___	___	___	14. Filing manually	___	___	___
___	___	___	15. Filing electronically	___	___	___
			16. Performing other functions on a computer			
___	___	___		___	___	___
___	___	___	17. Operating a photocopier	___	___	___
			18. Operating a microfiche reader/printer			
___	___	___		___	___	___
			19. Operating an optical disk system			
___	___	___		___	___	___
___	___	___	20. Other _____	___	___	___

Figure 36–6, Part B Appendix

example, then all headings at that level should begin with a noun. If one begins with a verb, then all others should begin with a verb. See the following example:

PARALLEL HEADINGS	UNPARALLEL HEADINGS
I. Steps in Planning (first-level heading)	I. Planning the Study
A. Defining the Objective (second-level heading)	A. Defining the Objective
B. Determining the Project Leader (second-level heading)	B. Determine Project Leader
1. Vendor (third-level heading)	1. Vendor
2. Outside Consultant (third-level heading)	2. Hiring an Outside Consultant
II. The Feasibility Study (first-level heading)	II. The Feasibility Study

Figure 36–7 shows one way to format report headings.

FIRST-LEVEL HEADING

Key the words of a first-level heading in capital letters and center the heading. Allow four spaces (three blank lines) before starting the first paragraph under a first-level heading.

Second-Level Heading

Place a second-level heading at the left margin of the report, capitalize all important words, and underline the heading or print it in bold. Side headings are always preceded and followed by a double space (one blank line).

Third-Level Heading. A third-level heading is actually part of the paragraph. Double space before it, underline it, capitalize the first letter of important words, and follow it with a period. Begin the text two spaces after the period.

Fourth-level headings may be needed in your report. If so, capitalize only the first word, underline it, and run the heading into the text of the paragraph.

Figure 36–7 Format for report headings

VISUAL AIDS

Most formal reports (and many informal reports) include **visual aids**, graphics such as charts, graphs, tables, and illustrations that help the reader understand and interpret the written information. With computers, the production of graphics is much easier and less expensive. All the visual aids described in this chapter can be produced with the appropriate computer software and hardware.

To plan the visual aids that will enhance your report, examine the outline of your report. Each major section of the outline probably represents a key point of your report. Decide if a visual aid would help the reader understand the data you are presenting in each section. No matter what type of data you are presenting, you have a wide choice of visual aids.

Types of Visual Aids

Among the most often used visual aids are tables, bar graphs, line graphs, pie charts, and illustrations. This section describes each of these visual aids.

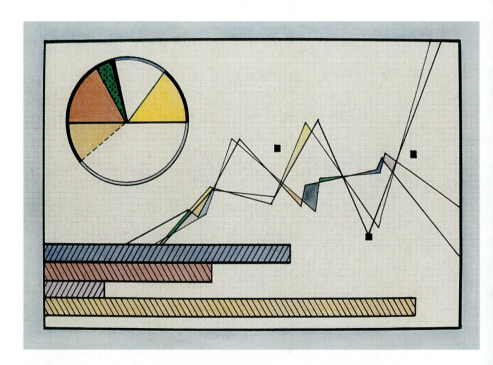

Tables

A **table** is an arrangement of data into columns and rows. Figure 36–8 shows a sample table. Complex numerical or verbal information often is easier to understand when it appears in tabular form rather than as textual copy. Tables are especially valuable when readers need to weigh several alternatives or to compare specific items. Headings help readers quickly and easily grasp the information in the table. All tables in a report should have a consistent look and should be numbered sequentially.

SALES OF PC PRINTERS
First and Second Quarter, 19—

TYPE OF PRINTER	FIRST QUARTER UNITS	SALES (000)	SECOND QUARTER UNITS	SALES (000)
Color Laser	30	9.1	46	13.8
Dot Matrix	476	280.8	521	416.8
Ink Jet	110	109.2	142	136.2
Laser	115	690.0	128	765.4

Figure 36–8 Table format

Bar Graphs

A **bar graph** can be used to compare the sizes of items and to show changes in items over time. A bar graph presents numerical values through the use of vertical or horizontal bars of varying length. Figure 36–9 shows a vertical and a horizontal bar graph. You can stack the bars to show the different components that make up the bar, as shown in the graph on the left in Figure 36–9. You can also double the bars to show comparisons or use the bars to show both positive and negative figures.

Line Graphs

A **line graph** is useful for showing changes in a quantity or value over time. This type of graph often is used to show fluctuations or trends in sales, costs, or production over a period of months or years. In graphs depicting trends, the horizontal axis is used to show the time or quantity measured; the vertical axis is used to show amounts. Figure 36–10 shows a sample line graph.

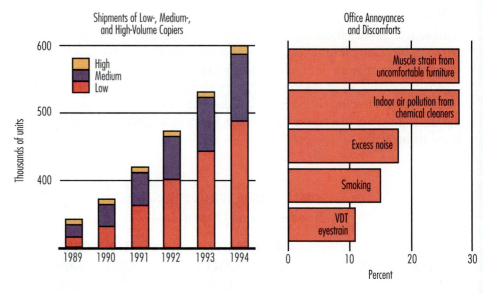

Figure 36–9 Vertical and horizontal bar graphs

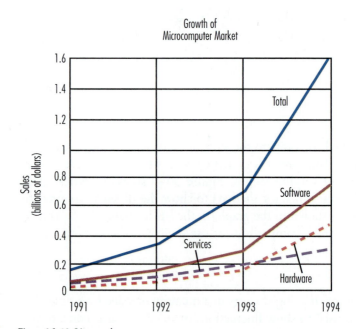

Figure 36–10 Line graph

Pie Charts

A **pie chart** shows how the parts of a whole are distributed and how the parts relate to one another. Figure 36–11 shows a sample pie chart. Generally, the parts (which should be limited to no more than seven) are represented by percentages. A pie chart can easily present such statistics as a breakdown of family income into various expense categories. When you construct a pie chart, place the largest part in the twelve o'clock position. Then place decreasing amounts clockwise from there.

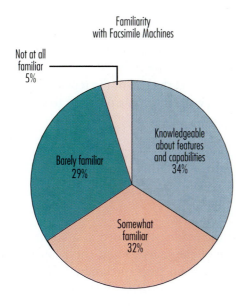

Familiarity
with Facsimile Machines

Not at all
familiar
5%

Knowledgeable
about features
and capabilities
34%

Barely familiar
29%

Somewhat
familiar
32%

Figure 36–11 Pie chart

Illustrations

Drawings and photographs can be very effective but are used less frequently than other visual aids because they are more difficult and expensive to produce. A drawing or diagram is a good way to show how something works. In annual reports, photographs can add visual impact to complement the main points.

Placement of Visual Aids

Introduce the visual aid in the text of the report before presenting the visual aid. The visual aid should appear immediately after the reference to it so that the

★ When you write a report on a technical subject such as manufacturing, you will find diagrams particularly useful for showing how equipment operates or how to follow the sequence of steps in a process.

reader can locate it easily. Unless you use layout services or computer software that can integrate text and visual aids, you may need to place a visual aid on the page after its reference in the text. Also, tables, graphs, and charts sometimes are placed in an appendix.

CHECKPOINT

Visual Aids

Indicate if each statement is true or false.

1. Visual aids can help the reader understand the text of the report.
2. Tables are useful for presenting complex numerical data.
3. Bar graphs are good for showing changes and trends over time.
4. Visual aids always appear at the end of the report.
5. Limit the number of parts shown in a pie chart to seven.

Check your answers in Appendix F.

Summary

The organization and the writing style used in a formal report can vary, depending on the nature of the message and the people who will receive it. Formal reports have three main parts: preliminary parts, the body, and supplementary parts. Visual aids can help illustrate and explain information included in a formal or an informal report. Tables, graphs, charts, and illustrations should be introduced in the text and placed as closely as possible after their first reference in the text.

Discussion Questions

1. What are the three major divisions of a formal report?
2. Why are visual aids used in a report?

Practical Applications

Part A

Plan a formal report to your instructor on one of the topics you selected in Practical Application A in Chapter 35.

1. How will this formal report differ from the informal report you prepared in Chapter 34?
2. Will this report have a section on findings and analysis? Will you include recommendations in your report? Why or why not?
3. Where in this formal report will you show your secondary research sources?

Part B

Prepare the letter of transmittal and the title page for the formal report you planned in Practical Application A.

Part C

What visual aids would help you convey your main points most effectively in the formal report you planned in Practical Application A? Develop visual aids to illustrate at least two major points.

Editing and Proofreading Application

Edit the following notes on secondary research sources and format them as they would appear in a report bibliography.

Re-inventing the Corporation written by John Naisbitt and Patricia Aburdene, published by Warner Books in New York, 1985.

The Leadership Factor was published by the Free Press, in New York in 1988. The author of this book is John P. Kotter.

A book published by Touchstone (located in New Yoork) in 1990: *When Giants Learn to Dance* by author Rosabeth Moss Kanter.

COMMUNICATION ACTIVITIES

Chapter 37

Creating Specialized Workplace Documents

OBJECTIVES

After studying this chapter and completing the chapter exercises, you will be able to do the following:

1. Plan, organize, and format news releases.
2. Differentiate between solicited and unsolicited proposals.
3. Develop and write meeting agendas.
4. Draft minutes to report meeting results.

SPECIALIZED EXTERNAL DOCUMENTS

As a business communicator, you will sometimes work with a variety of specialized workplace documents. In this chapter, you will learn how to plan, organize, and format news releases, proposals, meeting agendas, and minutes of meetings.

News Releases

A **news release** (also known as a *press release*) is a brief announcement sent to newspapers, magazines, and other media. Businesses use news releases to announce financial results and other information of interest to people outside the organization such as stockholders.

Planning News Releases

Press releases usually are prepared by public relations specialists or top managers. The objective is to present the company to the external audience in a positive way. If you draft a news release, remember that reporters expect to find the most important facts in the first paragraph. Introduce supporting facts in descending order of importance.

News releases should be both accurate and objective. Even when you deliver bad news such as employee layoffs, your news release should present the ideas fairly.

Organizing News Releases

News releases follow the direct-order organization. Start with the main idea and follow with supporting information. Answer "who, what, when, where, and why" about your newsworthy event. Include background information such as recent sales results in the final paragraph.

Even when you must communicate a bad news message, use the direct order and put the main idea first. Then offer supporting details to put the bad news into context. Use the goodwill closing to emphasize some positive aspects of your organization.

Formatting News Releases

You can increase the chances that a publication will include the information in your news release if you use the standard format to which reporters are accustomed. Refer to Figure 37–1 as you review the following format guidelines:

1. Use 1-inch side margins, a 1½-inch top margin, and double spacing (indent paragraphs ½ inch).
2. Use the company letterhead or a special news release letterhead.

LEGAL/Ethical

- Whether the announcement in a news release is good news or bad, be honest with your audience. Hiding bad news is not only unethical, it can also make the company look dishonest if and when unflattering details become public.

News Release

August 10, 19—

FOR IMMEDIATE RELEASE

STUDENT-FACULTY REUNION AT STACEY CORPORATION
MORROW, GA.

Two members of Clayton State College's faculty recently visited with Clayton State alumni employed at StaceyCorporation.

Office Technology faculty member, Ms. Gloria Ortiz, and Job Placement Counselor, Mr. Martin Long, were guests of Stacey Corporation for lunch.

Stacey Corporation actively recruits Office Technology majors from the College. In addition, Stacey Corporation employment representatives provide valuable services to the students and faculty. Ms. Paula Jackson, human resources manager at Stacey, regularly visits the campus to help students attain job-seeking skills by conducting simulated interviews.

Diana McDaniels

Diana McDaniels

2760 Industrial Parkway • Morrow, GA 31754-2028 • Public Relations Office • (912) 555-3996, Extension 408

Figure 37–1 Format for a news release

3. Key the current date and the release date (or the phrase *For Immediate Release*) at the top at the left margin.
4. Center the heading of the announcement in ALL CAPS four lines below the release date. Double-space after the heading.
5. Key the writer's name (or the name of the contact person) four lines below the message at the left margin.
6. Limit releases to one page if possible, although you may need more space for a complex message. If the release is longer than one page, key —*more*— at the end of all pages except the last.

★ The phrase *For Immediate Release* tells the media that the information in your news release can be announced right away. If you designate a release date, the media can announce the information on or after that date.

News Releases

Your company must relate some bad news for the Hillburn community in a press release. Rate each opening sentence as good or poor. If a sentence is **poor**, indicate the reason.

1. Nimco will close its Hillburn factory forever on January 1, putting 650 people out of work.
2. As part of a plan to eliminate excess manufacturing capacity and boost profitability, Nimco will close its Hillburn factory on January 1.
3. Nimco will close its Hillburn factory on January 1, lay off 650 workers, and transfer all managers to the Monroe plant.

Check your answers in Appendix F.

Proposals

Another external document frequently used in business is the **proposal**, an analysis of a problem and a recommendation for a solution. Examples of a problem include a need for new equipment or new designs. Possible solutions include buying a new machine or using a particular design.

In a proposal, the writer tries to convince someone to solve the problem by taking a specific action such as buying or donating something. As you learned in Chapter 34, company managers are the usual receivers of internal proposals. In contrast, external proposals are used to persuade people outside the organization to follow a particular course of action.

Using Solicited and Unsolicited Proposals

Many government agencies, nonprofit organizations, and corporations solicit proposals from suppliers who compete for the right to provide goods or services. By soliciting proposals, managers in these organizations can get details about price, delivery, quality, and other information they need to make an informed decision.

Unlike solicited proposals, unsolicited proposals are not requested by the receiver. In fact, the receiver may not even be aware of the project being suggested. For example, a medical researcher seeking money to investigate a specific problem will use an unsolicited proposal to request financial support from nonprofit foundations. Because the reader has little or no knowledge of the project, an unsolicited proposal must explain the proposed investigation thoroughly.

Planning Proposals

Use the psychology of persuasion when planning a proposal. Identify the objective and analyze the receiver to determine the most compelling benefits and to select the primary appeal. Then write an attention-getting opening that is both positive and receiver oriented.

Bear in mind that promises made in an external proposal may become legally binding on you and your company. Your proposal can become, in effect, a legal contract if the receiver accepts your terms. Therefore, be careful what you say in a proposal, and make sure that the data—especially numbers—are correct.

Organizing Proposals

Proposals may be organized in many ways. Most (but not all) contain the following elements:

1. **Objectives.** Explain what the project will accomplish.
2. **Need.** Describe the problem the project will solve or the need it will meet.
3. **Background.** Tell the reader why the project is important and why your solution makes sense.
4. **Scope of Project.** Indicate exactly what your proposal covers.
5. **Action Plan.** List the steps that must be taken to achieve the objectives.
6. **Schedule.** Discuss the amount of time needed to complete the project and note the deadline for each step in the action plan.
7. **Cost.** Explain the project's total cost and link it to the benefits the reader will receive.
8. **Qualifications.** Describe your company's qualifications.
9. **Supporting Information.** Include any necessary supporting information (such as the names of references) in an appendix.

ACROSS CULTURES

- When you submit a proposal to a company in another country, include details about your company's qualifications such as its history, its financial strength, and the technical training of its personnel.

Formatting Proposals

Typically, solicited proposals must follow a specific format. Follow formatting directions carefully because some organizations eliminate proposals that are formatted incorrectly. When the receiver does not specify a format, follow your company's proposal format. Figure 37–2 shows a solicited proposal in letter form.

MEETING DOCUMENTS

Meetings are an important method of exchanging information in any business setting. Whether you call a meeting or participate as an attendee, two internal documents you will use are agendas and minutes.

Agendas

An **agenda** is the order of business to be discussed during a particular meeting. The person who organizes the meeting usually prepares and distributes the agenda in advance so that participants can prepare for the meeting. Agendas also help keep people focused on the scheduled topics. Both the leader and the participants can use the agenda as a written guide.

Planning Agendas

To plan an agenda, determine the meeting objective and prepare a list of topics to be discussed. Determine if committee reports need to be reviewed during the meeting. Think, too, about any new topics that participants may introduce. Finally, allow time for routine announcements.

Organizing Agendas

Because an agenda is used as a discussion guide as well as a planning document, you will want to include every topic that should be discussed during the meeting. Also include information about the meeting date, time, and place.

Formatting Agendas

Agendas for formal meetings typically follow a structured format. Figure 37–3 shows a sample format for an agenda. Although formats vary, the name of the meeting generally is worded as a phrase. For example, a meeting about finding new employees could be titled "Recruitment Meeting." Center the day of the week, date, time, and location information under the meeting title.

The agendas for regular weekly or monthly meetings may vary little, so participants often can anticipate what topics will be discussed. In contrast, agendas for one-time meetings are less predictable; these agendas should be distributed in advance to allow participants time to prepare.

Teletalk 1000 Broadmoor Way Omaha, NE 68113-1844 Telephone: (402) 555-1000 Fax: (402) 555-1068

July 12, 19—

Ms. Gloria Quintero
Director of Consumer Affairs
The Foodworks Market
10 Dunstable Highway
Omaha, NE 68111-6496

Dear Ms. Quintero:

As you requested, here is our proposal for conducting a telephone survey to determine consumer interest in the posting of nutritional information in your store's produce department.

Objective

The objective of this project is to provide the research you need to decide whether to post nutritional information for produce.

Need

Your supermarket has positioned itself as the market leader in customer service. One aspect of customer service that you need to investigate is if detailed nutritional information posted in the produce department would be valuable to consumers.

Background

Consumers are more concerned than ever about their health. Many want to use more fresh fruits and vegetables in their home-cooked meals, but they do not have complete information about the nutritional value of these items. Because produce is not prepackaged in printed containers, consumers cannot check the labels for nutritional value. Consumers therefore have no source of nutritional information at the point of sale.

Scope of Project

To learn what adult consumers think about the posting of nutritional information in your store, we propose to plan and conduct a comprehensive survey.

Figure 37–2 Solicited proposal in letter form

Ms. Gloria Quintero
July 12, 19—
Page 2

This survey would include:

- identifying potential interviewees
- preparing a script for the telephone survey
- compiling and analyzing survey results
- preparing a final report to Foodworks' management

To get a balanced sampling of the local population, we recommend surveying at least 300 adults. Based on our experience, we will need the names and telephone numbers of up to 900 adults so that we can be assured of completing 300 interviews.

Action Plan

Once you approve the project, Teletalk will require three working days to prepare a script for the telephone survey. We will test this script on 25 telephone contacts, make any necessary revisions, and then proceed to complete 300 telephone interviews. These 300 interviews will be conducted over the course of five weekday evenings. One week after completing the survey, we will provide a statistical analysis of the results and a written summary of our findings and recommendations.

Cost

Our price for planning, completing, and analyzing this survey is $5,000. This price does not include additional costs such as telephone charges, postage, and other expenses, which will be billed later.

Teletalk has been privileged to conduct more than one dozen of Foodworks' surveys over the past three years. As always, we welcome the opportunity to help you better understand the needs of your local community. Thank you for asking Teletalk to submit this bid.

Sincerely,

Brad Altman

Brad Altman
Vice President

pn

Figure 37–2 Solicited proposal in letter form, *continued*

Agenda
Divisional Planning Meeting
Monday, October 3, 19—
10:30 a.m.
Executive Conference Room

1. Call to Order

2. Roll Call

3. Approval of Minutes From September Meeting

4. Chairperson's Report

5. Subcommittee Reports

   A. Sales Forecasting

   B. Supplier Evaluation

6. Unfinished Business

7. New Business

   A. Total Quality Management Program

   B. Product Distribution Analysis

   C. Other New Business

8. Announcements

9. Adjournment

Figure 37–3 Format for an agenda

Number the items in the agenda below the heading. The first item should be the call to order. After the roll call and approval of minutes from the previous meeting, add any entries for chairperson or subcommittee reports. Unfinished business—topics not resolved in prior meetings—is next, followed by new business. Most agendas end with announcements and adjournment.

Not every agenda contains every entry shown in Figure 37–3. On the other hand, many agendas are even more detailed. For example, the agenda for a major, ongoing project may show the name of the person who will report on each topic next to each entry.

Minutes

Minutes are the official record of the proceedings of a meeting. They summarize topics discussed, decisions made, and actions to be taken. Minutes are sent to every meeting participant as well as to people who were invited but could not attend. On occasion, minutes also are sent to nonparticipants such as senior managers or peers whose work is affected by decisions made during the meeting.

★ Minutes are intended only to summarize what occurred in a meeting, not to provide a word-for-word account of who said what and when.

★ Meeting participants also can take turns performing the role of secretary.

Planning the Minutes

Planning begins even before the meeting. Decide who will take notes during the meeting—either a company secretary or a volunteer from the group.

During the meeting, the secretary records the actual starting time, the location, and the names of the people who are present and absent, including the leader. (If the meeting is large, the secretary may simply note the number of people present.) Next, the secretary records the decision made or action taken for every item on the agenda. Finally, the secretary notes the time adjourned and the date and time of the next meeting, if another is needed.

Organizing the Minutes

Organize the minutes according to the order in which topics were discussed. Generally, items are discussed in the order shown on the agenda. The minutes also should reflect any topics that were discussed out of order.

Formatting the Minutes

By following a few formatting guidelines, you can make minutes easy to read. Figure 37–4 shows the format for minutes of a meeting. Use 1-inch side margins, a $1\frac{1}{2}$-inch top margin, and single spacing. Center the name of the meeting and/or organization in ALL CAPS at the top. Below that, center a subheading (optional) such as *Minutes of the Executive Board.* Center the date two lines below the heading. Use uppercase and lowercase letters for a subheading.

Key the body four lines below the subheading, single-spacing the text and double-spacing between paragraphs. Use headings to identify the various parts of the meeting. Key the headings in ALL CAPS or use uppercase and lowercase letters and underscore them as shown in Figure 37–4. Then key the name of the person who recorded the minutes and provide a signature line four lines below the last line.

MINUTES OF OFFICE TECHNOLOGY ADVISORY COMMITTEE

September 19, 19—

Call to Order

The meeting was called to order by Chairperson Sandra Clurman at 3:35 p.m. in Room C-47.

Members present were Sonia Berens, Dave Brown, Henry Fowler, Jane Keyes, Michael Nolan, Gloria Ortiz, Amy Resnick, and Dan Tripp. Ex-officio members present were Ann Barrett, Lu-yin Huang, and Martin Long.

Minutes of the April 30, 19—, meeting were approved.

Report From the Office of Technology Department

Dr. Keyes welcomed all new and returning committee members. She briefly discussed the new building proposal (near construction stage).

Mr. Nolan gave an update of the department. He provided an equipment inventory and distributed updated course guides for preview.

Program of Work/Goals

Dr. Clurman distributed the suggested program of Work/Goals for (1) Curriculum (2) Facilities and Equipment, and (3) College and Community. Members selected the committee on which they would prefer to serve.

Unfinished Business

Next Meeting

The Winter Quarter meeting will be held on January 28, 19—.

The meeting was adjourned at 4:55 p.m.

Adrian Cardona
Adrian Cardona, Secretary

Figure 37–4 Format for minutes of a meeting

Summary

Businesses use a variety of specialized workplace documents. A news release is a brief announcement sent to the media. A proposal is an analysis of a problem and a recommendation for a solution. An agenda is the order of business for a meeting. Minutes are the official record of the proceedings of a meeting.

Discussion Questions

1. What is the purpose of a news release?
2. How do solicited and unsolicited proposals differ?

Practical Application

Organize the following information into the news release format and suggest an appropriate attention-getting heading.

CONTACT: Gayle Smith, 555-1295

[Current Date]

For Immediate Release

San Francisco, CA

1. People, space, and technology will come together at the annual Office Design Conference, to be held May 15–17 at San Francisco's Moscone Convention Center.
2. This year's conference will feature more than 40 seminars, all designed to enhance the professional skills of office managers, interior designers, and other design professionals.
3. In addition, more than 200 exhibitors will show their office equipment and supplies.
4. Special features of the show include a photo gallery, which will exhibit photographs of the latest office design projects from all across the country.
5. Also, a video theater will offer daily presentations by Robert Byars, a design consultant.

Editing and Proofreading Application

Proofread the following memo and make any necessary corrections. Then prepare an agenda from the topics in the memo.

To: Joanna Burke

From: Benjamin Soto

Subject: New-product promotion meeting

Date: January 12, 19—

COMMUNICATION ACTIVITIES

With the national introduction of our Cool-Touch Toaster four months away, we need to complete our promotion plans. Please schedule a new-product promotion meeting for Thursday, January 19th, at 2:00 PM in Conference Room B. I would appreciate it if you would take notes during the meeting, which I will chair.

We should review the minites from last month's meeting and invite the chairpersons from the Advertising and In-store Promotion Subcommittees to report the results to date. I will report on the production schedule and show a sample of the new packaging.

Because we did not reach a decision about the warranty period, when we discussed it last month, we need to discuss this at the upcoming meeting. In addition, we should decide what to do about Sales Incentives, which was also discussed at last month's meeting. I may have announcements to make regarding new product ideas and we should allow time for any new topics.

Oral and Nonverbal Communication

Employees spend most of their working day communicating by writing, reading, speaking, or listening. Of these forms of communication, speaking and listening are used more than writing or reading. Part 8 focuses on listening and speaking.

Chapter 38 examines the importance of nonverbal communication—the messages you send without using words. Chapter 39 concentrates on listening—the most frequently used form of communication. Problems common to poor listeners are given and remedies for them are presented.

Chapters 40 through 42 center on oral communication in different settings. Chapter 40 provides guidelines for effective oral communication in a one-to-one conversation, a telephone call, and a group setting. Chapter 41 tells readers how to be effective in meetings. The roles of the participant, the organizer, and the leader are examined, and suggestions for effectiveness in each role are given. Chapter 42 contains information on short and formal oral presentations and provides guidelines for effective delivery.

Nonverbal Communication

OBJECTIVES

After studying this chapter and completing the chapter exercises, you will be able to do the following:

1. Describe the roles of nonverbal communication.
3. Describe nonverbal symbols sent in written messages.
4. List nonverbal symbols sent in spoken messages.
5. Describe the uses of nonverbal symbols in the environment.

THE ROLES OF NONVERBAL COMMUNICATION

Nonverbal communication can have a strong impact on the receiver. Sometimes actions speak so loudly that they drown out spoken words. Nonverbal symbols usually convey what the sender really feels and the degree of importance the sender attaches to the message and to the receiver. Spoken or written communication makes up the verbal part of a message and are always accompanied by nonverbal symbols. The unspoken or unwritten communication makes up the nonverbal part of a message. A nonverbal message may not have a verbal counterpoint. Nonverbal symbols include body language, appearance, touching, space, time, and voice. Nonverbal symbols exist in written and oral communication as well as in the environment.

Receivers interpret nonverbal symbols by using their senses: sight, hearing, touch, taste, and smell. If someone hears a secretary say, "Great!," and sees the secretary smile while a computer merges a list of addresses with a letter, the person will conclude that the mail merge is successful. If someone hears a secretary say, "Great!," in a disgusted tone and sees him or her frown, the person will conclude that the mail merge is unsuccessful. The receiver interprets the message based on sight (the secretary's smile or frown) and hearing (the tone of the secretary's voice). However, nonverbal symbols differ among cultures. In some cultures, for example, arriving late for a social or business engagement is polite; in others, it is considered rude. Be careful how you interpret nonverbal symbols.

People's opinions usually are based on the nonverbal symbols they observe and how they interpret them. Studies have found that when judging attitudes, people base 93 percent of their judgment on nonverbal symbols and 7 percent on spoken words. Verbal and nonverbal symbols should be interpreted in relation to each other. Nonverbal symbols may reinforce, contradict, substitute for, or regulate the verbal part of a message.

★ A firm handshake, a delicately seasoned sauce, the beep of a computer, or the stale smell of a creek all convey a message without a word being spoken.

ACROSS CULTURES

• Raising one's eyebrows in the North American culture means "I question what you are saying." In New Zealand, this same action means "yes."

Reinforcing the Verbal Message

Nonverbal symbols usually reinforce the verbal message. Pointing to the door as you state, "The office is the second door on the left," reinforces the verbal message. The secretary's statement of satisfaction in the earlier example was reinforced by a smile. Pounding the table while making a statement reinforces a verbal message and emphasizes it as well.

Contradicting the Verbal Message

Sometimes the verbal and nonverbal symbols do not agree. For example, you may say, "That's fine," but if your voice is strained and you look away from the receiver, which symbol will the receiver believe—the verbal or the nonverbal? Research indicates that when verbal and nonverbal symbols conflict, the receiver usually believes the nonverbal message.

Substituting for the Verbal Message

Nonverbal symbols sometimes act as substitutes for verbal messages. Gritting your teeth or throwing your hands in the air indicates frustration; clenching your fists, anger; tapping your foot or a pencil, impatience; and nodding or smiling, agreement. When nonverbal symbols act as substitutes, no words are spoken.

Regulating the Verbal Message

Nonverbal symbols may be used to regulate or control communication between the sender and receiver. In oral communication, these regulators may signal when you want to speak, when you want others to continue speaking, or when you want to withdraw from a conversation. For example, reestablishing eye contact with the receiver indicates that you will conclude your remarks shortly. The eye contact tells the receiver to prepare to take over the conversation.

Nodding in agreement encourages another person to continue; however, checking your watch or closing a portfolio means you are through listening. A chairperson of a meeting can regulate who will speak by looking directly at an individual.

CHECKPOINT 1

Roles of Nonverbal Symbols

Indicate if each statement is true or false.

1. All verbal symbols are accompanied by nonverbal symbols, and all nonverbal symbols are accompanied by verbal symbols.

(Continued on the next page)

NONVERBAL SYMBOLS IN WRITTEN MESSAGES

The appearance and correctness of a written document as well as the timeliness of the response send critical nonverbal messages and deserve careful attention. Letterhead stationery, plain sheets, and envelopes should have the same color and use high-quality bond paper. The typefaces and design of the letterhead and logo should convey a professional image. Drawings, photographs, charts, and graphs should be appropriate to the content and enhance the message. The print should be dark, crisp, and easy to read.

Documents should not include any errors in capitalization, grammar, number expression, punctuation, spelling, and word usage. Accuracy of content, especially amounts, addresses, dates, and other factual information, is essential. Correct documents send a nonverbal message that the sender is reliable and considers quality and the needs of the receiver important.

Incorrect documents send a negative message about the sender and his or her company. What messages does the document in Figure 38–1 send? How do you feel about the sender? Would you want to do business with this company? Probably not!

NONVERBAL SYMBOLS IN SPOKEN MESSAGES

Several nonverbal symbols—body language, appearance, touching, use of space and time, and voice and paralanguage—have an impact on oral messages. The following paragraphs discuss each of these symbols.

Rockingham First National Bank
3109 Wall Street Harrisonburg, VA 22814-0091

April 6, 19—

Mr. and Ms. Tony Jabobs
8902 YellOwsStone Rock Road
Bridgewater, VA 22812-3735

Dear Mr. amd Mrs. Jacobs

Congradulations! You're $25,000 home imporvement loan has been ap-
proved.

To receive the money, both of you need to come by the bank before April
20th and sign the loan agreement. After signing the agreement, the money
will be available to you immediately.

Because of your exceelent credit rating; other low-interest loans are open to
you. These include small investment, car, boat, vacation, etc. Should you be
interested in any of these or other loans, please call me at 555-38519.

Mr. and Mrs. Jacobs, thanks for using Rockingham First National Bank. I
look forward to seeing you in within 14 days.

Sincerely yours,

Juniper Jones

ROCKINGHAM FIRST NATIONAL BAKN
JUniper Jones Senior Loan Offcier

Figure 38–1 Nonverbal symbols in written communications sending negative messages

Body Language

Body language includes facial expressions, gestures, and posture. Interpreting body language is surprisingly complex because a single motion can have many different meanings.

Facial Expressions

People can reveal their feelings through various facial expressions. A frown usually indicates negative feelings; a smile, happy feelings. Smiles without eye contact and with closed lips can have the opposite effect. Nervous smiles convey weakness or insecurity.

Eyes are the most revealing facial expression and often are called "the windows of the soul." Eyes reveal feelings such as excitement, boredom, energy, fatigue, surprise or shock, intensity or concentration, and sadness. Eyebrows also send various messages. Raised eyebrows may mean nervousness, surprise, or questioning; pinched together they may imply confusion or indecision.

Direct eye contact may convey interest, friendship, or confidence; a lack of eye contact may mean disinterest or boredom. In business, the amount of eye

contact varies depending on a person's status. Because subordinates want to tell their supervisors that they like them, they generally make more eye contact.

Gestures

A gesture is the use of one's arms and hands to express an idea or feeling. Crossed arms may indicate concentration or withdrawal; a hand placed against the side of the head can imply forgetfulness; trembling or fidgeting hands sometimes indicate nervousness.

Leaning toward a person who is speaking conveys an open attitude. Nodding confirms listening and sometimes agreement. On the other hand, folding your arms or shaking your head from side to side indicates a closed attitude or disagreement.

Posture

A person conveys his or her level of confidence through posture. Poor posture may be a sign of timidity, laziness, or nervousness. To project a strong self-image, sit and stand straight and tall—no slumping, slouching, or leaning forward. To project confidence, act as if you believe you have a right to be where you are.

Appearance

To be viewed as acceptable, competent, and professional, you must project an appearance that is attractive and appropriate for the situation. According to research, people generally believe that attractive people of either gender have more socially desirable personality traits than do unattractive people.

Proper diet, rest, and consistent exercise are the keys to maintaining an attractive body. In addition, your clothing must be appropriate to your work and for your organization. In most businesses, appropriate clothes are conservative in fabric, color, and style.

Touching

The handshake is the most acceptable form of touching for both men and women in a business environment. It is a gesture used to greet someone or sometimes to close a discussion. A person who extends a firm handshake (and simultaneously establishes eye contact) projects a cordial, confident image. However, a weak, soft handshake suggests listlessness or mental dullness. A cold, wet handshake indicates nervousness and possibly a feeling of inferiority.

Other forms of touching such as hugging or backslapping are generally not acceptable in business. A person of higher rank, however, may put his or her hand on a subordinate's shoulder as a sign of encouragement or support. A coworker could do the same thing with another coworker; but a coworker should not put his or her hand on the shoulder of the supervisor. Such action could be considered too familiar. Businesspersons must take care, however, to avoid touching that can be interpreted as condescending, paternalistic, or sexual harassment. *Sexual harassment* can be defined as any unwanted verbal or physical actions associated with sex. A businessperson must be cautious when touching to prevent misinterpretation by anyone.

LEGAL/Ethical

• Sexual harassment is an ethical issue because it infringes on one's freedom and can have a demeaning or demoralizing affect.

Space

Space refers to the physical distance between individuals. In general, people stand relatively close to people they like and leave more space between themselves and people they fear or do not like. When unable to arrange space comfortably, as in a crowded elevator, people adjust other nonverbal symbols such as avoiding eye contact, staring at the passing floor numbers, or remaining silent.

People avoid speaking or making eye contact in such situations because their territory—their own space zone—is being violated. The size of this space depends on the activity and the relation with the other person(s) involved. For North Americans, the space zones are as follows:

1. **Intimate zone**—0 to 18 inches. To be comfortable at this close range, people must have an intimate relationship—close friends sharing confidences, a parent reassuring or scolding a child, a husband and wife having a disagreement. Touch and smell are the senses most used. Verbal communication is usually soft or even murmured.
2. **Personal zone**—18 inches to 4 feet. To stand this close, participants must be well acquainted. Words are spoken softly.
3. **Social zone**—4 to 12 feet. The social zone is common for most business meetings or social gatherings. When people converse in their social zone, they have some reason for speaking. If a stranger enters a social zone, people usually break eye contact or turn away. For example, if you notice a stranger as you walk on the sidewalk, you watch the stranger from a distance of about 20 feet. As the stranger approaches, however, you break eye contact. If you speak to a stranger who is within your social zone, you use a formal, businesslike voice.
4. **Public zone**—more than 12 feet. From a distance of more than 12 feet, people may look at each other, but they do not maintain eye contact. Interaction is avoided. Communication between a speaker and an audience is within the public zone.

When a co-worker stands too close or too far from you, he or she probably feels your relationship is on a different level. You may feel the relationship is on a personal level, but he or she feels it is on a social level. Standing too close to a co-worker consistently could be interpreted as sexual harassment.

In an office environment, the size, location (corner office, distance from the top manager's office, and so forth), and use of space may be a sign of a person's status. Generally, the more spacious an office, the higher the status. Persons of higher status also may enter a subordinate's space unannounced.

Meetings usually are held in the office of the person with the higher status because it is more convenient for that person.

Time

How you use time is another aspect of nonverbal communication. If someone asks you to do something as soon as possible, you feel urgency. If someone asks you to do something immediately, you might stop what you are doing and fulfill the request. Arriving on time for appointments and job interviews and responding promptly to requests communicate your sense of responsibility and respect for other people's time as well as your own.

The use of time also shows status. As mentioned earlier, persons of higher status have the freedom to interrupt subordinates. Higher-status persons typically determine the length of a meeting. On the other hand, executives often work longer hours than do lower-status persons.

Voice and Paralanguage

Maybe you have heard the saying, "It's not what you say, but how you say it that counts." **Paralanguage** is the nonverbal symbols that accompany a verbal message and reveal the difference between what is said and how it is said. Paralanguage includes pitch, stress, rate, volume, inflection, rhythm, and pronunciation. It also includes laughing, crying, sighing, grunting, yawning, belching, and coughing. Even silence, pauses, and hesitations are part of paralanguage. Paralanguage is critical to the correct interpretation of a message.

To understand the effect of paralanguage, repeat this sentence aloud four times. Each time stress the underlined word. Note how the meaning of the sentence changes.

<u>I</u> cannot do this.

I <u>cannot</u> do this.

I cannot <u>do</u> this.

I cannot do <u>this</u>.

NONVERBAL SYMBOLS IN THE ENVIRONMENT

The business environment is a form of nonverbal communication. Furnishings and decor; the arrangement of tables, chairs, and so forth; the level of lighting, temperature, and sound; and the use of color contribute to the way people feel in a setting.

Furnishings

Furnishings and decor are often a part of business strategy. For example, in a typical fast-food restaurant, the tables are close together, the lighting is bright,

ON THE JOB

Arriving late continually sends a nonverbal message that you are disorganized, lazy, or disrespectful.

ON THE JOB

Music can be used by businesses to influence customers. March music or music with a fast beat is used to move people quickly. Slow, mood music is used to encourage people to stay.

and the seats are molded plastic. The environment is carefully planned to encourage fast turnover of customers. In contrast, a fine restaurant may have a more spacious environment, dim lighting, padded armchairs, fine china, tablecloths, and fresh flowers.

Color

Color establishes a mood within an environment. Soothing colors such as beige, off-white, or light yellow are especially suitable where people perform stressful or tedious work. Excessive use of light blue can have a dulling effect, tending to make workers feel sluggish. Red and orange are stimulating colors, appropriate for areas where people spend a short amount of time (a cafeteria, for example) or perform creative work.

CHECKPOINT 2

The Use of Nonverbal Symbols

Indicate if each statement is true or false.

1. Body language is the study of how something is said.
2. Touching is a type of nonverbal communication that can be used to reinforce.
3. The typeface used to print a document is a nonverbal symbol of the written document.
4. In the North American culture, one's personal zone is 4 to 12 feet.
5. When measuring attitudes, the manner in which words are spoken is more important than the words themselves.

Check your answers in Appendix F.

Summary

All written and spoken messages consist of both verbal and nonverbal symbols. Nonverbal symbols help the receiver to interpret verbal symbols. Nonverbal symbols may reinforce, contradict, substitute for, or regulate a verbal message.

Nonverbal symbols are present in both written and oral communication as well as in the environment. In written messages, the nonverbal symbols of appearance, correctness, and timeliness reflect the sender's attitude and abilities. Nonverbal symbols used in spoken messages include body language, appearance, touching, space, time, voice, and paralanguage. Two nonverbal symbols used extensively in business environments are furnishings and color.

Discussion Questions

1. What are the roles of nonverbal communication symbols when they interact with verbal communication?
2. Are nonverbal symbols important in both written and spoken messages? Explain.
3. How are nonverbal symbols used in the environment?

Practical Applications

Part A

Identify the nonverbal symbols in each situation. Choose from the following list of nonverbal symbols:

a. furnishings   d. touching
b. body language   e. voice and paralanguage
c. space   f. appearance

1. a hand laid gently on a shoulder
2. a grunt
3. a young girl standing straight and tall
4. an elegant lamp
5. the distance between an employee and supervisor while conversing
6. a pressed shirt

Part B

Indicate the role of the nonverbal symbol in each situation. Choose from the following list of roles of nonverbal symbols:

a. contradict   c. reinforce
b. regulate   d. substitute

1. A subordinate asks you a question. Instead of saying, "I have to think about the question," you respond by folding your hands together and placing them behind your head.
2. After an exciting day, you arrive home, hug your spouse, and exclaim, "What a day!"
3. As you talk with a friend, your friend shakes his head, disagreeing with what you are saying.
4. While consoling your child, you gently pat her on the back.
5. You are speaking with one of your peers. When you finish what you want to say, you glance at your peer.

Part C

Visit an office, a retail store, or a restaurant. Write a short report describing the effect of the environmental factors and the image created by the environment.

Listening

OBJECTIVES

After studying this chapter and completing the chapter exercises, you will be able to do the following:

1. Identify the reasons for and the benefits of listening.
2. List barriers to effective listening.
3. Describe effective listening techniques.

THE IMPORTANCE OF LISTENING

What is the most frequent form of communication—reading, writing, speaking, or listening? If you said listening, you are correct. Research indicates that people spend about 70 to 80 percent of their awake time communicating; 45 percent, listening; 30 percent, speaking; 16 percent, reading; and 9 percent, writing. Managers, however, spend approximately 60 percent of their workday listening.[1] The higher one climbs in the corporate hierarchy, the more time one spends listening to others.

Reasons for Listening

People listen to relax, to obtain information, to express interest, and to discover attitudes. When you listen to good music and watch television, usually you are listening to relax. Listening to the sounds of summer or the rhythm of the tides helps clear your mind of worry and relieve stress.

People listen to gather information. Adults gain an estimated 90 percent of information by listening. Gathering information for an assignment, participating in an interview, and obtaining feedback from a customer are examples of listening for information.

You listen to let people know that you are interested in what they have to say and that they are important. Listening and responding as friends or associates over lunch is not only enjoyable but also conveys the message that their thoughts and feelings are important to you. Such informal conversations establish a bond between people that makes communication in formal situations easier.

Finally, people listen to discover attitudes. Attitudes often are expressed in the nonverbal cues of the message. Alert listeners observe these cues and try to identify the speaker's real feelings.

Benefits of Listening

Listening affects greatly the quality of your relationships with others. Through listening you can better understand your own feelings, attitudes, and beliefs, as well as those of others. Friendships thrive when people take the time to share and understand each other's feelings. Family members build strong bonds by responding to each other's needs. Likewise, good listening helps businesses develop

---

[1]Edward Wakin, "The Business of Listening," *Today's Office*, February 1984, p. 46.

their most important resource—their employees. Employees who believe their opinions count develop greater self-esteem and contribute more to the organization. Customers who think a company understands and meets their needs will return for future business dealings. Those who feel ignored do not return.

Listening affects the quality of decisions. To make good decisions, you must gather meaningful and accurate information. Gathering accurate information requires alertness and the ability to ask the right questions. Those who can listen to employees and managers at all levels will be able to make the best use of the information available to them.

Good listening skills are essential for success in business. Subordinates who receive and interpret instructions and information correctly win the respect of their supervisors. Successful supervisors listen to both their subordinates and their managers. Similarly, effective salespersons listen in order to gather meaningful feedback from customers and relay it to appropriate decision makers in the company. Employees who have good listening skills make prime candidates for promotion.

THE NATURE OF LISTENING

Some people assume they are good listeners because they have been listening all their lives. Yet, research by Ralph Nichols and others indicates that initially people remember and understand only about half of what they hear. After a few weeks, they remember only one-fourth of what they originally heard.[2] Effective listening requires remembering; and remembering, in turn, requires effective listening. To become a good listener, beware of barriers that make listening difficult, understand the listening process, and use the appropriate kind of listening.

Barriers to Effective Listening

Missing an important appointment, discounting a valuable suggestion, overlooking the feelings behind the words, and interpreting a situation incorrectly are just a few examples of problems that occur because of poor listening. Researchers have identified various barriers to good listening. As you read about these barriers, evaluate yourself as a listener. Do any of these barriers sound familiar?

---

[2]Bertha Collins, "Are You Listening?" *Journal of Business Education*, December 1982, p. 103.

★ Have you ever tuned out an instructor because of his or her appearance or teaching style? How much did you learn from that person? How much did you miss?

Attitudes Toward the Speaker

"My, he looks as if he didn't get enough sleep last night." "She speaks so slowly; doesn't she know I've got work to do?" "Oh! I wish he hadn't said that; I'm sure he's educated, but you would never know it from his language." When listeners have private conversations with themselves, they miss what the speaker is saying.

A speaker's appearance, mannerisms, tone of voice, and body language can distract the listener. Poor grammar or inappropriate word choice also can cause individuals to stop listening and mentally criticize the speaker.

Attitudes Toward the Topic

"I can't program using BASIC; programming is too complex." "Oh, insurance! Don't talk to me about that dull subject." "I couldn't stand to hear one more detail." Messages that sound technical often intimidate listeners. Uninteresting or boring messages cause people to tune out the speaker. In a similar manner, listeners often lose patience with messages that are too detailed or too long.

Environmental Distractions

Have you ever attended a luncheon at which the speaker began his or her presentation while the desserts or beverages were being served? Have you ever tried to finish a conversation with the telephone ringing in the background? If so, you know how unrelated activities and noise can interfere with your ability to listen. Likewise, excessive heat or coolness and noise are distracting.

Personal Barriers

Deafness or a partial hearing loss are physical barriers to listening. A headache or another temporary physical discomfort also inhibits listening. Each of us also tends to block out messages for various psychological reasons. Additional personal barriers include the following:

★ How do you feel when no one listens to you? Good listeners improve a speaker's ability to express thoughts clearly. Help the speaker—be focused listener.

1. *Prejudices or Differing Opinions.* Most people have preconceived ideas about certain topics. If a speaker challenges a strongly held belief, the listener may simply tune out the speaker. Often the listener begins preparing a rebuttal even before the speaker has finished.
2. *Assumptions.* Assumptions made in advance can account for a 75 percent decline in listening. People often disregard messages when they think they already know the information.
3. *Lack of Attention.* Mind wandering is another deterrent to effective listening. Worrying about a personal problem or daydreaming about more interesting ideas can cause your mind to wander.

Notetaking Techniques

Someone who tries to record everything that is said often hears only about one-third of what is said. Conversely, some listeners record only the main ideas and fail to record enough supporting information to make the main ideas meaningful or clear.

The Listening Process

Listening is the process of hearing and focusing attention to understand and remember an oral message. Four steps are required in the listening process:

1. *Hearing* is a function of the ears. In an office, you may hear people talking, telephones ringing, doors closing or opening, or other sounds.
2. *Focusing attention* involves concentrating on the speaker and what he or she says. To focus your attention, you must ignore unrelated sounds, background noise, and other distractions.

ACROSS
CULTURES

• Cultural differences make
effective listening—
understanding and recalling a
message—more complex.

3. *Understanding* means that you can attach meaning to the speaker's message. For example, a person may hear and focus on someone speaking in an unfamiliar foreign language, but the message is not understood and becomes meaningless.

4. *Remembering.* If you cannot paraphrase accurately something you have just heard, you have not really listened. Figure 39–1 illustrates the listening process.

Types of Listening

The two types of listening—casual and active—have different uses. Casual listening is what you do most frequently. **Casual listening** is listening associated with conversation and entertainment. Watching a movie or making small talk between classes or at lunch are examples of casual listening. The casual listener expends little energy or effort. Although the listener may comprehend the message, remembering it is not critical. Casual listening is relaxed. When you are engaged in informal conversations, however, you must be careful not to listen so casually that others think you are not paying attention.

Active listening requires remembering and has purpose. Doctors actively listen to their patients; interviewers actively listen to what an applicant says. To understand the difference between casual and active listening, recall a time that you listened very intently because you had something to gain from what was said— you were motivated to listen by your own self-interest.

When you listen actively, your mind is alert and absorbs what the speaker says. You empathize with the speaker by trying to understand the speaker's perspective, attitudes, and emotions. Empathetic listeners also realize the importance of listening rather than talking.

Active listening, however, involves an element of risk. The listener risks seeing the world as the speaker sees it. When a listener actually senses the feelings of another person and appreciates what the other person's experiences mean to that person, the listener may change his or her beliefs.

Active listening also requires the listener to notice and interpret the nonverbal cues of the message. Speakers express attitudes in various ways: pauses; tone of voice; emphasis given or not given to words; and nervous habits and utterances such as repeatedly saying "okay" and "um," fidgeting with pointers, grasping the lectern too tightly, and so forth. Figure 39–2 provides an example of active listening.

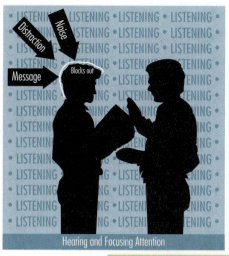

Hearing and Focusing Attention

You force distractions into the background. You keep the message in the foreground.

Understanding

You make the connections between important pieces of information.

Remembering

You bring back to mind the important points of the message.

Figure 39–1 The listening process

STEP	ACTION
1.	Ramon sends a message.
2.	Latisha listens to Ramon's words and to the way he uses them. She also watches the nonverbal cues sent by Ramon's face, hands, and so forth.
3.	Latisha analyzes the verbal and nonverbal messages received and decides what she thinks Ramon is saying.
4.	Latisha summarizes to Ramon what she thinks was his intended message.
5.	Ramon decides if Latisha's summary is a correct interpretation of the message he originally sent. If Latisha's summary is correct, Ramon agrees with the summary. If Latisha's summary is incorrect, Ramon says, "No, it is. . . ." At this point, Latisha repeats steps 2 through 5 until Ramon agrees with Latisha's summary.

Figure 39–2 Active listening

Facts About Listening

CHECKPOINT 1

Indicate if each statement is true or false.

1. Adults gather most of their information by listening.
2. Attitudes toward a speaker or toward a topic affect listening skills.
3. Preconceived ideas can create a barrier to effective listening.
4. The last step in listening is remembering.
5. Active listening may result in personal change.

Check your answers in Appendix F.

EFFECTIVE LISTENING TECHNIQUES

To be productive, people need to become effective listeners. Understanding the listening process and the barriers to effective listening is not enough. Listening is a skill that requires continuous practice. To become a good listener, you must know your own personal weaknesses and practice good listening habits. Follow these suggestions to improve your listening skills.

Share the Responsibility

Although the speaker has most of the responsibility for conveying meaning, effective listeners realize that they play a vital role in the communication process. Listeners must be able to attach meaning to what has been said.

People talk at a rate of about 100 to 150 words a minute and think at a rate of about 300 to 500 words a minute. Thus, the listener has spare time available. Rather than letting their minds wander, effective listeners use this spare time in ways that benefit comprehension. To increase comprehension, use your time effectively by focusing on the main idea, evaluating the message, and providing feedback.

★ Learn while listening by using spare time to review what has been said.

Focus on the Main Idea

Some speakers develop their points in a disorganized manner, mixing the unimportant with the important. Therefore, to be a good listener, you must be willing to wait for the main idea and not be distracted by unimportant details. Separate fact from opinion. When taking notes, record the main ideas and enough supporting information to make the main ideas meaningful. Concentrate on the message, not on the speaker's delivery or appearance.

Evaluate the Message

Compare the speaker's message with the information you already know or believe about the topic. When you have some knowledge of the topic, do not ignore the speaker by assuming you already know what he or she will say. Instead, relate what you already know to what the speaker is saying. Do not judge a speaker until he or she is finished.

Observe the speaker's nonverbal symbols. A natural, relaxed style and good eye contact show that the speaker feels confident about the message. On the other hand, nervous mannerisms may cause you to question the validity of the message.

Provide Feedback

When you understand the message, smile or nod your head to let the speaker know. Feedback tells the speaker that you are listening and that you understand the message. To assure understanding, ask questions for clarification, paraphrase the message, or restate the message as you understand it. Statements such as, "If I

understand you correctly, you mean that . . . ," can provide valuable feedback and aid understanding.

Overcome Poor Listening Habits

Listening is a skill that requires practice. Becoming an effective listener requires changing attitudes toward speakers, attitudes toward topics, and personal habits that result in poor listening. Figure 39–3 presents suggestions for becoming a better listener.

- Find common interests.
- Judge content, not delivery.
- Delay judgment until the speaker is finished.
- Listen for the main idea of the message.
- Take notes on only the important points.
- Concentrate on listening; stay alert.
- Avoid physical and environmental distractions.
- Listen with an open mind; do not let prejudices or assumptions cause you to miss the message.
- Use your spare listening time to analyze and evaluate the message.
- Talk less; listen more.

Figure 39–3 Keys to effective listening

CHECKPOINT 2

Effective Listening

Indicate if each statement is true or false.

1. Listeners have spare time when comprehending a message.
2. Effective listeners ignore a speaker if they already know what the speaker will say.
3. Feedback is important because it tells the speaker that you are listening to his or her message.
4. Effective listeners often must change their attitudes toward speakers.
5. Effective listeners delay judgments until speakers finish.

Check your answers in Appendix F.

Summary

Listening is an extremely important communication skill. You spend more time listening than writing, reading, or speaking. Your listening skills affect the quality of your relationships, the quality of your decisions, and your ability to succeed on the job.

People remember only half of what they hear and they forget much of that information. As a result, people miss appointments, take wrong turns, fail to respond to valuable suggestions, and misinterpret what people say. Factors such as a negative attitude toward the speaker or the topic, environmental distractions, and poor listening habits create barriers to effective listening.

The listening process involves hearing, focusing attention on the speaker and concentrating, understanding the message, and remembering the message. People can improve comprehension by (1) focusing on the main idea, (2) evaluating the message by comparing it with what they already know, and (3) providing feedback. To become an effective listener, share the responsibility for communication and overcome poor listening habits that inhibit good listening.

Discussion Questions

1. Why do people listen and what are the benefits of listening?
2. List five barriers to effective listening.
3. Describe effective listening techniques.

Practical Applications

Part A

Engage a friend or an acquaintance in a social listening experience. Then develop the conversation into a serious discussion. Try to maintain the serious discussion for three minutes. Write a one-page report. In the report, answer the following questions:

1. Were you able to maintain the conversation at the appropriate level? If so, how did you do it? If not, what prevented you from doing it?
2. Of the two types of listening, which was the easier to maintain, casual or active? Why?

Part B

Observe someone's listening skills for about 15 minutes. Indicate if the listener was involved in casual and/or active listening. Rate the listener as good, fair, or poor. Justify your answers by using the keys to effective listening and the characteristics of poor and good listening.

Part C

Ask students to observe the listening habits of others for two days. Then discuss their observations. Use the characteristics of poor listeners—listed in workbook exercise 1—as a basis for the discussion.

Part D

Select a moderately long newspaper article—more than 800 words. Develop a short test with five questions on the content of the article. Be prepared to read your article and administer the test in class. Determine the type of listening required by the situation.

Communication
with Others

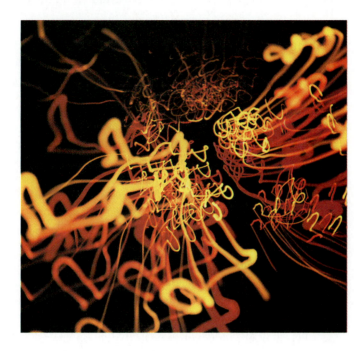

OBJECTIVES

After studying this chapter and completing the chapter exercises, you will be able to do the following:

1. Identify guidelines for one-to-one conversations.
2. List techniques for effective telephone usage.
3. Identify characteristics of an effective group.
4. Identify common group problems.

Chapter 40

ONE-TO-ONE CONVERSATION

Communication is a complex process. People often undergo change during communication. For example, mood, interest, alertness, respect, confidence, needs, concerns, beliefs, or opinions can change during a simple conversation. Consequently, oral communication between people is complex. The three most common business situations that involve oral communication with others are one-to-one conversations, telephone calls, and group discussions.

Some people believe one-to-one oral communication is the most important form of communication in the business world. Many important business decisions are made during conversations between two people. The following guidelines can help you communicate effectively in one-to-one conversations:

1. *Relax.* One-to-one communication is often relaxed and informal. One person shares or discusses information with another person. When you relax, you smile. Smiles during conversations tell others that you like them. A relaxed, friendly atmosphere encourages communication.

2. *Come prepared.* Although the extensive preparation for an informal speech is not necessary, you should have all necessary materials with you—notes, reports, letters, memos, and so forth.

3. *Think before you speak.* Speak clearly and distinctly and structure your words and sentences so that the receiver understands them.

4. *Listen carefully.* When you listen intently, you know if you understand the receiver's message and can ask the appropriate questions. Careful listening also tells the speaker that he or she is important. When you listen, the nonverbal message you send enables speakers to express themselves more effectively. Sometimes people fail to listen carefully or they interrupt speakers. If you do this too often, you will severely damage your relationships with others.

5. *Use names.* People like to hear their names. Call people by name to convey that they are important to you and that you care. Most of the time, the receiver will, in turn, call you by name.

6. *Look at others directly.* Effective eye contact encourages the receiver's close attention. By looking at others, you can receive feedback, which helps you understand how the receiver feels about what you are saying. Shifting eyes or limited eye contact communicates negative feelings—dishonesty, fear, or a lack of confidence (barriers to effective communication). Strong eye contact conveys strength and sincerity. When you maintain strong eye contact with others, you tell them they are important. Research on the North American culture indicates that people should maintain eye contact about 75 percent of the time they communicate with others.

7. *Use a conversational, pleasant tone of voice.* A conversational, sincere tone of voice helps receivers maintain interest in a conversation. In a business setting, you are expected to be calm, polite, and pleasant. Sarcasm and loud laughter are usually inappropriate.

8. *Act open, honest, and sincere.* When you are open, honest, and sincere, your receivers will value you and your ideas. People will know how you feel, and they will feel secure around you. If people view you as objective and competent, they will value your opinion. If your receivers believe you are dishonest or insincere, they will ignore and distrust you.

TELEPHONE CALLS

In the workplace, people communicate daily over the telephone. Here are some pointers for effective telephone communication.

1. *Plan calls.* Before dialing, gather all information available, including documents you need to discuss, names of people, telephone numbers, and possibly even a brief outline of points to discuss.

2. *Identify yourself and your organization.* Do not expect others to guess who you are and the reason for your call.

3. *Use a pleasant, low tone of voice.* You can even smile. Remember, your voice conveys your personality in a telephone conversation. If you have a pleasant attitude, your voice will sound pleasant.

4. *Speak clearly and courteously.* "Please" and "thank you" are not outdated terms. Enunciate words carefully. Hold the receiver one to two inches from your mouth and speak in a normal tone and loudly enough for the caller to hear you.

5. *Take messages accurately.* If necessary, offer to take a message or to locate information or other departments or people for the caller. When taking a message, supply all necessary information, including the name (and organization, if possible) of the caller, the name of person being called, the telephone number and extension, the message, the date and time of the call, and your name or initials as the person taking the message.

6. *Transfer calls.* When transferring a call, tell the caller to whom you are transferring the call, the reason for the transfer, and the telephone number to which you are transferring. Then, if for some reason the transfer does not go through, the caller can place his or her call without interrupting you again.

7. *Close conversations cordially.* Usually, the caller is expected to end the conversation. If a call comes at an inopportune time, politely tell the caller you cannot talk at this time but will call back as soon as possible. Then return the call as quickly as you can.

★ Use sarcasm only when you are with friends and when you are sure your words or tone will not offend anyone present.

One-to-One Conversations and Telephone Calls

Indicate if each statement is true or false.

1. One-to-one conversation in the workplace is usually formal.
2. People like to hear their names; effective one-to-one communicators use people's names.
3. Even telephone calls need planning.
4. Usually, the caller is expected to end a telephone call.
5. Preparation is not necessary for a one-to-one conversation.

Check your answers in Appendix F.

CHARACTERISTICS OF AN EFFECTIVE GROUP

Teamwork is increasing in the workplace because it offers two important advantages: (1) people learn more in groups than individually and (2) group decisions are generally better than individual decisions. Because business leaders are aware of these advantages, they are incorporating group activities into many work situations.

Poor leadership abilities can destroy the effectiveness of a group. Members who fear participating in a group, too, can destroy the effectiveness of a group. Nevertheless, learning to work in a group is important to your success.

In his book *The Human Side of Enterprise*, Douglas McGregor describes characteristics of an effective group. McGregor's characteristics of an effective group are as follows:

1. The atmosphere tends to be informal, comfortable, and relaxed. Tension is absent. Group members are interested and display no signs of boredom. The leader needs to create this atmosphere and make sure that all group members are involved. The leader can help create this atmosphere by being relaxed and involved in what the group is trying to accomplish. If the group becomes too tense, laughter will help relieve this tension.

2. All members of the group participate and focus on the objective. The activities remain pertinent to the task. If discussion strays from the subject, someone steers the discussion back to the subject. The leader is responsible for making assignments that keep group members involved. A group member also may make suggestions about group assignments. Group members should remember, however, that the leader is in charge of the group.

   The leader needs to make sure the group stays focused on its objective. If the group wanders off the topic, ask an appropriate, tactful question to refocus them. Suppose you are in a group that has the objective of exploring ways to improve productivity. Someone has just told a long, funny story that steers the group off from its objective. To get the group back on track, you could say, "What can we learn from that story that will help us to increase productivity?"

3. Group members understand and accept the objective. They discuss and modify the objective until they can commit to it. In the North American business culture, people are results oriented. Consequently, they want to devise quick solutions so that they can move on to other objectives. Effective group members make sure the objective of the group is clearly understood, that members are committed to the objective, and that the objective can be achieved.

4. Members of the group listen to each other. They do not interrupt one another and do not jump from related ideas to unrelated ones. They carefully evaluate all ideas. Being a good listener will help you and others learn. A good listener also enables others to speak clearly and encourages participation. Members generate and share many creative ideas when they do not fear ostracism, teasing, or other negative reactions. Help your group by being a good listener, and encourage others to do the same. Do not interrupt or cut off others when they are speaking.

5. Disagreement occurs often. The group is comfortable with disagreement and does not need to avoid conflict. Effective group members do not suppress or override

★ You may be a little tense at the first meeting of a new group, but that tension should subside quickly.

disagreements by premature group action. Instead, they carefully examine the reasons for disagreements and seek to resolve disagreements rather than to dominate the dissenter.

On the other hand, effective groups do not tolerate an overly outspoken minority. Group members who disagree should not try to dominate the group or to express hostility. Their disagreement should be a genuine difference of opinion that needs feedback from others and a resolution. Seek the solution through listening and through open, honest discussion.

Sometimes, groups cannot resolve basic disagreements. Effective groups can accept disagreements, thereby refusing to allow them to block their efforts. Under some conditions, groups defer actions to permit further study. On other occasions, when the group cannot resolve a disagreement, it takes necessary action and evaluates that action in the near future.

6. Groups reach most decisions by consensus. Make sure that the group knows your position when you oppose an action. By expressing any objections, you can make sure an apparent consensus does not hide real disagreement. An effective group rarely uses formal voting; the group does not accept a simple majority as a basis for action. Those who disagree with a group's decision may also lose their commitment to the group's objective and become uninvolved. Consensus agreements keep everyone committed to the group's objective.

7. Criticism is frequent, frank, comfortable, and impersonal. An effective group member provides both positive and negative criticism. However, criticism can prompt strong reactions. To make criticism effective, use two precautions: (1) make criticism constructive and oriented toward removing an obstacle that prevents the group from getting the job done and (2) make sure criticism is not a personal attack, either open or hidden. People accept criticism about ideas much easier than they accept personal criticisms.

8. Communications are open and honest. Group members should express their feelings openly about any problems and about the group's operation. If members have hidden agendas, they can lose the trust of group members. Make sure that group members share how they feel about all matters discussed.

9. Assignments are clear and accepted. Ask relevant questions to make sure that you understand your assignments. Once you feel you understand your assignment, paraphrase it back to the person who gave you the assignment. When you give an assignment to someone, ask that person to paraphrase the assignment back to you. These actions will ensure that group members understand their assignments and also provide an opportunity for them to express hesitation about accepting the assignment.

10. The leader does not dominate the group nor does the group defer unduly to the leader. If you are the leader, shift leadership responsibilities from person to per-

son. In fact, different members, because of their expertise or knowledge, should act as group resources. No struggle for power should exist. Your main concern is not who controls the group but instead how the group can achieve its objective.

Characteristics of an Effective Group

Indicate if each statement is true or false.

1. One person usually makes better decisions than a group.
2. In an effective group, every member understands and accepts its objective.
3. Effective groups vote a lot.
4. Effective groups do not disagree.
5. In an effective group, most decisions are reached by consensus.

Check your answers in Appendix F.

COMMON GROUP PROBLEMS

Sometimes groups are not as effective as they should or could be. Group members unknowingly do things that are counterproductive to the effectiveness of their group. The following paragraphs discuss six problems groups commonly encounter. By avoiding these problems, the group's productivity will increase.

Unclear Objective

When people form a group, they frequently assume the group's objective is clear to everyone. They try to determine what the group should do and quickly move on to other important responsibilities. Thus, the group's objective is never identified and members cannot commit to it. When groups do not clarify their objectives, they are usually less effective than they should or could be.

Groupthink

Groupthink occurs when group members have a tendency to take positions they think leaders want to hear, even when these positions are flawed or poorly con-

Groups can work productively or waste time. Two keys to productivity are leadership and participation.

ceived. Groupthink often results in poor decisions. However, leaders can prevent groupthink by taking the following measures:

1. Surround yourself with people who are not afraid to disagree with you. As a group member, define your role in terms of meeting group objectives, not just pleasing the leader.
2. Act impartial. Leaders who refuse to advocate a position are less likely to encourage groupthink than those who state strong opinions.
3. Encourage participants to evaluate their thinking critically and to air objections and doubts.
4. Assign one or more members the role of devil's advocate to challenge group thinking.
5. Hold a "second chance" meeting after a decision has been made to give everyone the opportunity to air any remaining doubts.

Conflicting Personal and Group Objectives

Personal objectives of group members must agree with the objectives of the group. Many businesspeople have high personal goals and may perceive their group's success as a stepping stone to their own success. Thus, some businesspeople believe that they can use a group to illustrate strong leadership skills and business competence. This mistake is based on the belief that they must dominate and control the group and its decisions. When people come into your group with this attitude, your group will have difficulty progressing towards its objective until it deals with the conflicting personal goal.

The solution to this problem is to select group members carefully and to measure the group's progress regularly. When a dominating person blocks the group's progress, the group may need to replace that person with someone else. If the person cannot be removed from the group, the group may need to dissolve.

Ineffective or No Leader

Groups need leaders to administer group procedures and to help guide the group towards its objective. However, the leader should not dominate the group's decision making. **Effective leaders control the group's operations but do not dominate decision making.** The person who appoints the group or the group itself should select the group's leader.

Time Constraints

As indicated previously, a consensus decision is the best kind of decision for a group. However, a consensus decision often takes considerable time to develop. Thus, group members must be aware of schedules and time constraints. If time allows, work toward a consensus decision; but if time is short, the group will have to vote.

Destructive Criticism

Although constructive criticism is a characteristic of an effective group, members must use it cautiously. If the receiver perceives criticism as personal, he or she will become defensive, which will hamper the objectivity of group members. As a result, the group probably will not reach the best decision. Disregard for the characteristics of effective groups and their members can cause communication within groups to break down and become ineffective.

The solution to this problem is to criticize carefully. Make criticism impersonal and inoffensive. To soften criticism of someone's ideas, ask thoughtful, relevant questions rather than making direct statements that question the quality of a person's thoughts.

CHECKPOINT 3

Common Group Problems

Indicate if each statement is true or false.

1. In the North American business culture, people want immediate results.
2. For the sake of speed, an effective group will sacrifice its objective so that it can solve a problem more quickly.
3. In an effective group, leaders only are needed sometimes.
4. Constructive criticism is part of an effective group.
5. Personal and group objectives that conflict have no affect on the effectiveness of a group.

Check your answers in Appendix F.

Summary

In the workplace, you will engage in one-to-one conversation, place and answer telephone calls, and work in groups. When engaging in one-to-one conversation, relax; come prepared; think before you speak; listen carefully; use the speaker's name; establish good eye contact; use a conversational, pleasant tone of voice; and be open, honest, and sincere. Using these suggestions will help you to become an effective conversationalist.

Effective telephone techniques are also important to the effective communicator. To make calls effective, identify yourself, your organization, and the reason for your call. Plan important telephone calls before you place them. When receiving telephone calls, take accurate messages and transfer calls if necessary; use a low, pleasant voice; be helpful and courteous; speak clearly; and end calls cordially.

Because groups generally make better decisions than individuals, sometime in your business career you probably will become part of a group. Helping your group use the characteristics of an effective group and helping them avoid the common problems of groups will aid your group's productivity.

Discussion Questions

1. List the guidelines for one-to-one conversations.
2. List the techniques for effective telephone usage.
3. What are the characteristics of an effective group?
4. Identify common group problems.

Practical Applications

Part A

Choose a member of your class as a partner. Attend a student government, city council, or civic organization meeting. **Do not use another student or school organization other than student government. Other student organizations are being used for a computer assignment.** Write a letter report to present your overall rating of the effectiveness of the meeting. Justify your rating using the characteristics of an effective group. Be prepared to present your report to the class.

Part B

Write a letter report on what the group members you observed in Practical Application Part A could have done to improve their group and its performance.

Part C

Pretend you are a member of a student organization in which the members seem to be afflicted with groupthink. Write a memo to the president of this organization expressing your opinion about what is happening. Suggest ways to overcome groupthink in this group.

Part D

Place a telephone call to the main telephone number of a retail store and ask to be transferred to a specific department. Observe the procedure followed by the person answering the telephone. List the errors this person makes when answering and transferring your call. List the effective techniques this person uses as well.

Editing and Proofreading Application

Proofread, edit, and revise the following message.

> On our vacation this passed year, we went to Florida. There, we went to Orlando and Lakefront. While their, I bought my friend, Cheryl, some stationary. Next year, we hope to go further; we want to go to southern Chile. I wonder what I can by Cheryl their and what the whether is like.

Effective Meetings

OBJECTIVES

After studying this chapter and completing the chapter activities, you will be able to do the following:

1. Identify guidelines for effective participation in meetings.
2. Organize a productive meeting.
3. Discuss guidelines for leading a meeting effectively.

Chapter 41

GUIDELINES FOR EFFECTIVE PARTICIPATION IN MEETINGS

When you attend a meeting, you send a message about who you are, your abilities, and your competence level. Meetings are a type of theater where managers observe and evaluate the performance and progress of subordinates. Even in the most ordinary meeting (a weekly staff meeting, for example), what you say and how you say it demonstrate your readiness for more responsibility—or less.

This chapter provides insights into the art of effective communication during meetings. Whether you are a leader or a participant, a meeting is expensive for a company but an opportunity for you. Effective meetings need competent participants, organization, and effective leadership.

Because managers constantly evaluate meeting participants, you need to be a productive participant. To be productive, follow these guidelines:

Arrive on Time

If you will arrive late for a meeting, notify the leader. When you enter the meeting, take your seat without interrupting. Timeliness sends a nonverbal message that you are dependable and that you believe the content of the meeting is important. Tardiness sends the opposite nonverbal message.

Participate Actively

Active participation means that you take the responsibility of partial ownership of the meeting. This type of participation requires involvement—a process that begins before you enter the room. For example, when you receive the agenda, prepare a list of questions to ask. If a meeting has been called to make a decision, prepare to support your point of view. Disagreement is okay. Few managers want "yes" people; instead, they want participants who have carefully formed opinions relevant to the topic. Come to a meeting prepared and remain focused on the objective of the meeting.

Improve Decision Making

When participants are reluctant to make a decision, an effective participant acts as an informal leader and tries to move them forward. Start by asking a probing question such as, "Does anyone need more information about the software?"

ACROSS CULTURES

- The importance of timeliness is based largely on culture. In some cultures, timeliness is important. In others, it is not. However, in the North American business culture, arriving on time for a meeting is extremely important.

Sometimes, people who make requests also prevent decisions. When the information is available, a participant should say something like, "Now that we have all the information we need about the software, we can proceed to costs."

The opposite problem occurs when the group makes a decision before you feel it is ready. In this case, use delaying tactics to postpone action. You could say, "I've listened carefully to all the information, but I still have some questions. Evelyn, tell me again why you think the software will help us maintain inventory." Even if the group does not agree with you, your hesitation probably will create more discussion.

Make a Positive Impact

Meeting participants have a responsibility for making a positive, helpful influence on the meeting. The following suggestions will help you improve your value as a group participant:

1. *Take a position but be willing to change it.* Groups work best when participants are open to new information and points of view.
2. *Speak briefly and directly.* Speak in a clear, organized manner so others will want to listen.
3. *Discuss ideas.* To discuss is to exchange ideas; to argue is to become emotional and leave reason behind. Arguments often start when participants put their ideas ahead of group objectives and refuse to listen to differing points of view. The moment you engage in an argument is also the moment the group stops functioning. When you argue, you lose credibility.
4. *Avoid personal attacks.* Mutual respect is a key to group functioning. A group cannot move toward its goal if members verbally attack each other.
5. *Engage in fair play.* Give everyone the opportunity to speak; not dominate the discussion.
6. *Use body language to your advantage.* Make eye contact when you begin speaking, speak slowly and calmly even when you are excited, and make sure your posture communicates authority and confidence.

Figure 41–1 summarizes the responsibilities of group members at meetings.

ORGANIZE PRODUCTIVE MEETINGS

If you are responsible for holding a meeting, ask yourself if the meeting is really necessary. Before scheduling a meeting, determine if the work can be accomplished without a meeting—if an information memo could suffice, or if the same

RESPONSIBILITIES	FAILURES
Arrive on time.	Arrive late continually.
Focus on the topic.	Engage in personal attacks.
Participate actively.	Fail to make the goals of the meeting personal goals.
Lead the group to competent conclusions.	Fail to help the group reach adequate conclusions.
State positions clearly.	Chooses not to share views with the group and remains uninvolved.
Follow an organized agenda.	Ramble from topic to topic. Speaks for too long.
Discuss ideas willingly.	Argue with people who disagree.
Engage in fair play.	Dominate the discussion and acts unfairly.

Figure 41–1 Responsibilities and failures of meeting participants

result can be achieved by calling a few people on the telephone. If you can accomplish a task without a meeting, do not call one. If a meeting is needed, define its tasks, determine the type of meeting to hold, choose participants carefully, and use the mechanics of an effective meeting.

Define the Tasks

Assuming that meetings require little or no planning is your first *and biggest* mistake. You must define the task or tasks of each meeting.

An effective leader recognizes what the group can and cannot do. For example, entry-level managers do not develop company policy. Corporate directors develop company policy but do not gather information; this job usually is done at a lower organizational level.

Trying to do too much ensures failure. Restrict the content of a meeting to its designated purpose. Although under certain conditions, a meeting can have two or more purposes, call separate meetings when goals become too broad. The general rule is "one objective—one meeting."

Determine the Type of Meeting

With the task of the meeting identified, you can easily determine the type of meeting you need to hold. Meetings can be held (1) to inform, (2) to develop

EXTRA, EXTRA!

★ As a new supervisor, should you cancel the weekly department meeting if it is not unnecessary?

EXTRA, EXTRA!

★ Entry-level employees who try to form company policy send the same offensive nonverbal message as new employees who try to change existing policies and procedures.

new ideas, (3) to make decisions, (4) to delegate work, (5) to collaborate, and (6) to persuade. Determining the type of meeting you need makes organizing it much easier.

To Inform

At meetings to inform, participants present oral reports that contain needed information. Use a meeting to inform for clarification of written information participants have received previously. This type of meeting also can be used to present new information. Figure 41–2 shows important aspects of a meeting to inform.

To Develop New Ideas

Brainstorming meetings are sessions in which participants suggest new ideas in an open, non-authoritarian atmosphere. Use brainstorming meetings to develop new procedures, programs, and so forth.

To Make Decisions

Decision-making meetings bring people and companies together to debate an issue, reconcile conflicting views, and make a decision. Hold a decision-making meeting before developing a new system. Collect information in advance to prepare for the decision-making stage. Critical features of decision-making meetings are listed in Figure 41–3.

To Delegate Work

Meetings to delegate are held to assign tasks to people or groups who are then responsible for completing those tasks. Although you can assign responsibilities

I. Agenda
  A. List speakers, subjects, and the length of time to speak
  B. Distribute the agenda to scheduled participants before the meeting

II. Meeting Procedure
  A. Indicate assent through silence
  B. Ensure everyone is present
  C. Discuss the information; stick to the topic
  D. Summarize new information, accomplishments, and
     follow-up actions

Figure 41–2 Important aspects of a meeting to inform

I. Agenda
   A. List problems
   B. Receive input and summarize it in a written document
   C. Distribute the written document before the meeting

II. Meeting Procedure
   A. Discuss each problem
   B. Allow junior members to vote first
   C. Summarize the decision

III. Action Minutes
   A. Summarize accomplishments and follow-up actions
   B. Set a follow-up date
   C. Include a preliminary agenda for the next meeting

Figure 41–3 Important aspects of decision-making meetings

over the telephone or by memo, you may need to hold a delegating meeting to clarify specific details. Meetings to delegate often are followed by informational and decision-making meetings.

To Collaborate

Collaborative meetings are sessions in which participants work together to organize complex memos, letters, or reports. Collaborative efforts succeed only if people work together as a team. These efforts waste time if members of a group are not open to improvement.

To Persuade Others

Persuasive meetings involve oral presentations to achieve a group consensus and support for a course of action. For example, a persuasive meeting may present the merits of specific computer hardware or build enthusiasm for purchasing the hardware.

Choose Participants Carefully

Group communication in a meeting works best when everyone has a reason for attending and can contribute to the discussion. When more than one person has the same expertise or point of view, choose only one to join the group to simplify communication. For best results, limit a group to seven people. A larger group often complicates communication.

Corporate culture may affect who can and who cannot be invited to a meeting. In formal, highly structured companies, meetings usually are attended by people on the same organizational level. In less structured companies, participants are more likely to span the entire organization, with less emphasis on seniority and position.

Use the Mechanics of an Effective Meeting

The mechanics of a meeting set the tone for the meeting and involve scheduling the meeting, selecting an appropriate site, and arranging the furniture.

Schedule Meetings Carefully

Although meetings can be scheduled at any time during the day, some times are preferable. Early in the morning and right after lunch are popular meeting times. Many businesspeople hold working breakfasts, lunches, and dinners to accomplish two things at once. Meals often are served or brought into the workplace for meetings.

LEGAL/Ethical

- When a scheduling conflict exists, leaders must make a choice by determining if personal preference or the preference of meeting participants is more important.

When scheduling a meeting, consider the travel needs of the participants. An 8:00 a.m. meeting that forces people to get up at 5:30 a.m. may be counterproductive. Even if participants arrive on time, they may be too tired to accomplish anything else during the day. Nevertheless, early morning scheduling is not unusual.

In a meeting that involves various presentations, talk with each presenter in advance to find out how much time he or she will need. The final agenda should reflect input from everyone participating in the meeting.

If you need to hold a series of meetings, schedule a time for the next meeting at the end of the current one. To schedule an initial meeting, write a memo or send an e-mail message instead of using the telephone. Scheduling by telephone may take two or three days as you call and recall participants with conflicting schedules.

Select an Appropriate Meeting Site

The decision to meet in your office, in a conference room, in someone else's office, or at an outside location depends on the amount of space needed and the environment that is best for the group. You many need a table to hold papers or an overhead projector available only in a conference room.

Political considerations also have an impact on meetings with clients. Holding a meeting at a client's office delivers the implicit message that you are committed to that client's needs. Think about the image you want to create and then choose the location for the meeting.

Arrange Furniture Appropriately

Furniture arrangement can enhance a meeting and help you avoid communication barriers. Here are some considerations:

1. The natural place to sit during a meeting in your office is behind your desk. However, the desk communicates that you are in charge of the discussion. To remove the message of power, move to a separate seating area or to a conference room where people can sit across from one another as peers.
2. Even when seating is informal, certain people have traditional places at the table. The leader, for example, usually sits at the head of the table; a key ally or the department manager may sit directly across. To avoid a mistake, wait for the key players to sit before choosing your place.
3. Choose your seat with your purpose in mind. Choose a controlling position if you want to influence the meeting. If you have little to say, choose a spot that allows you to remain relatively unnoticed.
4. Consider also where troublemakers will sit. When you expect dissention, orchestrate a seating arrangement that separates troublemakers from one another.

★ Seats in the front, in the center of a room, or at the head of a table imply power. Seats that allow participants to remain unnoticed are in the middle of a group or in the middle of a side of a table.

Effective Participants and Organization

Indicate if each statement is true or false.

1. Because meetings are inexpensive, they often are used by organizations to make decisions.
2. Active participants accept part ownership of a meeting.
3. Effective leaders know productive meetings must be long.
4. Effective meetings generally have two or three objectives.
5. When making seating arrangements for a meeting, separate potential troublemakers.

Check your answers in Appendix F.

LEAD MEETINGS EFFECTIVELY

Communication that takes place within meetings is defined by your role as leader. Enhance communication within a meeting by following these guidelines:

Begin Effectively

Convening the meeting is your first act of control in front of a group; do it with direction and purpose. Open the meeting by restating the specific tasks you want to accomplish. Although this information is part of the agenda, repetition will focus the group's attention. Make your statement positive and forward looking even if you anticipate problems. Never start by apologizing for previous mistakes or blaming others for problems. Convene the meeting on time to show your determination to get the job done.

ON THE JOB

An agenda can be used to direct participants back to the objective of a meeting if they stray.

Use an Agenda

Use an agenda to determine and control the direction of the meeting. Problems arise when meeting participants stray from the topic—when attention drifts to peripheral issues or personal stories. Remain polite and friendly, but keep the group on track. When participants ramble, summarize what you think they have said and ask a question to point them in a specific direction. An effective group leader looks for signs of confusion—puzzled looks, questions that ask for clarification, and drifting attention spans. When members are confused, summarize what the group has accomplished, what is now being discussed, and/or where the discussion is heading.

Stay Focused on the Task or Objective

Members of management are stunned by the number of people who do not know what type of meeting they are attending. For example, when a supervisor convenes a meeting to convey a decision, a staff member may persist in debating the decision. The time for discussion is past! Situations like this occur because the staff member does not realize the type of meeting he or she is attending. The purpose of this meeting is to inform and delegate—not to make a decision.

An agenda tells participants to prepare in advance for a specific type of discussion and to focus on that discussion during the meeting. The agenda is a promise you, as a leader, make to the participants that the meeting will deal with specific issues.

Balance the Discussion

Handling difficult people is the greatest challenge any meeting leader faces. Because you generally cannot handpick meeting participants, sooner or later you will encounter people whose personalities or hidden agendas make group success questionable.

Some people want to dominate conversations while others rarely say a word. An effective group leader tries to balance these contributions—to encourage extroverts to say less and introverts to say more. Without intervention, a meeting can become a platform for one person's point of view, thereby a true consensus difficult to achieve. Encourage people who say little to participate with direct, specific questions such as, "Gary, you are our computer expert. Will adding this program overload the existing computer system? Will we have to upgrade?"

When people talk about an area they know well, their shyness often disappears. Although you cannot force people to participate, you can ensure a positive climate and abundant opportunities.

Handling an overzealous contributor is more difficult. You could say something like, "Chris, as you can see by the agenda, we have a lot to cover. I can give you only five more minutes." If Chris continues to talk, redirect the discussion to another person. Interrupt Chris and say, "Your survey points to the need to communicate with consumers. Kelli, can you fill us in on the advertising plan?"

MAKE MEETINGS SUCCESSFUL

The leader sets the tone for the meeting through fairness, work ethic, and control. The following factors are critical to the success of your meetings.

Recognize Contributions

Recognize everyone's contributions. Participants who feel their discussion is valued will continue to contribute. Even if a proposal has problems, focus on the positive aspects and lead the group forward.

Maintain High Standards.

Do not accept slipshod work or opinions that masquerade as facts. When participants do not have information the group needs, postpone the meeting if possible.

Maintain Order

Follow the agenda as the discussion moves through the various meeting stages. At the conclusion of each item, summarize points of agreement and disagreement and include any actions that will be taken. These internal summaries improve communication. Allow only one person to speak at a time and discourage private conversations.

End Effectively

At the end of a meeting, summarize what happened and move the group ahead to future action. Your summary should review the discussion so that everyone understands how the group progressed from thought to action. Summarize items that need further consideration, review assignments and deadlines for future work, and set the time and place for the next meeting.

Lead Meetings Effectively

Indicate if each statement is true or false.

1. When opening a meeting, state its purpose.
2. The greatest challenge a leader faces is handling difficult people.
3. Effective leaders let participants ramble when they have creative ideas to share.
4. When participants are unprepared, effective leaders will postpone the meeting.
5. Summaries are effective tools when closing a meeting.

Check your answers in Appendix F.

Summary

Meetings provide opportunities for participants to show their abilities and strengths. Effective meeting participants arrive on time, focus on the task or objective, participate actively, and help the group make effective decisions. To organize a meeting, define the task or tasks; determine the type of meeting (to inform, to develop new ideas, to make decisions, to delegate work, to collaborate, or to persuade others); choose participants; and use the mechanics of an effective meeting. When leading a meeting, begin effectively, use an agenda, stay focused on the task or objective, balance the discussion, recognize contributions, maintain high standards, maintain control, and end effectively.

Discussion Questions

1. Identify the guidelines you should follow to be an effective meeting participant.
2. What are the steps to organizing a productive meeting?
3. Discuss three guidelines for leading an effective meeting.

Practical Applications

Part A

Write a memo announcing a meeting. Determine the objective and prepare an agenda for the meeting. Be ready to discuss your memo and agenda with the class.

Part B

Attend a meeting. Observe three or four participants at the meeting. Write a memo evaluating each person's level of participation.

Part C

Write a short report describing how you would organize the meeting you planned in Practical Application Part A.

Part D

Pretend you are the new president of the Business Club of your college. Write a memo describing what you will do to make the meetings of this club effective.

Part E

Prepare an agenda for the first Business Club meeting at which you will preside as president. Supply all necessary information.

Part F

Divide into teams of three or four students. Each group will prepare an agenda to discuss their assigned topic in a decision-making meeting to be held during the next class meeting. Assign each group one of the following topics: (1) What do you recommend for possible revision of affirmative action admission policies at your school? (2) What recycling programs do you recommend at your school? (3) What can be done on your campus to promote alcohol awareness and prevention programs? (4) Choose a current controversial topic local to your school. (5) Choose a current controversial topic specific to your state or across the country.

Part G

Prepare a memo to inform the appropriate people of the decision your team reached in Practical Application Part F.

Editing and Proofreading Application

Proofread, edit, and revise the following message.

Did you see the brochure and pamplet on the south Seas. They were extraordinary. There were pictures of waterfalls, beaches, and hotels that were uneque. Sarah is planing to go their on her vacation. I wish I was going with her.

Oral Presentations

OBJECTIVES

After studying this chapter and completing the chapter activities, you will be able to do the following:

1. Describe two types of short oral presentations.
2. Discuss planning, organizing, and outlining a formal presentation.
3. Describe three important factors in delivering speeches.

Chapter 42

SHORT ORAL PRESENTATIONS

Oral communication is a common business activity. The types of oral presentations you give will depend on your career path. If you supervise others, you may conduct training programs. If you work in a human resources department, you may conduct new employee orientation programs. If you become a high-level executive, you may make presentations to the board of directors, stockholders, media, and civic and professional organizations.

Most oral presentations are simple, straightforward, and short—15 minutes or less. Typical short speeches are introductions and briefings. Begin with an opening that creates interest and prepares the audience for what will follow. Then provide details in the body and summarize the main points in the closing.

★ When speakers stay focused, presentations often stay short.

Introductions

When planning an introduction of a speaker, determine if you should follow a specific format. Many organizations provide guidelines for introductions to keep them short and uniform. If no formal guidelines exist, consider adapting these suggestions to the situation:

Obtain Information About the Speaker

You will be given a resume or biographical sketch. If possible, find out what the speaker would like you to mention. Your purpose is to prepare the audience to accept the speaker and the speech. Too much information causes restlessness in the audience.

Introduce the Speaker and the Presentation

Mention information about the speaker, state the title of the presentation, and give an overview of the speech. Provide information that the audience can relate to and that will create interest in the presentation.

Briefings

A **briefing** is a short presentation usually given at a meeting or a conference to bring people up to date on business activities, projects, programs, or procedures. Because briefings are short, highlight key points and provide a few details to support each point.

FORMAL ORAL PRESENTATIONS

Preparing formal oral presentations is challenging. A long speech may last from 20 minutes to over an hour. As part of your preparation, determine the objective of your speech, analyze the audience, determine the time available for the speech, gather information, and determine the appropriate mode of delivery.

Planning the Presentation

Planning an oral presentation is like planning a written report. Oral presentations have an introduction, a body, and a closing. You may also use visual aids such as tables, charts, graphs, and photos.

Determine the Objective

What do you want to communicate to an audience? Answering this question will help you determine the objective of your presentation. Write the objective in sentence form. For example:

Marketing managers should learn about new products and sales goals.

A customer should place an order with us because we have a quality product and fast delivery.

Analyze the Audience

Analyze the expected audience in terms of size, knowledge level, and demographics. How do you want your audience to react to your presentation? How much does your audience already know about the topic?

The size of the audience determines the approach you take for delivery. If the audience is small (20 or fewer people), you may be able to have more audience interaction. If the audience is large (several hundred), you need a good sound system and some way to make visual aids visible to the entire audience.

If the audience has little or no knowledge of the subject, you need to provide background information. If the audience is familiar with the topic, you begin talking about the subject directly with little introduction.

Knowing the demographics of your audience can help when preparing your speech. What are the age ranges? How many are men and how many are women? What is their educational level? What are their occupations? Where do these people live or work? What socioeconomic and ethnic groups are represented?

Determine Time Available

Speakers often are allotted a specific amount of time to speak. If you have a few main points and 30 minutes in which to make a presentation, spend three to five minutes on opening remarks and the introduction. Take 15 to 20 minutes to develop the main points. Use 5 to 10 minutes for conclusions, summary, and questions.

Gather Information

Information for an oral presentation is gathered in much the same way as data for a formal written report. Refer to Chapter 34 for information on gathering data for reports.

Determine Mode of Delivery

Several modes of delivery are available to speakers—impromptu (also known as *extemporaneous*), textual (reading or speaking from notes), and memorization.

ON THE JOB

The more you focus on the objective, the more likely the success of the presentation.

ON THE JOB

To make sure you stay within the appropriate time frame, practice your presentation several times, noting its length.

When you speak without any advance notice, you make an **impromptu** speech. Take a few moments to gather your thoughts before speaking and avoid rambling by including an introduction, a body, and a closing.

When making a **textual presentation**, you read from a written copy of your speech, from an outline, or from note cards. Reading a speech is not recommended unless the material is highly technical. Even then, maintaining eye contact is essential. Speaking from an outline or notes is effective because you can maintain eye contact while referring to notes to make sure you cover major points.

Memorizing an entire speech is not recommended because of your chances of forgetting lines and becoming flustered. Also, a memorized speech often sounds stilted and formal. Memorizing a quotation or opening or closing remarks, however, can be effective.

★ The more you say, the less people remember. Plan carefully to make your presentations as concise as possible.

Organizing the Presentation

All presentations, formal and informal, should have three main parts: introduction, body, and closing.

Introduction

Open your speech by telling the audience the topic, the purpose, and the points that you will cover. You may want to use some proven attention-getters. Then, tell the audience your objective and give a preview of what you will cover in the presentation.

Attention-getters hold the audience's attention during a long presentation. Use reliable attention-getters in the opening and throughout your speech. Common attention-getting techniques include the following:

1. *Quotations.* Use a quotation to illustrate a point. If possible, memorize the quotation and cite the source.
2. *Anecdotes.* Tell a story related to the audience or the topic. People enjoy hearing stories and often understand a point better when they hear a related anecdote.
3. *Humor.* A little humor can relax a serious business atmosphere and make an audience more receptive. Many speakers warm up an audience with jokes and then proceed to a serious topic.
4. *Statistics.* Cite an interesting or unusual statistic when appropriate. People like details, but not too many!

Body

The middle part, or body, of a presentation should present the main points. Use the same organizational plans as those used in writing letters and memos—direct or indirect. Limit the main points to three or less, and arrange them in logical sequence. As you progress in the speech, summarize previous points and preview information to come. When you shift topics, provide a transition from one idea to the next.

Add variety to presentations to hold the audience's attention. You can vary the pace of a presentation by using visual aids, asking questions, and using examples to illustrate key points.

Closing

Close a presentation by reviewing or summarizing the main points. Your objective is to make sure the audience understands the topic and possibly takes some action as a result of your presentation.

Outlining the Presentation

An outline can be a very valuable tool when planning a speech. If you use the outline as notes for the presentation, you may find that complete sentences rather than one- or two-word topic headings are more helpful.

Develop the outline according to the organizational plan used for the speech—direct or indirect. Use direct order (main idea first) when you expect the audience to be receptive. Use the indirect order (main idea later) when you expect the audience to be skeptical or nonreceptive.

Suppose that you are the campaign manager for a political candidate and must make a speech on your candidate's chances of winning the election. If the polls indicate that your candidate probably will win, you would develop an outline using the direct order. Figure 42–1 shows a presentation outline using the direct order.

Suppose, however, that the election is too close to predict. You would use the indirect order, placing the main idea later in the speech. Figure 42–2 shows a presentation outline using the indirect order.

LEGAL/Ethical

- Speakers can use long, poorly organized speeches to confuse or cloud positions on issues or policies. Such actions may be self-serving, but are they ethical?

★ The more complex or long the presentation, the more important an outline becomes.

ACROSS **CULTURES**

- Remember, the use of the direct and indirect order varies according to culture.

I. Introduction
  A. Attention-getter—my candidate will win!
  B. Objective—to explain why you are going to win
  C. Preview—order the presentation by districts: District 1 and District 2
II. Body
  A. District 1
    1. Neutral district
    2. About 15,000 voters
    3. Opponent will receive 53 percent—8,000 votes
    4. My candidate will receive 47 percent—7,000 votes
    5. Opponent will carry District 1
  B. District 2
    1. Your home district
    2. About 15,000 voters
    3. Opponent will receive 27 percent—4,000 votes
    4. My candidate will receive 73 percent—11,000 votes
    5. My candidate will carry District 2 by a wide margin
III. Closing (Summary)
  A. Main idea—My candidate will win!
  B. Objective—to predict the outcome of the election
  C. Preview—paraphrased preview of the election
  D. Summary of data and conclusions

Figure 42–1 Presentation outline using direct order

I. Introduction
  A. Attention-getter
  B. Objective—to explain the anticipated results of tomorrow's election
  C. Preview—order the presentation by districts: District 1 and District 2
II. Body
  A. District 1
    1. Neutral district
    2. About 15,000 voters
    3. Opponent will receive 53 percent—8,000 votes
    4. My candidate will receive 47 percent—7,000 votes
    5. Opponent will carry District 1
  B. District 2
    1. Your home district
    2. About 15,000 voters
    3. Opponent claims 40 percent—6,000 votes
    4. My candidate's remaining share is 60 percent—9,000 votes
III. Closing (Summary)
  A. Objective—paraphrase objective
  B. Preview—paraphrase preview of the election
  C. Summary—summarize data and conclusions
  D. Main idea—election is too close to call. Let's really push to get voters out in District 2.

Figure 42–2 Presentation outline using indirect order

Short and Foraml Oral Presentations

Indicate if each statement is true or false.

1. In short presentations, the subject matter is generally simple and straightforward.
2. When planning a formal presentation, audience demographics are not important.
3. An attention-getter should be used only in the opening of a long, formal presentation.
4. A word outline is better for a formal presentation than a sentence outline.
5. The closing of a long, formal presentation should include a summary of the main points of the speech.

Check your answers in Appendix F.

DELIVERY

Delivery of a presentation is as important as content. Voice qualities, nonverbal symbols, and visual aids can enhance or inhibit delivery. Feedback can let you know if your audience understands and accepts your message. Figure 42–3 provides suggestions for delivering effective speeches.

Voice Qualities

Speak loudly enough for everyone to hear while still sounding natural. To achieve appropriate volume, look at the person farthest away and project your voice as though you were speaking to that person.

Speak at a moderate pace. If you talk too rapidly, the audience may not have time to consider all your points and may become confused.

Nonverbal Symbols

Nonverbal symbols add to or detract from an oral presentation. They indicate how the speaker feels about the situation—relaxed, nervous, or confident. Important nonverbal symbols during oral presentations include eye contact, facial expression, gestures, and posture.

ON THE JOB

Your delivery is critical to the success of your presentation.

EXTRA!

★ Speakers who speak softly give a nonverbal message that they are insecure or shy—neither message benefits a professional career.

- Know your subject regardless of the delivery mode you use (impromptu, textual presentation, or memorization).

- Practice your speech until you can present it comfortably. Consider audiotaping or videotaping your speech to provide feedback for improving your delivery.

- Dress appropriately and use good grooming techniques.

- Maintain your enthusiasm. Keep your energy level high.

- Start and finish your speech on time.

- Use your voice effectively. Speak clearly, project your voice, vary your tone, and use correct grammar.

- Use nonverbal gestures effectively.

- Maintain eye contact with the audience.

- Speak with enthusiasm and conviction. If you are excited about your topic and convey belief in it, you will be better able to convince skeptical audiences.

Figure 42–3 Tips for delivering effective oral presentations

Eye Contact

Maintaining eye contact with members of the audience keeps them involved in your speech. Focus on members of the audience to let them know you want to communicate with them and to read the feedback they give you.

Facial Expression

Use appropriate facial expressions to communicate with your audience. A smile, a frown, a look of concern, or a look of surprise can convey a message.

Gestures

Use gestures to emphasize important points in your speech. Gestures also indicate if you are nervous or calm. Actions such as playing with a visual aid pointer, repeatedly saying *ah* or *um*, tapping fingers, looking at visual aids instead of the audience, clutching the sides of a lectern, putting your hands in your pockets, and folding your arms indicate nervousness.

Presenters who appear very nervous send a nonverbal message that their fear of the situation exceeds the importance of their message.

You may be nervous about giving a speech because of your fear of public speaking. You can overcome this fear by doing what you are afraid of—speaking in public.

Posture

Good posture indicates self-confidence, an interest in your topic, and respect for the audience. Poor posture indicates poor self-esteem, a lack of interest in the topic, or a lack of respect for the audience.

Visual Aids

Visual aids should be used to emphasize, explain, or illustrate points of your presentation. Transparencies, flip charts, chalkboards or whiteboards, slides, and computer presentations are examples of visual aids.

Transparencies

Transparencies are projected onto a screen by an overhead projector. Normal lighting can be used, which allows continued eye contact with the audience.

Flip Charts

Flip charts are large sheets of paper bound at the top. Write on the sheets with felt-tip markers during a presentation or use previously prepared sheets and simply flip the pages during your speech.

Chalkboards or Whiteboards

Chalkboards or whiteboards can be used with small audiences to list major points of a speech or ideas from the audience. Colored pens are used to write on whiteboards.

Slides

Slides of photographs or drawings enhance a speech when they are coordinated with the speech. Showing slides requires a darkened room however, which prevents eye contact with the audience.

Computer Presentations

Computer graphics software can generate visuals for computer presentation. Other graphics software can generate printed handouts, slides, or transparencies.

Develop visual aids during the planning stage of the oral presentation; then use them when practicing the speech. When preparing visual aids, keep these points in mind:

★ Failing to practice your presentation with your visual aids becomes practice to fail.

1. Make sure all writing is large enough for everyone to read.
2. Keep visual aids simple and easy to understand by emphasizing a small number of points on each one.
3. Use color for emphasis and contrast.
4. Make sure visual aids look professional.
5. Check equipment before the speech to make sure it works.

★ Only feedback will tell you if your presentation really was effective.

Feedback

Oral presentations allow immediate feedback to the speaker in the form of questions from the audience. When planning a speech, allow time at the end for questions and answers. If the group is very small, you might encourage comments or questions during the presentation.

2 CHECKPOINT *Delivery*

Indicate if each statement is true or false.

1. Content of a speech is important, but delivery is more important.
2. Visual aids enhance a presentation.
3. Nonverbal symbols reveal how the speaker feels about the speaking situation.
4. Good posture during a presentation implies self-confidence.
5. When speaking to a large group, try to allow questions during rather than at the end of the presentation.

Check your answers in Appendix F.

Giving oral presentations is a common on-the-job activity. You may give short presentations such as introductions and briefings or give formal speeches. When preparing for a formal oral presentation, determine the objective of your speech, analyze the audience, determine the amount of time for the speech, and gather information as you would in preparing a formal written report.

Organize a formal speech into three parts—introduction, body, and closing. Develop an outline that you can use in the delivery of your speech. When delivering your presentation, make sure your vocal qualities, nonverbal communication, and visual aids enhance the delivery. Allow time for audience feedback through a question-and-answer period.

Discussion Questions

1. Describe two types of short oral presentations.
2. Discuss planning, organizing, and outlining a formal oral presentation.
3. Describe three important factors in speech delivery.

Practical Applications

Part A

Based on a report you have written for this or another class, prepare two outlines of an oral presentation you would give on this report. Prepare one outline in the direct order. Prepare the other in the indirect order. Which outline is better for this report? Justify your answer.

Part B

Select the better outline in Practical Application Part A. Prepare and deliver the oral presentation in class.

Part C

Listen to a speech and prepare a written evaluation of the speaker's effectiveness in delivering the speech. To help you, use the evaluation sheet provided in Chapter 42 of the workbook.

Part D

Assume that you work for the recruitment office of your school or college. Outline a presentation for student recruitment. Visit the appropriate office to obtain pamphlets, brochures, and so forth, to locate information for the presentation. Develop an outline and visual aids for the presentation.

Part E

Plan, develop, and deliver the oral presentation described in Practical Application Part D.

Part F

Divide the class into groups and give each group a resume for a fictitious person who will speak to the class. Students are to develop an introduction for the speaker. Groups should be prepared to present their introductions orally.

Part G

Bring a product to class. Divide the class into groups that will develop an introduction to a speech designed to persuade people to buy the product. The introduction should contain an attention-getter, an objective, and a preview.

Editing and Proofreading Application

Proofread, edit, and revise the following message.

Yesterday, I choose to enroll in the employers health insurance program. The affect of this decision is that teh cost of this insurance is consistant with what I can afford. Also, coverage of this policy will fullfill my family's needs.

Career Communication

Career communications such as resumes, letters of application, application forms, job interviews, and follow-up messages are useful tools for most workers throughout their working lives. As individuals progress in their careers, other job opportunities become available. Changes in industries and the economy often make it necessary for individuals to embark on new job searches, and for this they must update their resumes, send letters of application, complete application forms, and interview.

Part 9 discusses in detail the process of collecting personal information and analyzing personal and professional goals before preparing a resume. Special attention is given to formatting application letters and completing application forms.

Part 9 also presents tips on preparing for and interviewing successfully for job openings and stresses the importance of sending follow-up messages after job interviews.

Part 9

Chapter 43

Your Place in the Job Market

OBJECTIVES

After studying this chapter and completing the chapter exercises, you will be able to do the following:

1. Analyze your personal and career goals.
2. Identify your qualifications.
3. Analyze the job market.

ANALYZE YOUR GOALS

One of the most exciting and important challenges in your life will be the job search. Whether you are just starting your career or are reentering the job market, finding a job requires preparation and planning. Begin your job search at least three months before you want to start working.

This chapter explains how to start your job search. You will use the information you collect as you determine your place in the job market to prepare a resume, write an application letter, complete an application form, and prepare for a job interview. These steps will be examined in the chapters that follow.

The first step in any job search is to analyze your goals. Once you have established your goals, you are better equipped to target the jobs that make sense for you. As you start this self-analysis, you will consider both personal and career goals.

Personal Goals

Thinking about your personal goals will clarify what is important to you. Start by asking questions about your wants and needs. Answer these questions by writing personal goal statements. Sample questions and sample goal statements can include the following:

What do I most enjoy doing? (Sample goal statement: I like cars, and I want to continue learning more about them.)

Am I interested in government? (Sample goal statement: I want to serve my city.)

Am I interested in business or financial affairs? (Sample goal statement: I want to be involved in a business.)

Do I want to make humanitarian efforts an important part of my life? (Sample goal statement: I want to help other people.)

How important is material success and fame? (Sample goal statement: I want to become famous.)

Where do I want to live? In this country or in another country? (Sample goal statement: I want to live in Toronto.)

Do I want to travel? Do I want to travel domestically, internationally, or both? (Sample goal statement: I want to see all the major U.S. cities.)

★ Setting goals is not a one-time activity. You should review your goals from time to time, look at the progress you have made toward those goals, think about whether the goals are still important to you, and make any needed changes.

Do I want to work mainly with people? With machines? With ideas? (Sample goal statement: I want to work with people.)

Do I like frequent change or do I prefer consistency? (Sample goal statement: I want consistency, not frequent change.)

Add any questions that will help you identify your personal goals. Rank your goal statements so you have a sense of which goals are most important to you and which are less important. Now you can examine your career goals.

Career Goals

Just as you did with your personal goals, you should take time to think through what you want out of your chosen career. Write goal statements to answer the following questions:

What kind of work do I enjoy? What do I want to be doing five years from now? (Sample goal statement: I enjoy fixing cars, and I want to manage a car repair shop five years from now.)

Do I want to work for a business, a government agency, or a charity? (Sample goal statement: I want to work for a charity.)

Where do I want to work? (Sample goal statement: I want to work in a suburban community near a U.S. city.)

How much do I want to earn next year? Five years from now? (Sample goal statement: I want to earn $20,000 next year and earn $40,000 five years from now.)

How far do I want to advance? (Sample goal statement: I want to head an accounting department within ten years.)

What position would I like to hold in five years? (Sample goal statement: I want to be a store manager in five years.)

What is my ideal balance between personal and work obligations? (Sample goal statement: I want a career that allows a lot of free time for family and friends.)

Do I prefer steady, predictable work hours or a varied, flexible work schedule? (Sample goal statement: I want a work schedule that changes from week to week.)

Add any questions that help you clarify what you want from a career. Now put these career goals in order; list the most important goals before the less important goals. Compare this list to your list of personal goals to better understand what you want from life and work.

★ As you put your personal goals in order, think about which you would be willing to postpone or eliminate, if necessary. Be honest about what is important and what is not; only you know what you *really* want out of life.

ANALYZE YOUR QUALIFICATIONS

All of us have unique **qualifications**, skills, abilities, and accomplishments that make us fit for certain jobs. Many people, however, are not aware of all their qualifications. Analyzing your qualifications gives you the information you need to prepare a resume and to sell yourself during a job interview.

Begin by creating a file to hold information about your skills, abilities, and accomplishments. This file becomes the basis of your **portfolio**, a folder, notebook, or small briefcase containing samples of your work, transcripts, letters of recommendation, and other related items. Here are some items to include in your file:

Academic transcripts

Letters of recommendation and commendation (school, work, or organizations)

Previous resumes

Copies of job application forms

Awards

Test scores

Certificates or diplomas of coursework completed

Next, list at least ten skills, abilities, and accomplishments that have given you satisfaction and that make you marketable. Include accomplishments that reflect your creativity, initiative, and ability to work well with others. You might list a scholarship you have received, athletic activities you enjoy or excel in, your grade point average, and other information.

Take a close look at the items on your list. You may find that you most enjoy creative activities, such as art or writing, or that you have good communication skills. Consider how your skills, abilities, and accomplishments can be used on the job. Also think about how to represent these qualifications honestly, fairly, and positively when you write your resume or meet with a prospective employer.

Organizing information about yourself in one place will help you remember important facts as you write your resume. This information also will yield clues about the right career field for you. Your file should include details about qualifications such as education, work experience, achievements and activities, special skills, and personal traits.

LEGAL/Ethical

- As you analyze your qualifications, remember that few people are top performers in everything they do. Tell the truth about what you can and cannot do so that you and your potential employers can agree on a proper job match.

Education

Prospective employers are very interested in your educational preparation. Because many companies require technical school or college preparation for employment, show your educational background on all resumes or job applications you submit.

List the names of schools you attended (after high school), the city and state, certificates and degrees earned, and the dates attended (or expected graduation date). You also may include specific courses or skills that relate to your intended career and any special courses or programs you have completed. Include high school information if you have no post-secondary educational preparation; otherwise, you can omit information on your school education.

Work Experience

When identifying your qualifications, list all your work experience, including temporary or part-time jobs. Include the name, address, and telephone number of each employer; the full name of your supervisors; salaries earned; dates of employment; and, most important, the major tasks and responsibilities you had on each job.

If you have had little work experience, your first resume may list many jobs unrelated to your career goals. For example, you might list a job as a cashier even though you are applying to be a receptionist. As you gain more work experience, your resume will show only those jobs that relate to your intended career. Military experience may be included in this section.

If you have had no previous work experience, consider including unpaid volunteer activities such as teaching Bible school or raising funds for charity. Your experience as a volunteer shows prospective employers that you can complete work tasks. It also shows that you are committed, ambitious, and responsible.

For each job or volunteer activity, list any work-related skills you learned or applied. For example, if you learned or became more skilled in accounting while working at a paid or unpaid job, list this information. These skills are transferable and can be used in other work-related situations.

Achievements and Activities

In addition to your work and educational qualifications, list your other achievements and activities. For example, you may have been treasurer of your local Phi Beta Lambda student business organization. Perhaps your artwork won a local contest and was featured on a poster. List achievements and activities of this sort if they relate to your career goals.

Special Skills

Do not overlook other marketable skills you may have. You may be an experienced photographer, fluent in another language, or familiar with computer spreadsheet software programs. Other special skills include the ability to operate special machinery or vehicles, experience with woodworking, and certification to teach CPR. Employers often value such special skills.

Personal Traits

Before you complete your inventory of qualifications, think about your personal traits. Answer the following questions:

Do I have leadership ability?

Am I a perfectionist?

Can I meet deadlines?

No matter what types of jobs you may have held in the past, you are certain to have gained skills that other employers value. Similarly, as you search for a summer or part-time job, look carefully at jobs that will offer the opportunity to learn or to perfect skills you can use in your chosen career.

Do I work well under pressure?

Do I enjoy learning new skills? Do I enjoy teaching others?

What are my personal strengths and weaknesses?

These questions—and others that you come up with on your own—are designed to give you insight into who you are. With a thorough understanding of your own traits, you can make a better match with a suitable career field.

Many school placement offices and career counselors can help you with any part of this self-analysis by arranging for you to take aptitude and personality tests. Self-analysis can help you determine what you want, what you have to offer, and what career is right for you.

★ Once you match your goals and qualifications with a particular career field, you may find that you need additional education or work experience to get the job you really want. Consider working at a lower-level position or a part-time job in your field to obtain the experience you need.

CHECKPOINT 1

Analyzing Your Goals and Qualifications

Indicate if each statement is true or false.

1. The first step in any job search is to determine personal and career goals.
2. When analyzing your qualifications, include only those special skills and abilities that relate to your educational background.
3. An understanding of personal traits is one part of a self-analysis that can help you select a suitable career field.
4. Volunteer activities show prospective employers that you are not willing to assume responsibility.
5. Employers are not interested in your educational courses.

Check your answers in Appendix F.

ANALYZE THE JOB MARKET

Before you send your resume to prospective employers or schedule any interviews, you need to analyze the job market. Analyzing the job market involves determining actual job openings and gathering information about organizations for which you want to work.

Both types of research are important to your success in getting the job best suited for you. Interviewers are more likely to hire someone who knows something about their company than someone who has not taken time to do basic research. Research can also help you decide if a company is right for you.

Locate Employment Opportunities

During this phase of the job search, locate as much information about job openings in your chosen field as you can. Before you apply, compare job openings to the qualifications and goals you identified during your self-analysis; eliminate any that are unsuitable. The following sources should help.

School Placement Offices

Many schools provide job placement services. Placement offices assist both employers and student applicants by providing opportunities for both to meet. Employers frequently inform placement offices about job openings. They also may recruit applicants by visiting campuses and conducting interviews or by participating in job fairs on campus.

One advantage to a school placement office is that employers and applicants can be screened by knowledgeable personnel, providing a better opportunity for a good match between employer and employee. School placement offices also may have access to computerized job banks that allow students to search for openings or send resumes to many employers at one time.

★ Job fairs are a good opportunity to meet with several employers in your chosen field in one day. As you talk with company representatives, you can find out about these employers and, at the same time, learn how your qualifications match their needs.

Personal Contacts

An informal but often effective way to locate employment opportunities is to talk with people you know. Some of the best jobs are never advertised but instead are filled through personal referrals. Mention your job search to the many contacts you have, such as students and alumni of your school, former employers, business colleagues, relatives, instructors, and other people you know. When someone you have contacted learns of an appropriate opening, he or she will think of you.

Newspapers and Professional Publications

Check the job advertisements in your local newspaper as well as in any local, regional, or national business newspapers on the newsstand or at the library. Similarly, look through the advertisements in any professional or industry publications that serve your career field. Respond to these advertisements as quickly as possible and be sure to follow the instructions in each advertisement.

Employment Agencies

Both public and private employment agencies are available to match job seekers with job opportunities. Employment counselors at the agencies interview and sometimes test job applicants in order to match them with jobs listed with them by employers. You may find openings with specialized agencies that serve specific

fields such as accounting, computer programming, or word processing, as well as with agencies that work with companies in a variety of fields.

State employment agencies frequently have listings of jobs. To contact employment agencies, refer to the government section of your telephone directory under your state's name.

Private employment agencies charge a fee either to the employer or to the applicant. Before signing an agreement, find out who pays the fee and how the fee is calculated. If you are considering working with a particular agency, research its reputation, its success rate in placing job-seekers, the qualifications of its job counselors, and the services you will receive. Do not sign an agreement you may not wish to keep, such as an agreement to work for an employer for a certain length of time.

Libraries

Visit school and local public libraries to scan the many publications available to job seekers. For example, you can research individual organizations in *The 100 Best Companies to Work for in America* by Robert Levering, Milton Moskowitz, and Michael Katz, Doubleday, 1993. Check *Jobs '93: By Career, By Industry, By Region* by Kathryn and Ross Petras, Prentice Hall, 1993, for information about thousands of careers and organizations. If you want to work for an association, a charity, or another nonbusiness organization, you can look through the *Encyclopedia of Associations* published by Gale Research, 1993.

For information about requirements for more than 200 jobs, refer to the *Occupational Outlook Handbook* published by the U.S. Department of Labor. School libraries and placement offices also may have computer programs about building career.

Research Specific Organizations

Once you learn about a specific job opening in your career field, you need to prepare to submit a resume or arrange an interview by finding out more about that company. Visit a local or school library to check the publications mentioned previously, as well as company annual reports and *The Wall Street Journal* (locate articles through *The Wall Street Journal Index*). You also can find articles on individual companies on CD-ROM indexes such as *Business Periodicals on Disc* and *Business Newsbank* and on computer databases available in larger libraries.

In addition to conducting secondary research, try to talk with people who are familiar with the company, such as employees, suppliers, and customers. Figure 43–1 lists data that every job hunter should know about a prospective employer.

If you think you will work for a particular company for some time, you may want to investigate it in more detail. Find out about its financial situation (profit or loss), goals for the future, expansion plans, history, and philosophy. Also find out who owns and runs the company (parent organization, board of directors, top officers, and others). This information will help you decide if the company is right for you.

Organize Your Research

The research you conduct while exploring the job market will provide a valuable background to help you when applying for a job. Over time, you will have many notes, advertisements, articles, letters, and other items to which you can refer during the job search. Carefully organize your research so that the information is available when you need it.

Company Identification
- Name, city, and state of the home office.
- Local address and telephone number.
- Name of person (if possible) responsible for the department with which you will interview.
- Name and title of the person with whom you will interview.

Company Classification
- Business, government, or charitable organization?

Company Activities
- Production, sales, service-oriented, or a combination?
- Any brand names associated with the company?

Company Size
- Number of employees, which indicates the size of the organization.
- Annual sales or production output.

Location of Facilities
- Location of the company's branch or regional offices, plants, or outlets?

Figure 43–1 Company information

One way to organize your research is to use a separate file for each company. Each file should contain notes and any research materials about that company. As your job search progresses, you can add copies of job advertisements placed by the company, company letters, and other documents.

If you prefer, you can use a binder to organize your research. Use a separate divider for each company. File notes, letters, and other documents in each company's section. Allow space for additional entries such as telephone numbers, dates, and other information relating to your contacts with each company.

CHECKPOINT 2

Analyzing the Job Market

Indicate if each statement is true or false.

1. You should research the company identification, company activities, and company size before applying for a job.
2. Keep all company research together in the file you use to store information on your goals and qualifications.
3. The best jobs are advertised only in local newspapers.
4. Specialized agencies list jobs in various career fields.
5. Before you apply for a job, you should talk with employees, suppliers, and customers who are familiar with that company.

Check your answers in Appendix F.

Summary

The first step in any job search is to set personal and career goals. Next, you should analyze your qualifications. Create a special file and include in it a list of your employment qualifications and supporting documents, such as transcripts, letters of recommendation, awards, and copies of resumes and job applications. In addition, you should analyze your employment qualifications, such as education, work experience, achievements and activities, special skills, and personal traits. The final step is to analyze the job market. Gather information about industries, job openings, and requirements, as well as details about organizations to which you want to apply.

Discussion Questions

1. What items should you include in your qualifications file?
2. What five sources are useful when searching for employment opportunities?

Practical Applications

Part A

Write goal statements to answer the questions in the subsection titled "Personal Goals" (see pages 573 and 574). List two additional questions that pertain to your personal goals. Then write goal statements that answer both of your questions.

Part B

Write goal statements to answer the questions in the subsection titled "Career Goals" (see page 574). List two additional questions that pertain to your career goals. Then write goal statements that answer both of your questions.

Part C

Gather as many of the documents described in this chapter as you can. Look for school transcripts, letters of recommendation and commendation, previous resumes, copies of job application forms, awards, test scores, and certificates or diplomas. Next, list ten skills, abilities, and accomplishments that have given you satisfaction and that make you marketable. Set up a qualifications file for this information.

Part D

Select two companies or organizations you are interested in working for and list the following information: (1) name, city, and state of the home office, (2) local address and telephone number, if any, (3) classification, (4) activities, (5) size, and (6) city, state, and country location of facilities. Conduct your research using directories, annual reports, and other sources.

Part E

Select one of the two organizations you studied in Practical Application Part D. Using newspapers, business magazines, and other sources, research and list the following information: (1) current financial situation, (2) goals and philosophy, (3) company history, (3) person who owns and runs the company, and (4) recent acquisitions or expansion plans.

Editing and Proofreading Application

Using the guidelines in Chapter 34, edit the following information from a bibliography that was prepared for a report about job hunting. Provide a corrected copy.

Brockman, Terra; *The Job Hunter's Guide to Japan.* (New York, Kodansha): 1990.

U.S. News & World Report, December 23, 1991, "Selling Toys to Tokyo's Tots," by Jim Impoco on page 5.

"Fast-food's Blockbuster Chain." 13 June 1994, page 12, *Advertising Age*. Article written by Jeanne Whalen.

The Resume

OBJECTIVES

After studying this chapter and completing the chapter exercises, you will be able to do the following:

1. Describe how to organize information in a resume.
2. List the seven sections most resumes contain.

ORGANIZING YOUR RESUME

In the last chapter, you learned how to analyze your goals and qualifications and how to examine the job market in your chosen career field. Now that you know your personal and career goals, you are ready to apply for employment. This chapter focuses on how to organize, format, and write an effective resume.

A **resume** is a summary of an applicant's qualifications for employment. Think of a resume as a tool you can use to sell yourself to employers. A resume sometimes is called a *data sheet* or a *vita.*

A resume cannot guarantee that you will win an interview, or even a job, but it can highlight skills and abilities that you want employers to notice. An attractive, well-written resume may lead to an invitation for an interview. A poorly written or messy resume, however, could hurt your chances for getting an interview. Without an interview, you will not get the job.

Employers receive many resumes and must scan each of them quickly. Based on the resume's appearance, the reader forms a first impression. For that reason, a resume should be easy to read, attractive, crisp, and clean. Use the following guidelines when formatting your resume:

1. Use at least one-inch margins on all sides.
2. Print on high-quality, 20-lb. bond paper. Use colors that are appropriate to business, such as white, off-white, and gray. Use matching envelopes.
3. Use headings, boldface print, underscoring, listings, or capitalization to emphasize your qualifications.
4. Allow extra white space around headings.
5. Use bullets or asterisks for listings.
6. Use parallel structure for headings and listings.
7. Use sentence fragments rather than complete sentences. For example, say "Filed correspondence" rather than "I filed all correspondence."
8. Correct all spelling, grammar, and punctuation errors; make sure that errors are not visible behind your corrections.
9. Limit your resume to one page (unless you have extensive job-related experience).
10. Use a typewriter, personal computer, or word processor to prepare your resume. Make copies at a commercial printer, which also may prepare your resume for you.

Resume content may be either general or specific. Use a general resume if you are applying for a variety of jobs; use a specific resume if you have one particular job or type of job in mind. Later in the chapter you will learn how to tailor your resume for a specific job.

★ Many word-processing programs offer a variety of typefaces that can give your resume a professional look. Use a letter-quality or laser printer to make your resume readable. Remember to use the spell-checker to catch spelling errors before you print your resume.

Many resumes contain the following sections, which are discussed in more detail later in the chapter:

1. Heading
2. Job objective
3. Special qualifications
4. Education
5. Work experience
6. Activities, interests, and achievements
7. Personal information
8. References

When you organize your resume, think about its role as a selling tool. Choose an organization plan that highlights information that will impress employers. Your resume can be organized in one of two ways: in reverse chronological order or in functional order. The difference is the order in which you present information about your work experience.

Reverse Chronological Order

A resume organized in **reverse chronological order** presents the most recent work experience first and works backwards toward earlier jobs. Most resumes are organized this way. If much of your work experience is relevant to the job for which you are applying, use a resume organized in reverse chronlogical order to show an employer that your employment background fits the position. A resume in reverse chronological order is shown in Figure 44–1.

Functional Order

In a resume organized in **functional order**, you present your accomplishments or skills in order of their importance, showing the most important or impressive first. For example, if a job requires strong communication skills, you might organize your accomplishments under headings such as "Writing Experience" and "Public Speaking Experience." Your educational background and job history would appear in later sections of the resume. A resume in functional order is shown in Figure 44–2.

Many people, especially those who are just entering the job market or looking for work after a long period out of the job market, organize their resumes in functional order. The functional order is a good way to emphasize skills and capabilities rather than the order of jobs held.

ELENA DIAZ

145 Crabapple Road   (Day) 317/555-0148
Richmond, IN 47374-2187   (Night) 317/555-0182

Career Goal: To become a legal secretary at a large law firm
                       with opportunity for advancement.

Qualifications: Operate microcomputer. Key 70 wpm
                       Take shorthand at 100 wpm. Operate transcriber

Experience: <u>Legal Secretary.</u> Charles S. Ballard, Attorney-at-
                       Law, Richmond, Indiana, August 1994 to present.

                       Format and edit legal documents using computer
                       and word-processing software, file documents
                       with the courts, post to client accounts, make
                       bank deposits, answer telephone, greet clients,
                       make appointments, transcribe from machine
                       dictation, distribute incoming mail, and file
                       correspondence.

                       <u>Salesperson.</u> Carson's Department Store,
                       Richmond, Indiana, May 1990 to August 1994.

                       Operated computer terminal, handled transactions
                       with customers, set up displays, and stocked
                       merchandise.

Education: Waynesboro Junior College, Waynesboro, Indiana.
                       A.A.S. degree with major in Office Technology.
                       Will graduate June 1996. Worked full time while
                       attending college. Received Rotary scholarship.

                       Took elective courses in business law, business
                       application software, and business management.

Activities: Special Olympics volunteer, 1994. Responsible
                       for scheduling practice meets and coaching
                       sessions.

Figure 44–1 Sample resume in reverse chronological order

SAM S. GARVIN

3948 Sparrow Lane   (216) 555-0142 (home)
Cleveland Heights, OH 44121   (216) 555-0100 (work)

CAREER GOAL   To become a staff writer for a business
                           publication with opportunity for
                           advancement to the top editorial position.

SPECIAL   Experienced in using all major desktop
QUALIFICATIONS   publishing and word-processing programs.
EXPERIENCE

INTERVIEWING AND   As a reporter covering the small-business beat
REPORTING SKILLS   for the daily Cleveland Business Press (1995 to
                           present), interview local business owners, and
                           write three feature articles weekly. Cover
                           Chamber of Commerce meetings and
                           governmental activities. On the staff of the
                           Clermont Weekly, the student newspaper of
                           Clermont College, interview students
                           and faculty for a column titled "New on Campus"
                           (1993–1995). Write 25 columns.

RESEARCH SKILLS   On the staff of Cleveland Business Press,
                           research articles using computerized databases
                           such as Nexis, Lexis, and others.

EDUCATION   Clermont College of University of Cincinnati, Ohio
                           (1993–1995). Associate degree in English,
                           May 1995, 3.19 GPA. Coursework included
                           Journalism, Business Writing, and Technical
                           Writing.

ACTIVITIES AND   • Clermont College Award for Writing Excellence,
ACHIEVEMENTS   1995
                           • Member, Cleveland Business Journalism Society

REFERENCES   References are available upon request.

Figure 44–2 Sample resume in functional order

If you do not have much relevant work experience but have attended college or taken courses beyond the high school level, education is your most important qualification. In this case, you should present your educational qualifications before your work experience. In all sections of the resume, you may want to list items in descending order of importance to emphasize your strengths and deemphasize less important aspects of your background.

CHECKPOINT 1

Organizing Your Resume

Indicate if each statement is true or false.

1. A resume is a summary of a student's academic qualifications for employment.
2. An attractive, well-written resume can lead to an invitation for a job interview.
3. Leave at least a one-inch margin on all sides of a resume.
4. A resume in functional order lists the least important jobs or achievements first and progresses to the most important.
5. If much of your work experience relates to the job you want, you should organize your resume in reverse chronological order.

Check your answers in Appendix F.

PREPARING YOUR RESUME

Although the exact content of each resume may vary, employers are interested in all of the elements that present your background and experience in concise form. The subsections below discuss information you should include in each of the sections of your resume.

★ If you send out resumes while you are away at school, you may want to show both your school and home addresses (and the corresponding telephone numbers).

Heading

The heading or beginning section should include your name, address, and a telephone number where you may be reached during the day, in the evening, or both. The following example shows a heading appropriate for a general resume:

53 Country Way   501/555-0129 (Home)
Blytheville, AR 72315-0105   501/555-0111 (Work)

As an option, you also can change the first line as shown in the following two examples:

QUALIFICATIONS OF JONATHAN D. LASSER

RESUME OF JONATHAN D. LASSER

If you are applying for a specific position, your heading might look like this (followed by an address and telephone numbers):

ELAINE WILSON'S PREPARATION
for the Position of Account Executive
with Webster and Sorrell, Inc.

Job Objective

The **job objective** (or career goal) is a brief statement that describes the type of position for which you are applying. This section of the resume is optional. The job objective lets employers know immediately if your interests match their needs. On the other hand, employers also can use this section to screen you out if your objective does not fit their openings. When you are unsure of exactly what the employer is seeking, you may want to omit the job objective.

If you are interested in and qualified for different career fields, you can modify this section of the resume as needed. (Modifying your resume is easier if you use a computer or a word processor.) List only positions that you know are available within the organization to which you are applying. For example, do not identify your job objective as "legal secretary" if a target company does not have such a position. Make your job objective brief, as shown in the following example:

Career Goal   To secure a position as a word-processing specialist with opportunity for advancement into a supervisory position.

Special Qualifications

A condensed statement of your main qualifications may be placed at the beginning of your resume so that a prospective employer will not overlook them. This statement should cite your strengths and achievements. The following two examples show how to list your special qualifications:

Special Qualifications   Skilled at writing computer programs using object-oriented programming language. Extensive experience developing computer programs to analyze business expenses.

Special Qualifications   Three years' experience as a legal secretary. Promoted to administrative assistant. Have excellent word-processing skills, key 80 words a minute, have strong organizational skills, transcribe from machine dictation, and take shorthand at 120 words a minute.

Education

If you are still in school, your education may be your strongest qualification. Beginning with the most recent post-secondary school you have attended, list each school, the degree or certificate earned, the major area of study, and completion dates (month and year). Include credit and noncredit workshops, seminars, and classes if they relate to the job objective.

If you have excelled academically, include any scholarships, educational awards, and academic honors. If your grade point average is good (at least 3.0 on a 4.0 scale), include it on the resume. If your grade point average is under 3.0, do not show it on the resume. Include information on military service if pertinent and if space permits. An example of a good education section follows:

Education   Associate degree in Business Administration, May, 1994, Polk Community College, Winter Haven, Florida. Additional courses in management information systems and business communication. Worked full time while attending college.

Work Experience

The section on work experience should describe, in the order that makes you look best, all work experience you have had that relates to your job objective. For each job, list the name of the company or organization you worked for; the city and state; dates of employment (often shown but are not mandatory); the job title; and a description of your duties, responsibilities, and accomplishments. Show increased responsibilities or increased pay if possible.

In this section, you have the opportunity to describe your qualifications fully through a detailed listing of job duties. Emphasize your achievements, responsibilities, and initiative. Use action verbs such as the following:

★ You can group work experiences that are unrelated to your job objective (such as part-time or summer jobs) under a heading such as "Other Experience." Place this section after the section in which you described your work experience.

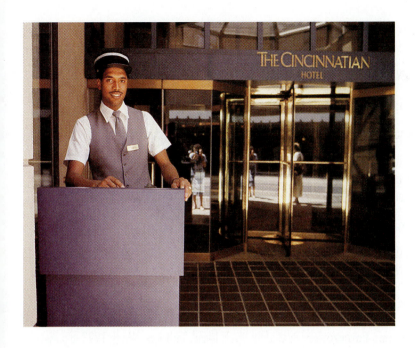

Action Verbs

administer	design	operate	revised
advance	develop	order	set up
analyze	direct	organize	supervise
calculate	increase	produce	supplied
complete	initiate	provide	train
create	key	recommend	verify

In addition to functional order, work experience may be presented by date, by job title, or by employer. The following examples show how you can list the jobs you have held by date:

September 1993
to Present

<u>Assistant to purchasing agent.</u> Agricultural Systems, Inc., Atlanta, Georgia. Assist in purchasing tools and materials, calculating payment terms, and scheduling deliveries. Developed a new inventory tracking system that reduced the time needed to account for items in stock.

June 1991 to	<u>Inventory Control Specialist.</u> Burns GMC Dealership, Morrow, Georgia.
August 1993	Ordered truck parts, maintained parts inventory, and checked supplier
	invoices. Designed several forms to simplify inventory procedures.

The following examples show how to list work experience by job title.

Assistant Manager, McDonald's restaurant, Raytown, Missouri, January 1994 to present.

Responsible for hiring, training, and scheduling a staff of 45 employees. Supervise food preparation, customer-service activities, and restaurant maintenance. Prepare franchise reports, cash accounting records, and payroll accounts.

Cashier, Wheeler's Variety Store, Independence, Missouri, October 1992 to January 1994.

Assisted customers in making purchases and returns, operated electronic cash register, and handled cash, check, and credit card transactions.

The examples below show how to list your work experience by employer:

TeleSystems Corporation, Pawtucket, Rhode Island, Technician, March 1993 to present.

Prepare repair estimates, repair cellular phones, and answer customer inquiries. Operate testing equipment, analyze repair records, schedule customer repairs, and order parts.

Radio Shack, Warwick, Rhode Island, Sales Representative, October 1991 to February 1993.

Sold telecommunications equipment, home electronics, and electronic components. Created instruction sheets showing customers how to set up stereo systems at home. Received sales awards in December 1991 and May 1992.

Including extensive detail about all your work experience on your resume is not necessary. You will provide a complete work history when you fill out the employer's application form. However, briefly mentioning summer and part-time jobs that are unrelated to your job objective is one way to show prospective employers that you are hard working.

Employers may ask about gaps in your employment history. If you are returning to work after a period of time, you should be able to account for the years you did not work. For example, you can explain that you left a particular job to attend school or that you returned to work after raising a family.

In general, emphasize all relevant full-time or part-time work experience. Also list military experience if it relates to the job you are seeking. You do not need to explain why you left a job; you will include this information on your application form. You will learn how to discuss negative work experiences in Chapter 46.

Activities, Interests, and Achievements

Employers are searching for applicants who are willing to work hard, who have creativity and initiative, who work well with others, and who have leadership qualities. If the information you have presented in the work experience and education sections does not demonstrate any of these qualities, you may have had other experiences that do.

For example, you may have been president of a school or civic organization, coach of a soccer team, or a reporter or photographer for a school newspaper or yearbook. These activities could reflect skills and qualities such as leadership, public speaking or organizational ability, and a positive attitude.

Refer to your self-analysis (see Chapter 43) for relevant information to include in this section. The following are possible headings for this section, according to the particular information you are including:

Achievements, Awards, and Honors

Interests

Activities and Achievements

Additional Interests and Qualifications

Personal Information

Personal information that has no bearing on your professional performance on the job should not be included on your resume. Personal information includes age, gender, national origin, religion, race, disability, marital status, and number of children. According to Title VII of the Civil Rights Act of 1965, the Age Discrimination in Employment Act of 1967, the Americans with Disabilities Act, and other federal legislation, employers cannot legally ask much of this information of job applicants. Handling personal questions during a job interview is discussed in Chapter 46.

In general, include personal information *only* if it is relevant and will help you get the job. Present any personal information just before the references heading on your resume. Do not include a picture of yourself unless physical appearance is a listed job qualification (for example, for a model).

References

Place your references on a separate page. Include a notation such as "References are available upon request" at the end of your resume (if you so desire; however, the notation is optional.) This notation alerts employers that you can provide the names, addresses, and telephone numbers of people who can discuss your qualifications.

Some employers are interested only in work-related references; others are interested in both employment and academic references. The following example shows an acceptable format for listing references on a separate sheet:

REFERENCES FOR YING NIU

Mr. Donald Rowe	Ms. Cindy Logan	Dr. Amelia Torres
Hatfield Corporation	Brady Enterprises	Chemistry Department
33 Mitchell Street	65 Palm Boulevard	Butte College
Chico, CA 95926-6432	Willows, CA 95988-4167	Oroville, CA 95965-1815
916/555-4523	916/555-3259	916/555-3578
(Employer)	(Former employer)	(College instructor)

Before you include people as references, ask their permission. Let them know what kind of job you are applying for so that they can describe their experiences with you appropriately. Employers *do* check references, so make sure your references are willing to talk about you—and that they have something good to say.

★ Make sure you are ready with the appropriate references when an employer asks by preparing two reference sheets. Show job references on one and both job and academic references on the other.

Summary

A resume is a summary of your qualifications for employment. An attractive, well-written resume can lead to an invitation for a job interview. Include the following sections: heading; job objective (optional); special qualifications; education; work experience; activities, interests, and achievements; and references. A resume organized in reverse chronological order presents the most recent work experience first and works backwards toward earlier jobs. A resume organized in functional order presents accomplishments or skills in order of their importance, showing the most important or impressive first.

Discussion Questions

1. When would you organize a resume in reverse chronological order? When would you use functional order?
2. What eight sections do many resumes contain?

Practical Applications

Part A

Select a help-wanted advertisement that interests you. Write a job objective for a resume tailored to that position.

Part B

Draft a summary of your work experience using the information in your qualifications file (see Chapter 43). List your work experience in reverse chronological order by date.

Part C

List your work experience in functional order according to achievements or skill using the information from Practical Application Part B.

Part D

Prepare your resume and format it according to the guidelines in this chapter. Tailor the contents to the job opening identified in Practical Application Part A.

Editing and Proofreading Application

Proofread the following work experience section of a resume and edit it to correct any errors. Provide a revised copy.

November 92 to today	<u>Assisstant to buyer of computers</u>, Business Systems, Inc. in downtown Atlanta, GA. Assist in in purchasing for 7 computer stores, negotiated with venders; compute price changes. Organise classes for computer training. Arrange for auto rentals, flite schedules, and hotel reservations.

Application Letters and Application Forms

OBJECTIVES

After studying this chapter and completing the chapter exercises, you will be able to do the following:

1. Describe two types of application letters.
2. Fill out an application form correctly.

APPLICATION LETTER

During your job search, you will need to write letters of application, sometimes called cover letters. When you answer a help-wanted advertisement, for example, you usually should send a letter of application as well as a resume. In addition, you may send letters to prospective employers who have *not* advertised positions. If you are invited to an interview as a result of your letter and resume, you probably will be asked to complete an application form. Learning to write a letter of application and to fill out an application form are essential to a successful job search.

Like resumes, application letters are sales tools that sell *you*. Application letters may be either solicited or unsolicited. A **solicited letter of application** is written to apply for a specific job opening which has been announced or advertised. For example, you may be applying for a job advertised in the newspaper or for a job you learned about from a current employee. An **unsolicited letter of application** is written to apply for a position that has not been advertised or announced and may or may not be open.

Every letter of application has three basic parts: an opening, a body, and a closing. The opening paragraph states that you are applying for a position and captures the reader's attention, the paragraphs of the body summarize your qualifications, and the closing paragraph asks for an interview.

★ When you write an unsolicited letter to an employer, remember that the job you are seeking may or may not be open.

Opening Paragraph

The openings of a solicited and unsolicited letter of application vary a little. However, in the opening paragraphs of either type, you must capture the reader's attention so that your letter will be read. Include the following information in your opening paragraph:

1. Indicate that you are applying for a position.
2. Name the position for which you are applying.
3. Tell how you learned of the opening (solicited letter).
4. Identify your abilities (unsolicited letter).

In the opening paragraph, indicate how your background and experience can benefit the employer, as in the following example:

> Kevin Miranda, a job placement counselor at Newark College, told me about an opening for a sales associate with your company. In June, I will graduate from a certificate program in marketing. My education and my three years of experience in sales qualify me for such a position. Please consider me an applicant.

Solicited Letter

If you are writing in response to an advertisement, you might open your letter as follows:

> In the July 21 issue of the *Sun-Times*, you advertised for a management trainee. My degree in management and my work experience as an assistant store manager qualify me for this position.

Often, an employee will tell you about an opening with his or her company. In such a situation, you might write an opening paragraph in the following way:

> When Terri Matsunaga, vice president of your bank, spoke to me about applying for a position as customer service representative, I became enthusiastic about the possibility of working with Second State Bank. My business administration degree and three years of customer service experience qualify me for the position.

Unsolicited Letter

Focus on your abilities in the opening paragraph of an unsolicited letter of application. You might open your letter in the following way:

> If you have an opening for an experienced truck mechanic, please consider me an applicant.

If appropriate, demonstrate your knowledge of the company's needs in an unsolicited letter:

> According to the February issue of *Changing Times*, many major companies need to fill positions for accountants. If your company has a need for accountants, I would like to be considered an applicant. I believe that my accounting degree, work experience in a CPA firm, and strong desire to succeed make me a qualified applicant.

★ Like a persuasive message, an unsolicited letter of application must have a relevant attention-getting opening. It also must create interest and desire to persuade the reader to interview the applicant.

CHECKPOINT 1

Opening Paragraph

Indicate if each opening paragraph is effective or weak.

1. My considerable experience and two years of technical training make me confident that I would fit in as a medical assistant in your office.
2. I would appreciate your letting me know of any openings in your factory that I am qualified to fill.

(Continued on the next page)

Opening Paragraph, Continued

3. Your advertisement in the February 28 *News Daily* for an office manager describes responsibilities for which I am well qualified through my college degree and work experience. Please consider me an applicant for the position.
4. The Placement Office at Kingston College has advised me of an opening in your company for a sales clerk. I believe that I am qualified. I hope you will consider me for this position.
5. Several years of legal secretarial experience, an associate degree in legal office administration, and a deep appreciation for the complexities of the legal system make me the ideal candidate for the paralegal assistant position for which you are advertising. Please consider me an applicant.

Check your answers in Appendix F.

Body Paragraphs

Your body paragraphs should convince the employer that you are right for the job. Instead of just repeating the facts presented in your resume, interpret these facts for the reader. The second—and possibly third—paragraph should demonstrate that your educational preparation, work experience, and/or qualifications are relevant to the job requirements.

When you respond to a published job opening, explain how your qualifications meet those mentioned in the advertisement. For example, an advertisement may indicate that the job requires four years of experience with computerized equipment. If you worked with such equipment for three years and completed a technical course on the same subject, you would include this information in the body of your application letter.

Here is an example of an effective body paragraph that focuses on the applicant's work experience:

> As a quality control inspector, I worked closely with the plant manager to improve quality and reduce costs. During my year in this position, my department was rated Number 1 in quality while costs went down by 8 percent.

If you have not had much work experience, then concentrate on other qualifications such as your education, related activities and honors, ability to learn quickly, or enthusiasm. Note the wording of the following section:

> During my second year of college, I was awarded a Rotary scholarship. While working toward my associate degree in data processing, I was vice president of the school's Phi Beta Lambda chapter. As vice president, I organized and hosted a fund-raising event for muscular dystrophy.
>
> As a computer programmer for Datacorp, I will offer these same qualities of involvement and commitment that I demonstrated while in school.

Although the applicant in the next example has had little work experience, the applicant highlights qualities that employers value:

> While studying for my associate degree in accounting, I worked on assignments that allowed me to learn more about cost accounting. I will bring my diligence in completing my coursework to my work as an accountant with your company. Also, I have extensive experience with computer accounting programs and spreadsheets. I work well with others and enjoy being a productive team member.

You should also explain any information in your resume that may raise questions or cause a negative reaction. For example, if you have an interrupted work history, provide an explanation in your letter. If you took an especially long time to complete your degree, explain why in your letter. Here is an example:

> While attending college, I worked full time to support myself and pay for all school expenses. I took two courses each quarter and completed my associate degree in three years.

★ When you explain any employment gaps on your resume, remember that you want to show your qualifications in the best possible light. Use the techniques you learned for conveying bad-news messages and maintain a positive tone throughout your application letter.

CHECKPOINT 2

Body Paragraphs

Indicate if each of the following body paragraph of an application letter is effective or weak.

1. Please review my resume, which is enclosed, for details about the type of training I have received at Marietta College.
2. My 13 years of work experience at Pacific Southern have prepared me to move into a position as office manager with your company. Starting as a records clerk, I was promoted several times and now hold the position of records supervisor.

(Continued on the next page)

Body Paragraphs, Continued

3. As my resume indicates, I will graduate from Housatonic Community Technical College in June with an associate degree in accounting. I have maintained a 3.4 grade point average while working full time as a bank teller for Midland State Bank.
4. The enclosed resume provides a complete description of my qualifications. The courses listed have given me an excellent background for the position you have available.
5. While in college, I acquired proficiency in using desktop publishing software. I also studied computer graphics, which I can apply on the job as a graphic artist with your company.

Check your answers in Appendix F.

Closing Paragraph

The closing paragraph should ask for an interview. Make it easy for the employer to contact you for an interview by providing your telephone number again (it also should appear in the heading of your resume). Avoid the overused phrase, "May I have an interview at your convenience?" Instead, your closing paragraph should lead up to a request for an interview. Note the following closing paragraph:

> You will see from the enclosed resume that my education and experience qualify me for this position. May I have an interview with you to discuss my qualifications for the job? You may reach me at 555-0184 between 8:30 a.m. and 4:30 p.m. any weekday.

If contacting you would be difficult, consider the following closing:

> I would appreciate the opportunity to discuss my qualifications with you. Because reaching me at school is difficult, I will call you early next week to see when we can arrange an interview.

If you are writing to an out-of-town company, mention if and when you will be in the area for an interview. For example:

> I would appreciate the opportunity to discuss my qualifications with you while visiting Tucson next week. On Monday, I will call your office to see when we can meet.

★ Think of the closing paragraph as an action ending in a persuasive message. Make sure you indicate the action to be taken—an interview.

Closing Paragraph

Indicate if each closing paragraph is effective or weak.

1. Because my qualifications are best described in person, I would appreciate an interview with you. Please telephone me between 2 and 5 p.m. any weekday at 555-0110 to let me know a day and time convenient for you to talk with me about this position.
2. In preparation for a personal interview to discuss the job, please send me information about your company and an application form. You can call me at 555-0121 to schedule an appointment.
3. May I come for an interview within the next two weeks? You can reach me at 555-0122 or at the above address. I look forward to discussing the possibility of joining your staff.
4. After you have reviewed my resume, I hope you will consider the possibility of putting my skills to work for your company. Please call me at (513) 555-0161, and I will try to meet with you.
5. As I complete my studies in March, I would like to know by March 10 if you have any job openings. Call me at 555-0128.

Check your answers in Appendix F.

General Guidelines for Application Letters

An employer will form a quick first impression of you from your letter of application. You can make your letters of application more effective by following these general guidelines:

1. Address the letter to a person. If you do not know the name of the person in charge of the department you will be joining (or in charge of employment), call the company to ask.
2. Use a simple writing style and indicate how your background and experience will benefit the employer. Make the letter brief and avoid using worn-out expressions.
3. Enclose a resume with your letter and refer your reader to it in the body or closing paragraphs.
4. Print your letter on the same high-quality, 20-lb., white, off-white, or grey bond paper you used for your resume. Also use matching envelopes.

Figure 45–1 shows a sample solicited letter of application. Figure 45–2 shows a sample unsolicited letter of application.

★ When you use a word processor or a computer to prepare an application letter, be sure to use the same letter-quality or laser printer you used for your resume. Before you print, use the spell-checker to find and correct any spelling errors.

506 Northwest Highway
Clovis, NM 88021-1304
April 30, 19—

Mrs. Sandra Markham
Director of Human Resources
Mountain Finance, Inc.
32 Commerce Way
Portales, NM 88130-5432

Dear Mrs. Markham

My bookkeeping experience and college degree in
Administrative Technologies have prepared me for the
position of accounts receivable clerk that you advertised in the
Chronicle on April 29.

In addition to more than two years of experience as a
bookkeeper for a busy sales office, I recently completed an
advanced workshop in collection techniques to supplement
my college studies. The skills I gained from this workshop will
enable me to work more effectively with Mountain Finance's
customers.

As you can see from the enclosed resume, my background fits
all the requirements mentioned in your advertisement. I would
appreciate the opportunity to discuss my qualifications in
person. After 2 p.m. on weekdays, you may reach me at (505)
555-0291.

Sincerely yours

Arnold Richter

Arnold Richter

Enclosure

Figure 45–1 Solicited letter of application

175 River Road
Hartford, WI 53027-1093
November 20, 19—

Dr. Anthony Marchi
Director of Medical Services
Atlantic Manufacturing
902 Main Street
Hartford, WI 53027-2951

Dear Dr. Marchi:

The Hartford News recently reported that Atlantic Manufacturing is expanding its medical services center. With this larger facility scheduled to open next month, will you have an opening for a recent college graduate trained in physical therapy?

The skills I developed from a combination of college coursework and hands-on experience during a six-month clinical internship will enable me to assist Atlantic Manufacturing employees who require physical therapy due to work injuries. While earning my associate in science degree as a physical therapy assistant, I also completed a special research project on human motor patterns in repetitive manufacturing.

During my internship at the Hartford Clinic, I learned to use hydrotherapy, electrotherapy, massage, and chest physical therapy to treat a variety of conditions. In addition, studying under registered physical therapists who have consulted with leading Wisconsin manufacturers gave me valuable insight into the nature and treatment of assembly line injuries.

My education and internship experience, along with my desire to meet new challenges, would make me an asset to your company's medical services center. After you have reviewed the enclosed resume, could we meet to discuss my qualifications? You may call me at 555-6684.

Sincerely yours,

Anne Monaco

Anne Monaco

Enclosure

Figure 45–2 Unsolicited letter of application

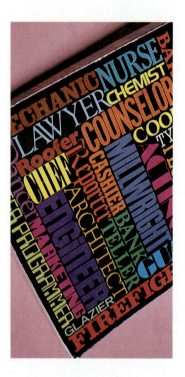

APPLICATION FORM

Most companies require applicants to complete an application form when applying for a job. An **application form** is a standardized data sheet that a company uses to compare qualifications of different job applicants. Employers invite candidates with the appropriate education and work background for an interview.

Using Sample Application Forms

If possible, fill out a sample application for practice. If you have none, look at a copy of an application form you have completed for a previous job. This sample application form should include information such as social security number, work experience (dates, addresses, supervisors, salaries), education (dates, schools, GPAs), and references (names, addresses, telephone numbers). If you have certifications or licenses, include the date granted and the number assigned for each.

If you can obtain a copy of the company's application form in advance, photocopy it to practice on. Type or print neatly. Photocopy the completed form for your qualifications file. Figure 45–3 shows a sample application form.

APPLICATION FOR EMPLOYMENT

Please print or type.   An Equal Opportunity Employer

Name	Address	City/State/Zip
Donna Monroe	602 Elm Street	Buffalo, NY 14240-1712

Telephone Number	Social Security Number	
(716) 555-0025	123-456-7890	

U.S. Citizen? Yes No	Position Applying for?	Desired Salary?
Yes	Bookkeeper	Open

WORK EXPERIENCE

Current/Most Recent Employer	Address
Corner Pharmacy	Buffalo Shopping Center, Buffalo, NY 14241-1342

Job Title	Dates of Employment from 10/93 to /Present
Cashier	

Supervisor	Salary	Reason for Leaving?
Mrs. Glenfield	$5.50/hour	Seeking full-time career position

Previous Employer	Address

Job Title	Dates of Employment from / to /

Supervisor	Salary	Reason for Leaving?

Previous Employer	Address

Job Title	Dates of Employment from / to /

Supervisor	Salary	Reason for Leaving?

EDUCATION

High School	City and State	Attended from 6/89 to 6/93
South Buffalo High School	Buffalo, NY	

GPA	Degree	Activities, Honors
B+	Diploma	Junior Achievement club member

College	City and State	Attended from 9/93 to 6/95
Lakeside Community College	Buffalo, NY	

GPA	Degree	Activities, Honors
3.5	A.S., Accounting	

SPECIAL SKILLS, LICENSES, TRAINING, OR MILITARY EXPERIENCE

Coursework in contemporary tax compliance, computer-assisted accounting.

REFERENCES (*Do not include the names of relatives or former employers*)

Name	Address	Telephone Number
1. James Lerner (instructor)	Lakeside Community College, Buffalo, NY 14242-6415	(716) 555-1100
2. Rosa Sanchez (instructor)	Lakeside Community College, Buffalo, NY 14242-6415	(716) 555-1100
3. Tom Rowan (neighbor)	605 Elm Street, Buffalo, NY 14240-1714	(716) 555-3854

CERTIFICATION

I certify that all information on this application is true. I understand that termination may result if any information is found to be untrue. I understand that employment is subject to passing drug tests conducted at the direction of the Company.

(sign) *Donna Monroe*   July 6, 19—

Signature   Date

Form 956 Rev. 8/95

Figure 45–3 Sample application form for employment

Completing the Employer's Application Form

When you visit an employer, take all the information needed to complete an application form. Bring a copy of your resume and your sample application form.

Use a pen with blue or black ink when you fill out an application form at the employer's office. Make sure your pen writes clearly and sharply. Neatly draw a line through any errors.

Skim through the application form before filling in any information to get an idea of the kinds of information you need to supply. A quick scan also will help you avoid repeating yourself in different sections.

Read all instructions before you start to write on the application form. Many applications begin with general instructions such as "Type or print in ink." You may be instructed to list your work experience beginning with the "current or most recent job." You can be sure you will be evaluated on your ability to follow instructions.

Answer all questions on the application form. If a question or section does not apply to you, write N/A (for *not applicable*) or put a dash in the space so that the employer will not think you have overlooked or omitted something. For example, if you have no military experience, simply write N/A or put a dash in the first space related to that section. The application form also may ask about convictions (and in some states, about arrests).

The applicant signs the application form to certify that all information is correct. This form then becomes a part of the applicant's permanent personnel record when that person is hired. Many items are verifiable, including work experience, job titles, and education record. Providing false information can hurt your career or even be grounds for dismissal.

Some application forms contain questions about desired salary. Research the market so that you are aware of the salary range possible. You may want to put a figure on the application form, but often the best response is to list a salary range, write "open," or write "appropriate for my education and experience." You can discuss salary at the appropriate time in the interview.

If the application form has space for references, list the names from the reference sheet you prepared for Chapter 44. If the application does not specify that references must be current or former employers, you may use a variety of references such as an employer, an instructor, and a business colleague.

LEGAL/Ethical

- Some application forms require prospective employees to certify that they have not omitted any significant information. Before you sign your application form, check once more to make sure you have not left out anything significant.

Take time and care in completing the application form to increase your chances of being offered the job.

Summary

As part of your job search, you may send letters of application. A solicited letter of application is written to apply for a specific job opening that has been advertised or announced. An unsolicited letter of application is written to apply for an unadvertised or unannounced position that may or may not be open. The opening paragraph of your letter of application should gain the reader's attention, indicate the position for which you are applying, state where you learned of the opening (solicited letter), and identify your abilities (unsolicited letter). In the body paragraphs, present your qualifications that relate to the job requirements. In the closing paragraph, ask for an interview.

Fill out a sample application form for practice, and take it when you visit an employment office. Complete the employer's application form carefully. Write clearly in blue or black ink. Skim through the application form before you complete it. Follow the instructions, complete all questions, and answer honestly.

Discussion Questions

1. How does a solicited letter of application differ from an unsolicited letter of application?
2. What is an application form and how is it used?

Practical Applications

Part A

Use the company research you conducted in Chapter 43 to write an unsolicited letter of application to an employer for which you are interested in working. Address this letter to the person in charge of the department you want to join.

Part B

Use the information in your qualifications file to fill out a sample application form provided by your instructor. If you are missing any information (such as dates of employment), call your former employers to request this information.

Editing and Proofreading Application

Edit and rewrite the following letter of application.

> Your company advertised for an administrative assistant in the December 9 issue of the *Weekly Herald*, which I subscribe to. I will be done with my studies in the Business Technology program at Central States Community College this month. And then I will be qualified for this position. Please consider me to be a formal applicant for this position.
>
> While attending school full time. I worked part-time as a secretary for Storrs Windows for over a year. In addition to my secretarial duties, I handled all payroll processing and petty cash. I supervised 1 clerical employee.
>
> If possible, please contact me at 555-0172 to arrange an interview at your earliest convenience. My background and education fit your requirements, and I would very much like to work for your company.

Job Interviews and Follow-Up Letters

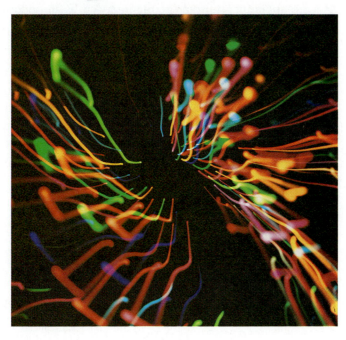

OBJECTIVES

After studying this chapter and completing the chapter exercises, you will be able to do the following:

1. Discuss the purpose of a job interview.
2. Explain how to prepare for an interview.
3. Write a follow-up letter.

Chapter 46

THE PURPOSE OF A JOB INTERVIEW

Employers generally do not hire solely on the basis of a resume or an application form. They want to talk with job applicants to determine if they are qualified for the position and if they are a good fit for the company. Every applicant is competing with other applicants who want the same job. The interview process helps an employer compare applicants and decide about which person to hire.

As a job applicant, you can use the interview as an opportunity to determine if you want to work for a particular company. Use the time spent in your interview to evaluate the organization and the job through your observations and questions.

Interviews may last anywhere from 20 minutes to several hours and take place on a single day or over several days. During the interview process, you may be interviewed by one person or by several persons. How you present yourself is crucial—as with resumes, first impressions count. An interviewer often makes a decision *not* to hire during the first 15 seconds of an interview. That is one reason why it is so important for you to be well prepared.

★ Use your research skills to uncover additional sources of information about the job, its requirements, and general salary levels. For example, you might learn more about the duties of a position by checking with the appropriate professional association or reading a career guide about the industry you are exploring.

JOB INTERVIEW PREPARATION

Your success in an interview depends in large part on your preparation. Preparation includes investigating the company and the position, anticipating questions that may be asked, preparing questions you want to ask, and other preliminary activities.

Investigate the Company and the Job

Before the interview, find out pertinent information about the company. Review the research you conducted before applying for the job and fill in any gaps about products, facilities, and other details that may be discussed during the interview.

Learn as much as you can about the job opening before you interview. Check with the person who suggested you apply at the company, ask current and former employees, or work with counselors in your placement office to get the following information: (1) job title and responsibilities, (2) qualifications, (3) salary range and benefits, and (4) advancement opportunities.

Anticipate Questions

Before interviewing for a job, prepare yourself for probable questions from the interviewer. Nervousness during an interview is natural. However, preparing to answer typical questions will help to relieve your anxiety. Expect to be asked about your work experience, education, goals, self-concept, and relationships with others. Figure 46–1 shows a list of frequently asked questions. Write down brief but complete answers to these questions, and practice the answers, possibly taping them to hear how you sound.

Prepare Questions to Ask

During the interview, you will be asked if you have any questions. Be prepared to ask questions that demonstrate your interest and professionalism. At the same time, your questions should help you learn more about how you might fit with the position and the company. Remember, you are trying to determine if you want to accept this position if it is offered to you. Keep your questions related to the job and the company. Until you are offered a position, avoid asking questions about salary or benefits. Here are some questions you might ask:

1. What would my major responsibilities be?
2. What qualities are you seeking in the person for this job?
3. Does your company have training programs?
4. What would you like to see a person accomplish in this job?
5. What are the major tasks to be accomplished in this job?
6. What is the typical career path for someone in this job?
7. What are the company's plans for new products? New services?
8. Where are the company's major markets? Will the company be expanding to new markets?

Practice for the Interview

If possible, ask someone to videotape you in a mock interview. Viewing the interview will help you assess your interview skills, particularly your nonverbal skills (body language), and improve them. You also will be able to analyze how your answers sound to an interviewer and then make any needed changes.

Educational Experiences

1. Why did you major in ________________?
2. Which courses did you like best? Least? Why?
3. What motivated you to seek a college education?

Work Experiences

4. Why do you want to work for our company?
5. What kind of work did you do in your last job? What were your responsibilities?
6. Describe a typical day on your last (or present) job.
7. What was the most difficult problem you encountered on your last (or present) job and how did you handle it?
8. What did you like best about your previous positions? Least?
9. Why did you leave your last job (or want to leave your previous job)?
10. What do you know about our company?
11. What aspects of this job appeal to you most?

Human Relations

12. What kind of people do you enjoy working with? Find difficult working with?
13. How do you get along with other students? With instructors? With co-workers or supervisors?
14. In your previous jobs, how much of your work did you do on your own? How much did you do as part of a team?

Goals

15. What are your career goals?
16. Why did you choose this particular field of work?

Self-Concept

17. What are your greatest strengths? Weaknesses?
18. What qualities do you need to strengthen?
19. Tell me about yourself.
20. Why do you think you are qualified for this job?
21. How do you spend your leisure time?
22. What do you consider to be your chief accomplishment in each of the jobs you have held?
23. What have your supervisors complimented you on? Criticized you for?

Figure 46–1 Sample interview questions

LEGAL/Ethical

- Many companies insist on seeing the documentation to prove an applicant's qualifications. For example, someone who claims to be a graduate of a particular college should be prepared to bring in a final transcript or degree as proof.

Bring Appropriate Information

Bring an extra copy or two of your resume and reference list, a completed sample application form (to help you fill in the employer's application form), two pens, a small notebook and calendar, and perhaps a portfolio containing samples of your work, transcripts, and letters of recommendation and commendation. If the interviewer asks questions related to these items, you may indicate that you have brought them with you and offer to show them.

Dress for the Interview

A good appearance will show your interviewer that you are professional. Here are some pointers:

1. Dress conservatively; avoid flamboyant styles or colors.
2. Wear a business suit in navy, gray, or brown when interviewing for office or professional jobs. If you do not have a suit, men should wear a sport coat and tie; women should wear a dress and jacket or skirt and jacket.
3. Avoid heavy fragrances and flashy jewelry. Women also should avoid bright nail polish, frilly clothes, and heavy make-up.
4. Choose a conservative, attractive hair style.
5. Make sure you are well groomed—good deodorant; clean clothes; polished shoes; trim, clean nails; and freshly brushed teeth.

Arrive on Time

If you are unfamiliar with the interview location, travel there before the day of the interview to learn the route. Allow plenty of time on the day of the interview. Remember, you may have to park, locate the building, and then find the right office. Allow extra time for heavy traffic or any problems that may occur, such as hunting for a parking spot or waiting for a bus. You will not impress an interviewer if you are late; therefore, plan on arriving a few minutes early.

CHECKPOINT 1

Preparing for the Interview

Indicate if each statement is true or false.

1. Before interviewing for a job, prepare yourself for probable questions from the interviewer.
2. Prepare questions to ask about the job and the company.
3. Dress casually for any interview.
4. Plan to arrive at the interview a little early.
5. All you need to take to the interview is your resume.

Check your answers in Appendix F.

THE INTERVIEW

At the interview site, you may be introduced to the interviewer by a receptionist or a secretary. As you wait in the reception area for the interview to begin, conduct yourself in a professional manner. The secretary may have an influence on whether or not you are hired. Some points to remember:

1. Avoid smoking.
2. Avoid chewing gum.
3. Greet the secretary cordially.
4. Avoid bringing friends or relatives to the interview.

The Introduction

Greet the interviewer with a smile and direct eye contact. Use the interviewer's name in a greeting such as "Glad to meet you, Dr. Wanamaker." A firm handshake is always appropriate and professional. Sit down only when you are asked. Then let the interviewer begin the interview and direct the discussion.

Nonverbal Skills

Your nonverbal skills are very important during the interview. From the time you meet, the interviewer will be assessing you for the job. Because the interviewer's first impression of you is crucial, you must look and act like someone the interviewer would like to hire. You will want to focus on such nonverbal signals as posture, facial expression, gestures, and eye contact.

Posture. Carry yourself erectly and confidently. Hold your head up and keep your shoulders back and straight. Maintain good posture when you sit. Make sure your back touches the back of the chair to avoid slumping.

Facial Expression. Keep a pleasant, interested expression on your face during the interview. A warm smile sends the message that you are someone the company would like on its team.

Gestures. Keep your gestures natural. Avoid extremes such as moving stiffly, making no arm movements, and waving your hands wildly. Minimize distinctive habits such as hand twisting or leg shaking.

Eye Contact. An important nonverbal communication skills is maintaining eye contact with the interviewer. Looking at the interviewer when he or she is talking communicates that you are interested.

Listening Skills.

Listen effectively so that you can answer questions and gather appropriate information. Here are some tips for effective listening during the interview:

1. Concentrate on what the interviewer is saying.
2. Look at the interviewer. Eye contact will let the interviewer know you are listening.
3. Be observant. Notice the interviewer's body language and pick up on nonverbal cues.
4. Listen eagerly. Show that you are interested by providing feedback, such as nodding or smiling, and giving verbal cues, such as saying "Yes" and "Uh-huh."
5. Listen carefully for the important points so that you can respond to them later; do not interrupt the interviewer.

ACROSS CULTURES

- If you are interviewing for jobs in other countries, be aware that certain hand gestures can convey different meanings in other cultures. For example, making a circle with finger and thumb usually indicates "okay" in the United States but has obscene connotations in some Hispanic cultures.

- Although direct eye contact is a sign of respect and attention in the United States, it has the opposite meaning in some other cultures. Investigate the meaning of nonverbal signals before you interview with an international company for a job in another country.

Interview Questions

From the time the interview begins, you will be expected to answer questions so that the interviewer can get to know you and your abilities. Speak clearly and distinctly as you answer these questions and use good grammar. The way you communicate with the interviewer indicates if you have good communication skills, an important qualification for most jobs.

Opening Questions

Many interviewers will begin with ice-breaker questions such as, "I see that you are in the school band. What instrument do you play?" These questions are intended to put you at ease. Answer them naturally and be yourself. Well-trained interviewers want you to be comfortable and natural so that they can get an accurate impression of your personality. Remember, the interviewer is as interested in finding the right person as you are in being selected for the position.

Main Questions

During the next stage, the interviewer gathers information about you by asking questions such as those in Figure 46–1. Listen to each question carefully, pause to gather your thoughts before answering, and elaborate on your answers. A simple "yes" or "no" is not enough. Use each answer as an opportunity to convince the interviewer that you are the best person for the job. Do not assume that the interviewer will learn all about you from your application form or resume. Talk about your accomplishments and abilities; employers want to hire people who are sincere, confident, and capable.

Illegal Questions

You may be asked personal questions that you do not want to answer. In general, you only should provide information that will be to your advantage. Federal laws such as Title VII of the Civil Rights Act of 1965 and the Americans with Disabilities Act prohibit employers from discriminating in job hiring on the basis of age, gender, national origin, religion, race, disability, marital status, number of children, or other factors unrelated to job performance. In some states, applicants may be asked about convictions but not about arrests.

The best way to handle illegal questions is to deflect them courteously, possibly providing some useful information. For example, if the interviewer asks you how your children will be taken care of while you work, you might answer, "If you are asking if I will arrive on time and do a good job, the answer is definitely 'Yes.'" You might also assure the interviewer that you have made child care arrangements. In addition, you might refer to a good performance and attendance record in your current job.

★ Remember to phrase the answers you offer during an interview like a persuasive message. Reflect the interests of the receiver rather than the needs of the sender.

Do not answer an inappropriate question if your response could hurt your chances of getting the job. Maintain your composure and be ready to provide information if the interviewer can show you that the question is job-related. If asked an inappropriate question, you might respond, "I do not understand how that question relates to my performance on the job. Can you explain?" Figure 46–2 provides some examples of illegal interview questions. Look them over and decide how you would answer these questions if asked.

Salary Question

Avoid mentioning salary requirements until you receive an offer for a position. However, if the interviewer asks your salary requirements early in the interview, indicate that you require the standard salary for the position in question or the salary that is appropriate for your education and experience. Letting the interviewer make a salary offer rather than naming a figure yourself puts you in a better position to negotiate.

The Closing

The interviewer will provide both verbal and nonverbal signals that the interview is over. Stand up, offer a handshake, and thank the interviewer. Usually a job is not offered at this point. However, asking the interviewer when a decision will be made is appropriate.

If you are offered the job, accept it only if you are sure you want it. This decision is important, and you may need some time to consider it. If you need more time, tell the interviewer that you need to think it over because you are interviewing for other positions. Then give your answer by the agreed-upon time. Ask for the

1. Are you married? Single? Divorced? Widowed?
2. Do you have small children? Do you plan to have children?
3. What is your date of birth?
4. Have you ever been arrested?
5. Where were you born?
6. Where does your husband (wife, father, mother) work?
7. Are you pregnant?
8. Do you belong to a religious organization? Which one?
9. Do you rent or own your home?
10. What is your maiden name?
11. Do you have a girlfriend? (boyfriend?)

Figure 46–2 Illegal interview questions

interviewer's business card before you leave; you will want to write a follow-up message.

FOLLOW-UP LETTERS

Within two days after the interview, write a brief follow-up letter thanking the interviewer. If you are sure you want the job, indicate your interest and ask for a decision. Follow-up letters are courteous and thoughtful, and they bring your name before the interviewer again.

Think back to the interview (or consult any notes you made) and identify one specific idea you can use to refresh the interviewer's memory about your conversation. You might emphasize how one of the qualifications you mentioned during the interview would benefit the company. Another approach is to provide the answer to a question that the interviewer asked you to consider. Incorporate the idea or answer into your letter to remind the interviewer of what you discussed during the interview.

Organize the letter as a goodwill message, as the example below illustrates:

Main Idea	Thank you for giving me the opportunity to interview yesterday for the position of legal secretary. After talking with you and seeing the office operations, I am convinced that I would like to join Powell and Martin's legal secretarial staff.
Supporting Information	During the interview, we discussed my availability for the northside office. After further consideration, I am happy to say that I would be able to work in any of the firm's locations in the city.
Helpful Closing	My education and experience make me confident that I would be able to perform the duties of the position well. If you need further information about my qualifications or have any questions, please call me at 555-7730.

Once the deadline for making a decision has passed, you may want to call the interviewer or write a second follow-up letter if you have not heard from the company. Make this second letter brief but not curt. Remind the interviewer that you still are interested in working for the company. Mention the decision date originally indicated, and politely inquire if the interviewer needs any additional information about your qualifications to help in this decision. Close by saying that you look forward to hearing from the interviewer soon.

The Interview and Follow-Up Letter

Indicate if each statement is true or false.

1. Maintaining eye contact with the interviewer is an important nonverbal skill.
2. During the main part of the interview, you will be asked questions about your abilities.
3. Be prepared to handle illegal questions and salary questions.
4. Ask about salary at the start of the interview.
5. Write a follow-up letter two weeks after the interview.

Check your answers in Appendix F.

Summary

Job interviews provide an opportunity for companies to find suitable employees and an opportunity for job applicants to locate appropriate employment. Prepare for the interview by investigating the company and the job, anticipating interview questions, and planning questions to ask. Make sure that you are well groomed and dressed appropriately for the interview. Take your resume and reference list, a completed sample application form, two pens, a small notebook and calendar, and perhaps a portfolio. Arrive on time.

During the interview, use good nonverbal and listening skills. Answer questions completely, and present yourself and your qualifications well. Be prepared to handle illegal questions and salary questions. After the interview, write the interviewer a short follow-up letter.

Discussion Questions

1. Why do employers interview applicants for positions?
2. What seven steps can you take to prepare for an interview?
3. Why should you send a follow-up letter after an interview?

Practical Applications

Part A

Team up with a classmate and stage mock interviews in which each student in turn plays the part of the interviewer and the applicant for a specific (real or imaginary) job. Videotape the interviews, if possible, and discuss each student's strengths and weaknesses after the playback.

Part B

Prepare answers to the interview questions in Figure 46–1.

Part C

Prepare your answers to the illegal interview questions in Figure 46–2. Exchange answers with a classmate and analyze the effectiveness of each answer.

Part D

Select a job that interests you and prepare five questions you would like to ask during an interview.

Editing and Proofreading Application

Proofread the following follow-up letter. Then edit and rewrite the letter.

Thank you for taking time from your buzy schedule to interview me me for the position of assisstant head Teller. I also enjoyed the toor of your mane branch.

As I mentioned during the interview, your computerized account system is really, really impressive. Because it is similar to the one I use in my current position at Western Bank, I am sure I could adopt to it in only a few days.

Given my years of experience with Western Bank, I believe that I would preform well and enjoy the challenje of serveing the customers of Ansonia Savings Bank. If you need addition references or other information, please just let me know.

FREQUENTLY MISSPELLED AND MISUSED WORDS

Words Frequently Misspelled

accidentally
accommodate
achievement
acknowledge
advertisement
all right
analysis
assistant

bankrupt
beneficial
bureau

calendar
canceled
census
changeable
clientele
confident
congratulate
conscientious
convenience
correspondence
courteous

development
disappear
discrepancy

efficiency
eighth

eligible
embarrass
envelope
exceed
extension

familiar
February
foreign
forty
freight

government
grammar
grateful
gratitude
guarantee
guidance

hindrance

illustrate
impatient
indispensable
intercede

language
length
liable
library

lieutenant
loose

maintenance
mathematics
mediocre
mileage
minimum
miscellaneous
misspell
mortgage

necessary
necessity
negotiable
nineteen
ninety
noticeable

occasion
occurred
occurrence

parallel
pastime
personnel
precede
preferred
privilege

receipt

receive
recommendations
referred
relevant
religious
rhythm

secretary
separate
similar
sincerely
situation
strategy
sufficient

transferred
treasurer
truly
Tuesday

unanimous
usually

vacuum

Wednesday
whether
withholding

Words Frequently Misused

Below is an alphabetized list of words that are misused frequently in business communication. To help you understand how to use these words, the list provides a definition of each word and an example of its usage.

a lot

n. many (Note that *a lot* consists of two words.)
> Ex. She owns *a lot* of books.

accept

v. to agree to; to receive
> Ex. He will *accept* your recommendation.

addition

n. increase; enlargement; part or thing added
> Ex. With the *addition* of the family room, the house is more comfortable. The new *addition* to the hospital provides more office space for the medical staff.

advice

n. counsel
> Ex. The college counsellor's *advice* helped the student.

advise

v. to give advice; to inform
> Ex. The attorney will *advise* you to write a will.

affect

v. to influence
> Ex. His new contract will *affect* his annual income.

all ready

adj. completely prepared
> Ex. The auditors are *all ready* to discuss their findings.

all together

adj. in a group; in unison
> Ex. Let us sing *all together* so that our voices ring out.

allot

v. to give or share in arbitrary amounts; to apportion
> Ex. They will *allot* each speaker only five minutes.

allude

v. to refer to something not specifically mentioned
> Ex. Did the article *allude* to her disinterest in the new product without actually stating it?

already

adv. by or before a specified or implied time
> Ex. He *already* called the bank officer.

altogether

adv. completely or thoroughly
> Ex. Raising the budget is *altogether* unwise in today's economy.

assure

v. to make sure
> Ex. We *assure* you that you can count on our support.

capital

n. money invested
> Ex. How much *capital* was invested in the business?

capitol

n. a government building
> Ex. She took her class to the *capitol* in Harrisburg.

choose

v. to select based on judgment
> Ex. They will *choose* Ted because of his skill and knowledge.

chose

v. past tense of *choose*

    Ex. Art *chose* Gloria to be on his team.

cite

v. to acknowledge; to quote as a reference

    Ex. You were asked to *cite* directly from your resource book.

complement

n. anything that completes a whole *v.* to complete or make perfect

    Ex. (*n.*) A *complement* of certified public accountants would enhance your staff.

    Ex. (*v.*) Her new hat will *complement* the outfit.

compliment

n. recognition; praise; flattery *v.* to praise

    Ex. (*n.*) The supervisor's *compliment* pleased the clerks.

    Ex. (*v.*) He will *compliment* his employees when they work overtime.

consul

n. an official appointed by the government to live in a foreign city to attend to the interests of the official's country.

    Ex. The *consul* from France helped the French tourists who had lost their passports.

continual

adj. taking place in close succession; frequently repeated

    Ex. The *continual* interruptions annoyed the music listeners.

continuous

adj. without break or letup

    Ex. The waterfall's *continuous* flow of water captivated the onlookers.

cooperation

n. assistance; help

    Ex. The *cooperation* of the parties is necessary in this situation.

corporation

n. type of business organization

    Ex. The four doctors formed a *corporation* to practice medicine.

council

n. group of people called together to provide counsel

    Ex. The vote of the *council* was divided.

counsel

n. advice *v.* to provide advice

    Ex. (*n.*) We must obtain legal *counsel* before we make a decision.

    Ex. (*v.*) Who is going to *counsel* them on the matter?

decent

adj. correct; proper

    Ex. We will accept any *decent* offer for the property.

descent

n. going from a high level to a lower level

    Ex. The *descent* of the asset's value is quite remarkable.

desert

v. to abandon *n.* a barren geographical area

    Ex. (*v.*) Don't *desert* a family that needs your support.

    Ex. (*n.*) He drove through the *desert* in the early morning hours.

dessert

n. a course at the end of a meal

    Ex. Chocolate ice cream is her favorite *dessert*.

disburse

v. to make payments; to allot

Ex. We will *disburse* the money after the project is completed.

disperse

v. to distribute

Ex. Did they *disperse* the pamphlets at the conference?

dissent

n. disagreement

Ex. The situation caused *dissent* between the parent and the teenager.

edition

n. an issue of a book or newspaper

Ex. The author is working on the second *edition* of his book.

effect

n. the result or outcome *v.* to bring about

Ex. (*n.*) The *effect* of the redistribution was felt by all the employees. (*v.*) The new leadership will *effect* massive changes.

elude

v. to escape notice or detection

Ex. By changing the subject, he was able to *elude* criticism.

ensure

v. to make sure; to guarantee

Ex. Bail is set to *ensure* the appearance of defendants in court.

envelop

v. to surround; to cover completely

Ex. The fog will *envelop* the area at daybreak.

envelope

n. containers for letters, reports, and so forth.

Ex. Send the memorandum in an interoffice *envelope*.

except

prep. with the exclusion of; other than

Ex. All staff members attended *except* Timothy.

farther

adj. more distant

Ex. Her home is *farther* from the school than Art's home.

forth

adv. forward; onward

Ex. From that day *forth*, he arrived at the airport one hour before departure time.

fourth

adj. any one of four equal parts; the item following the first three in a series

Ex. Randi is the *fourth* person to ask the same question.

further

adv. to a greater degree or extent

Ex. No *further* suggestions will be accepted at this time.

hear

v. perceive by the ear

Ex. Speak loudly so that everyone can *hear* you.

here

adv. in or at this place

Ex. Are all the speakers *here*?

hoard

v. to collect and keep

Ex. Aunt Rose does *hoard* all scarce items.

horde

n. a huge crowd

Ex. A *horde* of people blocked the street to prevent entrance.

insure

v. to secure from harm; to guarantee life or property

Ex. The company will not *insure* people who are poor risks.

its

pron. possessive form of *it*

Ex. When did you see *its* paw prints?

it's

contraction for *it is*

Ex. *It's* supposed to rain the day of our annual picnic.

lay

v. to place; to put (transitive verb—requires an object)

Ex. *Lay* the dictionary on my desk.

lie

v. to recline; to remain (intransitive verb—no object)

Ex. Glenn will *lie* down on the sofa.

loose

adj. not restrained; not fastened

Ex. The dogs are *loose* again despite all our efforts.

lose

v. to fail to win; to be deprived of

Ex. I play the lottery but always *lose*.

medal

n. a badge of honor

Ex. Faye deserves a *medal* for her kindness to others.

meddle

v. to interfere

Ex. Do not *meddle* in your adult children's business.

metal

n. a mineral substance

Ex. That item is made from *metal* not wood.

passed

v. past tense of *pass*

Ex. Sashi *passed* the final examination with a high grade.

past

adj. finished; gone by

Ex. The *past* season was good for the local retailers.

personal

adj. private; not public or general

Ex. Are you interested in my *personal* opinion on this subject?

personnel

n. the staff of an organization

Ex. A change in *personnel* is due the first of next month.

principal

n. the amount of the money borrowed in a loan; the head official in a court proceeding or school *adj.* most important or influential

Ex. (*n.*) The *principal* of the mortgage is about to be paid off. Ms. Landis is the new *principal* at the high school.
Ex. (*adj.*) What is the *principal* textbook used in biology?

principle

n. a basic belief or truth

Ex. Follow this *principle* to solve your first problem.

quiet

adj. still; calm

Ex. A librarian prefers *quiet* rooms to accommodate the readers.

quit

v. to stop; to discontinue

Ex. John will *quit* his job when he returns to college.

quite

adv. very or fairly; positively

  Ex. Miranda is *quite* ill and will not be able to attend.

sight

n. the ability to see; vision

  Ex. Joe's *sight* has improved with the treatment.

site

n. a place; a plot of land

  Ex. On what *site* are you planning to build?

stationary

adj. fixed; unmovable

  Ex. That huge piece of equipment is *stationary*.

stationery

n. paper for letters and envelopes

  Ex. The company is having new *stationery* printed.

taught

v. past tense of *teach*

  Ex. Len's father *taught* in the public schools in her city.

taut

adj. tight

  Ex. Make sure that the ropes are *taut* in order to hold the items.

than

conj. in comparison with *prep.* except; besides

  Ex. (*conj.*) Sean is older *than* Maria.
  Ex. (*prep.*) It was none other *than* Gayle who wallpapered the house.

their

pron. plural possessive form of *they*

  Ex. *Their* reports are on the receptionist's desk.

then

adv. at that time

  Ex. We will be ready *then* to discuss another investment.

there

adv. in or at that place

  Ex. Bob hesitates to go *there* to have his car repaired.

they're

contraction for *they are*

  Ex. *They're* interested in traveling to Spain this summer.

to

prep. in the direction of

  Ex. Go *to* the corner of South and Prescott Avenues.

too

adv. also; excessively

  Ex. *Too* many opinions are being offered on this matter.

two

adj. the number 2

  Ex. *Two* girls are being added to the team.

your

pron. possessive form of *you* (may be singular or plural)

  Ex. (*singular*) *Your* report card arrived in the mail. (*plural*) Let me help you with *your* roles before the auditions begin.

you're

contraction for *you are*

  Ex. *You're* very well qualified for the job.

TWO-LETTER POSTAL AND STANDARD ABBREVIATIONS

State	Two-Letter Abbreviation	Standard Abbreviation	State	Two-Letter Abbreviation	Standard Abbreviation
Alabama	AL	Ala.	Missouri	MO	Mo.
Alaska	AK	—	Montana	MT	Mont.
Arizona	AZ	Ariz.	Nebraska	NE	Nebr.
Arkansas	AR	Ark.	Nevada	NV	Nev.
California	CA	Calif.	New Hampshire	NH	N.H.
Colorado	CO	Colo.	New Jersey	NJ	N.J.
Connecticut	CT	Conn.	New Mexico	NM	N.Mex.
Delaware	DE	Del.	New York	NY	N.Y.
District of			North Carolina	NC	N.C.
Columbia	DC	D.C.	North Dakota	ND	N.Dak.
Florida	FL	Fla.	Ohio	OH	—
Georgia	GA	Ga.	Oklahoma	OK	Okla.
Hawaii	HI	—	Oregon	OR	Oreg.
Idaho	ID	—	Pennsylvania	PA	Pa.
Illinois	IL	Ill.	Rhode Island	RI	R.I.
Indiana	IN	Ind.	South Carolina	SC	S.C.
Iowa	IA	—	South Dakota	SD	S.Dak.
Kansas	KS	Kans.	Tennessee	TN	Tenn.
Kentucky	KY	Ky.	Texas	TX	Tex.
Louisiana	LA	La.	Utah	UT	—
Maine	ME	—	Vermont	VT	Vt.
Maryland	MD	Md.	Virginia	VA	Va.
Massachusetts	MA	Mass.	Washington	WA	Wash.
Michigan	MI	Mich.	West Virginia	WV	W.Va.
Minnesota	MN	Minn.	Wisconsin	WI	Wisc.
Mississippi	MS	Miss.	Wyoming	WY	Wyo.

Transcontinental
Chemical Supply

Interoffice
Memo

TO: All Employees

FROM: Richard Stafford, Personnel Director *RS.*

DATE: October 25, 19—

SUBJECT: **THINKING OF THANKSGIVING**

1 blank line

Can you think of Thanksgiving without a turkey
dinner? The Valley View Children's Home makes sure
there is a holiday dinner with turkey and all that
goes with it for the 45 children who live there.

Valley View is a nonprofit organization that
provides care for children who have lost their
parents. A brochure is enclosed describing the
facilities and services provided at the home.

A committee consisting of one member from each
department has considered many worthy causes. Their
decision is to pledge the support of Transcontinental this year to Valley View Children's Home.

You might recall that last year the employees of
Transcontinental generously gave $7,600 to our
local outreach organization, HelpLine. Please help
us meet this year's $8,000 goal for the Valley View
Home. Any generosity you show will once again be
tax deductible.

A pledge card is enclosed for your convenience.
Please return it by November 15. Feel free to call
for additional information.

1 blank line

Encs.

> This memo style uses a one-inch right-side
> margin. The TO, FROM, DATE, and
> SUBJECT lines are double-spaced to match the
> preprinted headings.
>
> The paragraphs are not indented but start at the
> left margin. They are single spaced, and there is a
> blank line between the paragraphs.

Traditional Memo on Preprinted Stationery

APPENDIX C

TO: Ms. Rebecca Riley, Courier, Word Processing Center

1 blank line

FROM: Brian Nichols, Administrative Manager   *BN.*

1 blank line

DATE: March 1, 19—

1 blank line

SUBJECT: Your Work Schedule

1 blank line

Rebecca, thank you for your memo about your work schedule. You have been doing excellent work for us as a courier in the Word Processing Center for the past five months since you transferred there. Continuing your service there and resolving your situation are important to all of us.

The good quality of your work as a courier has been possible for at least these three reasons:

1 blank line

1. Your interest in and enjoyment of the work

2. Your commitment to promptness and thoroughness during your rounds

3. The scheduling of your work at the time it is most needed—during our regular working hours

1 blank line

The flow of work in the Word Processing Center depends on this kind of courier service. Since your continued excellent performance requires that you be at work at 8 a.m., I want to assist you in any way I can in making the necessary arrangements to do so. Mark Harmine, my secretary, uses the ALL Child Care Center in the building next to ours. He said they are highly respected, and his child likes the Center very much. Mark checked and found they have openings for additional children now.

Rebecca, please contact Mark if you would like further information on the ALL Child Care Center. It seems to be a good alternative for you.

Your terrific work is appreciated, and I hope you stay with the Word Processing Center for many years to come.

> This memo format uses 1-1/2 inches for the top margin and 1 inch for the side margins.
>
> Note that the headings are keyed flush at the left margin and their information lines start ten spaces in from that left margin.
>
> Businesspeople often use this format because it is easy to produce and it saves time.

Traditional Memo Format on Plain Paper

Valley National Sporting Goods

4764 Euclid Avenue
Cleveland, Ohio 44104-3728
216/555-0162

1 blank line

August 11, 19—   **If on plain paper: line 10**

3 blank lines

Accounting Department
1 blank line
NEW LINE OF PRODUCTS
1 blank line
Many new products have been developed for our customers since we signed members of our city's winning baseball team as spokespersons. We have completed the data on producing these new items, such as the new line of sportswear that will be offered, and the costs have been determined.

Until they are entered on the mainframe system, however, each of you will have to work from lists prepared manually. We will be sending those figures to you as soon as we have the lists prepared.
3 blank lines

Tien Cheng-Wright

Tien Cheng-Wright

wb

> The use of personal computers and word processors has made this format increasingly popular.
>
> You can prepare this style of memo on either letterhead stationery or on plain paper.

Simplified Memo Format on Letterhead

Arthaus American Furniture
1710 Eudy Drive
Vicksburg, Mississippi 39180-9512
[601] 555-0164

December 11, 19—

3 blank lines

Mr. Thomas Underhill, Production Manager
Oak Works Company, Inc.
856 War Road
Vicksburg, MS 39180-6296

1 blank line

Dear Mr. Underhill

1 blank line

The good news is that Arthaus American Furniture has decided to approve the proposal submitted by Oak Works Company for supplying our dining room furniture for the coming year.

1 blank line

The purchase order agreement for your account is enclosed. Take a moment to read through it so that confusion does not occur later. Please call me if you have any questions concerning the agreement. In accordance with your request, I am having a copy of this agreement sent to Brad Powell.

The delivery schedules presented in your proposal were very impressive. The specifications that your proposal listed were well within the quality standards that we sought, and that was, by far, the deciding factor in your company's winning the bid.

You can be sure that we here at Arthaus American Furniture are pleased to have Oak Works as our supplier for this important part of our line. We have always been able to provide our customers with very high quality merchandise. All that we have learned about your organization has convinced us that working with Oak Works will help us maintain this level of quality.

1 blank line

Sincerely

3 blank lines

Raquel Sandoval

Raquel Sandoval
President

1 blank line

Enc.

1 blank line

c Brad Powell

1 blank line

tl

Notice that this letter models the block format style (all lines starting at the left margin) and open punctuation (no colon after the salutation and no comma after the complimentary close).

Letter in Block Format, Open Punctuation

Broadwerth Realty
839 Powder Circle
Lexington, Virginia 24450-3223
804/555-0172

January 11, 19—

3 blank lines

Ms. Sara Murphy
1270 Snowy Lane
Lexington, Virginia 24419-8752

1 blank line

Dear Ms. Murphy:

1 blank line

Thank you for recommending Broadwerth Realty to Mr. Harold Barnett.
You can be sure that we are doing our best to locate a home for Mr. Barnett
in which he will be comfortable and proud to live.

Mr. Barnett is a welcome addition to our community. You must be most
pleased to have hired a person of such caliber.

Sara, your confidence in Broadwerth Realty is appreciated. We welcome
seeing any clients that you can send us and will do everything we can to
locate a residence which is right for them.

1 blank line

Sincerely,

3 blank lines

Robert Broadwerth
President

1 blank line

tl

> Notice that this letter models the modified block
> format style (all lines begin at the left margin
> except for the dateline, complimentary close, and
> writer's name and title, which start at the center)
> and mixed punctuation.
>
> Since this is a short letter, the side margins were
> set at 1-1/2 inches.

Letter in Modified Block Format, Mixed Punctuation

D. H. Lowell Publishing Company
145 Rocky Lane
Stillwater, Oklahoma 74074-5557
(918) 555-0165

October 24, 19—

3 blank lines

Nathan Sauls
Queensport Editorial Services
975 Langdon Drive
Stillwater, OK 74074-4759

1 blank line

SCHEDULE FOR THE LAST OF THE PAGE PROOF

1 blank line

Thank you, Nathan, for your close contact with Carol Davidson while Anna Spence is on vacation. You know that this project is very complex and demanding. Cooperation between Carol and you will help in many ways.

It looks as though the challenges that Queensport Editorial is experiencing completing its stage in this project, nonetheless, have dropped us approximately five weeks behind our schedule.

Although you and Carol are working on resolving these difficulties, my concern remains as to how the end dates in our schedule will be met. Please provide Carol with what Queensport Editorial would consider a realistic schedule showing how we can catch up to where we will need to be in December.

Your attention to the details of this project are appreciated, Nathan. I am aware, of course, that challenges such as this occur in spite of all precautions. I am confident, however, that Queensport Editorial will be able to help us successfully work through this situation.

Patrick Sheng   *3 blank lines*

Patrick Sheng, Senior Production Editor

1 blank line

c Carol Davidson

1 blank line

mk

> The salutation and complimentary close are omitted in this letter since it is using the simplified block format style. Note how the adressee's name is used to personalize the message.
>
> This letter style is considered modern and time-saving.

Letter in Simplified Block Format

PROOFREADER'S MARKS

Symbol		Marked Copy	Corrected Copy
‖	Align	‖ $298,000 ‖ $298,000	$298,000 $298,000
∿	Bold	meaning of the message	**meaning** of the message
≡	Capitalize	bobby Johnson	Bobby Johnson
___	Change copy as shown	criteria ~~was~~ *were*	criteria were
∪	Close up space	con cise	concise
ℐ	Delete	happpy	happy
DS	Double space	Call me soon. DS Sincerely,	Call me soon. Sincerely,
∧	Insert	Make copy. *a*	Make a copy.
#	Insert space	alot of examples	a lot of examples
italic	Italicize or underline	The Sacramento Bee	The Sacramento Bee or *The Sacramento Bee*
stet	Ignore correction	~~effective~~ writer	effective writer
lc /	Lowercase	Sincerely Yours	Sincerely yours,
[ ] ⊏	Move in direction of bracket	Mr. Tony Smith 747 Oak Street Placerville, CA	Mr. Tony Smith 747 Oak Street Placerville, CA

Symbol	Marked Copy	Corrected Copy
No⁋ No paragraph	**No⁋** When expressing	When expressing
⁋ Paragraph	**⁋** In conclusion	In conclusion
ss Single space	Mr. Ron Pickard **ss** 590 Arizona Street	Mr. Pickard 590 Arizona Street
(sp) Spell out	7902 E. Oak Avenue **(sp)**	7902 East Oak Avenue
∼ Transpose	reclieve	receive
◯ Move as shown	to (completely) finish	to finish completely
⋀⋀ Remove bold face	**is not a factor**	is **not** a factor
⊬⊬⊬ Remove underscore	The Jungle by Stover	The Jungle by Stover
ts Triple space	in the selection. **ts** DELIVERY CAPABILITY	in the selection. DELIVERY CAPABILITY
——— Use initial capital only	A REMINGTON BRONZE	a Remington bronze

GLOSSARY

abbreviation A shortened form of a word or a group of words.

abridged dictionary A dictionary that contains nearly as many words but not as much information as an unabridged dictionary.

absolute adjective An adjective that cannot be compared because it is already at the maximum level of its potential.

acknowledgment A message telling a person that his or her message has been received.

acronym A special type of abbreviation that is a pronounceable word formed from the first letter or letters of a series of words.

action verb A verb that can take a direct object or an indirect object and helps to create lively, effective sentences.

active listening A type of listening that requires concentrated hearing and focusing to enhance understanding and memory.

active voice Verb voice that indicates the subject of a sentence is doing the action.

adjective A word that describes a noun (person, place, or thing).

adjustment A decision that is a positive settlement to a claim.

adverb A word that modifies an action verb, an adjective, or another adverb.

agenda A document that contains the order of business for a meeting.

analytical graphics software Computer programs that convert numbers, which may originate from a spreadsheet or database, into meaningful charts and graphs.

analytical reports Reports written to analyze a problem. These reports include interpretation of the facts as well as conclusions and recommendations.

antecedent A noun to which a pronoun refers.

antonyms Words that have the opposite meaning.

apostrophe A punctuation mark used to indicate the omission of a letter or number in a contraction; possession in nouns and indefinite pronouns, time, and money; and plurals of lowercase letters.

appendix A section of a formal report that contains material related to the report but too long to be included in the body.

application form A standardized data sheet that a company uses to compare qualifications of different job applicants.

application software A set of instructions for a computer that describes how to perform particular functions.

appositive A noun or pronoun that renames another noun or pronoun that immediately precedes it.

article The words *the*, *a*, or *an*, which act as adjectives.

attention line The part of the letter address that directs the correspondence to a particular person when the letter is addressed to an organization.

audioconference   A long-distance telephone conference call that involves two or more people.

bad news letter   A message in letter format that conveys news that will disappoint the receiver.

bar graph   A graph in which bars are used to compare the sizes of items and to show changes in items over time.

bibliography   A list of sources used in preparing a report, shown in alphabetic order by authors' names.

block format   Letter format in which all lines begin at the left margin.

body   The part of a message that contains its main idea and supporting information.

briefing   A short presentation usually given at a meeting or conference to bring people up to date on business activities, projects, programs, or procedures.

business communication   Communication that occurs within the business environment.

casual listening   A type of listening that requires some hearing and focusing; however, understanding and remembering are only somewhat important.

central processing unit (CPU)   A device that contains electronic computer chips that control the operating functions of a workstation.

claim   A special type of request in which a customer asks for a refund, exchange, or discount.

clause   A group of words that contains a subject and a predicate.

coherent paragraph   A set of sentences arranged in logical order in either a direct or an indirect pattern.

collection letter   A letter designed to motivate the receiver to pay his or her past-due bill.

colon   A punctuation mark that directs the reader's attention to the material following it.

common noun   A noun that identifies a person, place, or thing in a general way.

communication   The process used to send, receive, and interpret messages.

communication overload   A mental condition or attitude that occurs when people receive too many messages and, as a result, disregard or inaccurately interpret the messages.

communication software   Computer programs that enable a computer with a modem to send and receive messages over telephone lines.

comparison   A change in form and degree of an adjective that clarifies associations.

complete predicate   Everything in a sentence said by, to, or about the subject, including the main verb of the sentence.

complete subject   The simple subject plus all the sentence that is not part of the complete predicate.

complex sentence   A statement or question that contains one independent clause and one or more dependent clauses.

complimentary close   The formal closing of a letter, which follows the body.

compound adjective   Two or more hyphenated words that precede and modify a noun.

compound antecedent   An antecedent that consists of two or more elements.

compound noun   One noun composed of two or more words.

compound predicate   Two or more verbs with the same subject that are connected by conjunctions.

compound sentence   A statement or question that contains two or more related independent clauses.

compound subject   Two or more simple subjects joined by conjunctions.

compound-complex sentence   A sentence that contains two or more independent clauses and at least one dependent clause.

conclusion   An opinion based on interpretation of data.

concrete words   Specific and precise words.

condition linking verb   A verb that does not need an object or indirect object and that refers to a condition or appeals to the senses.

conjunction   A word that joins two or more sentence parts.

conjunctive adverb   A transitional word that joins two independent but related clauses.

considerate messages   Messages that address the receiver's level of interest, involvement, knowledge, or opinions about a subject.

consonant   All letters except vowels.

coordinate conjunction   A word that joins words, phrases, and clauses of equal grammatical rank, such as *for, and, nor, but, or,* and *yet.*

copy notation   An indication that someone besides the addressee is to receive a copy of a message.

correlative conjunction   Word used in pairs that connect words, phrases, and clauses of equal grammatical rank, such as *not only . . . but also, either . . . or, neither . . . nor.*

courteous request   A polite way to ask for action from the receiver.

courteous words   Polite, considerate, positive, and bias-free words that address the receiver by the proper title.

dash   A punctuation mark used with nonessential elements, before a summarizing statement, with a sudden change of thought, and before a detailed listing.

database management software   Computer programs that provide a way to store and retrieve information electronically.

dateline   The line in a written communication that shows the date of the message.

declarative sentence   A sentence that makes a statement.

degree   A name given to the positive, comparative, or superlative form of an adjective or adverb.

demonstrative pronoun   A pronoun such as *this, these, that,* and *those* that points to a specific person, place, or thing in a given sentence or answers *where.*

dependent clause   A clause that cannot stand alone as a complete sentence.

desktop publishing software   Computer programs that enable production of documents of typeset quality with a personal computer and high-quality printer.

dictionary   A book containing the words of a language, arranged in alphabetical order, as well as definitions and other information.

direct address   A reader's name that is mentioned in the beginning, middle, or end of a sentence.

direct object   A noun or pronoun directly affected by the action of a transitive verb.

direct paragraph   A paragraph in which the first sentence is the topic sentence.

discussion outline   An outline that provides detailed information about the topics and the subtopics.

document analysis software   Computer programs, sometimes called style checkers, that enable users to detect possible errors in grammar, punctuation, and spelling, as well as violations of effective writing principles.

double comparison   The use of two forms of comparative degree adjectives (or superlative degree adjectives) to describe a noun.

editing   The process of reviewing and revising a piece of writing to improve it grammatically and stylistically.

electronic mail (e-mail)   Written messages transmitted on a computer or a fax.

electronic workstation   Pieces of electronic equipment—usually a keyboard, a monitor or display screen, a printer, a logic or central processing unit, and a storage device—that enable computerized work to be performed.

enclosure notation   An indication that an additional item is included with a document.

equal grammatical rank   Elements in a sentence that are joined by a coordinate or correlative conjunction and are the same part of speech.

exclamation point   A punctuation mark that follows a word, a group of words, or a sentence that shows strong emotion.

executive summary   A brief overview of a formal report, sometimes called a *synopsis* or an *abstract*.

expletive   A word such as *there*, *it*, or *here* that is used to invert a sentence.

external barriers   Conditions that exist outside the receiver and/or the sender and detract from the communication process.

external communication   A message sent to receivers outside the organization.

facsimile (fax)   An electronic device that can send exact copies of documents, blueprints, drawings, or pictures.

feedback   The response to a message sent by the receiver.

flexible diskette   A removable storage medium that can store at least 260 pages.

formal communication   A message sent along established lines of authority.

formal reports   Reports that are long, analytical, and impersonal.

functional order   An order used in resumes that presents accomplishments or skills in order of their importance, showing the most important or impressive first.

future perfect tense verb   A verb form that indicates action that will be completed at a specific point in the future.

future tense verb   A verb form that expresses an action or condition yet to come.

gerund   A verb form that ends in *-ing* and serves as a noun.

good news letter   A message in letter format that contains good news for the receiver.

goodwill   The favorable reputation that a person or a business has with its customers.

goodwill letter   A friendship letter designed to build the receiver's goodwill toward the sender.

group decision support systems (GDSS) Computer programs that try to improve group performance or that enhance the computer's tremendous calculating capacity.

hard disk   A large-capacity storage medium usually built into the computer.

hyphen   A punctuation mark used in word division, in forming compound hyphenated words, and after some prefixes.

hypothesis   A statement that contains a possible cause or explanation of a problem.

image scanner   An electronic device that reads graphs, charts, or photographs and integrates them into documents.

indefinite pronoun   A pronoun such as *one* or *each* that refers in general terms to people, places, or things.

independent clause   A clause that can stand alone as a complete sentence.

indirect object   A noun or pronoun that receives a transitive verb's action.

indirect paragraph   A paragraph in which the topic sentence is at the middle or end.

indirect question   A sentence that contains a reference to a question but is actually a statement.

infinitive   A verb form consisting of a present tense verb preceded by the word *to*.

infinitive phrase   A group of words formed with an infinitive plus any modifiers the infinitive may have.

informal communication   A message sent along unrelated, established lines of authority.

informal reports   Reports that are shorter than

formal reports and are written in a less formal style.

informational reports   Reports written to present information (facts) and little analysis.

initial   The first letter used in a person's first or middle name.

integrated software   Computer programs that contain several types of computer programs such as word processing, spreadsheets, database, graphics, and communication software and can merge the products of each type of program.

intensive pronoun   A compound pronoun form created by joining a pronoun with *self* or *selves* that provides emphasis in a sentence.

interjection   A word or expression such as *No!* and *Help!* that has no grammatical relationship with other words in a sentence and is used to express strong emotion.

internal barriers   Conditions that exist within the receiver and/or the sender that impair the sender's willingness and ability to express messages and the receiver's ability to interpret them.

internal communication   A message sent to receivers within the organization.

interrogative pronoun   A pronoun such as *which* or *what* that begins a question that leads to a noun response.

intransitive verb   A verb that does not need an object to complete the meaning of a sentence.

irregular adjective   An adjective that does not form its comparison by adding *-er* or *more* or adding *-est* or *most*.

irregular noun   A noun that does not form its plural by adding *s* or *es*.

irregular plural noun   A plural noun that does not end in *s*.

irregular verb   A verb that has an irregular construction of its past and past participle forms.

irrelevant information   Words or phrases that are not necessary for understanding the main idea of a message.

job objective   A brief statement on a resume that describes the type of position for which an applicant is applying.

keyboard   An input device that has alphabetic, numeric, and functional keys that people can use to perform functions such as formatting or editing.

letter   A format used for external documents written to business associates, customers, or clients.

letter address   The part of a letter that shows the complete name and address of the receiver.

letter of transmittal   A document that transmits a formal report to the reader.

letterhead stationery   Paper that includes the printed company name, address, telephone number, and logo.

line graph   A graph that uses lines to show changes in a quantity or value over time.

listening   The process that requires hearing and focusing attention to achieve understanding and remembering.

local area network (LAN)   A group of connected workstations within a building or in nearby buildings.

machine dictation   A process in which the originator speaks into a microphone or telephone and the message is recorded onto a magnetic medium.

main idea   The central theme or most important thought contained in a message.

memorandums (memos)   A format used for written messages sent to others in the same organization.

message   A set of symbols that represent meaning.

microform   A medium used to store reduced images of paper documents or other data.

mild command   A stern request from the writer to the reader.

minutes   The official record of the proceedings of a meeting.

mixed punctuation   A style of punctuation used in letters in which a colon follows the salutation, and a comma follows the complimentary close.

modem   A device that converts computer signals into signals that can be transmitted over telephone lines.

modified block format   Letter format in which all lines begin at the left margin except for the dateline, the complimentary close, and the writer's name and title, which begin at the center.

modifier   A word that limits, describes, or defines.

modify   A verb that means to limit, describe, or define.

mouse   A device that enables quick and efficient movement on a computer screen.

news release   A brief announcement sent to newspapers, magazines, and other media to communicate information of interest to people outside the organization.

nominative case pronoun   A pronoun, also called a *subjective* pronoun, used as a subject or a predicate nominative.

nonessential element   An interrupting expression, nonrestrictive element, or appositive that is included in a sentence.

nonrestrictive phrase or clause   A phrase or clause that adds information that is not essential to the meaning of a sentence.

nonverbal symbols   Signs other than words that provide meaning to a message, such as gestures, posture, facial expressions, appearance, time, tone of voice, eye contact, and space.

noun   A word that names a person, place, or thing.

object of the preposition   The noun or noun substitute that ends a prepositional phrase.

objective   The purpose a message seeks to achieve.

objective case pronoun   A pronoun used as a direct or indirect object of a transitive verb and as an object of a preposition.

open punctuation   A style of punctuation used in letters in which no punctuation appears after the salutation or the complimentary close.

optical disk technology   An electronic device that enables a document to be scanned into the computer, viewed on a screen, indexed for accurate retrieval, and stored on a disk.

oral communication   Messages that use speaking and listening to convey meaning.

paragraph   A block of text containing one or more sentences that express one idea in a message.

paragraph unity   Sentences in a paragraph used to express one clear idea.

paralanguage   The nonverbal symbols that accompany a verbal message and reveal the difference between what is said and how it is said.

paraphrase   The process of modifying the words of material taken from another source.

parenthesis   A punctuation mark used in pairs to set off nonessential elements.

passive voice   Verb voice that indicates the subject of a sentence is receiving the action.

past perfect tense verb   A verb form that indicates an action that began in the past and continued to the more recent past when it was completed.

past tense verb   A verb form that expresses an action that was recently completed.

perfect tense verb   A verb form that describes the action of the main verb in relation to a specific time period, either present, past, or future.

period   A punctuation mark used at the end of sentences and abbreviations and after numbers or letters in enumerations.

personal computer/microcomputer   A common computer that can handle many different applications with a simple change of software.

personal pronoun   A pronoun that refers to people, places, or things.

phrase   A group of words that has no subject or predicate.

pie chart   A chart that shows how the parts of a whole are distributed and how the parts interrelate.

plagiarism   The act of presenting another person's ideas or writing as one's own.

plural noun form   A noun that represents two or more persons, places, or things.

plural possessive noun form   A noun that indicates ownership by two or more persons, places, or things.

pocket dictionary A small dictionary.

polite words Words that show appreciation for the receiver.

portfolio A folder, notebook, or small briefcase containing samples of work, academic transcripts, letters of recommendation, and other items.

possessive case pronoun A pronoun that indicates ownership or possession.

postscript A sentence or paragraph at the end of a letter that reinforces the message in the body.

precise words Words that give the exact and specific meaning.

predicate Everything in a sentence said by, to, or about the subject.

predicate nominative A noun or pronoun that refers to the subject and follows a form of the verb *to be*.

preliminary parts The first parts of a formal report, which provide information about the report body.

preposition A word that usually indicates direction, position, or time and is linked to a noun or noun substitute to form a phrase.

prepositional phrase A group of words that begins with a preposition and ends with a noun or noun substitute.

present perfect tense verb A verb form that indicates continuous action from the past to the present.

present tense verb A verb form that expresses present action.

presentation graphics software Computer programs that convert pictures, data, or numbers into visual aids for oral presentations.

primary research The act of gathering fresh data.

printer A machine that produces a printed copy.

pronoun A word that is a short, convenient substitute for a noun.

proofreading The process of reviewing and correcting the final draft of a message.

proper adjective A proper noun that precedes and modifies another noun.

proper noun A noun that names a specific person, place, or thing.

proposal An analysis of a problem and a recommendation for a solution.

qualifications Skills, abilities, and accomplishments that make people qualified for certain jobs.

question mark A punctuation mark used after a direct question or a series of questions.

quotation mark A punctuation mark used in pairs to set off a direct quotation, a definition, nonstandard English, a word used in an unusual way, or a title.

receiver The person or machine that receives a message.

recommendation A suggestion of a course of action.

reference initials Initials of the person who keyed a document.

reflexive pronoun A compound pronoun form that ends in *self* or *selves* and refers to a noun or pronoun that appears earlier in a sentence.

regular verb A verb that expresses its past and past participle forms by adding *ed* to its present form.

relative pronoun   A pronoun such as *who, whom,* or *which* that begins a dependent clause and relates to a person, place, or thing that appears earlier in a sentence.

report   A format used to send meaningful information to a group of people, such as research studies or proposals for top management.

restrictive phrase or clause   A phrase or clause that is essential to the meaning of a sentence.

resume   A document that summarizes an applicant's qualifications for employment.

reverse chronological order   The organization of a resume that presents the applicant's most recent work experience first, followed in reverse order by jobs held earlier.

revise   A verb that means to change or modify.

routine letter   A letter that makes no demands the receiver might view as a burden and that does not need to persuade the receiver to do something.

routine request   A request for action that the receiver will perform willingly.

sales letter   A letter that tries to persuade a receiver to purchase a product or service.

salutation   The part of a letter that acts as the greeting to the receiver.

scanner   An electronic device that converts printed text into digital form that another electronic workstation such as a computer or word processor can read.

scope   The boundaries that define what a report will include and will exclude.

screen   A device that displays material as it is keyboarded or recalled.

secondary research   The data that already has been gathered and reported.

semicolon   A punctuation mark used to denote a pause that is stronger than a comma but weaker than a period.

sender   The person or thing that originates a message and initiates the communication process.

sentence   A group of words that contains a subject and a predicate and expresses a complete thought.

sentence unity   The ability of a sentence to express one clear thought.

simple predicate   A verb that is a complete predicate.

simple sentence   A sentence that contains one independent clause and may contain phrases and compound subjects or verbs.

simple subject   The main word in the complete subject that specifically names what the sentence is about.

simplified block format   Letter format that omits the salutation and complimentary close.

singular noun form   A noun that refers to only one person, place, or thing.

singular possessive noun form   A noun that indicates ownership by one person, place, or thing.

soft sale   An attempt to sell a product or service that is not too strong or pushy.

solicited letter of application   A letter of application written to apply for a specific job opening that has been advertised or announced.

solicited persuasive message   A persuasive message requested by the receiver.

spreadsheet software   Computer programs that store data in rows and columns and allow mathematical manipulation of the stored data.

state-of-being linking verb   A verb, frequently called the verb *to be*, that does not take an object or indirect object.

statement   A sentence that states a fact.

style manual   A set of guidelines used for formatting documents to help writers plan appropriate margins, spacing, headings, and other details.

subject   A word or group of words that represents the person speaking, the person spoken to, or the person, place, or thing spoken about.

subject line   The part of a letter that contains the topic of the letter.

subordinate conjunction   A word such as *when, unless,* and *while* that is used to join elements of unequal grammatical rank and primarily to connect dependent clauses with independent clauses.

supplementary parts   The parts of a report that provide additional information and follow the report, such as a bibliography or an appendix.

supporting information   Essential facts that explain, reinforce, or justify the main idea.

synonyms   Words that have the same meaning.

table   A visual aid in which data is arranged into columns and rows.

table of contents   A listing that contains the contents of long documents such as a report, book, or magazine.

teleconference   A conference that uses the telephone or other media to allow two or more persons to communicate.

thesaurus   A book of words classified by meaning that contains synonyms and antonyms.

title page   The page of a report that shows the report title; the name, title, and organization of the person for whom the report was written; the writer's name, title, and organization; and the date the report is submitted.

topical outline   An outline in which the headings describe in a few words the topics investigated.

topics   The subjects discussed in a message.

transition   A word or phrase that connects sentences within paragraphs and connects paragraphs in business messages.

transitive verb   A verb that denotes action and requires an object.

unabridged dictionary   A dictionary contained in several volumes and that holds the most information about words.

underscore   A punctuation mark, also called an *underline*, that is used instead of italics to call attention to a word or expression.

unsolicited letter of application   A letter of application written to apply for a position that has not been advertised or announced and that may or may not be open.

unsolicited persuasive message   A persuasive message the receiver has not requested.

verb   A word that indicates an action, condition, or state of being.

verb phrase   A group of words that functions as one verb.

verb tense   A form of a verb that indicates time, such as present, past, and future.

verbal symbols   Words used when speaking or writing.

videoconference   A conference using telephone lines to transmit voices, images, and data so that conference members can see as well as hear each other.

visual aids Graphics such as charts, graphs, tables, and illustrations that help the reader understand and interpret information.

voice A verb form that indicates if the subject is performing the action or receiving the action of a verb.

voice mail Oral messages sent over the telephone but stored electronically in a computer for playback.

voice recognition technology The application of electronics that enables a speaker to reproduce his or her words on a computer screen.

vowel The letters *a, e, i, o,* and *u.*

wide area network (WAN) A group of workstations or computers connected in a nationwide or worldwide system.

word/information processing The steps used in moving information from origination to storage.

word-processing software Computer programs that enable the user to enter, format, revise, and print text efficiently.

ANSWERS TO CHECKPOINTS

Chapter 1

Checkpoint 1 *The Purposes and Process of Communication*

1. To select appropriate symbols
2. To interpret the symbols correctly
3. a. To share information and to build goodwill
   b. To build self-esteem and to build goodwill
   c. To persuade and to share information

Checkpoint 2 *Forms of Communication*

1. Lateral, internal, oral
2. Downward, internal, and written (possibly electronic)
3. Upward, internal, and oral
4. Lateral, external, and written (possibly electronic)
5. Upward, internal, and written (possibly electronic)

Chapter 2

Checkpoint 1 *Origination and Production of Documents*

1. g
2. e
3. d
4. a
5. b
6. c
7. f

Checkpoint 2 *Sending and Storing Documents*

1. e
2. a
3. f
4. c
5. b
6. d

Chapter 3

Checkpoint 1 *Nouns, Pronouns, and Verbs*

1. N
2. V
3. P
4. V
5. N
6. V
7. P
8. N

Checkpoint 2 *Adjectives and Adverbs*

1. An expert investment
2. a solid, excellent
3. An informative
4. progressive management
5. quickly
6. patiently
7. eagerly, seriously
8. very, only

Checkpoint 3 *Prepositions, Conjunctions, and Interjections*

1. I
2. PP
3. C
4. PP
5. PP
6. PP
7. C

Checkpoint 4 *Subjects and Predicates*

1. The Budget Committee
2. I
3. The panel
4. I
5. will receive a copy of the signed contract
6. are considering transfers to our new office
7. has been our supplier for years
8. used to audit our books

Checkpoint 5 *Clauses and Phrases*

1. PP	5. IP
2. DC	6. VP
3. PP	7. DC
4. IP	8. IC

Chapter 4

Checkpoint 1 *Proper and Common Nouns*

A. Students' lists will vary.
B.
1. clerks (CN), Silverman Building (PN)
2. terminal (CN), cable (CN), computer (CN)
3. photographer (CN), Amy Cordova (PN), proofs (CN), department (CN)
4. Star Industries (PN), products (CN), companies (CN), Tennessee (PN)
5. Fred Ausiello (PN), layouts (CN), president (CN), company (CN)
6. judge (CN), retirement (CN), September (PN)

Checkpoint 2 *Noun Forms*

1. four
2. singular
3. plural, singular possessive, and plural possessive
4. s
5. ' (the apostrophe)

Checkpoint 3 *Noun Plurals*

1. add *s*
2. adding *es*
3. adding *s*
4. changing the *y* to *i* and then adding *es*
5. banks
6. lunches
7. inventories
8. Kennedys

Checkpoint 4 *Special Plural Noun Forms*

1. bulletin boards
2. women
3. vice-presidents
4. the Misses DeGroat or the Miss DeGroats
5. the Williamsons
6. floppy disks
7. the Messrs. Ramirez or the Mr. Ramirezes
8. mottoes

Checkpoint 5 *Forming Possessive Nouns*

1. factory's
2. Cathy Ruiz's
3. children's
4. committees'
5. sales representatives'
6. nurses'
7. committee's
8. Personnel Department's

Checkpoint 6 *Identifying Correct Noun Forms*

1. managers (P)	5. memos (P)
2. supervisor's (SP)	6. president's (SP)
3. divisions' (PP)	7. Kleins' (PP)
4. memo's (SP)	

Chapter 5

Checkpoint 1 *Personal Pronouns*

1. I	5. I
2. me	6. He
3. him	7. them
4. They	

Checkpoint 2 *Possessive Case*

1. your	5. his, hers
2. It's, their	6. You're
3. His, our	7. ours
4. Their	

Checkpoint 3 *Who and Whom*

1. whom
2. Whoever
3. whom
4. whom
5. who
6. whomever
7. who

Checkpoint 4 *Selecting Pronouns*

1. yourselves
2. yourself
3. he
4. her
5. he
6. they
7. We

Checkpoint 5 *Identifying Correct Pronouns*

1. me
2. himself
3. I
4. herself
5. themselves
6. I
7. ourselves

Chapter 6

Checkpoint 1 *Agreement of Pronouns With Antecedents*

1. his
2. their
3. their
4. their
5. they
6. his or her
7. his or her

Checkpoint 2 *Indefinite Pronoun Agreement*

1. their
2. his or her
3. his or her
4. his or her
5. his or her
6. it

Checkpoint 3 *Relative Pronouns*

1. whom
2. who
3. whose
4. that
5. who
6. that
7. who

Checkpoint 4 *Demonstrative Pronouns*

1. These
2. Those
3. That
4. This
5. Those
6. those
7. This

Checkpoint 5 *Clear Pronoun Preference*

1. expert advice
2. Ms. Johnson is
3. the statement's issuance
4. the coaches
5. studying
6. the clients
7. accurate pronoun selection

Chapter 7

Checkpoint 1 *Verb Phrases*

1. has spent
2. was elected
3. was taking
4. might have been driving
5. had left
6. should have thought
7. have had

Checkpoint 2 *Verb Tenses*

1. will have visited
2. have
3. will have completed
4. OK
5. OK
6. do
7. will complete

Checkpoint 3 *Regular and Irregular Verbs*

1. held
2. has operated
3. goes

4. had flown
5. launder
6. have eaten
7. are calculating

Checkpoint 4   *Active and Passive Voice*

1. Julie painted . . .
2. The Company owners will increase . . .
3. The students took . . .
4. The creditor did not receive . . .
5. The copy center printed . . .
6. Mai gave . . .
7. Many French citizens ran . . .

Checkpoint 5   *Troublesome Verbs*

1. Set
2. sit
3. lie
4. lay
5. May
6. rise
7. Can

Chapter 8

Checkpoint 1   *Subjects and Predicates*

1. mother-in-law and father-in-law
2. suitcase
3. executive
4. Lloyd and Betty
5. have sung
6. has been redecorated
7. shopped, cooked, and set

Checkpoint 2   *Subject–Verb Agreement*

1. is having
2. are scheduled
3. are
4. is
5. is
6. are
7. are

Checkpoint 3   *A Number, The Number, Companies, Amounts*

1. were
2. prints
3. is
4. increases
5. is
6. is
7. is

Checkpoint 4   *Subject–Verb Agreement with And*

1. is enjoying
2. is covered
3. are
4. hopes
5. has been sent
6. are
7. is

Checkpoint 5   *Subject–Verb Agreement With Or/Not*

1. is
2. are
3. is
4. is
5. was
6. draws
7. has been

Chapter 9

Checkpoint 1   *Articles and Other Adjectives*

1. The tall Christmas, Gayle's colorful glass
2. a motivated
3. these three homework
4. Good, good, administrative
5. The new, tinted glass, a manual high-powered
6. The, Ms. Ortiz's consumer, four local
7. This Northern Italian, college-age, all

Checkpoint 2   *Comparison of Regular Adjectives*

1. Their, the largest (S), most beautiful (S), the
2. the kinder (C), your two, our
3. The antique, the most knowledgeable (S), the, the
4. the taller (C), the two new modern
5. A quick-witted, this
6. That, a better (C) British, the, the other, the
7. the latest (S), the most effective (S)

Checkpoint 3   *Helpful Guidelines and Irregular Adjectives*

1. most efficient
2. more nervous
3. worse
4. more reasonable
5. sweetest
6. better
7. cleaner

Checkpoint 4   *Double Comparisons and Absolute Adjectives*

1. more nearly immaculate
2. most nearly unique
3. quickest
4. more intense
5. less funny
6. hardest
7. more nearly round

Checkpoint 5   *More Adjective Pitfalls*

1. That, the handier, the
2. This maintenance
3. The manufacturing, fewer, less
4. My, best, my, the
5. more, any other

6. That surprise, a, a hot-air balloon
7. This, less, the original

Chapter 10

Checkpoint 1   *Action Verbs and Nouns Used as Adverbs*

1. beautifully—How?
2. Tuesday—When?
3. there—Where?
4. yesterday—When?
5. twice—How often?
6. very—To what extent? forcefully—How?
7. soon—When?

Checkpoint 2   *Adverbs as Modifiers*

1. very (soon) soon (will leave)
2. exceptionally (are concerned)
3. not (happy)—too (not happy)
4. not (right)—quite (not right)
5. extremely (quickly) quickly (to think)
6. here (to meet) tomorrow (to meet)
7. always (had visited)

Checkpoint 3   *Adverbs and Comparisons*

1. fast
2. later
3. more friendly
4. very carefully
5. most efficiently
6. earliest
7. quickly

Checkpoint 4   *Adverb Pitfalls*

1. real
2. bad
3. that
4. not
5. really
6. badly
7. where

Checkpoint 5 *More Adverb Pitfalls*

1. really good
2. good
3. Surely
4. well
5. really well
6. surely
7. bad

Chapter 11

Checkpoint 1 *Prepositional Phrases*

(The word that the phrase modifies is in parentheses.)

1. without empathy (acted) (ADV)
2. to your favorite charity (donation) (ADJ)
3. until tomorrow (call) (ADV)
4. on break (had gone) (ADV)
5. between the two new computers (Place) (ADV)
6. around the corner (store) (ADJ)
7. behind my desk (cabinet) (ADJ)

Checkpoint 2 *Troublesome Prepositions*

1. *beside* instead of *besides*
2. *among* instead of *between*
3. *Besides* instead of *Beside*
4. *in* instead of *into*
5. *between* instead of *among*
6. *Besides* instead of *Beside*
7. *Among* instead of *Between*

Checkpoint 3 *Additional Troublesome Prepositions*

1. As regards
2. Like
3. over
4. With regard to
5. As
6. over
7. like

Checkpoint 4 *Selecting Prepositions*

1. studying
2. opposite of
3. like
4. off
5. going
6. opposite
7. like

Checkpoint 5 *Prepositions With Other Words*

1. identical with
2. agreed upon
3. part with
4. different from
5. to tour
6. angry with
7. discrepancy between

Chapter 12

Checkpoint 1 *Coordinate Conjunctions*

1. and
2. for
3. and
4. nor
5. but
6. or
7. yet

Checkpoint 2 *Correlative Conjunctions*

1. nor
2. but also
3. or
4. and
5. or
6. nor
7. but also

Checkpoint 3 *Subordinate Conjunctions*

1. while/after/before
2. and/after/when/since/before
3. if
4. after/when
5. If
6. after/as/because
7. because

Checkpoint 4   *Pitfalls*

1. Because
2. speedily
3. that
4. painting
5. Because
6. or
7. with accuracy

Chapter 13

Checkpoint 1   *Noun Plurals and Possesives*

1. employees
2. operator's
3. accountants
4. women's
5. actuaries
6. executives
7. managers'

Checkpoint 2   *Verb Form and Agreement*

1. had written/wrote
2. was taken
3. had grown/has grown/grew
4. had seen/saw
5. is providing
6. is joining
7. are

Checkpoint 3   *Agreement*

1. are impatiently awaiting
2. have started
3. were discarded
4. wrote/has written
5. Where are
6. Here are
7. Who are

Checkpoint 4   *Pronoun Selection and Agreement*

1. he or she
2. they
3. his or her
4. them
5. me
6. she
7. He

Chapter 14

Checkpoint 1   *Pronoun Selection*

1. me
2. she
3. him
4. them
5. they
6. her
7. he

Checkpoint 2   *Pronoun and Noun Possessives*

1. your helping
2. Dave's writing
3. Rose's printing
4. Gerald's speaking
5. its trademark
6. theirs
7. Your check

Checkpoint 3   *Adjectives and* Good *and* Well

1. well
2. good
3. well
4. those
5. Those
6. This
7. those

Checkpoint 4   *Were, Was, and Like*

1. as if he were
2. As I
3. like Carol
4. were a cat
5. I were a
6. if he were
7. as if he

Chapter 15

Checkpoint 1   *Using Periods*

1. mild command
2. courteous request
3. declarative sentence
4. indirect question
5. mild command

6. courteous request

7. indirect question

Checkpoint 2 *Periods and Question Marks*

1. .   5. .
2. .   6. .
3. ?   7. ?
4. ?

Checkpoint 3 *Selecting Punctuation*

1. ! !   5. .
2. ?   6. .
3. ! !   7. ?
4. .

Chapter 16

Checkpoint 1 *Introductory Elements and Compound Sentences*

1. no comma   5. Personally,
2. train,   6. no comma
3. Yes,   7. interested,
4. well,

Checkpoint 2 *Comma Usage*

1. winter,/schedule,
2. Kim,/newscaster,
3. no commas
4. scholarship, Maria,
5. modern, comfortable,
6. Road, Dayton, Ohio,
7. no commas

Checkpoint 3 *Identifying Comma Use*

1. in numbers
2. indicate omission of words
3. between adjectives
4. with an appositive
5. in a series
6. with direct address
7. with an interrupting expression

Checkpoint 4 *Clarity, Abbreviations, Repeated Words, and Direct Address*

1. before, no comma after *stated*
2. appearance, etc.,
3. big, big
4. 1,000
5. under,
6. hard, hard
7. sure, Dr. Thomas,

Checkpoint 5 *Comma Pitfalls*

1. suits and/case and
2. no comma
3. no comma
4. no comma
5. replace the comma with a semicolon or a period
6. no comma
7. James, the receptionist,

Chapter 17

Checkpoint 1 *Semicolons*

1. session;
2. April;
3. office;
4. insurance and
5. strangers;
6. interview;
7. States;

Checkpoint 2 *Interesting Semicolons*

1. restaurant;
2. Florida; Louisiana;
3. Meredith;
4. fund-raising;
5. consider;
6. me;
7. manager; Sara Chan; head;

Checkpoint 3 *Colons*

1. these:
2. 6:30/7:30
3. stated:
4. beautiful:
5. following:

Checkpoint 4 *Dashes*

1. maturity—
2. that—
3. patience—
4. graduates—/Jeffrey—
5. Flaherty—/Boise—
6. change—

Checkpoint 5 *Hyphens*

1. attorney-at-law
2. president-elect
3. cure-all
4. father-in-law
5. up-to-date
6. ex-president
7. self-made

Chapter 18

Checkpoint 1 *Inserting Punctuation*

1. "They/allowance,"/Meg./"He/it."
2. stated, "The/yelled, 'Leave/once!'"
3. remarked, "I/May."
4. "We believe,"/Charles, "that/co-ed."
5. "This/work"?
6. inquired, "Are/Kenya?"
7. exclaimed, "Bring/home!"

Checkpoint 2 *Quotation Marks*

1. "down/dumps."
2. "Software/Offices."
3. "You/Destiny"
4. "master chef"
5. "sight/eyes."
6. "Sunscreen/Children"
7. "I/Francisco"

Checkpoint 3 *Parentheses*

1. (one or the other)
2. (six)
3. (May issue of *Photography Digest*),
4. (girl's).
5. (the black sheep of our family)
6. (GM)
7. (pages 11–21)

Checkpoint 4 *Apostrophes and Underscores*

1. <u>shalom</u>
2. It's
3. <u>Newsweek</u>
4. can't
5. <u>Tips for Word Processors</u>
6. '93
7. Don't/we'll

Checkpoint 5 *Apostrophes*

1. years'
2. t's
3. company's/'94
4. th's
5. week's
6. dollar's
7. father-in-law's

Chapter 19

Checkpoint 1 *Abbreviations*

1. Mr.
2. Mrs.
3. Dr.
4. Esq.
5. CPA
6. doctor of veterinary medicine
7. Honorable

Checkpoint 2 *Addresses and States*

1. avenue
2. Boulevard, NW

3. Street, Road
4. Wyoming, West Virginia
5. LA
6. Puerto Rico
7. highway, hours

Checkpoint 3   *Applying Abbreviation Guidelines*

1. OK
2. organization
3. IBM
4. UPS
5. corporation
6. a.m.
7. CEO, company

Checkpoint 4   *Technical Communications and Acronyms*

1. company, manufacturing
2. paid, merchandise, month
3. pounds, ounces
4. EPCOT
5. Monday, Tuesday, a.m.
6. Friday, October
7. NASA's

Chapter 20

Checkpoint 1   *Capitalizing First Words*

1. I
2. their
3. Let
4. Sir, very truly
5. "When
6. "but
7. All

Checkpoint 2   *Capitalizing Titles*

1. the
2. The Creature
3. Dr.

4. mayor
5. President's
6. "A, for
7. **and**, "The Value of a Modem for All."

Checkpoint 3   *Capitalizing Proper Nouns*

1. Biology
2. Delaware River
3. Ugly Duckling
4. Mustang
5. brother's, Sean
6. Declaration of Independence, Holmes Junior High School
7. Paris, French

Checkpoint 4   *Capitalizing Names*

1. headache medicine
2. Cross pen and pencil set
3. south, bridge, recreational
4. reservation, Southwest
5. Tuesday's, labor negotiations
6. Thanksgiving
7. Winter Ice Carnival

Checkpoint 5   *Capitalizing Names*

1. building, Empire State Building, New York
2. Ph.D., Brandeis University
3. Chinese, Chinese
4. Catholic, Jewish, Protestant
5. Indian, African-American, Asian-American, Caucasian
6. Memorial Day
7. Spanish, Italian, German

Chapter 21

Checkpoint 1   *Ten and Under/Eleven and Over*

1. four
2. 16
3. two hundred

4. nine
5. 8
6. 57
7. twelve

Checkpoint 2 *To Begin Sentences and Express Dates*

1. Sixteen
2. Fifty
3. January 23, 1995
4. 1996
5. 4
6. either
7. 10th

Checkpoint 3 *Addresses and Money*

1. Seventh
2. One
3. 75th
4. $350
5. 89 cents
6. $1 million
7. $.25

Checkpoint 4 *Percentages, Decimals, Fractions, and Time*

1. two-thirds
2. ten o'clock
3. 11:30
4. Six and three-quarter
5. 0.1532
6. 2:00 p.m.
7. four

Checkpoint 5 *Miscellaneous Situations*

1. 10
2. two-thirds
3. 20, 20
4. 1
5. eighties
6. 135
7. Twenty-third

Chapter 22

Checkpoint 1 *Identify the Objective of a Message*

1. inform
2. persuade
3. request
4. record
5. inform

Checkpoint 2 *Determine the Main Idea, Choose Supporting Information, and Adjust the Message for the Receiver*

A. 1. c
   2. a
B. 1. a
   2. c
C. 2.

Checkpoint 3 *Organizing Messages*

1. Direct
2. Direct
3. Indirect
4. Indirect

Chapter 23

Checkpoint 1 *Courteous Words*

1. Please bring me the report.
2. Reverend Chang will conduct the session.
3. The attorney was an expert trial lawyer.
4. The professor has Lymes Disease.
5. People think, therefore they worry.

Checkpoint 2 *Correct Words*

1. Topek Motor Scooters get 30 miles a gallon.
2. Please ask Bill to reserve the hotel for our conference.
3. I do not know if I will apply for that job.
4. If we have to recall the product, compile a customer list.

5. Customers who place their orders by November 30 will receive a gift.

Checkpoint 3 *Dictionary and Thesaurus*

1. book, words, alphabetical, definitions.
2. historic or most frequently used
3. pocket, abridged, unabridged
4. words, meaning
5. synonyms, antonyms

Chapter 24

Checkpoint 1 *Unnecessary Sentence Elements*

1. Overall, in my opinion, by far, qualified, that is open.
2. that was painted a nice blue
3. The many helpful new, for work
4. Let it be known that I believe, which were recently reupholstered at great expense by the Save-A-Chair Company, that are in the cafeteria
5. that was

Checkpoint 2 *Conversational Tone*

1. All employees will receive a 5-percent raise as a reward for hard work.
2. Ms. Lewis wrote a memo to copywriters asking them to suggest names for the new dog food.
3. Please send me 30 pairs of red gloves for the Christmas season.
4. The correspondence contained errors.
5. Chien, the new sales manager, likes to play squash, ride unicycles, and fly light airplanes.

Checkpoint 3 *Concrete Sentences*

1. Describe how today's breakfast is better.
2. Eliminate *clearly*.
3. Describe what makes the brownies great.

4. Give the specific date, time, and place of arrival.
5. Clarify the word *good*.

Chapter 25

Checkpoint 1 *Complete Paragraphs*

1. False	4. True
2. True	5. True
3. False	

Checkpoint 2 *Clear Paragraphs*

A. The type of developmental paragraph is to provide specific facts or details or to provide an example.
B. (1) pronoun—this
   (2) key word—programs

Chapter 26

Checkpoint 1 *Editing Communications (Answers will vary)*

1. Welcome to the company; here is your pass to the cafeteria.
2. Your office equipment will be moved tomorrow at (time).
3. Please ask Reverend Lewis to speak at the dinner.
4. Please meet my train at (date, time, and place).
5. Visitors must have a pass to enter the building.

Checkpoint 2 *Revising on a Word Processor or a Computer*

1. f	4. d
2. e	5. c
3. b	6. a

Checkpoint 3 *Proofreading Checklist*

1. is
2. Dr.; delete one *the*
3. salary; insert period at end of sentence
4. brakes
5. business

Checkpoint 4 *Proofreading Methods*

1. scroll the screen
2. compare drafts
3. Read aloud
4. proofread backwards
5. Use two proofreaders

Checkpoint 5 *Proofreading on a Word Processor or a Computer*

1. SRF
2. SF
3. TAF
4. TAF
5. TAF

Checkpoint 6 *Using Proofreaders' Marks*

1. The memo has been sent.
2. The meeting will be held in the board room.
3. Mr. Sanchis of Sanchis and Sanchis, Ltd., is speaking.
4. Dear Dr. Lei, Ph.D: Please have patience with our billing department.
5. Company sales have increased, but profits have declined.

Chapter 27

Checkpoint 1 *Using Memos*

1. True
2. False
3. False
4. False
5. True

Checkpoint 2 *Traditional and Simplified Memo Formats*

1. False
2. True
3. False
4. True
5. True

Chapter 28

Checkpoint 1 *Uses of Memos*

1. to state policy and to inform
2. to inform
3. to promote goodwill
4. to provide a record

Checkpoint 2 *When to Use a Memo*

1. Do not send a memo. Employees might be suffering from communication overload. Call them to ask for the information.
2. Send a memo. Its purpose would be to inform and to state policy.
3. Do not send a memo. Either have a one-to-one conversation or call him or her on the telephone.
4. Send a memo. Its purpose would be to promote goodwill.

Chapter 29

Checkpoint 1 *Planning Memos*

1. **Objective**—to advise and inform. **Main Idea**—here is the report with recommendations.
2. **Objective**—to inform and state policy. **Main Idea**—the ad hoc committee is responsible for developing three procedures.

3. **Objective**—to inform and to provide a
   record. **Main Idea**—I still do not have the
   Jones report.

Checkpoint 2 *Organizing Memos*

1. Direct order; this message makes a routine
   request
2. Indirect order; this is a bad-news message
3. Indirect order; this is a bad-news message
4. Indirect order; this is a bad-news message

Checkpoint 3 *Guidelines for Writing Effective Memos*

1. True   4. True
2. False   5. False
3. False   6. False

Chapter 30

Checkpoint 1 *Letter Parts*

1. subject line
2. enclosure notation
3. salutation
4. copy notation
5. complimentary close

Checkpoint 2 *Letter Formats and Business Envelopes*

1. True   4. True
2. False   5. False
3. False

Chapter 31

Checkpoint 1 *Main Idea*

1. Poor—does not introduce or reveal the
   main idea
2. Poor—does not introduce or reveal the
   main idea
3. Good

4. Poor—does not introduce or reveal the
   main idea
5. Good

Checkpoint 2 *Goodwill Closing*

1. Poor—does not help the receiver
2. Good
3. Good
4. Poor—does not help the receiver
5. Poor—does not help the receiver

Checkpoint 3 *Routine, Good News, and Goodwill Letters*

1. True   4. True
2. True   5. False
3. False

Chapter 32

Checkpoint 1 *Neutral Openings*

1. Poor—does not introduce the topic of the
   letter
2. Good—introduces the topic of letter and
   does not infer a positive or negative
   response
3. Poor—implies the answer will give the
   receiver what he wants
4. Good—introduces the topic of the letter
   and does not infer a positive or negative
   response
5. Poor—implies the answer is "no"

Checkpoint 2 *Reasons for the Bad News*

1. Good—provides a logical, receiver-oriented
   reason for the negative response
2. Good—provides a logical, receiver-oriented
   reason for the negative response
3. Poor—provides a reason that is sender
   oriented, not receiver oriented

4. Poor—provides a reason that is short and company oriented
5. Good—provides a customer-oriented, logical reason for the negative response

Checkpoint 3 *The Bad News*

1. Good—implies the answer and avoids using negative language
2. Poor—states the answer directly, uses negative language, and uses personal pronouns with negative language
3. Good—implies the answer and avoids using negative language
4. Poor—states the answer directly, uses negative language, and uses personal pronouns with negative language
5. Good—implies the answer and avoids using negative language

Checkpoint 4 *The Closing*

1. Poor—uses the word *hope* and does not contain a soft sale
2. Good—contains a soft sale, provides motivation for the receiver to say "yes," and makes his or her response easy
3. Good—tries to help even while providing a negative response
4. Poor—contains an apology and does not contain a soft sale
5. Good—offers another option

Chapter 33

Checkpoint 1 *Attention-Getting Opening*

1. Poor—sounds insincere because of "fantastic"; no supporting information precedes this opening
2. Good—gains attention and introduces the topic of the letter

3. Good—gains attention and introduces the topic of the letter
4. Good—gains attention and introduces the topic of the letter
5. Poor—sounds like a form letter; the opening does not gain attention and does not introduce the topic of the letter

Checkpoint 2 *Supporting Information*

1. Poor—sounds insincere; words such as "tremendous" and "expert" sound like exaggerations
2. Good—motivates the receiver
3. Good—motivates the receiver
4. Poor—creates little interest and does not motivate the receiver
5. Poor—gives the price in a large unit and includes statements that sound like exaggerations

Checkpoint 3 *Action Closing*

1. Good—creates interest and shows benefits
2. Poor—gives the receiver no specific action to perform; the receiver must determine what he or she should do
3. Good—creates interest and shows benefits.
4. Poor—allows easy action, but does nothing to help the receiver visualize or feel the pleasing consequences of doing that which is asked
5. Poor—provides a negative statement and seems to encourage a negative response

Chapter 34

Checkpoint 1 *Planning a Report*

1. False   4. True
2. False   5. True
3. False

Checkpoint 2 *Collecting and Analyzing Data*

1. True   4. True
2. True   5. False
3. False

Chapter 35

Checkpoint 1 *Organizing and Writing Informal Reports*

1. True   4. True
2. False   5. False
3. True   6. True

Checkpoint 2 *Formatting Informal Reports*

1. False   4. True
2. True   5. True
3. False   6. True

Chapter 36

Checkpoint 1 *Organizing, Writing, and Formatting Formal Reports*

1. False   4. False
2. True   5. True
3. False

Checkpoint 2 *Visual Aids*

1. True   4. False
2. True   5. True
3. False

Chapter 37

Checkpoint 1 *News Releases*

1. Poor—this opening is not receiver-oriented
2. Good
3. Poor—this opening is not receiver-oriented

Checkpoint 2 *Proposals, Agendas, and Minutes*

1. False   4. False
2. True   5. True
3. False

Chapter 38

Checkpoint 1 *Roles of Nonverbal Symbols*

1. False   4. True
2. False   5. True
3. True

Checkpoint 2 *The Use of Nonverbal Symbols*

1. False
2. True   4. False
3. True   5. True

Chapter 39

Checkpoint 1 *Facts About Listening*

1. True
2. True   4. True
3. True   5. True

Checkpoint 2 *Effective Listening*

1. True
2. False   4. True
3. True   5. True

Chapter 40

Checkpoint 1 *One-to-One Conversations and Telephone Calls*

1. False
2. True   4. True
3. True   5. False

Checkpoint 2 *Characteristics of an Effective Group*

1. False
2. True
3. False
4. False
5. True

Checkpoint 3 *Common Group Problems*

1. True
2. False
3. False
4. True
5. False

Chapter 41

Checkpoint 1 *Effective Participation and Organization*

1. False
2. True
3. False
4. False
5. True

Checkpoint 2 *Lead Meetings Effectively*

1. True
2. True
3. False
4. True
5. True

Chapter 42

Checkpoint 1 *Short and Formal Presentations*

1. True
2. False
3. False
4. False
5. True

Checkpoint 2 *Delivery*

1. False
2. True
3. True
4. True
5. False

Chapter 43

Checkpoint 1 *Analyzing Your Goals and Qualifications*

1. True
2. False
3. True
4. False
5. False

Checkpoint 2 *Analyzing the Job Market*

1. True
2. False
3. False
4. False
5. True

Chapter 44

Checkpoint 1 *Organizing Your Resume*

1. False
2. True
3. True
4. False
5. True

Checkpoint 2 *Preparing Your Resume*

1. False
2. True
3. False
4. False
5. True

Chapter 45

Checkpoint 1 *Opening Paragraph*

1. Weak
2. Weak
3. Effective
4. Weak
5. Effective

Checkpoint 2 *Body Paragraphs*

1. Weak
2. Effective
3. Effective
4. Weak
5. Effective

Checkpoint 3 *Closing Paragraph*

1. Effective
2. Weak
3. Effective
4. Weak
5. Weak

Chapter 46

Checkpoint 1 *Preparing for the Interview*

1. True
2. True
3. False
4. True
5. False

Checkpoint 2 *The Interview and Follow-Up Letter*

1. True
2. True
3. True
4. False
5. False

INTERNET@A.GLANCE

E-mail pals from across the globe "chat" while experiencing virtually no delay in transmission. A student in Australia researching archaeology locates and transfers files from a remote computer in Iceland. A business executive in Paris obtains the most recent stock market values in Tokyo as the changes occur. These examples are made reality through using the Internet.

This Appendix provides an overview of the Internet. It introduces terms and navigational tools that lend themselves to specific business applications. A glossary of basic Internet terms and a bibliography of books, which provide more practical advice on how to use the Internet, are included at the end of this Appendix.

What Is the Internet?

The information "superhighway" is probably the best analogy for the Internet. The information system is named the "Internet" because of the connection, not only between computers, but also among computer networks. A network is two or more computers connected to each other with the capability of exchanging information.

Currently, the Internet is the world's largest computer network. Composed of smaller networks linked together, the Internet has become a community of people using computers to interact with each other. In addition to being a communication tool, the Internet also provides a method for obtaining information from a variety of sources worldwide. This information covers a multitude of topics from governments to academic research to businesses and corporations.

Where Did the Internet Originate?

The Internet started as a network for the Defense Department. The Defense Department used a technique to transfer data in information packets from one computer system to another. This technique is known as TCP/IP (Transmission Control Protocol/Internet Protocol). The Internet still uses TCP/IP as a standard method for information transfer.

Both NASA and National Science Foundation developed their own computer networks in the 1980s. This development provided easier information access for research scientists.

Then, universities and academic institutions expanded their own networks. The academic links included both intrastate and interstate computers for larger data sources.

During the late 1980s, a tremendous growth occurred in the number of networked computers. The most recent development in the Internet system is the expanded access available to the general public. This access is provided through commercial carriers (America Online, Prodigy, Delphi, CompuServe, and others) and through direct access. The Internet seems destined to continue expanding as more and more people use the system.

What Can You Do with the Internet?

You can use three basic programs on the Internet. You can communicate (primarily through e-mail), research information, and transfer information files.

All communication modes allow you to correspond without any delay in sending or receiving. Electronic mail or e-mail is probably the most used feature of the Internet. In order to use e-mail, you must know (or be able to find) the receiver's address.

E-mail addresses will always have two parts—the name and the location of the user. An example of an address is:

cpbrantley@aol.com

This means that the username is *cpbrantley*, who is located at America Online (*aol*), which is a commercial carrier (*com*). The location part of the address is known as the domain.

Seven different organizational domains exist as shown in Figure G–1.

Another address example is:

tclesc32@mail.firn.edu

In this address, the *tclesc32* is a username assigned by the carrier. The domains (to the right of the @ symbol) indicate this is an educational carrier (*edu*) through the Florida Information Resource Network (*firn*) routed to the mail program (*mail*).

Geographic domains represent addresses outside the United States. Some examples are: *au* (Australia), *jp* (Japan), *es* (Spain), and *fr* (France).

DOMAIN	PURPOSE
com	Commercial entities
edu	Educational institutions
gov	Non-military US government institutions
int	International institutions
mil	US military institutions
net	Network resources
org	Non-profit organizations

Figure G–1 Organizational domains

You may use a number of tools to search for information on any topic imaginable from computers around the world. Some of these tools include GOPHER, ARCHIE, WAIS, VERONICA, WWW, and JUGHEAD.

Once the desired information has been located, another tool transfers the data you have located from the host computer to your location. FTP (File Transfer Protocol) is the primary program that retrieves information from global sources.

How Do You Get Connected?

You must have one of two systems to connect into the Internet. The first system is from your personal computer via a modem. The second system is through direct wiring to larger computers, which are usually available on academic campuses or in large businesses. Internet connections may be complete service (able to access worldwide databases) or may be limited to electronic mail functions.

In order to connect, you need a computer, a modem, communications software with proper settings or parameters, a login/user name, a password, and an Internet account. An Internet account may be provided through one of several carriers. The following are frequently used carriers:

1. Commercial carriers such as America Online, CompuServe, Delphi, and Prodigy (require a monthly fee)
2. Universities and other educational institutions (usually free to staff and students)
3. Statewide networks, which may also connect academic institutions (CORE in California, PEN in Virginia, FIRN in Florida)
4. Governmental agencies
5. Internet access sites (require a monthly fee)

How Can You Use the Internet?

When you use the Internet, you select appropriate navigation tools, follow navigation basics, and observe Internet etiquette.

Navigation Tools

Navigation tools enhance your ability to communicate, research information, and transfer files.

Communication Tools. Communication tools include the following:

1. *Electronic mail* (e-mail) has many advantages over standard postal service or "snail-mail." e-mail is paperless, instantaneous, private, and requires no postage.
2. *TALK* (chat mode) allows real-time dialogue between users.
3. *TELNET* connects you to other host computers; then, you proceed as if you were at that site. One example of TELNET use is to access the National Weather Service weather report through a computer at the University of Michigan.
4. *USENET* is a group of users who share information on a central theme. People contributing to this "net" may be located anywhere in the world.
5. *IRC* (Internet Relay Chat) enables many users to communicate simultaneously.
6. The *FINGER* command allows you to find information on other users. Another feature of this command enables you to list everyone logged on at a specific site. If you are trying to send a message to someone and are unsure of the address, the finger command may be used.

Research Tools. Research tools include the following:

1. *ARCHIE* electronically searches directories of other computers and gives you the location or FTP (see Transfer Tool on page G-5) site of the desired information. You may access ARCHIE directly; or you may go through a GOPHER command, through a TELNET command, or through e-mail.
2. *GOPHER* (named after a human "go-fer" and after the University of Minnesota mascot where the program was developed) also searches by keyword or topic. In addition to finding matching files, GOPHER also displays the files in a menu format. You can access GOPHER directly or TELNET to a public GOPHER client.
3. *WAIS* (Wide Area Information Server) does keyword searches and lists files containing keywords. WAIS provides a slightly broader source of information than GOPHER because WAIS includes indexes from a number of databases rather than just one or a few.

4. *WWW* (World Wide Web) searches a larger number of databases using "hypertext" links. Hypertext simply means that certain words or graphics are highlighted on the screen. Clicking these highlighted areas automatically sends you into another set of files with further information on that topic.
5. *VERONICA* acts as an index for GOPHER menus. While GOPHER may only access the information in one particular database, VERONICA searches all the titles in GOPHER sites and then displays a menu.
6. *JUGHEAD* operates as a limiting factor for the number of articles listed. In conjunction with the GOPHER command, JUGHEAD allows you to narrow a data search to finer parameters.

Many of these tools simply give a listing of sites where files of interest are found. If you want to read the file, you may then TELNET to that site. If you want to transfer the file to your computer, you use a transfer tool.

Transfer Tool. The primary file transfer tool is FTP, a program that sends and receives information between computers. Using FTP, you can transfer text as well as graphics from anywhere in the world to your computer. When transferring any files, you must include both the address where the file is coming from and the address where the file is going.

Navigation Basics

UNIX is the language of the Internet, just as DOS is the operating language for many computer systems. In order to "surf" the Internet, you do not need to know UNIX, but a basic understanding could be helpful. Most commercial carriers provide help screens.

The first step in using the Internet is to **login** or **logon** to a host computer. This procedure varies depending on the type of carrier used. A sample logon screen is shown in Figure G–2.

The screen may then include a menu or may show only a command prompt (similar to a DOS prompt). From this beginning screen, you may enter into a variety of programs.

Communicate. When you send an e-mail message, the procedure is relatively the same, no matter what system you use. Basically, the message needs an **address** (where the message will be sent) and a command to **send**. You may send messages to anyone on the Internet. The receiver does not have to be on the same carrier as you are.

Figure G–2 America Online logon screen

When receiving a message, the screen may appear as shown in Figure G–3.

If you had actually received this message from America Online, additional "header" information would appear below the signature. This information tells the computer pathways that the message traveled.

Subject: Word Usage

Date: 95-06-07 20:07:52 EDT

From: millermg@aol.com (Miller, Michele)

To: cpbrantley@aol.com

Clarice,

You are right. Midwesterners use some unique words. A water fountain is called a "bubbler." I'm not sure where this name originated, but I have not heard anyone from a different part of the country use the same term. Please share some of the unique terms used by Southerners.

Michele

Figure G–3 An e-mail message using America Online

Research. Of the many research tools listed, you will probably use GOPHER and WWW the most. You may use WWW to "browse" many different systems simply by clicking on the highlighted text or graphics. If you are using a GOPHER command, you need to know which GOPHER site to select. If you are unsure of the site, you may use one of the additional research tools, such as VERONICA, to search more than one site.

Transfer. When using FTP, you must first login to the system or host holding the desired files. In most systems, you may login as a guest by using "anonymous" at the login prompt. When asked for a password, you may respond with your e-mail address. Although some systems may allow you in without your address, supplying the address is an Internet courtesy.

The major commands needed to use FTP are **get** and **put**. As these commands imply, **get** retrieves a file from the host and brings the file to the local host. Sometimes the local host is not your personal computer. Further transferring may be required; follow the guidelines given to you by your local provider. **Put** takes a file from your computer to another host.

When you are finished, you must break the connection. This is accomplished by using either the **close** command or the **quit** command. Both will break the connection; however, **quit** will also end the FTP program.

The methods of proceeding from the original login may vary, but one aspect is constant—etiquette.

Navigation Etiquette or "Netiquette"

Even though you send messages electronically, the communication rules still hold true. Be sure your messages are courteous, clear, concise, concrete, correct, considerate, and complete. If you communicate in a USENET, listen (or lurk) before you talk. Many of the frequently asked questions (FAQs) for a specific newsgroup are posted in that newsgroup. Many newsgroups or USENETs have particular interests. If you disagree with any statement, simply get out of that net. Also, you must be very careful when using sarcasm or humor. Without the benefit of facial expressions, many statements may be misinterpreted.

Additional guidelines include the following:

1. Do not give your password to anyone.
2. Do not use all capital letters in e-mail. Using all caps is comparable to shouting. Also, use limited exclamation marks. These marks also indicate excessive volume.

3. Comply with the system's "Acceptable Use Policy" that is available online.
4. Make sure the address is properly designated with the username correctly spelled and separated from the domain by an @ symbol.
5. Include a signature line on all messages.
6. Limit the use of graphics. Some people have to pay for downloading messages; graphics require extended downloading time.

MAY YOU COMMUNICATE WITH THE AUTHORS THROUGH E-MAIL?

Yes, you may. Please communicate with the textbook authors. Use whatever system you have available; send your messages to any of the following addresses:

Carol Henson

henson@gg.csc.peachnet.edu

Thomas L. Means

means@cab.latech.edu

SOURCE: Adapted from Brantley, Clarice Pennebaker, and Michele Goulet Miller. *Effective Communication for Colleges.* 7th ed. Cincinnati: South-Western Publishing Co., 1994, 1996. 373–80.

Internet Glossary

A

Address   The number sequence that identifies a unique user or computer on a network. Every computer and user on the Internet must have a different address for the system to know where to send e-mail and other computer data. (See Names.)

Archie   A tool (software) for finding files stored on anonymous FTP sites. You need to know the exact file name or a sub-string of it.

Articles   Information, ideas, and comments posted on USENET and e-mail lists.

B

BBS   Bulletin Board System. A computerized meeting and announcement system that allows people to carry on discussions, upload and download files, and make announcements without the people being connected to the computer at the same time.

Backbone   The Internet backbone was created by the National Science Foundation. The backbone links major computer centers together with a high-speed telecommunication connection. Subnetworks attach to the backbone.

BITNET   Because It's Time Network. A network of educational sites separate from the Internet, but e-mail is freely exchanged between BITNET and the Internet. Listservs, the most popular form of e-mail discussion groups, originated on BITNET. BITNET machines are IBM VMS machines, and the network is probably the only international network that is getting smaller.

Bits Per Second   A measurement of speed for network telecommunications systems. A bit is the smallest piece of information communicated by computers. The number of bits that pass through a modem determines the speed of a modem.

Bookmark   A means of collecting favorite Home Pages and addresses in Netscape and in other Gopher and Internet Clients for future reference.

bps   See Bits Per Second.

Browsers   Browsers are the newest and most significant new software tools on the Internet. Browsers, like Netscape and Mosaic, are user-friendly viewers and are required to navigate the World Wide Web and to manipulate hypertext documents. Well-designed Browsers have the other major Internet software tools built right into their software.

C

Category   Collection of related Newsgroups.

Client   The term given to any computer that is connected to the Internet and has the software it needs to share information over the Internet.

Client Software   Software that allows your computer to talk, communicate, and share information with Internet host computers and Internet servers.

com   Indicates a commercial domain.

Connections   The software and hardware links between computers are called connections. The speed and compatibility of your computer's connection to your Internet host computer will determine the efficiency with which you can access Internet resources. (See SLIP and PPP)

Cybernetics   The science that compares the functions of the brain with those of a computer.

Cyberspace   A term given to the electronic, computerized world of the Internet. Often called virtual reality. When you are on the Internet or the World Wide Web, you are in Cyberspace.

D

Directory   A storage location, like a file folder, where related data and files are stored.

Distributed Network   The Internet is a distributed network, meaning that there is not one central authority or group guiding its growth, use, and development. If one part of the Internet goes down, as in a natural disaster like an earthquake, Internet communications can be transferred to other lines of communication, and the downed portion of the network can be bypassed until repairs are made.

DNS   See Domain Name System.

Domain Name System   A system of computers and software that allows Internet names like karl@dixon.edu to be converted into a number like 158.90.62.25 and back again.

Domains   A division or section of the Internet. For example, the military is one domain, education is another. Service providers like America Online and Prodigy have their own domains. Domains can be divided geographically by country, region, or state, or by other similarities such as business, commerce, government agencies, or private organizations.

Download   To copy files, data, information, and software from a remote host computer to your computer or to another computer.

Dumb Terminal   A dumb terminal is attached to a mainframe or minicomputer. The terminal does not do any of the computer processing.

Dumb terminals allow input from the user and display the processing taking place on a host computer.

Dynamic   Constantly changing.

E

edu   Indicates an educational domain.

E-Mail   E-mail is short for electronic mail. Electronic mail is the most widely used feature of the Internet. Mail is written in an e-mail program and transmitted over networks to other users with compatible e-mail software.

Emulate   To imitate. (See Dumb Terminal.)

Etiquette   Rules of conduct and behavior. (See Netiquette.)

F

FAQs   Frequently Asked Questions. Hosts will post answers to their most frequently asked questions.

Finger   An Internet software tool for locating people (via e-mail addresses) on other Internet sites.

Flamers   Newsgroup or e-mail users who send flames or written rebukes.

Flames   Rebukes sent by agitated Internet users to people who violate rules of Internet "netiquette," or who "spam" the Internet.

FTP   File Transfer Protocol. FTP software transfers files, information, and data from one computer to another.

G

Gateways   Tools that allow commercial e-mail software to communicate with each other.

Gopher   A system of menus that allow users with Gopher Client software to access information on computers called Gopher Servers.

Gopher Client   Software that allows users access to Gopher Servers.

Gopher Servers   Software that allows Gopher Clients access to Gopher files, directories, and menus.

Gopherspace   The Internet pathways available from a Gopher Client.

gov   Indicates a governmental domain.

Groups   USENET Newsgroups.

GUI   Graphical User Interface. GUI, pronounced gooie, replaces commands with pictures, or icons, in software usually associated with Windows or Macintosh computers.

H

Hits   A hit is recorded anytime someone connects to a remote computer, site, or Home Page.

Home Page   A Home Page is like an index that contains related information on a single topic in a hypertext WWW environment.

Host   Any computer providing network services and resources to other computers is called a host. Host computers are also called servers. Servers are the key computers in networks.

Hotlist   A catalog or list of Home Pages in Mosaic.

HTML   (See HyperText Markup Language.)

HTTP   (See HyperText Transfer Protocol.)

Hypermedia   Computer data that creates hypertext links between more than one kind of media. Types of media include video, pictures, graphics, animation, and text. (See Multimedia.)

Hypertext   A system of information retrieval, where selected keywords are linked to text and other information in the same document or in another document. Clicking on a hypertext word will execute a command to find the text you have selected. Hypertext links are not limited to the local computer network. Hypertext links can take you to information located on another computer in another part of the world.

HyperText Markup Language   A set of commands that describe a file to a GUI Browser.

HyperText Transfer Protocol   Protocols are instructions that tell computers how to handle and send hypertext documents and data from one computer to another.

I

Icon   A picture or graphic that represents something. For example, an icon of a printer may represent the Print command. (See GUI.)

Incompatability   When software from a client computer does not communicate with the software on an Internet host, there is an incompatibility. Incompatibilities exist with different versions of software, when internal software settings do not correspond, or for a variety of other reasons. Hardware may also be incompatible, limiting Internet access.

Internet   The name given to the current telecommunications system between networks of computers. The Internet is often called a "network of networks." The Internet will grow into the electronic superhighway of the future. The Internet is often called the Net because it is the largest computer network in the world.

IP   Internet Protocol, an address label for Internet packages called packets. IP makes sure the packets arrive at the correct destination.

L

Links   Hypertext Words that jump automatically to another selection of text.

Listserv   The most common kind of maillist, Listervs originated on BITNET, but they are now common on the Internet.

Lurkers   Newsgroup or e-mail users who read groups but don't post their own articles.

M

Maillist (or Mailing List)   A (usually automated) system that allows people to send e-mail to one address, whereupon their message is copied and sent to all of the other subscribers to the maillist.

Menu   A menu is a list of choices.

mil   Indicates a military domain.

Modem   A simple communications tool that converts computer signals into signals that can travel over telephone lines.

Moderated   Screened by a person or group for anything going into a Newsgroup for distribution to its readers. Moderators cut out unnecessary postings and articles that do not fit the topic of the group.

Mosaic   The popular and widespread WWW browser or client software. The source-code to Mosaic has been licensed by several companies.

Multimedia   Systems that use more than one medium. A multimedia computer can utilize various types of media including video, sound, pictures, graphics, animation, and text.

N

Names   A unique or different name is required for Internet users. In common speech, the words "name" and "address" are often used interchangeably. Technically speaking, a name involves the use of words (eugene@dixon.edu), and an address is a number like 158.95.6.2.

net   Indicates a network provider domain.

Net   Short for Network.

Netiquette   Internet rules of behavior and conduct.

Network   Two or more computers linked together to share information and data.

Network Administrators   The most important person on a network is the Network Administrator. These people manage all the hardware and software issues on a network and keep things running. They manage the security of the network and grant network rights to users. Network Administrators are often overworked and underpaid, but they usually have some really cool computers.

Newbies   New members of discussion groups.

Newsgroup   Participants who follow threads of a particular topic with the help of a USENET newsreader.

Newsreader   Software tool required to read and participate in USENET Newsgroups.

NIC   Network Information Center. Generally, any office that handles information for a network. The most famous of these on the Internet is the InterNIC, which is where new domain names are registered.

O

On-line   Using computer connections to networks.

org   Indicates an organizational domain.

P

Packets   The bundles of data that can be transmitted over the Internet.

Password   A special word used to secure computer systems. Passwords are usually created by authorized users under the directions of a Network Administrator. Hosts use passwords to distinguish users that are allowed on a computer network from those that are trying to gain illegal or unauthorized entry.

Platforms   There are many different and sometimes incompatible computer hardware and software systems, called platforms.

Post   To send articles to Newsgroups or to electronic bulletin board systems.

PPP   Point-to-Point Protocol. One of the types of connections that allow Internet communications over a modem. PPP allows your computer to act like you have a direct connection to the Internet. (See SLIP.)

R

Resources   Anything you can find on the Internet is a resource, including software, files, data, information, services, and people.

S

Saints   People who provide help to new members of discussion groups.

Server   Any computer providing network services and resources to other computers. Server computers are also called "hosts." Servers are the key computers in networks.

Service Providers   Companies that provide Internet connections.

Site   A computer connected to the Internet that contains information that can be accessed using a navigation tool such as gopher or FTP.

SLIP   Serial Line Internet Protocol. One of the types of connections that allow Internet communications over a modem. SLIP allows your computer to act as if you have a direct connection to the Internet. (See PPP.)

Spam   Unwanted Internet garbage, particularly advertising on the public Internet.

Subject Line   The title of a Newsgroup posting or article.

Subscribers   Participants in a Newsgroup or e-mail discussion list.

Superhighway   Another name for Cyberspace. Also, the name given to the Internet of the future.

Surf   Exploring the Internet. When you surf, you are looking for interesting information.

T

TCP   Transmission Control Protocol. TCP keeps track of every item in a packet or package that is transmitted over the Internet. If an item arrives broken or incomplete, TCP asks the host computer to send the packet over again.

Telnet   Telnet provides the ability to log in to remote servers or host computers and to use its resources as if you were a computer terminal on that particular host computer.

Telnet Session   Anytime you log in to a Telnet computer, you start a Telnet session. When you log out of Telnet, you end the session.

Text-Based   Internet systems that rely on words rather than on graphics and pictures.

Thread   A series of messages on the same theme or topic.

Title The particular name of a Newsgroup within its category.

Transfer Rate The speed at which data is exchanged between computers.

U

Uniform Resource Locator An address or reference code that makes it possible for a GUI Browser like Mosaic or Netscape to locate hypertext and hypermedia documents on any WWW host server in the world.

Unique Different, individualized.

Unmoderated Not screened for anything going into a Newsgroup for distribution to its readers. Therefore, group members must be more aware of what is and is not appropriate for the group.

URL See Uniform Resource Locator.

USENET A huge collection of computers that allow you to post, distribute, or publish Newsgroup articles. USENET is one of the most widely used Internet services.

User-Friendly Easy-to-use software. User-friendly software is intuitive; in other words, people are able to figure out by the name, icon, or location of a command what a particular software command will do.

V

Veronica Very Easy Rodent Oriented Net-wide Index to Computerized Archives. Developed at the University of Nevada, Veronica is a constantly updated database of the names of almost every menu item on thousands of gopher servers. The Veronica database can be searched from most major gopher menus.

W

WAIS Wide Area Information Servers. A commercial software package that allows the indexing of huge quantities of information, and then making those indexes searchable across networks such as the Internet. A prominent feature of WAIS is that the search results are ranked according to how relevant the "hits" are, and that subsequent searches can find similar topics and thus refine the search process. WAIS database searches take you inside the documents or files you're interested in; whereas Gopher and Archie searches only look at key words in the file title and description.

WAN Wide Area Network. Any internet or network that covers an area larger than a single building or campus.

Wizards Newsgroup experts.

WWW The World Wide Web, or W3. WWW is a system of computers that can share information by means of hypertext links.

SOURCE: Adapted from Ashton, Gary L., Karl Barksdale, Michael Rutter, and Earl Jay Stephens. *Internet Activities: Adventures on the Superhighway.* Cincinnati: South-Western Educational Publishing, 1995. 239–44.

SELECTED INTERNET PUBLICATIONS

Books

Ashton, Gary L., Karl Barksdale, Michael Rutter, and Earl Jay Stephens. *Internet Activities: Adventures on the Superhighway.* Cincinnati: South-Western Educational Publishing, 1995.

Dern, Daniel P. *The New User's Guide to the Internet.* New York: McGraw-Hill, 1993.

Kehoe, Brendan P. *Zen and the Art of the Internet: A Beginners Guide.* Englewood Cliffs, N.J.: Prentice Hall, 1992.

Krol, Ed. *The Whole Internet: User's Guide and Catalog.* Sebastopol, Calif.: O'Reilly and Associates, Inc., 1992.

Lane, Elizabeth S., and Craig A. Summerhill. *An Internet Primer for Information Professionals: A Basic Guide to Networking Technology.* Westport, Conn.: Meckler, 1992.

Lynch, Daniel C., and Marshall T. Rose. *Internet System Handbook.* Greenwich, Conn.: Manning Publications Co., 1993.

Malamud, Carl. *Exploring the Internet: A Technical Travelogue.* Englewood Cliffs, N.J.: Prentice Hall, 1992.

Strangelove, Michael, and Diane Kovacs. *Directory of Electronic Journals, Newsletters and Academic Discussion Lists.* Washington, D.C.: Association of Research Libraries, Office of Scientific and Academic Publishing, 1993.

Tennant, Roy, John Ober, and Anne G. Lipow. *Crossing the Internet Threshold: An Instructional Handbook.* Berkeley, Calif.: Library Solutions Institute and Press, 1993.

Veljkov, Mark, and George Hartnell. *Pocket Guides to the Internet.* Westport, Conn.: Meckler, 1993. Vol. 1: *Telneting*; Vol. 2: *Transferring Files with File Transfer Protocol*; Vol. 3: *Using and Navigating News Nets*; Vol. 4: *The Internet e-mail System*; Vol. 5: *Accessing Internet Front Ends and General Utilities*; Vol. 6: *Physical Connections.*

Periodicals

The Cook Report on Internet—NREN. Cook Network Consultants: Ewing, N.J. cook@path.net.

The Internet Business Journal. Strangelove Press: Ottawa, Ontario, Canada K1M-1C7. 72302.3062@CompuServe.Com.

Internet Business Report. CMP Publications: Manhasset, N.Y. locke@cmp.com

The Internet Letter. NetWeek: Washington, D.C. 20045. helen@access.digex.com

Internet World. Meckler: Westport, Conn. 06880. meckler@jvnc.net.

Note: The letter *f* following a page number indicates that the term appears in a figure.

Delete text function, 330
Delivery, of oral presentation, 563–566, 564*f*
  modes of, 559–560
Desire, creating, in persuasive letter, 427–429
Desktop publishing software, 19
Developmental paragraph, 315
Dictating machine, 15
Dictionaries
  information in, 297–298
  types and sizes of, 299
Difficult people, handling, at meetings, 551–552
Direct address, commas with, 201
Direct-indirect order organization
  for memos, 367
  for messages, 285–286
Directions, within parentheses, 229
Direct object, 60
Direct order organization
  for informal reports, 454, 456*f*–457*f*
  for memos, 367, 367*f*–368*f*
  for messages, 284
  for orders, 399–401
  for positive responses, 401–402
  for requests, 397–398
  for routine, good news, and goodwill letters, 394, 396*f*
Direct paragraph, 320
Direct questions, 191
Direct quotations, quotation marks with, 225
Disability designations, 293

Discussion outlines, 445
Distances, numbers in, 272
Distribution list. *See also* Copy notation
  in memos, 344
Document analysis software, 18
Documents. *See also* Letters; Memorandums; Proposals; Reports
  creating on computer, 15–16
  editing on computer, 16–20, 329–330, 335–336
  for meetings, 495–499
  nonverbal messages in, 509, 510*f*
  sending on computer, 20–23
  specialized external, 491–495
  storing on computer, 15, 23
  technical, abbreviations used in, 245–246
Downward communication, 9
Dress, for job interview, 617

E
Editing, 328, 336
  on computer, 16–20, 329–330, 335–336
  seven Cs in, 328*f*
Education, as job qualification, 576
  describing in resume, 592
Electronic communication, 11, 15–24
  application software, 17–20
  dictating machine, 15
  electronic mail, 21
  electronic workstations, 16
  facsimile devices, 21–22

Electronic Communication (*Contd.*)
  keyboard and mouse, 15
  local area networks, 21
  magnetic disks, 23
  microforms, 23
  optical disk technology, 23
  personal computers, 16–17
  scanners, 15
  teleconferencing, 22
  videoconferencing, 22
  voice mail, 23
  voice recognition technology, 16
  word/information processing, 15–17
Electronic mail, 11, 21, 341, 341*f*
Electronic workstation, 16
E-mail. *See* Electronic mail
Employment. *See* Job interview; Job market; Job search
Employment agencies, 579–580
Employment opportunities, locating, 579–580
Empty phrases, 304
Enclosure notation, 386
Enumerations. *See also* Lists; Series
  in memos, 373
  periods with, 191
  semicolons in, 211
Envelopes, addressing, 389, 391*f*
Exclamation points, 193
  quotation marks with, 226
Executive summary, 472, 473*f*–474*f*
Explanation, transitions for, 321*f*
Extemporaneous speech, 559–560

Voice mail, 11, 23
Voice recognition equipment, 16

W

well, good, 132–133, 179–180
where, that, 131
where, where at, where to, 143
which, 78
Whiteboards, 565
whoever, whomever, 65
who, whom, 64–65, 78
Windows, 19
Wishes, sentences expressing, 182–183
with regard to, in regard to, as regards, 141
Word division, 218–219, 298
Wordiness, eliminating, 304, 307
Word/information processing, 15
   software for, 17
Word processor, 16. *See also* Electronic communication

Word processor *(Contd.)*
   creating documents on, 15–16
   dedicated, 16
   editing on, 16–20
   proofreading on, 335–336
   revising on, 329–330
   sending documents with, 20–23
   storing documents with, 15, 23
Words, choosing, 291–300. *See also specific parts of speech*
   bias-free, 292–293
   concise vs. redundant, 296
   concrete, 307–310
   correct, 294–299
   courteous, 291–293
   familiar vs. unfamiliar, 295
   frequently misused, 62–63
   positive vs. negative, 291
   precise vs. imprecise, 295
   unconventional, quotation

Words *(Contd.)*
   marks with, 226–227
   up-to-date vs. out-of-date, 295–296
   using dictionary for, 297–299
   using thesaurus for, 299
Work delegation meetings, 546–547
Work experience
   analyzing for job search, 576–577
   describing in resume, 592–595
Written works, titles of
   capitalization in, 252–253
   quotation marks for, 227
   underscores for, 231
Ws, five, 316–317

Y

your vs. *you're,* 63, 177–178

PHOTO CREDITS